Printing Statement:

Due to the very old age and scarcity of this book,
many of the pages may be hard to read due to the
blurring of the original text, possible missing pages,
missing text and other issues beyond our control.

Because this is such an important and rare work, we
believe it is best to reproduce this book regardless of
its original condition.

Thank you for your understanding.

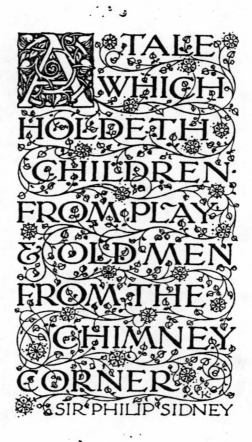

A TALE WHICH HOLDETH CHILDREN FROM PLAY & OLD MEN FROM THE CHIMNEY CORNER

SIR PHILIP SIDNEY

The ADMIRABLE CRICHTON BY WILLIAM HARRISON AINSWORTH

LONDON & TORONTO
PUBLISHED BY J·M·DENT
& SONS L.T.D & IN NEW YORK
BY E·P·DUTTON & CO

PRINTED IN GREAT BRITAIN

EVERYMAN'S LIBRARY
EDITED BY ERNEST RHYS

FICTION

HARRISON AINSWORTH'S
THE ADMIRABLE CRICHTON
WITH AN INTRODUCTION BY
ERNEST RHYS

THIS IS NO. 804 OF *EVERYMAN'S LIBRARY*. THE PUBLISHERS WILL BE PLEASED TO SEND FREELY TO ALL APPLICANTS A LIST OF THE PUBLISHED AND PROJECTED VOLUMES ARRANGED UNDER THE FOLLOWING SECTIONS:

TRAVEL ❧ SCIENCE ❧ FICTION
THEOLOGY & PHILOSOPHY
HISTORY ❧ CLASSICAL
FOR YOUNG PEOPLE
ESSAYS ❧ ORATORY
POETRY & DRAMA
BIOGRAPHY
REFERENCE
ROMANCE

THE ORDINARY EDITION IS BOUND IN CLOTH WITH GILT DESIGN AND COLOURED TOP. THERE IS ALSO A LIBRARY EDITION IN REINFORCED CLOTH

LONDON: J. M. DENT & SONS LTD.
NEW YORK: E. P. DUTTON & CO.

INSCRIBED

TO

MRS. JAMES TOUCHET,

IN

KINDLY REMEMBRANCE OF THE DAYS

WHEN THIS

ROMANCE WAS WRITTEN

* 804

Ergo, flos juvenum, Scotiæ spes, Palladis ingens,
Ereptumque decus Musarum e dulcibus ulnis,
Te, quamvis sileant alii, Critone, poetæ,
Teque, tuamque necem nunquam mea Musa silebit.

ABERNETHY, *Musa Campestris.*

INTRODUCTION

IN an early volume of *Fraser's Magazine* there is a portrait
of Harrison Ainsworth at the time when he was writing his
romance—*The Admirable Crichton*. It sketches him in outline
after the piquant manner of that monthly—a handsome
young buck seated very much at his ease on the end of a
table. The accompanying squib or article is written by "Oliver
Yorke." "You see," says he, "what a pretty fellow THE young
novelist of the season is. . . . We may without swagger apply
to Ainsworth what Theodore Hook has sung of D'Orsay:

> . . . gallant and gay,
> With the chest of Apollo, the waist of a gnat,
> The delight of the ball, the assembly, the play."

It was the success of *Rookwood* which had brought the young
romancer into the London limelight. Dick Turpin's Ride to
York, with Cruikshank's drawing of Black Bess in the act
of leaping donkey and donkey-cart at Edmonton, was the
choice morsel in the story, which won the readers of
that day.

In the succeeding saga of the invincible Scot, who was
descended from the Crichtons of Sanquhar, and the Royal
Stewarts, Ainsworth has to add learned disputations to
physical combats in realising his hero. The scene is shifted
from Dick Turpin's England to the France of Henri de Valois
and the lengthening sixteenth-century stage. He draws freely
on the extravagant life of Crichton which is found in the
history entitled a *Jewel . . . serving to frontal a Vindica-
tion of the Honour of Scotland*, by Sir Thomas Urquhart,
translator of Rabelais. Ainsworth takes his own "high-falutin'"
note from its magnification of "James Crichtoun . . . who
for his learning, judgement, valour, eloquence, beauty and
good fellowship was the perfectest result of the joynt labour
of the perfect number of those six deities, Pallas, Apollo,
Mars, Mercury, Venus and Bacchus."

Urquhart outdoes himself in describing the tragic close
at Mantua of Crichton's amazing career. It befell, as he de-
scribes it, upon a Shrove Tuesday, after a night of carnival
followed by a passionate love-scene, written in erotic hyper-

bole. As for the lovers, "the visuriency of either," we are told, "by ushering the tacturiency of both, made the attrectation of either cosequent to the inspection of either; here was it that passion was active, and action passive, they both being overcome by other, and each the conqueror." We see by this euphuistic passage where Harrison Ainsworth got some of the fine flowers of his style, adding a store of expletives and swashbuckling oaths from the old transpontine drama. In Urquhart's brief romance, the death-scene pictures Crichton facing terrible odds. One of the prince's men cries, as he draws on them, "Do not you see how he dandleth the sword in his hand, as if he were about to braveer us?" This prince Vincenzo is, we should say, the son of the Duke of Mantua, who has put him under Crichton's tutelage. The Scottish hero had already laid six of the prince's men on their backs, and had got within the prince's own guard, when one of the four remaining courtiers cried, "Hold, hold, kill not the prince!" At that Crichton, who has not in the dark recognised his opponent, makes the prince a low obeisance and offers him his sword, which the other, being half drunk, seizes, and with it "runs Crichtoun through the heart and so kills him."

Nothing of this appears in Ainsworth's romance, for he keeps his hero alive to the end according to rule in melodrama. Thus we lose the tragic last fillip given to the legend of the Admirable Crichton, by his early death at Mantua in a midnight brawl. Ainsworth in his appendix does refer to the book inscribed *memoriæ Jacobi Crichtonii*—in honour of James Crichton's memory. The book was an edition of Cicero's *De Universitate*, and its editor, Aldus Manutius, either misdated it or Crichton's death.

That event no doubt took place soon after 1585, when he was only twenty-three or twenty-four years old. A younger brother, Robert, had already succeeded to the family estate at Cluny before 1591.

For the rest Harrison Ainsworth has cast the saga in the exuberant mode which best goes with its hero's character, and which singularly agreed with his own mood and time. He borrowed properties freely from Victor Hugo, Dumas and the early Victorian English romancers, and he has given us a novel which, in its way, is a masterpiece of splendid swashbuckling and derring-do, based upon that historic fact which is the surest foundation for romance.

E. R.

The following is a list of the works of William Harrison Ainsworth:

Works of Cheviot Tichburn (pseudonym), 1822, 1824; December Tales, 1823; Poems (published under pseudonym), 1824; A Summer Evening Tale, 1825; Considerations of the best Means of affording immediate Relief to the Operative Classes in the Manufacturing Districts, 1826; Sir John Chiverton (? in collaboration with John Partington Aston), 1826; Rookwood, 1834; Crichton, 1837; Jack Sheppard, 1839; Tower of London, 1840; Guy Fawkes, 1841; Old St. Paul's, a Tale of the Plague and Fire of London (from the *Sunday Times*), 1841; The Miser's Daughter, 1842; Windsor Castle, 1843; St. James's, or the Court of Queen Anne, 1844; Lancashire Witches (from the *Sunday Times*), 1848; Star Chamber, 1854; James the Second, or the Revolution of 1688, etc., 1854; The Flitch of Bacon, or the Custom of Dunmow, 1854; Ballads, romantic, fantastical, and humorous, 1855; Spendthrift, 1856; Mervyn Clitheroe, 1857; The Combat of the Thirty. From a Breton Lay of fourteenth century, with introduction comprising a new chapter of Froissart, by W. H. A., 1859; Ovingdean Grange, A Tale of the South Downs, 1860; Constable of the Tower, 1861; The Lord Mayor of London, or City Life in the Last Century, 1862; Cardinal Pole, 1863; John Law the Projector, 1864; The Spanish Match, or Charles Stuart in Madrid, 1865; Myddleton Pomfret, 1865; Auriol, or the Elixir of Life, 1865; The Constable de Bourbon, 1866; Old Court, 1867; The South Sea Bubble, 1868; Hilary St. Ives, 1869; Talbot Harland, 1870; Tower Hill, 1871; Boscobel, 1872; The Good Old Times, the story of the Manchester Rebels, 1873; Merry England, 1874; The Goldsmith's Wife, 1874; Preston Fight, or the Insurrection of 1715, 1875; Chetywnd Calverley, 1876; The League of Lathom, a tale of the Civil War in Lancashire, 1876; The Fall of Somerset, 1877; Beatrice Tyldesley, 1878; Beau Nash, 1879 (?) or 1880; Auriol and other Tales, 1880; Stanley Brereton, 1881.

Editor of *Bentley's Miscellany*, 1838-41, 1854, etc. (in which several of his novels first appeared); of *Ainsworth's Magazine*, 1842-54 (when it was incorporated with *Bentley's Miscellany*); of *New Monthly Magazine and Humourist*, vols. 73-147. He also started *The Bœotian* in 1824, but the magazine only ran through a few numbers. Contributor to *Fraser, London Magazine, Edinburgh Magazine*, etc.

LIFE.—Memoir by Laman Blanchard, the *Mirror*, 1842; prefixed to later editions of Rookwood; John Evans, Early Life of William Harrison Ainsworth, *Manchester Quarterly*, 1882; W. E. Axon, William Harrison Ainsworth, A Memoir, 1902.

CONTENTS

BOOK III—*continued*

PREFACE TO THE FIRST EDITION

THERE is a passage in David Buchanan's memorial of Crichton, in which, alluding to the deadly enmity borne towards the Admirable Scot by Vincenzo di Gonzaga, he assigns as the cause: "quod amasiam principis deperiret." This passage may be regarded as the text of the narrative of Sir Thomas Urquhart, and of the following romance. To a certain extent I have pursued the course taken by the never-sufficiently-to-be-admired Knight of Cromarty, whose *Discoverie of a Jewel* is, indeed, a jewel of a book. Urquhart's descriptions of the masque and duel at Mantua are inimitable. So thoroughly was this singular writer imbued with the spirit of Rabelais (of whom he has left an unfinished, but, so far as it goes, most exquisite translation), that in his account of the disputation in the college of Navarre, he seems to have unconsciously imitated Panurge's controversy with Thaumast, the Englishman, while, in the "true pedigree and lineal descent of the ancient and honourable family of Urquhart," he appears anxious to emulate the mighty genealogical honours of the good Pantagruel. Sir Thomas, however, is a joyous spirit—a right Pantagruelist; and if he occasionally

Projicit ampullas et sesquipedalia verba,

he has an exuberance of wit and playfulness of fancy that amply redeems his tendency to fanfaronade.

In my endeavour to illustrate the various shades of Crichton's many-coloured character, I have, perhaps, touched too lightly on its scholastic features. But feeling that adequately to exhibit one of the scenes of intellectual digladiation in which he was so frequently and so triumphantly engaged, it would require the possession of a depth of learning little inferior to that of the invincible disputant himself, I have elected as the safer and more suitable course to portray him as the *preux chevalier* and all-accomplished gallant, rather than as the philosopher and dialectician.

Boccalini's *Satiric Sketch*, Sir Thomas Urquhart's *Jewel*, and other allusions of more accredited biographers, would justify me in giving my hero an air of gallantry, were it possible to

1

conceive that he who surpassed all the aspiring spirits of the age in which he flourished in the feats of arts and arms (and whose aim was to excel in everything), could be behind them in their excesses, especially when those very excesses tended to advance his reputation. The manners of the time were corrupt in the extreme; and the fascinations of the *belles et honnêtes dames et demoiselles* of the Court of Catherine de Medicis were such as required more stoicism to withstand than the handsome Scot cared to practise. The reader may, if he chooses, speedily gather a notion of the universal profligacy of the period from the *bons contes* of Brantôme, and the different memoirs included in the *Journal of Henri III*.

What I have advanced respecting Margaret de Valois is fully borne out by the *Divorce Satirique*, and the details of Scipio Dupleix. The majestic and terrible figure of Catherine de Medicis is too deeply impressed upon the page of history to make it necessary to advert to the sources whence I have transferred its lineaments to my canvas.

It only now remains to speak of Vincenzo di Gonzaga, whose cause has been warmly but unsuccessfully advocated by Dr. Black. Notwithstanding his patronage of men of letters (extended towards them as much from ostentation as any other motive by the various Italian rulers of the time), this prince was, we learn from Muratori, exceedingly luxurious and profuse in his habits: "gran giocatore, grande scialacquator del danaro, sempre involto fra il lusso, e gli amori, sempre in lieti passatempi o di festi, o di balli, o di musiche, o di commedie." Sismondi, who has given an excellent summary of his character, says: "il aimait avec passion les femmes, le jeu, la danse, le théâtre." And Possevino, the annalist (and, therefore, the panegyrist) of his family, expressly alludes to his vindictive disposition: "quidam vindictæ nimium, ideoque in abrupta tractum opinantur." For the rest, I may affirm with Victor Hugo: "que souvent les fables du peuple font la vérité du poète."

THE ADMIRABLE CRICHTON

BOOK I

CHAPTER I

THE SCHOLARS

Tu viens doncques de Paris? dist Pantagruel—Et à quoy passez-vous le temps vous aultres Messieurs Estudians au dict Paris?—RABELAIS, *Pantagruel*, liv. ii. chap. vi.

TOWARDS the close of Wednesday, the 4th of February, 1579, a vast assemblage of scholars was collected before the Gothic gateway of the ancient college of Navarre. So numerous was this concourse, that it not merely blocked up the area in front of the renowned seminary in question, but extended far down the Rue de la Montagne Sainte-Geneviève, in which it is situated. Never had such a disorderly rout been brought together since the days of the uproar in 1557, when the predecessors of these turbulent students took up arms, marched in a body to the Pré-aux-Clercs, set fire to three houses in the vicinity, and slew a sergeant of the guard, who vainly endeavoured to restrain their fury. Their last election of a rector, Messire Adrien d'Amboise, "pater eruditionum," as he is described in his epitaph, when the same body congregated within the cloisters of the Mathurins, and thence proceeded, in tumultuous array, to the church of Saint-Louis, in the isle of the same name, had been nothing to it. Every scholastic hive sent forth its drones. Sorbonne and Montaigu, Cluny, Harcourt, the Four Nations, and a host of minor establishments—in all, amounting to forty-two—each added its swarms; and a pretty buzzing they created! The fair of Saint-Germain had only commenced the day before; but though its festivities were to continue till Palm Sunday, and though it was the constant resort of the scholars, who committed, during their days of carnival, ten thousand excesses, it was now absolutely deserted.

The Pomme-de-Pin, the Castel, the Magdaleine and the Mule, those *tabernes méritoires*, celebrated in Pantagruel's

3

conference with the Limosin student, which has conferred upon them an immortality like that of our own hostel, the Mermaid, were wholly neglected; the dice-box was laid aside for the nonce; and the well-used cards were thrust into the doublets of these thirsty tipplers of the schools.

But not alone did the crowd consist of the brawler, the gambler, the bully, and the debauchee, though these, it must be confessed, predominated. It was a grand medley of all sects and classes. The modest demeanour of the retiring, pale-browed student was contrasted with the ferocious aspect and reckless bearing of his immediate neighbour, whose appearance was little better than that of a bravo. The grave theologian and embryo ecclesiastic were placed in juxtaposition with the scoffing and licentious acolyte; while lawyer *in posse*, and the law-breaker *in esse*, were numbered amongst a group whose pursuits were those of violence and fraud.

Various as were the characters that composed it, not less diversified were the costumes of this heterogeneous assemblage. Subject to no particular regulations as to dress, or rather openly infracting them, if any such were attempted to be enforced, each scholar, to whatever college he belonged, attired himself in such garments as best suited his taste or his finances. Taking it altogether, the mob was neither remarkable for the fashion nor the cleanliness of the apparel of its members.

From Rabelais we learn that the passion of play was so strongly implanted in the students of his day, that they would frequently stake the points of their doublets at tric-trac or trou-madame; and but little improvement had taken place in their morals or manners some half-century afterwards. The buckle at their girdle—the mantle on their shoulders—the shirt to their back—often stood the hazard of the die; and hence it not unfrequently happened, that a rusty pourpoint and ragged *chausses* were all the covering which the luckless dicers could enumerate, owing, no doubt, "to the extreme rarity and penury of *pecune* in their *marsupies*."

Round or square caps, hoods and cloaks of black, grey, or other sombre hue, were, however, the prevalent garb of the members of the university; but here and there might be seen some gayer specimen of the tribe, whose broad-brimmed, high-crowned felt hat and flaunting feather; whose puffed-out sleeves and exaggerated ruff—with starched plaits of such amplitude that they had been not inappropriately named *plats de Saint Jean Baptiste,* from the resemblance which the wearer's head bore to that of the saint, when deposited in the charger of the daughter of Herodias, were intended to ape the leading mode of the elegant court of their sovereign Henri Trois.

To such an extent had these insolent youngsters carried their licence of imitation, that certain of their members, fresh from the fair of Saint-Germain, and not wholly unacquainted with the hippocras of the sutlers crowding its mart, wore around their throats enormous collars of paper, cut in rivalry of the legitimate plaits of muslin, and bore in their hands long hollow sticks, from which they discharged peas and other missiles in imitation of the sarbacanes then in vogue with the monarch and his favourites.

Thus fantastically tricked out, on that same day—nay, only a few hours before, and at the fair above-mentioned, had these facetious wights, with more merriment than discretion, ventured to exhibit themselves before the cortège of Henri, and to exclaim loud enough to reach the ears of royalty, "à la fraise on connoit le veau!"—a piece of pleasantry for which they subsequently paid dear.

Notwithstanding its shabby appearance in detail, the general effect of this scholastic rabble was striking and picturesque. The thick moustaches and pointed beards with which the lips and chins of most of them were decorated, gave to their physiognomies a manly and determined air, fully borne out by their unrestrained carriage and deportment. To a man, almost all were armed with a tough vine-wood bludgeon, called in their language an *estoc volant*, tipped and shod with steel—a weapon fully understood by them, and rendered, by their dexterity in the use of it, formidable to their adversaries. Not a few carried at their girdles the short rapier, so celebrated in their duels and brawls, or concealed within their bosom a poniard or a two-edged knife.

The scholars of Paris have ever been a turbulent and ungovernable race; and at the period of which this history treats, and, indeed, long before, were little better than a licensed horde of robbers, consisting of a pack of idle and wayward youths drafted from all parts of Europe, as well as from the remoter provinces of their own nation. There was little in common between the mass of students and their brethren, excepting the fellowship resulting from the universal licence in which all indulged. Hence their thousand combats amongst themselves—combats almost invariably attended with fatal consequences—and which the heads of the university found it impossible to check.

Their own scanty resources, eked out by what little they could derive from beggary or robbery, formed their chief subsistence; for many of them were positive mendicants, and were so denominated; and, being possessed of a sanctuary within their own quarters, to which they could at convenience retire, they submitted to the constraint of no laws except those enforced within the jurisdiction of the university, and hesitated at no means of enriching themselves at the expense of their neighbours. Hence, the frequent warfare waged between them and the brethren of Saint-Germain-des-Prés, whose monastic domains adjoined their territories, and whose meadows were the constant *champ clos* of their skirmishes; according to Dulaure—*presque toujours un théâtre de tumulte, de galanterie, de combats, de duels, de débauches, et de sédition.* Hence their sanguinary conflicts with the good citizens of Paris, to whom they were wholly obnoxious, and who occasionally repaid their aggressions with interest. In 1407, two of their number, convicted of assassination and robbery, were condemned to the gibbet, and the sentence was carried into execution; but so great was the uproar occasioned in the university by this violation of its immunities, that the Provost of Paris, Guillaume de Tignonville, was compelled to take down their bodies from Montfaucon, and see them honourably and ceremoniously interred. This recognition of their rights only served to make matters worse, and for a series of years the nuisance continued unabated.

It is not our purpose to record all the excesses of the university, nor the means taken for their suppression. Vainly were the civil authorities arrayed against them. Vainly were bulls thundered from the Vatican. No amendment was effected. The weed might be cut down, but was never entirely extirpated. Their feuds were transmitted from generation to generation, and their old bone of contention with the abbot of Saint-Germain (the Pré-aux-Clercs) was, after an uninterrupted strife for thirty years, submitted to the arbitration of the Pope, who very equitably refused to pronounce judgment in favour of either party.

Such were the scholars of Paris in the sixteenth century—such the character of the clamorous crew who besieged the portals of the college of Navarre.

The object that summoned together this unruly multitude, was, it appears, a desire on the part of the scholars to be present at a public controversy, or learned disputation, then occurring within the great hall of the college before which they were congregated, and the disappointment caused by their finding the gates closed, and all entrance denied to them, occasioned their present disposition to riot.

It was in vain they were assured by the halberdiers stationed at the gates, and who, with crossed pikes, strove to resist the onward pressure of the mob, that the hall and court were already crammed to overflowing, that there was not room even for the sole of a foot of a doctor of the faculties, and that their orders were positive and imperative that none beneath the degree of a bachelor or licentiate should be admitted, and that a troop of martinets[1] and *Béjaunes*[2] could have no possible claim to admission. In vain they were told this was no ordinary disputation, no common controversy, that all were alike entitled to licence of ingress, that the disputant was no undistinguished scholar, whose renown did not extend beyond his own trifling sphere, and whose opinions, therefore, few would care to hear, and still fewer to oppugn, but a foreigner of high rank, in high favour and fashion, and not more remarkable for his extraordinary intellectual endowments, than for his brilliant personal accomplishments. In vain the trembling officials sought to clinch their arguments by stating, that not alone did the conclave consist of the chief members of the university, the senior doctors of theology, medicine and law, the professors of the humanities, rhetoric and philosophy, and all the various other dignitaries; but that the debate was honoured by the presence of Monsieur Christophe de Thou, first president of parliament; by that of the learned Jacques Augustin, of the same name; by one of the secretaries of state and governor of Paris, M. René de Villequier; by the ambassadors of Elizabeth, Queen of England; and of Philip II., King of Spain, and several of their suite; by Abbé de Brantôme; by M. Miron, the court physician; by Cosmo Ruggieri, the Queen-Mother's astrologer; by the renowned poets and masque writers, Maîtres Ronsard, Baïf, and Philippe Desportes; by the well-known advocate of parliament, Messire Etienne Pasquier; but, also (and here came the gravamen of the objection to their admission) by the two especial favourites of his majesty and leaders of affairs, the *seigneurs* of Joyeuse and D'Epernon.

It was in vain the students were informed that, for the preservation of strict decorum, they had been commanded by

---

[1] Scholars either not living within the walls of the university, or not being *en pension* at the colleges.

[2] Yellow-beaks; a nickname applied to newly admitted students.

the rector to make fast the gates. No excuses would avail them. The scholars were cogent reasoners, and a show of staves soon brought their opponents to a nonplus. In this line of argument they were perfectly aware of their ability to prove a major.

"To the wall with them—to the wall!" cried a hundred infuriated voices. "Down with the halberdiers—down with the gates—down with the disputants—down with the rector himself!—Deny our privileges! To the wall with old Adrien d'Amboise—exclude the disciples of the university from their own halls!—curry favour with the court minions!—hold a public controversy in private!—down with him! We will issue a mandamus for a new election on the spot!"

Whereupon a deep groan resounded throughout the crowd. It was succeeded by a volley of fresh execrations against the rector, and an angry demonstration of bludgeons, accompanied by a brisk shower of peas from the sarbacanes.

The officials turned pale, and calculated the chance of a broken neck in reversion, with that of a broken crown in immediate possession. The former being at least contingent, appeared the milder alternative, and they might have been inclined to adopt it, had not a further obstacle stood in their way. The gate was barred withinside, and the vergers and beadles who had the custody of the door, though alarmed at the tumult without, positively refused to unfasten it.

Again, the threats of the scholars were renewed, and further intimations of violence were exhibited. Again the peas rattled upon the hands and faces of the halberdiers, till their ears tingled with pain. "Prate to us of the king's favourites," cried one of the foremost of the scholars, a youth decorated with a paper collar; "they may rule within the precincts of the Louvre, but not within the walls of the university. *Maugrebleu!* We hold them cheap enough. We heed not the idle bark of these full-fed court lapdogs. What to us is the bearer of a *bilboquet?* By the four evangelists, we will have none of them here! Let the Gascon cadet, D'Epernon, reflect on the fate of Quélus and Maugiron, and let our gay Joyeuse beware of the dog's death of Saint-Mégrin. Place for better men—place for the schools— away with frills and sarbacanes!"

"What to us is a president of parliament, or a governor of the city?" shouted another of the same gentry. "We care nothing for their ministration. We recognise them not, save in their own courts. All their authority fell to the ground at the gate of the Rue Saint Jacques, when they entered our dominions. We care for no parties. We are *politiques*, and steer a middle course. We hold the Guisards as cheap as the Huguenots, and the brethren of the League weigh as little with us as the followers of Calvin. Our only sovereign is Gregory XIII., Pontiff of Rome. Away with the Guise and the Béarnais!"

"Away with Henri of Navarre, if you please," cried a scholar of Harcourt; "or Henri of Valois, if you list, but, by all the saints, not with Henri of Lorraine, he is the fast friend of the true faith. No!—no!—live the Guise—live the Holy Union!"

"Away with Elizabeth of England," cried a scholar of Cluny; "what doth her representative here? Seeks he a spouse for her amongst our schools? She will have no great bargain, I own, if she bestows her royal hand upon our Duc d'Anjou."

"If you value your buff jerkin, I counsel you to say nothing slighting of the Queen of England in my hearing," returned a bluff, broad-shouldered fellow, raising his bludgeon after a menacing fashion. He was an Englishman belonging to the Four Nations, and had a huge bull-dog at his heels.

"Away with Philip of Spain and his ambassador," cried a Bernardin.

"*Por los ojos de mi Dama!*" cried a Spaniard belonging to the College of Narbonne, with huge moustaches curled half-way up his bronzed and insolent visage, and a slouched hat pulled over his brow. "This may not pass muster. The representative of the King of Spain must be respected even by the Academics of Lutetia. Which of you shall gainsay me?—ha!"

"What business has he here with his suite, on occasions like to the present?" returned the Bernardin. "*Tête-Dieu!* this disputation is one that little concerns the interest of your politic king; and methinks Dom Philip, or his representative, has regard for little else than whatsoever advances his own interest. Your ambassador hath, I doubt not, some latent motive for his present attendance in our schools."

"Perchance," returned the Spaniard. "We will discuss that point anon."

"And what doth the pander of the Sybarite within the dusty halls of learning?" ejaculated a scholar of Lemoine. "What doth the jealous-pated slayer of his wife and unborn child within the reach of free-spoken voices, and mayhap of well-directed blades? Methinks it were more prudent to tarry within the bowers of his harem, than to hazard his perfumed person among us."

"Well said," rejoined the scholar of Cluny, "down with René de Villequier, though he be Governor of Paris."

"What title hath the Abbé de Brantôme to a seat amongst us?" said the scion of Harcourt; "certes he hath a reputation for wit, and scholarship, and gallantry. But what is that to us? His place might now be filled by worthier men."

"And what, in the devil's name, brings Cosmo Ruggieri hither?" asked the Bernardin. "What doth the wrinkled old dealer in the black art hope to learn from us? We are not given to alchemy, and the occult sciences; we practise no hidden mysteries; we brew no philtres; we compound no slow poisons; we vend no waxen images. What doth he here, I say! 'Tis a scandal in the rector to permit his presence. And what if he came under the safeguard, and by the authority of his mistress, Catherine de Medicis! Shall we regard her passport? Down with the heathen abbé, his abominations have been endured too long; they smell rank in our nostrils. Think how he ensnared La Mole—think on his numberless victims. Who mixed the infernal potion of Charles IX.? Let him answer that. Down with the infidel—the Jew—the sorcerer! The stake were too good for him. Down with Ruggieri, I say."

"Ay, down with the accursed astrologer," echoed the whole crew. "He has done abundant mischief in his time. A day of reckoning has arrived. Hath he cast his own horoscope? Did he foresee his own fate? Ha! ha!"

"And then the poets," cried another member of the Four Nations—"a plague on all three. Would they were elsewhere. In what does this disputation concern them? Pierre Ronsard, being an offshoot of this same College of Navarre, hath indubitably a claim upon our consideration. But he is old, and I marvel that his gout permitted him to hobble so far. O, the mercenary old scribbler! His late verses halt like himself, yet he lowereth not the price of his masques. Besides which he is grown moral, and unsays all his former good things. *Mort-Dieu!* your superannuated bards ever recant the indiscretions of their nonage. Clement Marot took to psalm-writing in his old age. As to Baïf, his name will scarce outlast the scenery of his ballets, his plays are out of fashion since the Gelosi arrived. He deserves no place amongst us. And Philippe Desportes owes all his present preferment to the Vicomte de Joyeuse. However, he is not altogether devoid of merit—let him wear his bays, so he trouble us not with his company. Room for the sophisters of Narbonne, I say. To the dogs with poetry!"

"*Morbleu!*" exclaimed another. "What are the sophisters of Narbonne to the decretists of the Sorbonne, who will discuss you a position of Cornelius à Lapide, or a sentence of Peter Lombard, as readily as you would a flask of hippocras, or a slice of botargo. Ay, and cry *transeat* to a thesis of Aristotle, though it be against rule. What sayst thou, Capète?" continued he, addressing his neighbour, a scholar of Montaigu, whose modest grey capuchin procured him this appellation. "Are we the men to be thus scurvily entreated?".

"I see not that your merits are greater than ours," returned he of the capuch, "though our boasting be less. The followers of the lowly John Standoncht are as well able to maintain their tenets in controversy as those of Robert of Sorbon, and I see no reason why entrance should be denied us. The honour of the university is at stake, and all its strength should be mustered to assert it."

"Rightly spoken," returned the Bernardin, "and it were a lasting disgrace to our schools were this arrogant Scot to carry off their laurels when so many who might have been found to lower his crest are allowed no share in their defence. The contest is one that concerns us all alike. We at least can arbitrate in case of need."

"I care not for the honours of the university," rejoined one of the Ecossais, or Scotch College, then existing in the Rue des Amandiers, "but I care much for the glory of my countryman, and I would gladly have witnessed the triumph of the disciples of Rutherford, and of the classic Buchanan. But if the arbitrament to which you would resort is to be that of voices merely, I am glad the rector in his wisdom has thought fit to keep you without, even though I myself be personally inconvenienced by it."

"*Hijo de Dios!* what fine talking is this?" retorted the Spaniard. "There is little chance of the triumph you predicate for your countryman. Trust me, we shall have to greet his departure from the debate with many hisses and few cheers; and if we could penetrate through the plates of yon iron door and gaze into the court it conceals from our view, we should find the loftiness of his pretensions has been already humbled, and his arguments gravelled. *Por la Litania de los Santos!* to think of comparing an obscure student of the pitiful College of Saint Andrew with the erudite doctors of the most erudite university in the world, always excepting those of Valencia and Salamanca. It needs all thy country's assurance to keep the blush of shame from mantling in thy cheeks."

"The seminary you revile," replied the Scot, haughtily, "has been the nursery of our Scottish kings. Nay, the youthful James Stuart pursued his studies under the same roof, beneath the same wise instruction, and at the self-same time as our noble and gifted James Crichton, whom you have falsely denominated an adventurer, but whose lineage is not less distinguished than his learning. His renown has preceded him hither, and he was not unknown to your doctors when he affixed his programme to these college walls. Hark!" continued the speaker, exultingly, "and listen to yon evidence of his triumph."

And as he spoke, a loud and continued clapping of hands proceeding from within was distinctly heard above the roar of the students.

"That may be at his defeat," muttered the Spaniard, between his teeth.

"No such thing," replied the Scot. "I heard the name of Crichton mingled with the plaudits."

"And who may be this Phœnix—this Gargantua of intellect —who is to vanquish us all, as Panurge did Thaumast, the Englishman?" asked the Sorbonist of the Scot.—"Who is he that is more philosophic than Pythagoras?—ha!"

"Who is more studious than Carneades!" said the Bernardin.

"More versatile than Alcibiades!" said Montaigu.

"More subtle than Averroës!" cried Harcourt.

"More mystical than Plotinus!" said one of the Four Nations.

"More visionary than Artemidorus!" said Cluny.

"More infallible than the Pope!" added Lemoine.

"And who pretends to dispute *de omni scibili*!" shouted the Spaniard.

"*Et quolibet ente!*" added the Sorbonist.

"Mine ears are stunned with your vociferations," replied the Scot. "You ask me who James Crichton is, and yourselves give the response. You have mockingly said he is a *rara avis*; a prodigy of wit and learning; and you have unintentionally spoken the truth. He is so. But I will tell you that of him which you are wholly ignorant, or which you have designedly overlooked. His condition is that of a Scottish gentleman of high rank. Like your Spanish grandee, he need not doff his cap to kings. On either side hath he the best of blood in his veins. His mother was a Stuart directly descended from that regal line. His father, who owneth the fair domains of Eliock and Cluny, was Lord Advocate to our bonny and luckless Mary (whom Heaven assoilzie!) and still holds his high office. Methinks the Lairds of Crichton might have been heard of here. Howbeit, they are well known to me, who being an Ogilvy of Balfour, have often heard tell of a certain contract or obligation, whereby——"

"*Basta!*" interrupted the Spaniard, "heed not thine own affairs, worthy Scot. Tell us of this Crichton—ha!"

"I have told you already more than I ought to have told," replied Ogilvy, sullenly. "And if you lack further information respecting James Crichton's favour at the Louvre, his feats of arms, and the esteem in which he is held by all the dames of honour in attendance upon your Queen-Mother, Catherine de Medicis—and moreover," he added, with somewhat of sarcasm, "with her fair daughter, Marguerite de Valois—you will do well to address yourself to the king's buffoon Maître Chicot, whom I see not far off. Few there are, methinks, who could in such short space have won so much favour, or acquired such bright renown."

"Humph!" muttered the Englishman, "your Scotsmen stick by each other all the world over. This James Crichton may or may not be the hero he is vaunted, but I shall mistrust his praises from that quarter, till I find their truth confirmed."

"He has, to be sure, acquired the character of a stout swordsman," said the Bernardin, "to give the devil his due."

"He has not met with his match at the *salle-d'armes*, though he has crossed blades with the first in France," replied Ogilvy.

"I have seen him at the *manège*," said the Sorbonist, "go through his course of equitation, and being a not altogether unskilful horseman myself, I can report favourably of his performance."

"There is none among your youth can sit a steed like him," returned Ogilvy, "nor can any of the jousters carry off the ring with more certainty at the lists. I would fain hold my tongue, but you enforce me to speak in his praise."

"*Cuerpo de Dios!*" exclaimed the Spaniard, half unsheathing the lengthy weapon that hung by his side. "I will hold you a wager of ten rose-nobles to as many silver reals of Spain, that with this staunch Toledo I will overcome your vaunted Crichton in close fight in any manner or practice of fence or digladiation which he may appoint—sword and dagger, or sword only—stripped to the girdle or armed to the teeth. *Por la santa Trinidad!* I will have satisfaction for the contumelious affront he hath put upon the very learned gymnasium to which I belong; and it would gladden me to clip the wings of this loud-crowing cock, or of any of his dunghill crew," added he, with a scornful gesture at the Scotsman.

"If that be all you seek, you shall not need to go far in your quest," returned Ogilvy. "Tarry till this controversy be ended, and if I match not your Spanish blade with a Scottish broadsword, and approve you as recreant at heart as you are boastful and injurious of speech, may Saint Andrew for ever after withhold from me his protection."

"*Diablo!*" exclaimed the Spaniard. "Thy Scottish saint will little avail thee, since thou hast incurred my indignation. Betake thee, therefore, to thy paternosters, if thou hast grace withal to mutter them; for within the hour thou art assuredly food for the kites of the Pré-aux-Clercs—sa-ha!"

"Look to thyself, vile braggart!" rejoined Ogilvy, scornfully; "I promise thee thou shalt need other intercession than thine own to purchase safety at my hands."

"Courage, Master Ogilvy," said the Englishman, "thou wilt do well to slit the ears of this Spanish swashbuckler. I warrant me he hides a craven spirit beneath that slashed pourpoint. Thou art in the right, man, to make him eat his words. Be this Crichton what he may, he is, at least, thy countryman, and in part mine own."

"And as such I will uphold him," said Ogilvy, "against any odds."

"Bravo! my valorous Don Diego Caravaja," said the Sorbonist, slapping the Spaniard on the shoulder, and speaking in his ear. "Shall these scurvy Scots carry all before them?— I warrant me, no. We will make common cause against the whole beggarly nation; and in the meanwhile we entrust thee with this particular quarrel. See thou acquit thyself in it as beseemeth a descendant of the Cid."

"Account him already abased," returned Caravaja. "By Pelayo, I would the other were at his back, that both might be transfixed at a blow—ha!"

"To return to the subject of difference," said the Sorbonist, who was too much delighted with the prospect of a duel to allow the quarrel a chance of subsiding, while it was in his power to fan the flame; "to return to the difference," said he, aloud, glancing at Ogilvy; "it must be conceded that, as a wassailer, this Crichton is without a peer. None of us may presume to cope with him in the matter of the flask and the flagon, though we number amongst us some jolly topers. Friar John, with the Priestess of Bacbuc, was a washy bibber compared with him."

"He worships at the shrines of other priestesses besides hers of Bacbuc, if I be not wrongly informed," added Montaigu, who understood the drift of his companion.

"Else wherefore our rejoinder to his cartels?" returned the Sorbonist. "Do you not call to mind that beneath his arrogant defiance of our learned body, affixed to the walls of the Sorbonne, it was written, 'That he who would behold this miracle of learning must hie to the tavern or the bordel'? Was it not so, my hidalgo?"

"I have myself seen him at the temulentive tavern of the Falcon," returned Caravaja, "and at the lupanarian haunts in the Champ - Gaillard and the Val - d'Amour. You understand me—ha!"

"Ha! ha! ha!" chorused the scholars. "James Crichton is no stoic. He is a disciple of Epicurus. *Vel in puellam impingit, vel in poculum*—ha! ha!"

"'Tis said that he hath dealings with the Evil One," observed the man of Harcourt, with a mysterious air; "and that, like Jeanne d'Arc, he hath surrendered his soul for his temporal welfare. Hence his wondrous lore; hence his supernatural beauty and accomplishments; hence his power of fascinating the fair sex; hence his constant run of luck with the dice; hence, also, his invulnerableness to the sword."

"'Tis said, also, that he has a familiar spirit, who attends him in the semblance of a black dog," said Montaigu.

"Or in that of a dwarf, like the sooty imp of Cosmo Ruggieri," said Harcourt. "Is it not so?" he asked, turning to the Scot.

"He lies in his throat who says so," cried Ogilvy, losing all patience. "To one and all of you I breathe defiance; and there is not a brother in the college to which I belong who will not maintain my quarrel."

A loud laugh of derision followed this sally; and, ashamed of having justly exposed himself to ridicule by his idle and unworthy display of passion, the Scotsman held his peace and endeavoured to turn a deaf ear to their taunts.

CHAPTER II

THE GELOSO

Ham. Will you play upon this pipe?
Guil. My lord, I cannot.
Ham. I pray you.   SHAKESPEARE.

WHILE his eye glanced fiercely round upon his tormentors, Ogilvy suddenly encountered the dark and earnest orbs of a youth, standing at a little distance from him, but fully within hearing of their contention, who appeared to take a lively interest in the cause of quarrel, though his sympathy was evidently strongly enlisted in behalf of the Scotsman. There was something in the appearance of this youth that, despite the excitement of his feelings, at once arrested the attention of Ogilvy.

In age, the youth could not be more than eighteen, perhaps not so much, as his slight, though exquisitely symmetrical figure, fragile even to effeminacy, denoted immaturity. But the fire and intelligence of his glances showed that his spirit and resolution were far in advance of his years. Tresses of jetty hair overshadowed his flushed cheek — the olive tint of which, together with his intensely black eyes, proclaimed him a native of some more southern clime — while his attire, though not otherwise singular, was neither that of a member of the university nor accordant with any of the received usages then adopted by the good citizens of Paris. A cap of green Genoa velvet fell on one side of his head; a mantle of the same material, and of ampler fold than was the mode, was clasped with a chain of gold, and disposed so as best to hide his slender shape, and to give a semblance of more manly width to his narrow proportion of shoulder.

"You are moved in my behalf, young sir," said Ogilvy, remarking that the youth still kept his eye fixed upon him, forcing his way at the same time towards the spot where he stood. "May I ask to which of our academies you belong?"

"I belong to none of your schools," replied the youth, now shrinking from the Scot's approach as much as he had courted his attention from afar. "I came hither as a stranger, attracted solely by curiosity to learn the result of a disputation with which all Paris rings; and having unwittingly entered this crowd, though I would fain retire, I must now perforce abide its issue, which," he added, with some hesitation, and a slight increase of colour, "will, I trust, result in the triumph of your peerless countryman, in whose success I am, I own, nearly as much interested as yourself."

There was a music in the tones that vibrated in a strange manner upon the heart of Ogilvy.

"As I have a soul to be saved," he thought, "but that they are boy's lips that uttered that speech, I could have sworn it was the very voice of Marion; and, but that the eyes are darker, and it may be larger, I could swear they had the same look too. By Saint Andrew, but it is singular how like they are. I would gladly know, if he be not from my own country, what can make him express himself so warmly in behalf of James Crichton. Hark ye, young sir," he cried aloud, "you are not, I suppose, from Scotland, are you?"

The youth could scarce forbear a smile at the inquiry; but he shook his head in denial. The smile that severed the lips displayed a row of pearls. "The very teeth are Marion's," thought Ogilvy.

"From Scotland?" shouted the Sorbonist. "Can any good come from out that rascal country? I know this youth well—he is one of the Gelosi—one of the Venetian troop who have the king's licence to enact their plays at the Hôtel de Bourbon. I thought I knew the face and figure, but the voice was not to be mistaken. 'Tis he who singeth the airs in the comedies; and right well, too, I warrant him. Ah!—a thought strikes me—we have a minute or two to spare—why not employ it in a song? What say you, comrades, shall we lose this golden opportunity?—A song!—a song!"

"Bravo!—bravo!" cried the scholars, clapping their hands. "Nothing can be better. A song by all means"; and a circle of faces was presently formed round the Geloso.

Meanwhile Ogilvy, not less annoyed at the turn which affairs had taken, than at the supposed imputations thrown out against the stranger, for, not being untinctured by the prejudices of his country, as to the morality of stage representations, he entertained a feeling of contempt, amounting almost to abhorrence, for the vocation of an actor, thus addressed him: "Hath he not belied thee?" he said, with something of distrust. "Say he hath spoken falsely—say thou art no player—no hired mimic, and, by the pious memory of John Knox, I will hurl back the foul aspersion in his teeth."

"Peace!" cried the scholar of Montaigu. "Down with the froward Scot, if he offer further interruption."

"Let him answer me, and I am dumb," returned the resolute Ogilvy. "Once more, stranger—have I misconstrued thee?"

"You have done so if you supposed me other than I am," replied the youth, raising his head. "I am one of the Gelosi!"

"You hear him," cried the Sorbonist. "He admits it. Now, give us the song without more ado."

"I deny not my calling," replied the Geloso, "but I will not sing at your bidding."

"We will see that," returned the Sorbonist. "There are pumps within our courts whose waters are as song-compelling as those of Helicon. Their virtue is marvellous."

"*Sangre de Dios!* let us drag the young spark thither," cried Caravaja; "he'll find his voice, I'll engage, rather than brook the catarrhs likely to be engendered by the gelid fount."

So saying he laid his hand rudely upon the Geloso's shoulder. The latter started back—his dark eyes shot lightnings at the aggressor, while, quick as thought, he drew forth a stiletto, and placed it at Caravaja's throat.

"Withdraw thy hand from my person," he cried, "or by St. Mark I will strike!"

And Caravaja, seeing from his manner that the Geloso was in earnest, deemed it prudent to relinquish his hold, which he did with a shrug and his habitual braggadocio exclamation.

"*Bravissimo!*" shouted the bystanders with renewed acclamation; "a capital *tableau*. It would tell famously at the Hôtel de Bourbon."

"By my faith!" said the Englishman, laughing heartily, "our Spaniard hath the worst of it."

"I pray you, *signori*," said the Geloso, heedless of their sarcasm, taking off his cap and displaying at the same time a shower of raven ringlets. "I beseech you to let me depart without further molestation; I have it in not my power to comply with your wishes, neither do I see your title to require my compliance. Though a player, I am not wholly unfriended; and if——"

"He threatens us," said the Sorbonist; "marked you that *if?* It will never do to give up our point. The song, Signor Geloso, and then depart as soon as you list."

"Never!" replied the Geloso; "and I counsel you to beware how you drive me to extremities."

"If none other will take the youth's part I will," said the Englishman. "I care not if he be Geloso or Diaboloso. If all are against him I am for him. The Blounts ever take the weaker side, and Simon Blount will not disgrace the name he bears. Come, Sir Scot, this quarrel is partly yours. Draw your blade, man, and stand by this poor lad, who looks as if he had never seen a blow struck before."

A blithe jingle of small silver bells was heard amongst the crowd, offering a seasonable interruption to the brawl, and a very fantastic personage, from whom the sound proceeded, strove to press forward. He was clad in a singular parti-coloured raiment, composed of white, crimson and blue damask, so quaintly fashioned, and striped with such numberless straight and horizontal lines, that it produced the most whimsical effect imaginable. His slashed *juste-au-corps* was puffed out at the hips in the most extravagant style, and served as an admirable foil to his thin misshapen legs, decked in hose of amaranthine hue. Over his shoulders was thrown a surcoat which resembled nothing so nearly as the vestment wherewith the knave of clubs is arrayed, and which depended in huge sleeves over his arms.

At the back of this surcoat the royal arms were emblazoned in gold tissue, and again displayed on either sleeve. Innumerable tags, to which, as well as to the edges of his sleeves, hung the bells in question, adorned each knee. Around his neck he wore a chain of small medallions, stamped with devices *à la folie,* the gift of his *cher Henriot,* as he fraternally termed his royal master, and his tall conical cap—which had superseded the old orthodox cock's-comb, then quite out of date—had the triple points *à la cornette,* borne by all the servitors of the court. In his hand he carried his ensign of office—the bauble, an ebony truncheon decorated with the fool's head, cast in wrought silver. A huge escarcelle, or pouch, filled with confectionery, of which he was immoderately fond, hung at his girdle, and near it was stuck a formidable dagger of lath.

This bizarre figure was the king's favourite buffoon Chicot.

"By your leave, my masters," he cried, shouldering his way through the crowd, and bestowing buffets with his bauble upon all who opposed his progress. "Why would you stop me? Folly was ever current in the University of Paris. Besides, all my wisdom is needed. They are about to souse a singer in cold water to give him a voice. That were a feat worthy the first fool in France. I should lose my post were I not to assist. Have a care, I say. Make way for the Abbé of the Béjaunes, though he be not mounted on his ass as at the Feast of the Innocents."

And planting himself immediately before the Geloso, to whom he nodded in the most familiar manner, Chicot drew his lathen dagger and, with abundance of gesticulations and grimaces, brandished it in the face of the students. "This youth, who is my foster-brother," said the jester (here there was a loud laugh), "is in the right to refuse you. He is engaged for the masque to-night, and must not exhibit himself beforehand. Our gossip Henriot is chary of his services. If you want music, come with us to the gates of the Louvre. The band of the Swiss Guard is celebrated for its quick movement."

"Exasperate them not, kind sir," whispered the Geloso, "I will rather comply with their demands, unreasonable though they be, than endanger another's safety by refusal. *Signori*," he continued, addressing his persecutors, "I will do your bidding, provided I am free to depart when my song is ended."

"Agreed!" shouted the scholars, waving their caps. In an instant the clamour ceased. A dense ring was formed around the Geloso, while in a voice of the most exquisite modulation, though with something of sarcasm in its tone, he sang the following strain, evidently the inspiration of the moment:

THE SCOTTISH CAVALIER

I

From Scotia's clime to laughing France
    The peerless Crichton came;
Like him no knight could shiver lance,
    Wield sword, or worship dame.
Alas! each maiden sighs in vain,
    He turns a careless ear:
For *queenly* fetters fast enchain
    The Scottish cavalier!

II

But not o'er camp and court, alone,
    Resistless Crichton rules;
Logicians next, defeated, own
    His empire o'er the Schools.
'Gainst sophists shrewd shall wit prevail,
    Though tome on tome they rear;
And pedants pale, as victor, hail
    The Scottish cavalier!

"No more of this," cried the Sorbonist, "this is not the song we bargained for. We will have thy favourite air from *La Maddalena*, or the canzonet from *La Florinda*, or thou stirrest not, *mon mignon*."

"Bah!" ejaculated Chicot; "you are no judges. The song was charming, and I vote for its repetition. But the buffoonery of the troop at the *hôtel* of the Abbé de Clugni, in the Rue des Mathurins, would be more in your way. What say you to a motet from their last *sotie—La Farce joyeuse des béjaunes sophistes?*"

"*Ventrebleu!* What mockery is this?" cried one of the scholars with the preposterous paper collars. "Are we to be chaffered out of our projects by yon magot-pie, who, having newly escaped his cage, hath flown hither to babble at his ease?"

"'Tis well," returned Chicot, "that, like some I wot of, I have not arrayed myself in peacock's plumes. Strut as it may, the daw will out; and roar as loudly and lion-like as he may, the ass is an ass still. Fool as I am, I am not folly's counterfeit. The ape, but not the ape's shadow, *compère.* 'By the caul you may know the calf'; that is your cry, they tell me. Now, were your calf-ship to be judged by that rule, we could scarce find subject fitter for the shambles."

"A thousand devils!" cried the enraged scholar. "Were you ten times the licensed fool you are, you shall repent this insolence."

"Back!" exclaimed Blount, interposing his bludgeon so as to ward off the blow aimed at the jester's sconce. "A bloody cock's-comb were an unseemly consummation to such gay apparel. Reserve your blows for one more able to requite them. See you not his weapon is of lath?"

"Let him keep better rule over his tongue, then," replied the angry scholar.

"Ha! ha! ha!" cried Chicot, screaming with laughter, "stay me not. I will combat with him to the outrance. My marotte to his ruff, but I slay him on the exchange of a stoccata. My *feeble* shall prove his *reverse.*"

"In the meantime we are losing sight of our songster," said the Sorbonist. "What hath become of the Geloso?"

"Vanished, as I think," exclaimed Caravaja. "I nowhere behold him."

"I had not remarked his departure," thought Ogilvy, "but 'tis better thus. I could not have refused the poor youth aid in case of need, and yet my soul revolts at the thought of being embroiled in the quarrel of a stage-player. 'Tis strange the face should haunt me so much. I will think of him no more."

But, in spite of his resolution, Ogilvy could not prevent his eyes from wandering amongst the distant ranks of the scholars in search of the fugitive. His quest was vain. During the confusion created by the jester's defiance of the student, and not improbably by his connivance, or that of the Englishman, the Geloso had contrived, unobserved, to make good his retreat.

"Hath Maître Chicot secreted him in his escarcelle? It is large enough," said Harcourt.

"Or in the sleeves of his surcoat," said the Bernardin.

"Or swallowed him, as Gargantua did the pilgrim," added Caravaja, laughing.

"Or as thou wouldst a cup of *Val de Peñas*, were it proffered thee; or thine own words, if need be, Señor Caballero," said the jester.

"Señor Satan!" roared Caravaja, unsheathing his sword; "I will carve thee into as many slices as there are patches in thy jerkin—sa-ha!"

"Or as there are dints on thy sword, of thine own notching," rejoined Chicot, with a malignant grin; "or oaths in thy mouth, of thine own coining. Or lies in thy brain, of thine own hatching. Or dice in thy pocket, of thine own loading. Or pence in thy pouch, of thine own pilfering. Or scars in thy back, of thine own procuring—ha! ha! Shred me into as many pieces as a Spanish onion, and the number shall yet be far below thy own countless peccadilloes—sa-ha!"

"*Sangre de Dios!* Give me way to the scurrilous ribald," vociferated Caravaja, furious as a bull chafed by the matador, flourishing his rapier and stamping on the ground, and with difficulty withheld by the students. But nothing could check the wild exhilaration of the jester, who was nigh convulsed with laughter at the ineffectual attempts of the vindictive Spaniard to reach him. He exhibited no alarm, but stood his ground as carelessly as if no danger threatened him. Nay, he even continued his galling mockery, and might, in all probability, have paid the penalty of his rashness, if a new incident had not occurred, which operated as a diversion in his favour.

The gates of the College of Navarre were suddenly thrown open, and a long-continued thunder of applause bursting from within, announced the conclusion of the debate. That it had terminated in favour of Crichton could no longer be doubted, as his name formed the burden of all the plaudits with which the courts were ringing. All was excitement: there was a general movement. Ogilvy could no longer restrain himself. Pushing forward by prodigious efforts, he secured himself a position at the portal.

The first person who presented himself to his inquiring eyes was a gallant figure in a glittering steel corslet, crossed by a silken sash, who bore at his side a long sword with a magnificent handle, and upon his shoulder a lance of some six feet in length, headed with a long scarlet tassel, and brass half-moon pendant. "Is not Crichton victorious?" asked Ogilvy of Captain Larchant, for he it was.

"He hath acquitted himself to admiration," replied the
guardsman, who, contrary to the custom of such gentry (for
captains of the guard have been fine gentlemen in all ages),
did not appear to be displeased at this appeal to his courtesy,
"and the rector hath adjudged him all the honours that can be
bestowed by the university."

"Hurrah for old Scotland," shouted Ogilvy, throwing his bonnet in the air. "I was sure it would be so; this is a day worth
living for. *Hæc olim meminisse juvabit!*"

"Thou at least shall have reason to remember it," muttered
Caravaja, who being opposite to him, heard the exclamation—
"and he too, perchance," he added, frowning gloomily, and
drawing his cloak over his shoulder.

"If the noble Crichton be compatriot of yours, you are in the
right to be proud of him," replied Captain Larchant, "for the
memory of his deeds of this day will live as long as learning shall
be held in reverence. Never before hath such a marvellous display
of universal erudition been heard within these schools. By my
faith, I am absolutely wonder-stricken, and not I alone, but all.
In proof of which I need only tell you, that coupling his matchless scholarship with his extraordinary accomplishments, the
professors in their address to him at the close of the controversy,
have bestowed upon him the epithet of 'ADMIRABLE'—an
appellation by which he will ever after be distinguished."

"The Admirable Crichton!" echoed Ogilvy—"hear you that!
—a title adjudged to him by the whole conclave of the university—hurrah! THE ADMIRABLE CRICHTON! 'Tis a name will
find an echo in the heart of every true Scot. By Saint Andrew!
this is a proud day for us."

"In the meantime," said Larchant, smiling at Ogilvy's exulta-
tions, and describing a circle with the point of his lance, "I must
trouble you to stand back, Messieurs Scholars, and leave free
passage for the rector and his train.—Archers advance, and make
clear the way, and let the companies of the Baron d'Epernon
and of the Vicomte de Joyeuse be summoned as well as the guard
of his excellency, Seigneur René de Villequier. Patience,
messieurs, you will hear all particulars anon."

So saying, he retired, and the men-at-arms, less complaisant
than their leaders, soon succeeded in forcing back the crowd.

CHAPTER III

THE RECTOR OF THE UNIVERSITY OF PARIS

The rector now finding it high time to give some relaxation to these
worthy spirits, which, during such a long space had been so intensely
bent upon the abstrusest speculations, rose up, and saluting the divine
Crichton, after he had made an elegant panegyric, or encomiastic speech
of half an hour's continuance, tending to nothing else but the extolling
of him for the rare and most singular gifts with which God and Nature
had endowed him, presented him with a diamond ring, and a purse full
of gold.—Sir Thomas Urquhart.

As the archers advanced and posted one of their number at
every interval of ten paces, the scholars drew back and, with
almost military precision, formed themselves into two solid
bodies.

A profound hush of expectation reigned throughout their
lines. Each eye was directed towards the embrowned archway
of the Academy, but not a word was uttered. All remained in
postures as motionless as those of the statues of Philippe-le-Bel
and Jeanne de Navarre his spouse (the foundress of the Institution), who looked from their niches on the portal like mute
spectators of the scene.

Meanwhile, from out the gateway there issued such a constant
stream of grave and gowned dignitaries, that the space between
the two files of students was presently filled up by a moving mass
of robes and caps. First, flourishing his rod of office, a blue wand
plentifully besprinkled with fleurs-de-lis of gold, alternately
planting it on the ground or elevating it in the air, with a strut
and simper worthy of Malvolio, strode forth the clerk of the messengers, who bore upon his tunic the blazon of the university,
namely, a hand descending from the sky, holding a book,
surrounded by three fleurs-de-lis *or*, on a field, *azure*. Glancing
at the scholars with a supercilious smile, the herald passed on.
Next came the bedels and the minor bedels of all Faculties, who
by some accident were so jumbled together that it was impossible to determine or arrange any order of precedence. All
put their best feet foremost. Medicine trod hard on the heels of
Theology and the Arts, while Civil Law appeared most uncivilly
inclined to outstrip all three. These bedels or greffiers were jolly
robustious souls, bending beneath the weight of their ponderous
silver maces, and attired in gowns of black, blue, violet, or dark
red, each colour denoting the Faculty to which the wearer per-
tained. To the bedels succeeded a confusion worse confounded,

in the heads of the Faculties themselves, who strove in vain to collect together their scattered forces, or to form them into anything like processional array.

Violations of collegiate etiquette took place each instant. Here was a Doctor of Theology in his black cope edged with ermine, by the side of a procureur of the Nations, in his red robe of office; a propinquity which the Theologian internally execrated, and openly resented. There a Doctor of Medicine in his scarlet cope, trimmed with minever, was elbowed by a Licentiate of Theology, who happened to be suppler of joint, and who was arrayed in cope of sable bordered with white fur. No degrees were respected. The Doctors of the Canon and Civil Law, who had kept together during the debate, and whose costume consisted of scarlet robes with hoods of fur, were most scandalously hustled in maintaining their ground against a rush of youthful Bachelors of Medicine.

Notwithstanding all this confusion of raiments, which were so massed and heaped together as to present an almost rainbow variety of tints in the rays of the setting sun—notwithstanding the utter want of order which occasioned much objurgation on the part of the seniors, and not a little expenditure of patience as well as of ermine, by their too close proximity to each other—notwithstanding all this, the whole body of Doctors, Professors, Bachelors, and Licentiates, were unanimous upon one point—namely that the disputation at which they had assisted had been more admirably contested than any controversy since the days of Petrus Abelardus, and Berengarius, and that in vanquishing them Crichton had vanquished the whole world of science and learning.

Suddenly the shrill blast of a trumpet shook the air, and echoed far down the hill of Sainte-Geneviève. The call was immediately answered by the trampling of a troop of horsemen in the distance. Presently the clatter of hoofs drew nearer, and a few seconds had not elapsed ere two companies, each consisting of fifty archers of the bodyguard, fully accoutred and superbly mounted, rode into the area and drew up in the rear of the students. Besides this array of soldiery might be seen the numerous retinue of René de Villequier, composed not merely of his own lackeys and attendants in their sumptuous apparel of blue and red cloth, but of certain armed cross-bowmen of the *Guet Royal,* headed by their chevalier, who surrounded the governor's huge unwieldly caroche of state and richly caparisoned Flanders horses. Altogether it was a gallant sight; and the scholars, though not entirely satisfied with the presence of so many intruders, and perhaps not wholly unawed by their numbers, manifested no further show of discontent.

A pause now took place in the procession. The foremost in advance came to a halt, and the whole body wheeled round and faced the college. Three semicircles were thus formed, of which the professors described the inner and the lesser, the archers on horseback the outer and wider, and the students the intermediate and denser circle. Still, however, a small vacant space was preserved before the portal.

At this instant a murmur arose amongst the schoolmen. "He comes—he comes"—flew from one to other with the rapidity of lightning. Four other mace-bearers, walking abreast, strode deliberately through the gateway, as if they had been the only objects of interest, and drew up two on either side.

The course was now completely unobstructed. The rector appeared. He was a man of venerable aspect and majestic mien, and well became the magnificent apparel—the ample stole of scarlet, and mantle of snowy ermine, in which, as chief of the university, he was clad. A sash of sky-blue silk crossed his robe, and sustained a sumptuous velvet escarcelle, fringed with lace and decorated with buttons of gold. Upon his head he wore the square cap of a Doctor of Theology.

At his side, and on his right, walked one on whom all eyes were bent with wonder and curiosity. The rector and his companion stopped without the gateway, when, as if they were influenced by some sudden and uncontrollable impulse, one long, loud, continuous acclamation burst from the ranks of the scholars. Nor were the graver members of the university silent. Even the Doctors of Theology lent the aid of their voices; while the archers, raising themselves in their stirrups, lifted their helmets from their brows, and waving them in the air, increased and prolonged the clamour by their vociferations.

James Crichton possessed an exterior so striking and a manner so eminently prepossessing, that his mere appearance seemed to act like a spell on the beholders. The strongest sympathy was instantly and universally excited in his favour. Youth is ever interesting; but youth so richly graced as his could not fail to produce an extraordinary impression. At the sight of him the whole aspect of things was changed. Enthusiasm, amounting almost to devotion, usurped the place of animosity, and all vindictive feelings resulting from wounded pride or other petty annoyances, were obliterated or forgotten. Even discomfiture wore the aspect of victory.

But in the demeanour of the victor no external sign of self-elation was perceptible. He might not be insensible to the distinction of his achievement, but he did not plume himself upon it, or rather, with the modesty ever inherent in true greatness, appeared to underrate his own success. His cheek was slightly flushed, and a smile of tempered satisfaction played upon his countenance as he acknowledged the stunning applauses of the concourse before him. No traces of over-exertion or excitement were visible in his features or deportment. His brow was unclouded, his look serene, his step buoyant—and, as his bright eye wandered over the multitude, there was not an individual upon whom his gaze momentarily rested, but he felt his heart leap within his breast.

The countenance of Crichton was one that Phidias might have portrayed, so nearly did its elevated character of beauty approach to the standard of perfection erected by the great Athenian sculptor. Chiselled like those of some ancient head of the Delphic god, the features were wrought with the utmost fineness and precision—the contour of the face was classical and harmonious—the lips were firm, full, and fraught with sensibility, yet giving token of dauntless resolution—the chin was proudly curved—the nose Grecian—the nostril thin and haughty—the brow ample and majestical, shaded by hair of light brown, disposed in thick ringlets, after the manner of the antique.[1] There was a brilliancy and freshness in Crichton's complexion, the more surprising, as the pallid hue and debilitated look of the toil-worn student might more naturally be expected in his features than the sparkling bloom of health. A slight moustache feathered his upper lip, and a short, pointed beard clothed his chin, and added to the manliness of his aspect.

Crichton's attire, which partook more of his chivalrous than of his scholastic character, was that of a complete gentleman of the period, and was calculated to display to the utmost advantage the faultless symmetry of figure with which Nature, not less lavish than art and science in her gifts, had endowed him. A doublet of white damask, slashed with black bands of the same material, crossed by other bands, so as to form a sort of grating, buttoned from the throat to the girdle, and fitting closely to the person, revealed the outline of his full Antinous-like chest, as well as his slender circumference of waist; while the just

---

[1] Crichton is described in the letter of Aldus Manutius to the Duke of Sora elsewhere quoted, as "grande di statura, di pelo biondo, e d'aspetto bellissimo."

proportions of his lower limbs were as accurately defined by the satin hose, similar in colour to his doublet, and similarly slashed, in which they were enveloped. A short Spanish cloak of black velvet, edged with gold lace, hung from his left shoulder, and descended as low as the elbow. His arms were a rapier and a poniard, suspended from a richly ornamented girdle. Boots of buff-skin, sharply pointed at the top, as was then the mode, were fitted upon feet that seemed almost diminutive in comparison with the lofty stature of the wearer. His hat was looped with a diamond buckle, and crested by a single green feather.

To the modern observer, perhaps, the triple folds of his ruff and the voluminous width of his sleeve might appear formal and redundant; but these exuberances were then altogether unnoticed, or possibly regarded with as much complacency as a sleeve *à gigot* might be at the present time. In sooth, despite its stiffness and extravagance there was something picturesque and imposing in the court costume of Henri Trois (who, if he had no especial genius for monarchy, had unquestionably a great talent for the toilet), that amply redeemed its incongruities of taste. Crichton's figure, however, owed little to the adventitious circumstance of dress, and in fact was wholly independent of it.

As Crichton lingered for an instant beneath the shadow of the archway, the rector laid his hand upon his shoulder, with the intention, apparently, of arresting for a short space his further progress. He was not, perhaps, unwilling to afford the junior members of the university, who had been debarred from attending the disputation, a momentary opportunity of noting the striking personal appearance of one, whose name would long be associated with its annals, or it might be that he was influenced by some ulterior motive. Whatever occasioned the delay, it was a matter of gratulation to the scholars, who renewed their applauses in consequence.

"By the rood!" exclaimed the Sorbonist, "I am glad they have come to a pause. We were out in our reckoning, Don Diego; this Crichton is a perfect knight of romance, a Bayard as well as a Politian. Was there ever such a combination of qualities? I can scarce credit my senses when I look at him. Why, he hath barely a beard upon his chin, and yet to vanquish all our reverend doctors! Shame and confusion to *them*, and glory and renown to *him*."

"Hump!" muttered Caravaja. "Will he pass by *us*, think you?"

"I know not," returned the Sorbonist, "let us, if possible,

get nearer. Methinks old Adrien is making up his mouth to a speech. He deserves to be hooted for his pains—the toothless mumbler! But we will hear what he has to say. Perhaps he may make out a good case. Our Scot, I see, is in the fore-ranks, and shouting loud enough to split our ears and his own lungs. Peace, in front, I say! Keep him in view, my hidalgo, or we may lose him in the confusion."

"I will do more," returned Caravaja, "I will dog him like his own shadow. *Cuerpo!* he 'scapes me not, rely on it. Canst thou not aid me to approach him?"

"My elbows are at your service," replied the Sorbonist, "bravely done! We have effected a passage with more ease than I anticipated, thanks to thy sharp bones. By my faith, we are in the very nick of time. Look at the Seigneurs d'Epernon and Joyeuse. They are accounted the handsomest, as they are the bravest of our king's court; and yet, certes, peerless cavaliers though they be, they bear no comparison with this northern luminary."

"You own it!" cried Ogilvy, whom the speakers had approached; "you admit my countryman's superiority—I am satisfied. Let not our quarrel go farther. How say you, Sir Spaniard, will you refuse me your hand? I was hasty, and reck'd not what I said. We will drown the remembrance of our brawl over a stoop of claret. I would willingly drink a cup to the health of our admirable Crichton."

Ogilvy stretched out his hand. Caravaja, however, hesitated to accept it. "By the cinders of Saint Anthony!" he muttered, "the *duélo* must take its course."

"Saint Anthony forfend!" whispered the Sorbonist. "A cup of claret shed in the tavern is better than blood spilt in the *duélo*. Besides," he added, in a still lower key; "that need be no hindrance to the subsequent arrangement of the affair, if you see fitting. I warrant me, you will readily find new grounds for offence. Swallow thy indignation," he continued, aloud, "and take the hand of the valiant Scot."

"*Bien*," said Caravaja, apparently convinced by the reasoning of the Sorbonist; "I assent. We will compotate to the health of 'The Admirable Crichton,' since such is the epithet by which he is henceforth to be distinguished."

"Enough," said Ogilvy, grasping the hand of the Spaniard; "quit not my side in the press—or meet me anon at the Pine Apple."

"Conclude me there already," returned Caravaja.

Meantime, all the more distinguished auditors of the disputation, including the Governor of Paris, the ambassadors, the Vicomte de Joyeuse, and the Baron d'Epernon, who, with some others (ushered forth by the grand master of the College of Navarre, Doctor Launoi, and escorted by the two principals of dialectics and philosophy), had followed close upon the steps of the rector, were drawn up in a small phalanx beside them, and appeared to await their further movements. Amidst this group, the stately figures and magnificent accoutrements of the two favourites of the king stood out conspicuously. Both were esteemed the flower of the chivalry of their time, and both were equally remarkable for their gallantry, their good looks, and reckless courage. Jean-Louis de Nogaret de la Valette, Baron d'Epernon, possessed many brilliant qualities. To his vigour and address, Henri was subsequently indebted for the preservation of his throne; and to him might be traced the ultimate overthrow of the Guises, whom he bitterly hated, and uniformly opposed. D'Epernon still wore a suit of sables in memory of his brother-in-arms, Saint-Mégrin, assassinated by order of the Duke of Mayenne, on suspicion of an amour with his sister-in-law, the Duchess of Guise. His mourning, however, was of the most costly description, and his black mantle was embroidered with the cross of the Holy Ghost in orange-coloured velvet, passmented with silver, of which newly instituted order, he, as well as his companion, was a knight-commander. Joyeuse was radiant in orange-coloured satin, and velvet of the most dazzling hues. Nothing could be more splendid than his attire, unless, perhaps, it was that of René de Villequier, who, being also a Knight Commander of the Holy Ghost, was upon this occasion bedizened in all the finery of its full paraphernalia, the doublet and hose of silver tissuè, and the sweeping mantle of black velvet bordered with fleurs-de-lis of gold and tongues of flame intermingled with the royal cipher. From the necks of all three, suspended by a blue riband, hung the decoration of the lesser order, a small elaborately chased cross and dove of silver.

Amongst this group also were to be seen the Abbé de Brantôme and the poet Ronsard. Brantôme had a piercing eye, a thin visage, and a nose slightly aquiline. Immense moustaches clothed his long upper lip, but his lofty brow was almost entirely destitute of hair. There was much of the courtier in his manner, but his smile was sarcastic, and a vein of irony might be detected even in his most flowery compliments. A sneer was habitual to his lips, and his eye, though full and keen, was enclosed within lids of a pinkish hue and blear expression, sufficiently indicating the libertinage of his character. His attire was in the court fashion. His doublet was of a deep blue, slashed with white, the colours of Marguerite de Valois, whose miniature he wore attached to a chain of medallions. He bore, also, the Order of St. Michael, then, however, in great disrepute, and called *le Collier à toute bête*. The Abbé de Brantôme was then a man of middle-age, somewhat on the wane; and his frame appeared prematurely withered. His shoulders were bent, and his legs shrunk within his hose. His look was sharp, suspicious, penetrating; and his general manner that of a shrewd and accurate observer.

Age, and perhaps the life of sensuality he was known to have led, had, indeed, committed sad havoc upon the once well-favoured person of the poet Ronsard. He was no longer the *beau Page* whose manner fascinated James of Scotland, and, perchance, his queen. Nor was he what he sung of himself, when, near his fortieth year, he said:

> "Trente et sept ans passez, et encore n'ai-je atteint
> D'ans, ni de maladie, et en toutes les sortes
> Mes nerfs sont bien tendus, et mes veines bien fortes;
> Et si j'ai le teint pâle et le cheveu grison,
> Mes membres toutefois sont hors de saison."

He now complained both of ill-health and years. Such locks as remained had become "sable silvered." His tint of skin was dull and deadly pale; and, so grievously tormented was he with his old enemy the gout, that he was compelled to support his frame, at least on the present occasion, upon a crutch. Nevertheless, though gross of person, the countenance of the poet was handsome and intelligent, and, except when an awkward twinge crossed it, expressive of extreme good humour.

"Methinks, my dear Abbé," said Ronsard, looking around with some uneasiness, and addressing Brantôme, "it were scarce wise to have called together this tumultuous array. Our Cæsar may be crowned in the Capitol while we are sacrificed at his ovation. I am too well acquainted with the force of the poet's words:

> Monstrari digito et dicier 'hic est,'

as occasionally exemplified towards me by the students, to desire any further illustration of their abilities in my own person."

"You have changed your tune since the reception of your last masque, brother bard," said Chicot, who had forced himself, unperceived, amongst them. "These same scholars, I remember,

were once the only patrons of the Muses. Now they have lost
their discrimination. But give yourself no trouble: you will pass
unnoticed this time, depend on't, gossip. Even I, you see, for a
marvel, have escaped attention."

"Then, of a surety, I will put myself under thy escort," said
the poet, seizing the arm of the jester. "It was the abandonment
of folly that hath brought me into disrepute. Thou shalt help
me to amend. But what hath brought one of thy calling into the
haunts of wisdom, my merry gossip?"

"Wisdom and folly are nearer akin than you suppose,"
returned Chicot; "and fools who have soared to a greater height
than I can ever aspire, have been caught within these owl-roosts.
I like a fine sight as well as my neighbours; and though I care
not to be bespattered with a shower of *ans* and *utrums*, or sit
out a twelve-hour's bout of rhetoric and philosophy, where, if
one man hath not all the talk to himself, he, at least, doth his
best to silence his comrades, I am mightily pleased to come in,
as it were, for the last act of a dull comedy, and to enjoy a laugh
at the veteran stagers who have been driven off the boards by a
youthful actor, who, though he hath spent but a tithe of the time
in the service, understandeth their craft better than themselves."

"Have a care, sirrah," said Brantôme; ".thou art within
hearing of James Crichton."

"James Crichton will acquit me of flattery, then," rejoined
the jester. "I am one of those who speak truth behind a man's
back, and falsehood to his face, and care not to avouch it. Pierre
de Bourdeille, a word in thine ear! Thou wearest thy mistress's
colours on thy pourpoint, and her miniature at thy neck, but she
hath another image than thine at her heart. Take a fool's counsel,
and forget her."

Brantôme reddened with anger; but Chicot, who had all the
galling pertinacity of a gadfly, continued:

"You who are so well versed in history, seigneur, will assuredly
recollect the tradition of the fair queen, who founded this old
pile, and whose statue graces its doorway, how, above all her
courtly train, she smiled upon the *scholar* Buridan; and how,
within her bower upon the Seine, she—but you mind the tale,
I see—methinks we might find a modern parallel to that
ancient legend. After all, Jeanne de Navarre was but a fickle
jade, and played her lovers scurvy tricks. Ha! ha!" And bursting
into a loud laugh, the jester flew to the side of the Vicomte de
Joyeuse for protection.

"Well encountered, cousin D'Arques," he said; "our dear

Henriot needed thy presence at the fair of Saint-Germain this morning. Hadst thou or D'Epernon been with him, the insult he brooked would not have passed unnoticed."

"What insult do you allude to?" asked the vicomte, eagerly. "Let me hear it, that I may yet avenge it!"

"'Tis a matter of little moment," returned Chicot; "you shall know anon—that is, when your escort draws up to the gateway. It relates to yon graceless students, who have been studying court fashions rather than scholarly discourse; and having plucked a leaf out of your books, have twisted it fool-fashion round their necks, as you perceive."

"I observe them," replied Joyeuse. "'Tis an insolent device of the Guise or his faction. I would brain the knaves, but it were idle to bestow a thought on the puppets while the charlatan showman is to be met with."

"Our gossip, Henriot, thought otherwise," said the jester, "when these varlets roared within ear-shot of him, '*à la fraise on connoît le veau!*'"

"*Mort-Dieu!*" exclaimed Joyeuse. "What ho! there, Captain Larchant! Summon my company of archers, and give me my horse! To the saddle, D'Epernon, and bring up thy *Quarante-Cinq.* We will disperse this rabble rout! We will bind them hand and heel—scourge them to the bone—slay in case of resistance! —to the saddle, I say!"

"Moderate your choler, Joyeuse," said D'Epernon, holding back the vicomte, and addressing him in a low tone. "You will only incur his majesty's displeasure by involving yourself in a broil with the university, and gladden the hearts of the Guisards and the Leaguers, who would rejoice in your rashness. The present is not fitting season for retaliation. We will find surer means of vengeance."

"I would spurn the *canaille* beneath my charger's feet," replied Joyeuse, "but be it as you will. The rector, I know, is as jealous of his privileges as the Guise of his duchess, and we might not, perhaps, have sufficient plea of justification. Let him hang the knaves himself, and I am satisfied. 'Twill save the provost-marshal a labour."

"All in good time," replied D'Epernon, "and his conference with Crichton concluded, the rector appears inclined to address his *cari alumni.* I trust in terms of sufficient reprobation."

The rector, who had, apparently much against Crichton's inclination, detained him in earnest conversation at the portal, now turned towards the scholars, intimating his intention of addressing them. The clamour ceased as soon as his gestures were understood.

"Messieurs scholars of the University of Paris," he said, "you have already learned, I doubt not, that your most erudite doctors and professors have this day sustained a defeat; a defeat, however, which, while it reflects no disgrace on the conquered, enhances the glory of the victor. In the whole circle of science and learning James Crichton hath approved his supremacy, and we willingly surrender to him our laurels. May he long continue to wear them, and may his career, the dawn of which is so brilliant, be equally glorious at its close! Like the great poet Dante he came hither unknown. Like Dante he departeth with a reputation which will be blazed throughout all the schools of Europe. In earnest of the profound admiration which, in common with all the principals of the university, I entertain for his transcendent abilities and matchless scholarship, in their names and in my own name, in your behalf and in that of every member of the university by whom learning is reverenced, and with whom genius is held sacred, I would tender for his acceptance, as a mark of our esteem and veneration, this ring; which I trust he will not disdain to wear upon his person as a trophy of the conquest he has this day achieved, and in remembrance of the university he has vanquished. And that every member of the university may participate in this expression of our sentiments towards the Admirable Crichton, I have taken this public opportunity of their manifestation. Scholars of Paris, have I not your approval and concurrence?"

A thunder of applause succeeded the rector's oration, and a thousand hurrahs responded to his appeal. All eyes were now turned to Crichton, who, it was evident, only awaited a cessation of the clamour to address the assemblage in his turn. Silence was instantly commanded; and scarce a breath was drawn as he spoke, so intent were all upon catching each syllable that fell from his lips.

"When the Phœnix of his age," began Crichton, in a voice distinct and musical, "and the favourite of the Muses, Picus of Mirandula, was proffered all the honours of the Roman School, he declined them, saying that he felt his own unworthiness, and that he had acquired more distinction than was his due in having obtained a hearing at their hands. In imitation of the conduct of this illustrious prince, though with far less claim to the same honourable note, I would say that I neither deserve nor desire further distinction than I have gained. Fortune has already favoured me beyond my deserts. I have engaged in amicable strife with men whose intellectual superiority I am ready to acknowledge, and who, if I have worsted them in argument, have been foiled solely because I made a better choice of weapons, and happened to be the more skilful in their use. I am not blinded by self-esteem. I do not attribute my victory to other than its right causes. Like most of the great events of life, its issue has been the result of chance, which has upon this occasion declared itself in my favour. Were the contest to be renewed on the morrow, I might be placed in the position of my opponents. Courtesy to a stranger, and consideration for his youth, have restrained my adversaries from putting forth their strength. Some such feelings must have had their influence. Grant, however, that I have triumphed. You have bestowed upon me your applause. I am fully requited. Trophies of victory which may be wrested from me as soon as won are of little avail. Better men may appear—*Plures habet Sparta Brasidâ meliores.* My ambition has a hundred goals, which it would fain reach.

Magnum iter intendo, sed dat mihi gloria vires."

"Live Crichton! Live the Admirable Crichton!—*Euge Optime! Euge! Euge!*" shouted the scholars.

Crichton gracefully saluted the assemblage and would have retired, if he had not been withheld by the rector. "You must perforce accept this gem," said the latter; "the gifts of the University of Paris are not wont to be slighted," and taking a brilliant diamond ring from his forefinger, and loosening the velvet escarcelle from his sash, Messire Adrien d'Amboise presented them to Crichton.

"I may not decline your offer," replied Crichton, reluctantly receiving the proffered gem, "since you thus press it upon me, though I feel how little I merit it. The ring I shall prize, but as to the contents of the purse, you must suffer me to dispose of them as I shall see fitting."

"The purse is yours; do with its contents what you think proper," said the rector.

Crichton removed the ring, and taking forth the crowns of gold with which the escarcelle was filled, threw them amongst the crowd of scholars. A violent commotion ensued, during which many of the students broke through the lines and approached close to the persons of Crichton and the rector. One of these, a youth, who for some space had held his green mantle before his face, now rushed forward, and prostrating himself before Crichton, threw down a garland of twisted bay-leaves at his feet.

"Disdain not my offering, Seigneur Crichton," he said, in a low and timid voice, "simple though it be, and all unworthy your acceptance, I will myself wind it round your brows, if I receive your gracious permission to do so."

"Retire, thou forward youth," said the rector, gravely. "This is presumption."

"I pray you excuse him," said Crichton, "the compliment is too flattering to be declined, and, let me add, the mode in which it is conveyed is too graceful to be unwelcome. I accept your wreath, young sir, and beg you to arise. But wherefore," he added, with a smile, "did you imagine I should come off victorious? Surely there was nothing to warrant such a conclusion. And had I returned ingloriously, this garland would have been wholly thrown away."

The youth arose, and fixed his dark eyes full upon Crichton's countenance. "Whatever the Admirable Crichton shall undertake, in that he will excel all men," he said. "With him to engage in a conflict is to obtain a victory. I was assured of his success."

"Your looks are sincere, and I will not distrust your words," replied Crichton. "Your face resembles one I have seen, though where I cannot call to mind. Are you of these colleges?"

"He is one of the Gelosi, sir," said Ogilvy, who, together with Caravaja and the Sorbonist, had forced himself into the vicinity of Crichton. "Be not deceived by his honest look, as I have been. Hence, youth, and take thy mummeries with thee."

"One of the Gelosi!" exclaimed Crichton. "Ha! now I remember the features. 'Tis the youth I have seen so oft. But why avert thy head, gentle boy? I have said nothing, I trust, to wound thy feelings?"

The Geloso appeared crimsoned with shame. "Tell me," continued Crichton, "what may mean that masked figure whom I have seen for ever hovering nigh thee in thy walks? nay, that seems like thy shadow at the Hôtel de Bourbon. Is it a device of thine own to attract curiosity, young sir? If so, I can tell thee thou hast succeeded. Even the royal Henri has noticed the singularity of the figure."

"Have you, likewise, remarked that mask, signor?" replied the Geloso, with an expression of uneasiness almost amounting to terror. "I have often thought it a trick of my own imagination. But you have seen it likewise!"

"I have," replied Crichton; "but methinks you answer

evasively. I thought more of sincerity dwelt in those earnest eyes. Your present action is but, I fear, an artifice to win attention."

So saying he turned from him. The Geloso attempted to reply, but retired abashed. Ogilvy was about to thrust him back, but perceiving that the youth had shrouded his face with his mantle, and voluntarily withdrawn himself, he desisted.

There was something in the manner of the youth that struck Crichton; and his feelings reproached him with undue severity towards him. Laying his hand upon his shoulder, he addressed a few words to him in a more kindly tone.

The Geloso raised his eyes. The black orbs were filled with tears. He looked with a blinded gaze on Crichton, and thence at the hand which he still suffered to remain upon his shoulder. Suddenly he started. He pressed his hand across his eyes. He pointed to Crichton's finger. "The ring!" he exclaimed. "Did you not place it there?"

Surprised at the youth's emotion, and at the inquiry, Crichton looked at the finger upon which he had scarcely a moment ago placed the gift of the rector. The ring was wanting.

Unable to account for this extraordinary occurrence, and not without some suspicions of the youth himself, Crichton fixed a cold scrutinising glance upon him. The Geloso shuddered slightly at the expression of his glance, but quailed not beneath it. "He cannot have done it," thought Crichton. "Falsehood could not dwell in looks so guileless."

At this instant there was a further rush amongst the scholars. Ogilvy and the Geloso were forcibly propelled against Crichton. A knife was seen to glitter in the air. From its position it seemed to be grasped by the hand of Ogilvy. For an instant the steel was suspended over the head of Crichton. The Geloso saw it. Uttering a loud cry of warning, he threw himself in the way of the blow. The blade descended. The arms of the youth were entwined round Crichton's neck. In an instant he found himself deluged in blood.

With Crichton to draw his sword—to sustain the almost inanimate body of the Geloso, was the work of an instant.

"This is the assassin!" he shouted. And with the hand that was still at liberty, and with a force that seemed almost superhuman, he grasped the throat of the paralysed Ogilvy.

CHAPTER IV

AN ENGLISH BULL-DOG

As sure a dog as ever fought at head.—*Titus Andronicus.*

A CRY arose amongst the scholars that Crichton had been assassinated, and such was the confusion that prevailed in his vicinity, that for some space the truth or falsehood of the report could not be ascertained.

The crowd was fearfully incensed. They demanded that the assassin should be given up to their vengeance. Yelling, groaning, uttering threats and imprecations, they pressed forward—at the sides, in front, in all directions. The archers, stationed as a foot-guard around the doctors and professors, were incontinently carried off their legs. The principals of the colleges immediately beat a retreat, and betook themselves for refuge to the hall of the institution they had so recently quitted. Affairs assumed a very ominous aspect. Bludgeons were waved in the air; blows were dealt indiscriminately, and many a pretended random stroke wiped off old scores with some rigid disciplinarian who had not been sufficiently alert to effect his escape. In vain did the rector strive to check this rising storm. His voice, wont to be listened to with awe, was unheard or unheeded amid the tumult.

"*Los aux Ecoles!*" shouted the scholars, pressing forward.

"*Los aux Ecoles!*" cried Chicot, who, safely ensconced within the gateway, eyed the raging mob at a distance. "I never hear that cry but I think of the screaming of a pack of gulls before a tempest. Mischief is sure to be brewing."

"Their cursed croaking resembles that of the frogs in Aristophanes," said Ronsard; "would it might end in crocitation! I prophesied evil from the moment I beheld this rabble."

"I trust you will rather approve yourself *Vates* in its poetic than its prophetic sense," replied Brantôme. "I own my mind misgives me."

"Methinks, my lord," said René de Villequier to the rector, "it were well to nip this riot in the bud. Some lives may else be lost. See—they approach the assassin—they seize him—they drag him from the grasp of Crichton. *Mort-Dieu!* my lord, they will tear him in pieces—this must be prevented, we must not stand by and see outrage like this committed."

"The butchers!" shouted Joyeuse. "Crichton himself will be endangered. By my halidom! I will bring down my archers upon them!——"

"Stay, my lord, an instant, I implore of you," said the rector, "my presence will restrain their violence. I will go amongst them myself—they dare not disobey my mandates."

And accompanied by the grand master of the College of Navarre, the rector forced his way towards the principal scene of strife.

"Give them this further chance," said D'Epernon to the vicomte, who was chafing like a high-mettled steed with impatience. "If they heed not their rector then——"

"*Los aux Ecoles*," replied Chicot, with a laugh. "We shall have a pleasant specimen of their chivalry anon. By my marotte, they are in no mood to listen to a dissertation now."

"'Tis a waste of time," cried Joyeuse, "forbearance is thrown away. When the king's majesty is not held sacred by these felon scholars, how can their rector expect obedience from them? To my side, Larchant—*en avant!*" And drawing his sword, and attended by the captain of the guard, the vicomte flung himself headlong into the press.

Intelligence that Crichton was unhurt somewhat abated the frenzy of the multitude. Still they were vehemently excited. Ogilvy had been dragged from Crichton's grasp, and was threatened with instant immolation. Deprived of utterance by the choking grip of Crichton; stunned by the buffets of the students, it was only in this perilous extremity that he recovered his power of speech. With a force that could only have been given him by despair, he burst from their hold and shouted to Crichton for aid. He was instantly retaken, and his cries drowned by a roar of mockery from the ruthless mob.

"Call on Crichton for protection!" shouted Caravaja, who had been a prominent instrument in assailing the unfortunate Scot, and who indulged in a savage rejoicing at his situation. "As well might the serpent sue for protection to the heel it hath bitten, as thou implore succour from him thou wouldst have slain. But thy countryman, thou seest, turns a deaf ear to thy plaints—ha! ha!"

"Surely mine ears deceived me," said Crichton, who, with his broidered kerchief was busied in staunching the wound of the Geloso, and who had only caught this latter exclamation of the Spaniard. "Can it be that the assassin is countryman of mine?"

"'Tis even so, Señor Crichton," replied Caravaja. "To his eternal infamy be it spoken."

"Hear me, noble Crichton!" shouted Ogilvy, whom the

Spaniard vainly endeavoured to silence. "Think me not guilty of this foul offence. I care not for death, but I would not die dishonoured. I would not perish charged with a deed which my soul abhorreth. I am no assassin. I am Jasper Ogilvy, of Balfour."

"Hold!" exclaimed Crichton, consigning his yet inanimate burden to the care of a bystander, and pressing towards Ogilvy, "let me speak with this man. Give me some token that I may know thou art he whom thou callest thyself. Thy voice brings back bygone days; but I can discern naught of Jasper Ogilvy in those blood-stained features."

"You would not know my visage, were it freed from its stain," returned Ogilvy. "We both have grown to manhood since we met; but you will call to mind a moonlight cruise upon the Lake of Cluny, years ago, when a noble youth was saved from perishing in its waters. To me the recollection of that deed hath been ever sweet; to-day it hath been proud. Let me but establish my truth with you, honoured sir, and these hell-hounds may do their worst."

"You have said enough; I am satisfied, more than satisfied," replied Crichton. "Messieurs, release this young man. He is wholly guiltless of the crime laid to his charge. I will answer for him with my life."

The scholars replied with a laugh of incredulity.

"We have only his bare word for his innocence," replied the Bernardin. "Appearances are sadly against him."

"This knife was within his vest when we dragged him from the Señor Crichton," added Caravaja, holding up an ensanguined blade. "*Por los Revelaciones de San Juan!* this, methinks, is proof unanswerable."

A volley of execrations answered this appeal to the passions of the multitude.

"Thou liest," cried Ogilvy, struggling to set free his hands; "that poniard is thine own; my dirk hangs at my girdle—would it were now within my grasp!"

"Produce the weapon, then," said Caravaja. And he thrust his hand into the Scot's torn doublet. "Ha!" exclaimed he, suddenly, what have I found? *Por nuestra Señora!* 'tis the diamond ring, with the cipher of the university. He is a robber as well as an assassin."

A sudden light seemed to break upon Crichton.

"Let the accuser and the accused both be brought before the rector," he cried.

A murmur arose amongst the scholars.

"He would shield his countryman," they vociferated; "we are satisfied of his guilt."

"But you are not to constitute yourselves his judges," replied Crichton sternly. "Deliver him to the proper authorities; let that Spaniard, who stands forth his accuser, be secured; and I am satisfied."

"Mighty well!" returned Caravaja. "All I get for my exertions in seizing the assassin is to be accused of the crime myself. But if you are so readily gulled by your countryman's subterfuge, Señor Crichton, my comrades are not so easily imposed upon. *Hijo de Dios!* they know me too well to suspect me of any such enormity."

"The scholars of Paris are apt to take the law into their own hands upon occasions like the present, where the guilt of the offender is manifestly established," said the Sorbonist. "It is the part of their privileges to adjudicate their own causes, and they are always willing to abide by the consequences of their own decisions. We have sentenced this man to run the gauntlet of the schools, and he shall not escape. Wherefore do we delay, comrades?"

"Ay, wherefore?" rejoined Caravaja.

"Beware," shouted Crichton, in a voice of thunder, "how you proceed to further acts of violence. My respect for your university has thus long withheld me; but I will not stand by and see outrage committed."

"I am with you," said the English student, Simon Blount, advancing towards him, and still followed by his huge bull-dog. "Your countryman shall suffer no wrong, while I have staff to wield or blade to draw in his defence. And as to the merits of his case, I have as little doubt of his innocence, as I have assurance of yon cut-throat Spaniard's guilt. But, in any case, he shall not be put to death without judge or jury. What, ho! Druid," added he, glancing significantly at his dog, "it will be time to slip thy muzzle in case these curs show their teeth."

At this juncture, the rector and the Doctor Launoy made their appearance.

"Hear me, my children," said the rector, in a loud voice, "justice shall be dealt upon this Scot. Deliver him into the custody of the sergeant of the guard now in attendance upon me, and I pledge myself to the instant examination of his case. What more can you require? By your threatened violence, you will only add one crime to another, and increase the scandal you have already brought upon the university."

Crichton conferred an instant with the rector, who apparently acquiesced in the propriety of the suggestion made to him.

"Disperse at once; and let each man seek his respective college," continued Adrien d'Amboise, with some severity. "Sergeant, advance, and seize upon the persons of Jasper Ogilvy, of the Ecossais, and Diego Caravaja, of the College of Narbonne. Messieurs Scholars, give him your aid. Ah! do you hesitate?—is it possible that you venture to disobey the paternal injunction of the father of the university—what frenzy is this?"

A sullen murmur ran through the battalion of the scholars; and such was their threatening aspect, that the sergeant of the guard hesitated to obey the command of the rector.

"Why should we respect his mandates?" muttered the Sorbonist. "'Tis plain we are but lightly considered at his paternal hands. Let the father of the university tell us why his children were excluded from the disputation this morning, and we will then perpend the propriety of compliance with his request."

"Ay, let him answer that," said the Bernardin.

"'Twould shrewdly perplex him to do so," returned Caravaja. "By the perdition of the world! I will surrender myself to no man living, sergeant or rector, Scot or Englishman; and to show them how little I regard their threats, if no other can be found to smite this starveling bravo, my hand shall deal the first blow."

Caravaja raised his knife with the intent to strike. At that instant, however, he was seized by a nervous grasp, and hurled backwards with such force that, muttering an oath, he fell heavily to the ground. Crichton, for it was by his hand that the Spaniard had been prostrated, threw himself amongst the ranks of the scholars with such irresistible force, that their united efforts were unable to withstand him. Shaking off Ogilvy's captors, he placed a poniard within his grasp, and, drawing his own sword, calmly awaited the further assault of the students.

Rugged and resolute as the bull-dog at his heels, Blount followed closely in his rear. Confining himself to the warding off a few blows, aimed at Crichton, he at first dealt none in return; but he could not long act upon the defensive. A rude buffet on the head aroused his ire. He then laid about him with such good-will and determination, that an opponent dropped for every blow of his cudgel, which was not a vine-wood staff, but a huge English crab-stick, seasoned, knotty and substantial. The might of twenty threshers seemed to reside in Blount's single arm.

Sconces were cracked by him with as much ease as a boy for pastime would beat in pieces as many gourds. The Sorbonist ventured to oppose his estoc against the Englishman's club. The sophister, however, had now a more difficult thesis to maintain than any he had hitherto defended. His postulate was effectually blanked by Blount's knotty rejoinder. Yielding to the weighty blow, the supple vine-staff fled from his grasp, spinning through the air to a considerable distance, while the arm that sustained it, shattered by the stroke, sank powerless to his side.

Meantime, Ogilvy and Crichton were not left unmolested. Placed back to back, both stood in postures of defence. Uttering frightful yells, and brandishing their staves, the scholars furiously commenced the assault. Caravaja, who had regained his feet, was amongst the foremost of the assailants.

"By Saint James of Compostella!" he roared, "I will wash out, in blood, the stain he hath put on our academies, and on myself. Give way; look to thyself, proud Scot." And pressing forward, he made a desperate thrust at Crichton.

Caravaja was no contemptible swordsman; but he had to do with an antagonist unequalled in the art of self-defence. His thrust was parried with infinite dexterity, and after the exchange of a few fierce and rapid passes, his long Toledo was twisted from his grasp, and he lay at the mercy of his adversary. Crichton, however, forbore to strike; but dismissed his foe as one unworthy of his steel. Gnashing his teeth with rage, Caravaja sought a new weapon; and encouraging each other by shouts and cries, the scholars still pressed madly on.

One amongst their number, of colossal stature, noted amongst his brethren for extraordinary athletic feats, and rejoicing in the Rabelaisian sobriquet of Loupgarou, advanced deliberately towards him. He wielded a bar of iron, and while Crichton was engaged on all sides, he discharged a tremendous blow full at his head. The ponderous weapon descended, but Crichton had foreseen the stroke and averted it, not, however, without some loss. Such was the force of the blow, that his sword blade, though of the best tempered steel, was shivered at the hilt.

It was now that Crichton's great personal strength and remarkable activity stood him in admirable stead. Without allowing his gigantic antagonist time to repeat his blow, he sprang forward and grappled him with an energy that shook his Herculean frame to its foundation. The Antæus of the schools reeled. For the first time he had met with his match.

Locked in Crichton's grip, Loupgarou could neither disentangle his right arm, nor bring his unwieldy powers into play. He could scarcely even draw breath, and his brawny chest heaved like a labouring mountain.

Confident of the result of the strife, and unwilling to deprive their champion of the entire honours of conquest, the scholars suspended further hostilities against Crichton, and directed their attacks upon Ogilvy and Blount. Abandoned by his comrades, Loupgarou was ashamed to roar for aid, and experienced some such qualms as fell to the share of his namesake when struggling within the clutch of the redoubted Pantagruel. Like a tower shaken from its equilibrium by the blast of the miner, he tottered on his base, and with a concussion heard above the din of the fray, he fell to the ground, deprived of sense and motion.

Snatching the bar from the relaxed grasp of his adversary, Crichton was about to rejoin his comrades when his attention was suddenly drawn to a new quarter. Hearing his own name called upon, as he thought, by the voice of the Geloso, followed by a loud shriek for help, he strove to force his way in the direction of the sound.

Ogilvy, meantime, found an unexpected and most efficient ally in the Englishman's dog, Druid. Galled by the fierce and pertinacious assaults of his enemies, Blount suddenly slipped the muzzle of the savage animal, and he rushed at the scholars. Blount directed his attacks, and cheered him on. Blows availed nothing against the tough hide of the hardy animal, and served only to incense him. He raged amongst them like a wolf in a lamb-pasture.

Fain would the students have taken to their heels, but retreat was impossible. Those behind pushed forward the ranks in front. Shrieks and execrations evidenced the devastation of the relentless pursuer. His teeth met in the legs of one, in the arms of another, in the throat of a third.

A space was quickly cleared around Blount and Ogilvy by their staunch partisan. With his back on the ground—his face shielded by his hands to protect himself from the teeth of the dog, by whom he had been pinned to the earth, lay the prostrate form of the Bernardin. Planting his heavy paws upon his neck, and sprawling over the body of the half-dead scholar, Druid upturned his glowing eyeballs to his master, as if to inquire whether or not he should complete his work of destruction. It was a critical moment for the Bernardin.

Just then, however, the clatter of swords, the trampling of steeds, and shouts of "Joyeuse, to the rescue!" announced that the vicomte had reached his company of archers. With a swoop like that of an eagle upon a flock of meaner fowl—and with his charger rearing into the air, Joyeuse dashed amongst the multitude.

On the other hand came the halberdiers of the rector and the lackeys of René de Villequier with bills and partisans; and, furthermore, the crowd was invested to the right by the well disciplined *Quarante-Cinq*, under the command of the Baron D'Epernon. Thus menaced on all sides, the scholars found themselves in an awkward predicament. At first there was a murmur of "Down with the minions!—Down with the Gascon *coupe-jarrets!*" but these cries were speedily silenced. A few strokes from the blunt edges of the swords of the guardsmen, and their staves were thrown to the ground in token of submission.

CHAPTER V

COSMO RUGGIERI

Icy près, dist Epistémon, demoure Her Trippa: vous sçavez comment par art d'Astrologie, Géomancie, Chiromancie, et aultres de pareille farine, il prédict toutes choses futures; conférons de vostre affaire avec lui. De cela, respondit Panurge, je ne sçay rien.—RABELAIS, *Pantagruel*, liv. iii.

THE bystander to whom Crichton committed the inanimate Geloso, when he rushed to the assistance of Ogilvy, received his charge with an eager readiness that almost appeared as if he had anticipated the event. Shielding his burden with his arms, and unwilling, it would seem, to attract further attention, he endeavoured to extricate himself from the crowd.

He was a little old man, of singular and inauspicious appearance, dressed in a flowing robe of black taffeta, lined with flame-coloured silk, and edged with sable fur. In lieu of doublet and hose, he wore a rich gown of crimson velvet, fastened round the waist with a silken cord, in the which was stuck a costly purse, embroidered with the arms of Catherine de Medicis. A collar of medallions, graven with cabalistic characters, hung over his shoulder, and upon his head he wore a small skull-cap of purple velvet. He bore neither arms nor device of any sort beyond the blazon of the Queen-Mother. His forehead would have appeared venerable from its height, baldness and innumerable wrinkles, had not his black scowling brows given it a sinister and portentous look. His temples were hollow and sunken; his cheeks emaciated; the colour of his skin was sallow and jaundiced, and its texture like that of shrivelled parchment. His nose was high and aquiline, tufted between the eyes with a clump of dusky hair; and the whole expression of his features was crafty, suspicious and malignant. When erect, his stature might have been lofty, but his height was now dwindled to insignificance by his stooping shoulders and contracted spine. His distorted limbs were concealed from view by the ample folds of his drapery; but his joints had been wrenched from their sockets, and but ill-restored, during his confinement in the Bastille, where he had been incarcerated and tortured for supposed practices of sorcery, during the reign of Charles IX.

Cosmo Ruggieri, the forbidding personage described—by birth a Florentine, by vocation a mathematician, alchemist, nay, even bard, as may be gathered from the *Anagramatographie* of Nicolas Clément Tréleau, secretary to the Duc d'Anjou, where he is eulogised as "Florentinum, mathematicum, et poetam lectissimum";—officiated as chief astrologer to Catherine de Medicis, by whom he was brought to Paris. It was to the influence of the Queen-Mother that he owed his deliverance from the rack and the dungeon; his escape with life; his subsequent advancement to court favour under her third son, Henri, for whose accession to the throne, it was said, indeed, he had paved the way by the removal of his brothers, Francis II. and Charles IX., and by whom, latitudinarian and heretical, if not wholly heathenish and abominable as his tenets were known to be, he was advanced to the ecclesiastical dignity of Abbé of Saint-Mahé, in Brittany. It was to the protection of Catherine's powerful arm that, although surrounded by open and secret foes, he was enabled to pursue his mysterious career unmolested; and it was to her he was indebted for the wonderful State information he possessed.

In return for these obligations, the stars were nightly consulted for her by him, and on all emergencies Catherine had recourse to his counsel. Ruggieri was blindly devoted to her will, and mainly instrumental in the execution of her hidden projects and machinations.

Ruggieri, however, did not stand alone. To such an extent did the practice of judicial astrology prevail at the time, that the number of professors in the science was estimated at thirty thousand; a calculation almost incredible, if the number of

dupes necessarily required for their support be taken into
consideration.

Be this as it may, Ruggieri flourished. But then it was whispered, that he had another and more terrible source of lucre.
The slow and subtle poisons of Florentine origin, whose treacherous effect was manifested in the gradual decay of the
victim, were said to be brewed by him. The blood that nightly
bathed the couch of Charles IX. was supposed to be the consequence of one of these diabolical potions; and such was the
dread entertained of his villainous drugs, that a cup of wine
would have fallen from the grasp of the boldest bacchanal, if
it had been thought to be medicated by Cosmo Ruggieri.

By the side of the astrologer was a dumb African slave of
the most diminutive size and fantastic configuration, who had
the reputation of being his familiar; and strange as was the
appearance of the sorcerer, that of his page was many degrees
more grotesque. Hideously deformed and hunchbacked, Elberich
was so short in comparison with his width and girth that, when
moving, his squat rotundity of figure looked like a rolling ball
of soot, in which, in place of eyes, two flaming carbuncles had
been set; and when motionless, he appeared like a black,
bloated baboon.

Aided by his dwarf, from whose contact all recoiled with
disgust, Ruggieri had but little difficulty in making good his
retreat; and having gained the shelter of a flying buttress of
the college wall, in the angle of which he was secure from
interruption, he turned his attention to the restoration of
his charge.

As he removed the black and clustering ringlets, fallen in
disorder over the features of the Geloso, Ruggieri could not
help being struck by their exceeding loveliness. The cheek had
indeed lost the warm suffusion that, like a glow of sunshine
on a snowy peak, had lit up its bright southern complexion;
but the face was not less beautiful; and Ruggieri perused its
lineaments with the rapture of a virtuoso. He peered into every
line with increasing wonder. It was not so much the harmony
and regularity of the youth's features that struck him with
astonishment, as the softness of the skin, and the polished
whiteness of the throat, on which the azure veins were traced
like wandering threads. These were what chiefly excited his
admiration. He grew so much absorbed in contemplation of the
countenance, that he wholly neglected to apply the phial of
pungent spirit, which he held extended in his grasp.

Throwing back the hair as far as it would admit, Ruggieri examined more narrowly the snowy forehead of the Geloso. Thence his glance wandered to the face with renewed surprise. The eyes were closed; but the dark orbs could almost be seen through the thin lids. Then, those long silken lashes—that dark and pencilled brow—those nostrils, fine and thin—those lips so delicately carved! The astrologer was lost in amazement. Taking the small white hand that hung listlessly at the youth's side, he opened it, and intently perused its lines. A shade came over his countenance as he pursued his study.

"Spirit of Sambethe!" he exclaimed, "can this be? Can I have been so long in error? Can the heavenly influences have so long deceived their votary?—Impossible! True, the planets have of late assumed malevolent aspects—menacing me with ill. Saturn hath rule within the Chamber of Death. The Lord of the Third House was combust and retrograde within the Eleventh, presaging peril from the hand of a stranger. This day, this hour, is pregnant with calamity. I foresaw my danger, but I foresaw likewise the means whereby it might be averted. Within my path stands Crichton. He is the foe by whom I am threatened. This day links his fate with mine, and with that of another. That other is my safeguard—that other is within my arms. One of us must perish. A thick curtain hangs between me and the event. Curses on my own imperfect skill, which will only enable me to see so far and no farther. But I may ward off the stroke."

And he again returned to the scrutiny of the Geloso's countenance. "Wherefore is it," he continued, musingly, "that as I gaze upon these beautiful features, a thousand forgotten fancies should be awakened within my bosom? This face, though lovelier far, recalls to me the image of one long since buried in oblivion—it recalls dreams of youth, of passion, fever, delirium; of a deed of which I will not even think. Who is this youth? or rather, unless mine eyes are wholly sightless, or dim to aught save the midnight glories of the heavens, who is this——"

The reverie of the astrologer was here interrupted by a slight convulsive attempt at respiration on the part of the Geloso. Ruggieri applied the phial and, with a trembling hand, proceeded to unclasp the youth's doublet to give him greater freedom in breathing. In removing the folds of the blood-stained linen, the heaving bosom of a young and lovely female was revealed. His eye glistened through its film. "It is as I suspected," he muttered

—"a girl in masquerade attire. Most probably the fool hath lost her heart to Crichton—if so, she will be a useful agent. I have need of such an one in my designs upon him. Ha! what have we here?—an amulet—no, by Hermes, a small key of gold, of antique fashioning, attached to a chain of the same metal, which, from its exquisite workmanship, I judge to be Venetian. Ah, fair maiden, I have here, no doubt, a clue to your history, of which I may avail myself hereafter! by your leave, this key is mine."

And little scrupulous as to the means of accomplishing any object, Ruggieri, without hesitation, unfastened the chain, and was about to commit it to the custody of his pouch, when he was alarmed by a monitory signal from his sable attendant.

The sound uttered by the dwarf resembled the hissing of a startled snake. Indeed, the vocal powers of the wretched creature only ranged between gibbering and sibilation. By the former he expressed his rejoicing, by the latter his fears. The astrologer well knew how to interpret the present boding noise. Following the direction of the dwarf's red and glowing orbs, he caught sight of a figure, upon which the angry manikin was glowering, puffing, and spitting like an owl disturbed by some prowling specimen of the furry tribe. The figure was masked, and muffled within the folds of a large sable cloak; and ere Ruggieri could thrust the chain of gold into his girdle, the intruder was by his side.

CHAPTER VI

THE MASK

Don Garcia. Qu'est-ce alors
Que ce masque?—Tenez, le voilà.
VICTOR HUGO, *Hernani.*

"BE not alarmed, father," said the mask, addressing Ruggieri, "I am a friend."

"What assurance have I of that?" returned the astrologer, doubtfully. "Your speech is fair, but your guise and deportment are not calculated to inspire confidence. We are not now in Venice, Signor Maschera; neither is this the season of carnival. The good citizens of Paris deem the mask but an indifferent excuse for intrusion; and I have been long enough amongst them to acquire some of their foolish notions on this head. Your pardon, signor, if I misconceive you. Much treachery has made me distrustful."

"You are in the right to be cautious, father," replied the mask; "distrust becomes your years and character; yet, methinks, the science you profess should enable you to detect a friend from a foe."

"I read not men's looks beneath a vizard, my son," replied Ruggieri, "that were, indeed, to see through a glass darkly. Let me behold your features, and I will tell you whether or not you are a friend."

"You wrong me by your doubts, father," replied the mask—"that I am well known to you, you shall have ample assurance presently; and that I have some claim to the service I am about to require at your hands, you will then, I doubt not, admit. Meantime, as secrecy is my object, and as the disclosure of my features, or even of my name, would only be attended with risk, you will, perhaps, suffer me to preserve my incognito."

"Assuredly, my son," replied Ruggieri, who had now regained his confidence. "I have no desire to penetrate your mystery. Were it an object with me, I could readily gain information. What do you require of me?"

"Before we proceed," returned the mask, "I pray you, father, to accept this purse as an earnest of my sincerity. It will give you a clearer insight into my character than even the display of my features." And as he spoke, he thrust a well-lined purse into the hands of the astrologer, who received it, nothing loth.

"You have said well, my son," he returned; "this is a medium through which I clearly distinguish the false from the true friend. How can I assist you? Whatsoever comes within the scope of my art is yours to command."

"In a word, then," returned the mask, "I love——"

"Ah! I understand," replied Ruggieri, significantly, "you love without requital."

"Precisely so, father."

"And would subdue the heart of her for whom you sigh. Is it not so?"

The mask nodded assent.

"Doubt not its accomplishment. Be she chilly as Caucasian snow, I will engage to create a flame within her bosom that shall burn with an ardour fiercer than that created by the cestus of Venus."

"Swear to me, you will do this."

"By Orimasis! she shall be yours."

"Enough—I am content."

"Tell the damsel's name and dwelling——?"

"Neither are needed—she is here." And the mask pointed to the Venetian girl.

"Jabamiah!" exclaimed the surprised astrologer.

"Nay, I know all," pursued the mask. "Plead not ignorance. I witnessed the discovery you made."

"And—and you love her——"

"Love her!" echoed the mask—"Hear me, father," he continued, with impetuosity. "You, who are of our fiery land, need not be told with what fierceness we Italians love. With all the ardour of overwhelming passion I pursued this damsel. She was deaf to my entreaties. In vain I used every blandishment, every artifice—in vain lavished gifts upon her that might have won a princess. All my efforts were ineffectual. For me she had no smile. Nay, more, the fury of my suit affrighted her. Indifference grew to fear, and fear to hate. Hate in some bosoms is akin to love, but not in hers. She fled my sight. Stung by resentment, I formed plans, that had they not been foiled in execution, must have placed her within my power. By some means she became acquainted with my projects, and sought safety in flight. Her disappearance added to my torture—I was frantic. While plunged in this despair, I received intelligence that she had flown to Paris. Thither I repaired—traced her— saw through her disguise—hovered round her dwelling—haunted her like her shadow, in the hope that chance would, in the end, befriend me. It has befriended me when least expected. The moment has arrived—she has fallen into your power—no further obstacle exists—she *is mine*."

And the mask would have seized upon the inanimate girl, if he had not been withheld by the astrologer.

"One obstacle yet exists, my son," said Ruggieri, coldly; "you have a rival."

"A rival!" echoed the mask. "Name him!"

"For whom did she wreathe that garland? For whom endanger her life?"

"Ha!"

"For Crichton!"

"Perdition seize him! But he loves her not—knows her not— they must meet no more."

"Take back your purse, signor," said Ruggieri; "I cannot aid you in this matter."

"How?" exclaimed the mask—"Have I not your oath?"

"True; but I knew not what I swore."

" 'Tis binding, nevertheless. That is, if aught can be binding on a conscience supple as your own. What interest can you have in this maiden? Are your services already purchased by this accursed Crichton, or do you hope to make a better market with him?"

"Put no further affront upon me, signor," returned Ruggieri. "I am not easily appeased, as you will learn, if you provoke my anger. I am no friend to Crichton, nor is this maiden aught to me. Beyond the accidental discovery of her sex, and what you yourself have told me, I am wholly ignorant in all relating to her; but Fate has thrown her upon my protection, and to violence like yours I will never betray her. Take back your purse, signor, and trouble me no longer."

"Away!" exclaimed the mask. "Think not to impose upon me by these idle pretences. Why should I stoop to solicit when I can command? A word from me—and thou art plunged within a dungeon—whence not even Catherine's mighty arm can accomplish thy deliverance. Of all men living, Ruggieri, thou hast most cause of dread of me; but of all agents of iniquity, I have most need of thee, therefore thou art safe; but tremble if thou disobeyest me. My vengeance is swifter and more certain than thine own."

"Who, in the devil's name, are you that talk thus?" inquired the astrologer.

"Were I the devil himself, I could not occasion you more disquietude than I should were I to reveal myself," replied the mask. "Be satisfied, and seek to know nothing further of me."

The haughty imperiousness of tone suddenly assumed by the mask was not without its effect upon the astrologer; but he struggled to maintain a composed demeanour.

"What if I still refuse compliance?" he demanded.

The mask whispered in his ear. The astrologer started, and trembled from head to foot.

"I am content," he said, after a pause. "Command me as you see fitting. My life is at your disposal."

"I do not require so much," returned the mask, scornfully. "Deliver up the girl. Yet stay, I am not unattended here. Hast thou no place of refuge, to which thou couldst convey her?"

"I have," replied Ruggieri, after an instant's reflection; "if it be your pleasure, I will convey her to the mystic tower, near the Hôtel de Soissons, whither alone her majesty, Catherine de Medicis, and I have access. There she can remain concealed, till I am acquainted with your further wishes. But can it be that she hath refused your suit? There must be witchcraft in the case. You may be spell-bound, noble signor. The Emperor Charlemagne was similarly enslaved to a foul hag—and now I mind me of a strangely-fashioned key, which I discovered upon her bosom. Perchance the charm resides in that. It may be a talisman of potent virtue. I will put it to the proof. In any case we must have a counter-enchantment."

"As thou wilt," interrupted the mask, "be that thy business. Ha! she stirs—quick, we lose time."

For some moments before it was remarked by the astrologer and his companion, the return of animation had been perceptible in the Venetian girl. Heaving a deep sigh, she opened her large and languid eyes, and fixed them upon Ruggieri and Elberich; the former of whom was bending over her, at the instant of her restoration to consciousness, while the latter sustained her within his grasp. In this crouching posture, with his unbared, yellow arms twined around her person, the hideous dwarf resembled a messenger from Eblis, sent to bear her to perdition. The objects before her looked like visions in a dream. In vain did Ruggieri raise his finger to his lips; she neither comprehended her own situation, nor perceived necessity for silence. Just then her wandering gaze chanced upon the mask, and with a wild laugh she pointed to the dusky figure, and muttered some incoherent ejaculations.

"Away," exclaimed the mask, "about it quickly. Why listen to her ravings? Remove her to the turret."

"That voice!" shrieked the maiden, starting to her feet, and spreading her hand before her eyes, "it is—it must be he!— where am I? Ha!"

"Seize her," vociferated the mask.

"He haunts me even while life is ebbing," screamed the distracted girl; "I am dying, yet cannot escape him. Save me from him, Crichton—save me." And, with a wild scream, she broke from the grasp of Ruggieri.

The mask ineffectually endeavoured to stay her flight.

"Miscreants!" he cried, "you have let her go."

"The bird hath only fluttered forth," returned the astrologer; "we can easily retake it."

It was at this juncture that the cry reached the ears of Crichton. Like a frail barque amidst troubled waters, the enfeebled maid strove against the tumultuous mob, who little heeded either her plaints or frantic ejaculations.

"Poor youth!" cried one of the scholars, "his hurt hath turned his brain. Get hence, foolish boy! Crichton hath his hands too full to give attention to thy shouts. He hath more need of help than thou. Dost see yon tall green plume?—It is Crichton's. Be advised, and venture not where blows shower thick as hail, and where thou mayst come in for thy share of them. Seek shelter in the rear."

But the girl heeded him not, but still continued to cry, "Save me, Crichton, save me!"

A thick battalion of scholars opposed themselves to Crichton's progress. "Stand aside!" he vociferated, nothing daunted by their numbers. And, whirling the iron bar over his head, he dashed in the direction of the girl.

She beheld him approach. She saw the scholars give way before his resistless efforts. She heard his shout of encouragement; and at the very instant when her bosom throbbed highest with hope, and when she almost deemed herself secure beneath his protecting arm, she felt her waist encircled by a sudden clasp. ·She looked up. Her eyes encountered two dark orbs flashing from a sable mask. Her brain reeled. She saw no more.

Crichton, meanwhile, pressed fiercely forward. Fresh difficulties were thrown in his path—fresh ranks obstinately opposed themselves to his progress; but all were at length overcome, and he reached the spot where he beheld the Geloso. It was void. A roar of mockery from the students testified their satisfaction at his disappointment. "You have arrived too late to succour your friend," shouted a voice from out the crowd; "he is beyond your reach, and in the care of one who will not readily surrender him, *Higados de Dios!* you are foiled, most puissant *caballero*, nor shall it be my fault if you do not ever find a stumbling-block within your path."

Turning towards the quarter whence the voice proceeded, Crichton beheld the retreating figure of Caravaja. "By Saint Andrew," he murmured, glancing fiercely round, "I would give all the laurels I have this day won to effect that poor youth's deliverance. Curses upon these brawling scholars! It were a labour of Hercules to pursue the quest amidst a scene of such confusion; and yet I would fain continue it if I saw a chance of success. Why did Ruggieri, who so eagerly accepted the charge of this wounded boy, suffer him to incur such peril? The old astrologer shall render me an explanation of his conduct."

Crichton's further self-communion was cut short by the shouts of the archers and the trampling of their steeds. After a brief, but ineffectual, resistance, as before stated, the scholars threw down their arms and, shouting for quarter, fled. Crichton was left alone. No sooner did Joyeuse, who was careering among the crowd, perceive him, than he reined his charger by his side.

"Now Heaven and Our Lady be praised," exclaimed the vicomte gaily, "you are unhurt, Seigneur Crichton. By my blazon, it had, indeed, been a blot upon the fair page of chivalry, if its brightest mirror had perished amid a rascal rout like this. *Tête-Dieu!* if the Lord Rector reprove not his froward children, our sergeants shall take the task from his hands, and give him a lesson. But see, your page is at hand; your charger paws the ground. Ah, Crichton! brave steed—fair page—both pledges of a royal lady's favour—you are twice fortunate!"

"Thrice fortunate, Joyeuse, in a brother-in-arms who flies to my rescue in extremities like the present," returned Crichton, in the same lively tone as his companion, vaulting at the same time into the saddle of a superb charger in rich housings, which was led towards him by a page, mounted upon a milk-white palfrey, and bedecked in doublet of white satin and velvet mantle of deepest azure, the colours of Marguerite de Valois. "Methinks," he added, smiling, "this hard-fought field is at length our own; and yet, after enacting more wonders than ever were achieved by the doughtiest champions of Romance —Tristan or Launfal, Huon or Parthenopex, when struggling against the powers of sorcelrie and darkness—it moves me to tears to think in what light esteem my exploits will be held by *preux chevaliers* like yourself, who think there is no honour to be won in such perilous conflicts. Trust me a legion of swarthy gnomes, with the fay Urganda at their head, were more easily vanquished than these disloyal varlets. I have now encountered this university alike in hall and field; disputed it with them by rule of rhetoric, and by rule of fence; and will freely admit that I prefer the weapons of the principals to those of their disciples, and plume myself rather upon my conquest, if conquest it be, over these hard-headed, cudgel-wielding neophytes, whose stubborn brains were more difficult to be convinced than their renowned and learned seniors. But it is time to bestow a thought upon my luckless countryman, the original cause of all this scene of discord. I think I discern him and his staunch ally, amid the thickest turmoil. Forward, Joyeuse, I must speak with them."

A few bounds of his steed brought Crichton beside Ogilvy and Blount. The latter, perceiving that the fray was at an end, called off his dog from the Bernardin, but finding that his intimation was not attended to by the stubborn animal, he seconded the hint with a heavy blow of his crab-stick, which produced the desired effect. Druid quitted his hold, and with a surly growl plumped down at his master's feet.

"We meet to-morrow, then, Ogilvy," said Crichton, "and such service as I can render, you may command. Meantime, you shall suffer no further molestation. Monsieur le Vicomte, hath he your safeguard?"

"He has," replied Joyeuse. "The brave Scot shall have a post amongst my company of archers, if he choose to barter his gown of grey serge for a steel breast-plate. He will not be the first of his countrymen who hath found the change to his advantage."

"I will reflect upon your offer, my lord," replied Ogilvy, with characteristic caution. "Meantime, my best thanks are due to you for the proposal."

"As you please, sir," replied Joyeuse, haughtily; "nor are your acknowledgments due to me, but to the Seigneur Crichton. To him alone you are indebted for my offer."

"He knows not what he declines, Joyeuse," returned Crichton. "I will reason with him on the morrow. And now," he continued, "I would desire better acquaintance with your valiant comrade, whom I judge to be an Englishman."

"I am so," returned Blount, "but I deserve not to be called valiant. Had you bestowed the epithet on my dog the term might not have been misapplied—on me 'tis wholly thrown away. Druid hath some pretensions to valour—he will never disgrace the soil from which he sprung—nor will his master, for that matter. But since you have honoured me with your notice, worthy sir, let us join hands upon our new-struck friendship, if I be not too bold in assuming such a feeling on your part to me, and you shall find, if you need them, that in Simon Blount and his dog, for I must not except Druid, who is part and parcel of myself, and indeed the best part, you will have two followers upon whose faith you may rely. *Audacter et fideliter* is my device."

"And a cordial and constant one it is," replied Crichton, as he warmly returned the pressure of the Englishman's huge hand. "I gladly embrace your offer. Come to my hotel with Ogilvy on the morrow, and neglect not to bring with you my new and trusty follower."

"Doubt not that," returned Blount; "Druid and I are inseparable."

Further conversation was interrupted by the sudden arrival of Chicot, who, contrary to his wont, had a somewhat serious countenance.

"Ah! my gay gossip," said Crichton, "why that portentous look? hast thou lost thy bauble in the fray?"

"Far worse than that, brother droll," returned Chicot, "I have lost my reputation. Thou hast fairly won my cap and bells, and shall have them by pre-eminence of wisdom. But bend down thy lordly neck to me, I have somewhat for thy private hearing."

And approaching Crichton, the jester breathed his information in a low tone.

"What!" exclaimed Crichton, who appeared struck with surprise at Chicot's intelligence, "art sure this Geloso is——?"

"Hush!" muttered the jester, "who is now the fool? Would you betray the secret?"

"And it was the mask who seized her?" asked Crichton, in a whisper. "Whose features doth that vizard hide?"

"I know not," replied Chicot, "it may be the Balafré, or the Béarnais, for aught I can tell. But this I will venture to assert, that it is neither my gossip, Henriot, nor thou, nor I, nor even the Seigneur Joyeuse; I will not say as much for the Duc d'Anjou, whom perchance it *may* be."

"But Ruggieri, thou sayest——"

"Was with him. I beheld him and his dwarf Elberich. Both lent assistance to the mask."

"He is gone, thou sayest?"

"I will seek the astrologer in his tower, and compel him to some explanation of this mystery," said Crichton.

"That tower is the kennel of the she-wolf Catherine—take heed what you do. Many a hand has been thrust into a cage, the bearer whereof would have gladly withdrawn it unscathed. But as you will, fools are leaders, wise men receders."

"Adieu, Ogilvy!" said Crichton; "remember our appointment of the morrow. Joyeuse, our rendezvous is at the fête to-night.— Au revoir!"

So saying, Crichton plunged spurs into his horse's sides and, followed by his page, rode swiftly down the Montagne Sainte-Geneviève. Chicot shrugged his shoulders.

"Knight-errantry is not wholly extinct, I perceive," he muttered. "My gossip, Crichton, is born at least half a century too late. He should have flourished in the good old times of Triboulet, and the first Francis. He is caught at once by the silken meshes of this dark-haired siren. What will Queen Margot

say if this new adventure reach her jealous ears? But I must
to the Louvre. This scholastic brawl will divert Henri's spleen.
And as I descend this Parnassian steep of Sainte-Geneviève, to
beguile the time I'll invoke the Muses in honour of—

THE ADMIRABLE SCOT

A song I'll write on
Matchless Crichton;
In wit a bright one,
Form, a slight one,
Love, a light one!
Who talketh Greek with us
Like great Busbequius;
Knoweth the Cabala
Well as Mirandola;
Fate can reveal to us,
Like wise Cornelius;
Reasoneth like Socrates,
Or old Xenocrates;
Whose system ethical,
Sound, dialectical,
Aristotelian,
Pantagruelian,
Like to chameleon,
Choppeth and changeth,
Everywhere rangeth!
Who rides like Centaur,
Preaches like Mentor,
Drinks like Lyæus,
Sings like Tyrtæus,
Reads like Budæus,
Vaulteth like Tuccaro,
Painteth like Zucchero,
Diceth like Spaniard,
Danceth like galliard,
Tilts like Orlando,
Does all man can do!
Qui pupas nobiles
Innumerabiles,
Amat amabiles
Atque Reginam
Navarræ divinam!
Whose rare prosperity,
Grace and dexterity,
Courage, temerity,
Shall, for a verity
Puzzle posterity!

"Ough, ough," gasped the jester, "I am fairly out of breath
—as old Marot sings, 'en rimant bien souvent je m'enroue.'"

BOOK II

CHAPTER I

THE COURT OF HENRI TROIS

Les peuples pipés de leur mine,
Les voyant ainsi s'enfermer,
Jugeoient qu'ils parloient de s'armer
Pour conquérir la Palestine.
Et toutefois leur entreprise
Etoit le parfum d'un collet;
Le point coupé d'une chemise
Et la figure d'un ballet.
De leur mollesse léthargique,
Le discord sortant des enfers,
Des maux que nous avons soufferts
Nous ourdit la toile tragique.

MALHERBE.

ON the same night that the event previously narrated occurred, high festival was held within the Louvre, by its effeminate and voluptuous sovereign, who assembled upon the occasion the whole of his brilliant court, then without a rival in Europe, either for the number and loveliness of the dames who frequented it, or for the bravery and gallantry of the youthful chivalry, by which it was graced. To Henri Trois the lighter amusements of the revel, the ballet, and the masque, were as captivating as the more manly sports of the chase were to his brother and predecessor, Charles Neuf, of execrable memory. His fêtes were sumptuous and frequent—so frequent, indeed, that the chief part of his time was occupied in the arrangement of these magnificent spectacles. The sums lavished upon the marriage-feasts of his favourites were enormous: the royal coffers were often drained by his inordinate extravagance; and, while the State groaned beneath the weight of the burdens constantly imposed upon it, the unbridled licence that reigned at his orgies occasioned scandal and discontent throughout the reputable portion of the community, of which his enemies were not slow to take advantage.

Two years before the period of which we treat, Henri gave an entertainment to his brother, the Duc d'Alençon, at which the ladies assisted, "vestues de verd, en habits d'homme, à moitié nues, et ayant leurs cheveux épars comme épousées." [1] The cost of this banquet exceeded a hundred thousand francs! In December 1576, as we learn from the *Journal* of his reign, he went *en masque* to the Hôtel de Guise, accompanied by thirty princesses and ladies of the court, richly attired in silks and silver tissue, braided with pearls and gems of price; and such was the confusion that prevailed, that the more discreet part were obliged to retire, by reason of the licence of the maskers; for, as it is significantly observed, by Pierre de l'Estoile, "could the walls and tapestry have spoken, they would have, doubtless, found many pleasant particulars to communicate." Subsequently, in 1583, upon Shrove Tuesday, attended by his favourites, masked like himself, Henri rushed into the streets, where he committed such frantic and unheard-of follies and insolences, that he was publicly reprimanded the next day by all the preachers in Paris.

Louise de Lorraine, or de Vaudemont, his queen, a princess of amiable but feeble character, entirely without ambition (on which account she was selected as a suitable spouse to her son by the crafty Catherine de Medicis, ever apprehensive of a rival near the throne), and possessing the negative merit of passive submission, offered no opposition to the wishes of her royal husband, though she took little part in his festivities. Her gentle existence was divided between her oratory, her garden, the establishment of *confréries*, and other religious institutions, and the retirement of a secluded apartment; her daily occupations were embroidery, or the perusal of her book of prayer; her attire was of the simplest material, fashioned chiefly of woollen cloth; and, though her complexion had become deathly pale, she refused the aid of rouge. Her immediate attendants and ladies of honour were recommended to her regard rather by their piety and decorum of conduct, than for any other dazzling qualifications. Of this queen many pleasing traits are narrated—one, in particular, of a reproof conveyed to the flaunting and over-dressed lady of a president, to whom, in the unpretending garb she had adopted, she was wholly unknown. But taken altogether, her nature was too easy and acquiescent, and her frame of mind too infirm, to promote in any way the welfare of the kingdom, or to accomplish the reformation of the monarch to whom she was united. That she found rather sorrow than happiness in her exalted station can scarce be

[1] *Journal de Henri III.*, mai 1577.

doubted; indeed, her woes have been thus embalmed in verse by the Jesuit, Le Moine:

> Son esprit fut gêné dans la couche royale;
> La couronne lui fut une chaine fatale,
> Le Louvre une prison, le trône un échafaud
> Erigé pour montrer son tourment de plus haut.

But, perhaps, the severest of her afflictions consisted in her being denied the blessing of children.

The position which Louise de Vaudemont should have occupied was assumed by the Queen-Mother, who amply supplied whatever might be wanting in her daughter-in-law. In her hands, her sons were mere puppets; they filled the throne, while she wielded the sceptre. Hers was truly, what it has been described, "a soul of bronze, or of iron." Subtle, secret, Machiavellian—the *Prince* of the plotting Florentine was her constant study—her policy worked in the dark; none could detect her movements till they were disclosed by the results. Inheriting many of the nobler qualities of the Medicis, her hatred was implacable as that of the Borgias; and, like that dread race, her schemes were not suffered to be restrained by any ties of affinity. Rumour attributed to her agency the mysterious removal of her two elder sons[1] from the path of the third, who was unquestionably her favourite; and she was afterwards accused of being accessory to the sudden death of another, the Duc d'Alençon, who perished at Château-Thierry, from smelling at a bouquet of poisoned flowers.

The court of Henri Trois numbered three hundred of the loveliest and most illustrious damsels of the land, a list of whom will be found in the pages of Brantôme, who falls into raptures in describing the charms of this galaxy of beauties, proclaiming them to be little short of goddesses, and declaring that the palace which they enlightened was "un vray paradis du monde, escole de toute honnesteté et vertu et ornement de la France." Now, however, we may differ from the vivacious chronicler of the *Dames Galantes* in our estimate of the *honnesteté et vertu* of the ladies in question, remembering, as we do, the adventure of the Demoiselle de Limeuil with the Prince de Condé, and the libellous verses which it occasioned, we are quite satisfied that his enthusiastic admiration of these dames

---

[1] See what Thuanus says, upon the post-mortem examination of Charles IX., lib. lvii.—*ex causâ incognitâ reperti livores*. The end of Charles was, indeed, awful; but its horror would be increased, if we could be assured that his excruciating pangs were occasioned by his mother.

was fully warranted by their personal attractions. In later times the sparkling court of our own Charles II. did not boast so much beauty as that of Henri III.

Surrounded by this fair phalanx, Catherine felt herself irresistible. As in the case of the unfortunate Demoiselle de Limeuil, she only punished their indiscretions when concealment was impossible. An accurate judge of human nature, she knew that the most inflexible bosom was no proof against female blandishment, and, armed with this "petite bande des dames de la cour," as they were called, she made use of their agency to counteract the plans of her enemies, and by their unsuspected influence, which extended over the whole court, became acquainted with the most guarded secrets of all parties. The profound dissimulation that enveloped her conduct, has left the character of Catherine a problem which the historian would in vain attempt to solve; and equally futile would be his endeavours to trace to their hidden sources the springs of all her actions. Blindly superstitious, bigoted, yet sceptical, and, if her enemies are at all to be believed, addicted to the idolatrous worship of false gods; proud, yet never guilty of meanness; a fond wife—an Italian woman, yet exhibiting no jealousy of an inconstant husband; a tender mother, yet accused of sacrificing three of her sons to her ambitious views; a rigid observer of etiquette, yet not unfrequently overlooking its neglect; fiery and vindictive, yet never roused to betray her emotions by any gesture of impatience, but veiling her indignation under a mask of calmness, her supposititious character and actions were a perpetual contradiction to each other.

Catherine's was a genius of a high order. No portion of her time was left unoccupied. She was a lover of letters and of men of letters, a cultivator of the arts, and the most perfect horsewoman of her time. To her the ladies are indebted for the introduction of the pommel in the saddle (female equitation being, up to that period, conducted à la planchette), a mode which, according to Brantôme, she introduced for the better display of her unequalled symmetry of person.

If Catherine was a paradox, not less so was her son, Henri III., whose youth held forth a brilliant promise not destined to be realised in his riper years. The victor of Jarnac and Montcontour —the envy of the warlike youth of his time—the idol of those whose swords had been fleshed in many battles—the chosen monarch of Poland—a well-judging statesman—a fluent and felicitous orator, endowed with courage, natural grace, a fine

person, universally accomplished in all the exercises of the
tilting-yard, the *manège*, and the hall-of-arms—this chivalrous
and courageous prince, as soon as he ascended the throne of
France, sank into a voluptuous lethargy, from which, except
upon extraordinary occasions, he was never afterwards aroused:
his powers of mind—his resolution—his courage, moral and
physical, fading beneath the enervating life of sensuality in
which he indulged.

Governed by his mother and his favourites, who were
Catherine's chief opponents, and of whose overweening influence
she stood most in fear; threatened by the Duc de Guise, who
scarcely deigned to conceal his bold designs upon the throne;
distrusted by the members of the League, of which he had named
himself chief, and who were, for the most part, instruments of
the Guise; dreaded by the Huguenots, to whom he had always
shown himself a relentless persecutor, and who remembered
with horror his cruelties at the massacre of Saint-Barthélemy,
of which dismal tragedy he has avowed himself a principal
instrument; opposed by the Pope, and by Philip II. of Spain
(his brother-in-law), both of whom were favourable to the
claims of Guise; with Henri of Navarre in the field, and his
brother the Duc d'Alençon disaffected; fulminated against by
the Sorbonne; assailed by one of its doctors, in a pamphlet
endeavouring to prove the necessity of his deposition; Henri,
with his crown tottering upon his head, still maintained an
exterior of the same easy indifference, abandoned none of his
pleasures, or his devotions (for devotion with him took the
semblance of amusement—and the oratory and the ball-room
were but a step asunder—the mass and the masquerade each
the division of an hour)—turned a deaf ear to the remonstrances
of his counsellors, and could only be awakened, like the Assyrian
monarch, from his luxurious trance, when the armed hand
was put forth to grasp his sceptre. Then, indeed, for a brief
space, he showed himself a king.

It is not, however, with this portion of his reign that we have
to do; but with that in which this Sybaritic prince was altogether
sunk in indolence and dreamy enjoyment.

On the night in question he had gathered together, within
his gorgeous halls, the loveliest and the proudest of his capital.
Catherine de Medicis was there with her brilliant bevy of beauties.
Marguerite de Valois, the fair Queen of Navarre, then in her
seven-and-twentieth summer, and glowing in the noontide
warmth of her resplendent charms, was present, attended by

her train; nor were the gentle Louise de Vaudemont and her demure and discreet dames of honour absent. All that Henri's court could boast, of grace, wit, youth, beauty, or distinction, were assembled.

Perfumes exhaled from a thousand aromatic lamps; fragrant exotics filled the air with sweets; music, soft and low, breathed from a band of unseen minstrels; lofty plumes waved to the cadences of the melody; small elastic feet twinkled in the varied elastic movements of the figure—now attuned to the rapid whirl of the bransle—now to the graceful and majestic pauses of the Spanish pavane, or to the grave, slow, and dignified deportment of the Italian pazzameno.

It was a masked fête, and all, save the monarch and a few of his privileged followers, wore the vizard. The costumes were endless and diversified, but chosen rather with a view to display the person of the wearer to the best advantage in a guise different from his wont, than with that bizarre taste which characterises a carnival. Bright eyes, not less bright that they were seen peeping like stars through the dusky loopholes of the pretty velvet mask called the *touret de nez*, which gave additional piquancy and effect, when none was needed, to the ruby lips and polished chin of the wearer, rained their influence around. Of all favourers to flirtation, commend us to the mask. Beneath its shadow a thousand random darts may be shot that would fall pointless, or never be aimed at all were it not for the friendly covering. Blessings, therefore, upon him that invented the mask, who has thereby furnished the bashful and timid lover with a shield to fight under.

The splendid company dispersed throughout the long suite of gilded saloons—listening to the ravishing notes of a concert of harmonious voices—gathering round the tables where vast sums were lost at tric-trac, primero, and other forgotten games of hazard—pausing beneath a scented arcade of flowers—loitering within the deep embrasure of a tapestried window, or partaking of the sumptuous banquet set forth within the great hall of carousal. The laugh and the jest were loud and high; the love speech and its response faint and low.

Amidst the glittering throng might be discerned a group who had laid aside their masks, and who held themselves slightly aloof from the proceedings of the assemblage. More mirth, however, might be observed amongst this party than otherwise. Their laughter was heard above the conversation; and few were there, whether dames or seigneurs, who passed in review before them, if their gait or features could be detected, but were exposed to a galling fire of raillery and sarcastic remarks.

One amongst their number was treated with marked deference and respect by the others; and it would appear that it was for his amusement that all these witticisms were uttered, as, whenever a successful hit was made, he bestowed upon it his applause. A man of middle height, slender figure, with a slight stoop in the shoulders, he had a countenance charged with an undefinable but sinister expression, something between a sneer and a smile. His features were not handsome; the nose being heavy and clubbed, and the lips coarse and thick; but his complexion was remarkable for its delicacy and freshness of tint; neither were his eyes deficient in lustre, though their glances were shifting, suspicious and equivocal. He wore short moustaches curled upwards from the lips, and a beard *à la royale* tufted his chin. From either ear depended long pearls, adding to his effeminate appearance, while, in lieu of plumes, his black toquet, placed upon the summit of his head, and so adjusted as not to disturb the arrangement of his well-curled hair, was adorned with a brilliant aigrette of many-coloured gems. Around his neck he wore a superb necklace of pearls, together with a chain of medallions intermingled with ciphers, from which was suspended the lesser Order of the Saint-Esprit radiant with diamonds of inestimable value. In fact, the jewels flaming from his belt, the buckles, and the various fastenings of his magnificent attire, were almost beyond computation. On one side this girdle sustained a pouch filled with small silver flacons filled with perfumes, together with a sword with rich hilt and velvet scabbard, and on the other, a chaplet of death's-heads, which, ever mindful of a vow to that effect, he constantly carried about his person, and which indicated the strange mixture of religion, that, together with depravity, went to the composition of the wearer's character. Adorned with the Grand Order of the Saint-Esprit, and edged with silver lace, his chestnut-coloured velvet mantle, cut in the extremity of the mode, was a full inch shorter than that of his companions. His ruff was of ampler circumference, and enjoyed the happiest and most becoming *don de la rotonde*. Fitting as close to the figure as loops and buttons could make it, his exquisitely worked and slashed pourpoint sat to a miracle, not less studied was the appointment of the balloon-like hose, swelling over his reins, and which, together with the doublet, were of yellow satin.

Far be it from us to attempt to portray the exuberant splendour of his sleeve; the nice investiture of the graceful limb, with the hose of purple silk, or the sharp point of the satin shoe. No part of his attire was left unstudied, and the *élégant* of the nineteenth century might aspire in vain to emulate the finished decorative taste of the royal exquisite of the sixteenth.

Henri III., for it was the monarch whom we have endeavoured to describe, conferred, as before stated, infinite attention upon the *minutiæ* of the toilet, and carried his consideration of dress somewhat to an extreme. Upon the solemnisation of his espousals with the Queen Louise, so much time was occupied in the arrangement of himself and his spouse for the ceremonial, that mass could not be celebrated until five o'clock in the evening; and the *Te Deum* was in consequence neglected to be sung, an omission which was regarded as a most unfortunate augury. Of his personal appearance, moreover, he was excessively vain; and so anxious was he to preserve the delicacy and freshness of his complexion, and the smoothness of his skin, that during the night he always wore a mask and gloves prepared with unguents and softening pastes. Few ladies of his court could compete with him in the beauty and smallness of his hand; a personal grace which he inherited from his mother, and which was enjoyed in common with him by Marguerite de Valois.

Upon the present occasion he had withdrawn one glove, of silk, woven with silver tissue, and pinked with satin, in colours of white and incarnadine; and suffered his small and snowy fingers, loaded with sumptuous rings, to stray negligently through the luxuriant ears of a little lap-dog, sustained by the jester Chicot, who stood by his side. Of dogs, Henri was so passionately fond that he generally drove out with a carriage full of the most beautiful of the species, and took possession of any others that pleased his fancy in the course of the ride. Of his forcible abduction of their favourites, loud complaints were made by the nuns, the convents being the best canine storehouses, in the days of this great "dog-fancier," and frequently resorted to by him for fresh supplies.

Scarcely less splendidly equipped than their sovereign, were the courtiers stationed around him. Upon the right of Henri, who supported himself upon the shoulder of his chief valet, Du Halde, was placed the portly person of the Marquis de Villequier, surnamed "le jeune et le gros," though now laying little claim to the former epithet, near to whom was his son-in-law, D'O, superintendent of the finance, occupied in the childish amusement of the bilboquet, then in vogue with all the courtiers, in consequence of their monarch's partiality for it. Even the gallant Joyeuse and the stately D'Epernon disdained not to indulge in this frivolous pastime; and both of them carried long silver sarbacanes in their hands, with which, like the modern Italians at a carnival, they occasionally pelted the masquers with confectionery and sugar-plums, displaying infinite quickness of aim.

Engaged in converse with D'Epernon, was François d'Epinay de Saint-Luc, Baron de Crèvecœur, another favourite of Henri, and equally distinguished with his companions for a courage, which, in its wild and fierce display, amounted almost to ferocity. Saint-Luc was accounted the handsomest man of his time, and universally obtained the epithet of *le beau*. Many pages and lackeys, in the sumptuous liveries and emblazoned array of their lords, were in attendance.

"Joyeuse," said the king, addressing the young vicomte in a soft and melodious tone, "canst inform me whose lovely face lurks beneath yon violet mask?—for lovely 'tis, or else the lips and throat belie it—there, within the train of her majesty, our mother—thou seest whom I mean?"

"I do, sire," replied Joyeuse; "and I quite concur in your majesty's opinion, that the face must be divine which that envious mask shrouds. The throat is superb, the figure that of a Venus. But as to the angelic owner, though I flatter myself I am sufficiently acquainted with the dames of her majesty's suite to offer a correct conjecture as to nine out of ten of them, let them be ever so carefully disguised, I own I am puzzled by this fair incognita. Her gait is charming. *Vive Dieu!* with your majesty's permission, I will ascertain the point."

"Stay," said the king. "'Tis needless. Saint-Luc will resolve our doubts at once; 'twas she with whom he danced the pavane. How name you your fair partner, baron?"

"I am equally at a loss with yourself, sire, as to her name," replied Saint-Luc, "my efforts were in vain to obtain a glimpse of the features, and with the tones of the voice I was wholly unacquainted."

"Madame la baronne may well be jealous of her handsome husband," said the king, smiling (the baroness, according to the memoirs of the time, was "bossue, laide et contrefaite et encore pis," if worse can be well conceived); "but if thou, Saint-Luc, hast failed in making an impression upon the fair unknown, which of us shall hope to succeed? It cannot be, though the figure somewhat resembles hers, the Demoiselle de Chastaigneraye, or the fair La Bretesche, Villequier would be able to peer through any disguise she might assume; nor Surgères, Ronsard's divinity, nor Teligni, nor Mirande—*Mort-Dieu!*—not one of them is to compare with her. She floats in the dance as if she moved on air."

"You appear interested, sire," said Saint-Luc, smiling, to show his superb teeth, "are we to infer that the damsel may plume herself upon a royal conquest?"

"The damsel hath already made another conquest, upon which she has more reason to plume herself," said Chicot.

"Indeed!" exclaimed Saint-Luc. "Who may that be?"

"Nay, it refers not to thee, *beau* François," returned the jester. "Thou, like our dear Henriot, art the victim of ever-passing glance; and neither of ye are a conquest upon which a damsel might especially congratulate herself. Now, he whose love she hath won is one of whose homage a damsel might be proud."

"Ha!" exclaimed the king, "thou art in the secret, I perceive. Who is the damsel, and which of my gentlemen is her admirer?"

"All appear to be so, sire," returned Chicot; "but were I to point out the most devoted of her admirers, I should indicate your majesty's jester; if the most audacious, Saint-Luc; if the most fickle, Joyeuse; if the most grave, D'Epernon; if the most overweening, D'O; if the most bulky, Villequier; if the most imperious, your majesty——"

"And the most successful, thou shouldst add," interrupted Henri.

"No," replied Chicot. "In love affairs kings are never successful. They have no *bonnes fortunes*."

"Wherefore not?" asked Henri, smiling.

"Because their success is due not to themselves but to their station," returned the jester, "and is therefore wholly unworthy of the name good fortune. Can it be termed a triumph to obtain that which may not be refused?"

"My ancestor, the great Francis, found it otherwise," returned the king. "He at least was tolerably successful, even in thy sense of the word."

"I doubt it," replied Chicot. "And so did my ancestor Triboulet. Poh! kings are always detected. Did you ever find it otherwise, Henriot?"

"I shall not make thee my confessor, *compère*," said Henri; "but what wouldst thou say were I to hazard the experiment in the case of yon fair unknown? What wager wilt thou hold, that I do not succeed *en masque?*"

"Never throw away the best card, gossip," returned the jester, "that were poor play indeed. Approach her *en roi*, if you would be assured of triumph. Even then I have my doubts. But I will stake my sceptre against yours that in the other case your majesty is foiled."

"I may put it to the proof anon," replied the king; "I am not accustomed to defeat. Meantime, I command thee to disclose all thou knowest concerning the damsel in question."

"All I know may be told in a breath, gossip."

"Her name?"

"Esclairmonde."

"A fair beginning. The name likes us well—Esclairmonde de—give me the surname?"

"*Le diable m'emporte!* there I am at fault, sire—she has no surname."

"*Sang-Dieu!* be serious, *compère.*"

"By your father, the great Pantagruel—an oath I never ejaculate without due reverence—I swear to you, sire, I am serious. The lovely Esclairmonde hath no patronymic. She hath little occasion to consult the herald for her escutcheon."

"How, sirrah! and one of the attendants on our mother?"

"Pardon, sire. You require information—and I am literal in my replies. There is a trifling mystery attached to her birth. Esclairmonde is an orphan—a Huguenot."

"A Huguenot!" exclaimed the king, with an expression of disgust, and hastily crossing himself. "*Pardieu!* thou must be in error."

"The daughter of a Huguenot, I should have said," returned Chicot. "No one would look for heretics in the train of her most Catholic Majesty, Catherine de Medicis. They would flee from her as the fiend from holy water. Martin Luther or John Calvin have few disciples within the Louvre."

"Heaven forbid!" ejaculated the monarch, fervently grasping his chaplet of mort-heads. "'Tis strange," he added, after a moment's pause, "that I have never before heard of this girl, or of her story. Are you sure you are not amusing us with some silly fable?"

"Does Madame Catherine trust you with all her secrets, gossip?" demanded Chicot. "I trow not. But attend to me, and you shall have the story of Esclairmonde in the true style of a chronicler. Immured within her chamber, carefully watched by her majesty's attendants, suffered to hold no intercourse with any of the palace and, above all, no communion with any suspected of heresy, Esclairmonde until within these few days has led a life of entire seclusion. Whoever her father may have been—and that he was of rank, and a veritable Huguenot, cannot, methinks, be doubted—he perished by the edge of the sword at the day of Saint Barthélemy, of blessed memory. While yet a child she was placed within the hands of your royal parent, by whom she hath been reared in the true Catholic and Apostolic faith, and in the manner I have related."

"*Mort-Dieu!* the tale is curious," replied the king; "and I now remember somewhat of the details thou hast given, though they had long since escaped my memory. I must see and converse with the fair Esclairmonde. Our mother hath not used us well in neglecting to present the damsel to us."

"Your royal mother hath usually good reason for her actions, sire, and I will answer for it in the present instance she had the best of motives for her apparent neglect."

"Beshrew thy ribald tongue, sirrah," returned Henri, laughing; "I have yet, however, another question to put to thee. Have a care thou answerest it not lightly. Of what particular cavalier hath Esclairmonde made conquest? Of which of these gentlemen? Take no heed of their glances, but reply without fear."

"I should not fear to speak, were it to any of them that I alluded," replied Chicot; "but it was not so. Let these gentlemen withdraw a few paces, and thou shalt learn thy rival's name."

At a gesture from the king the courtiers retired to a little distance.—"'Tis Crichton," said Chicot.

"Crichton!" echoed the king in surprise—"the peerless— the Admirable Crichton, as he hath this day been surnamed— who hath vanquished our university in close conflict—he were indeed a rival to be feared. But thou art wrong in naming him, gossip. Crichton is ensnared within the toils of our sister of Navarre, and she is as little likely to brook inconstancy as any dame within the land. We are safe, therefore, on that score. Besides, he hath no thought of other beauty. Apropos of Crichton, it now occurs to me that I have not seen him to-night. Will he not grace our festival? Our sister Marguerite languishes in his absence like a pining floweret, nor will she force a smile for Brantôme's sprightliest sally, or Ronsard's most fanciful rhapsody. What hath become of him?"

"I am wholly ignorant, sire," replied the jester. "He started at full speed from the College of Navarre after our affray with those disloyal scholars, *ces bons rustres*, as mine uncle Panurge would call them; several of whom, as I already informed your majesty, are safely lodged within the Grand-Châtelet awaiting your disposal. But what hath since befallen him I know not, save that he may by accident have thrust his hand into the hornet's nest."

"Thou speakest in riddles, *compère*," said the king, gravely.

"Here cometh one who shall read them for you, sire," returned Chicot: "One more learned than Œdipus—Le Ramoneur d'Astrologie—you will hear all from him."

"Ruggieri!" exclaimed the king. "Is it indeed our astrologer, or hath some masker assumed his garb?"

"A circumstance not very likely," replied Chicot, "unless the wearer has a fancy for being poniarded by *accident*, as will, in all probability, be the case with Ruggieri, provided he escape the stake. What hath happened, father?" asked the jester, surveying Ruggieri with a malignant grin. "Are the stars overcast—is the moon eclipsed—or hath a bearded comet risen in the heavens?—What prodigy hath occurred? Have thy philters failed—are thine images molten—or hast thou poisoned a friend by mistake?—Hath thy dwarf eloped with a succuba or salamander—thy gold turned to withered leaves—thy jewels proved counterfeit—thy drugs lost their virtues?—By Trismegistus, what hath gone amiss?"

"Can I have an instant's speech with your majesty?" said Ruggieri, with a profound obeisance, and disregarding the taunts of the jester. "What I have to say imports you much."

"Say on, then," replied the king.

Ruggieri looked at Chicot. Henri waved his hand, and the jester reluctantly withdrew.

"I warrant me it is to speak of Crichton and the Geloso that the accursed old owl hath quitted his roost," he muttered. "Would I could catch a syllable of his speech. Methinks I am afflicted with a more than wonted deafness, or the crafty knave hath practised the art of talking in an under-key to some purpose. His majesty looks wonder-stricken, yet not displeased. He smiles; what pretended secret can the lying old miscreant have to make known?"

Henri, meanwhile, listened with evident surprise to the communication of Ruggieri, but offered no interruption beyond an occasional exclamation of astonishment, accompanied by a slight shrug of the shoulders. As the astrologer concluded, he mused for a moment, and then addressed him.

"I have observed that mask, Ruggieri," he said, smiling, "at the Hôtel de Bourbon, but little thought whose visage it shrouded. *Mort-Dieu!* thou hast let me into a pretty confidence. I have sufficient, methinks, to answer for in my own indiscretions, without making myself responsible for those of others. However, this young galliard shall have my assistance. Hath he seen the Duc de Nevers?"

"No, sire," returned Ruggieri; "and whatever may betide, into whatever perils his youth and hot blood may lead him, I implore your majesty to maintain his secret and afford him your protection."

"Fear not. You have our royal word. *Corbleu!* I delight in mysteries and intrigue of all kinds, and will lend him a helping hand with pleasure. He is a youth after my own heart, to engage in such a madcap frolic. I am charmed with his story, yet I own I can scarce comprehend how a player-girl like this can occasion him so much trouble. Our actresses are not wont to be so hard-hearted—ha, ha, especially to one of our masker's consequence— eh, Ruggieri? This is new, methinks."

"There is magic in the case, sire," replied Ruggieri, mysteriously; "he is spell-bound."

"Mary Mother!" said the king, crossing himself devoutly. "Shield us from the devices of the evil one! And yet, Ruggieri, I must own I am somewhat sceptical as to these imaginary temptations. More witchcraft resides in the dark eyes of that Gelosa than in thy subtlest compounds. But from whatever source her attraction originates, it is clear that the charm is sufficiently potent to drive our mask to his wits' ends, or he would never have committed such extravagances in her pursuit."

"Sire, I have now fulfilled my mission," returned Ruggieri. "I have put your majesty upon your guard against what may be urged by Crichton. Have I your permission to depart?"

"Stay!" said the king, "a thought strikes me. Du Halde," he exclaimed, motioning to the chief valet, "say to the queen, our mother, that we would confer an instant with her; and add our request that her majesty will, at the same time, take an opportunity of presenting the Demoiselle Esclairmonde."

Du Halde bowed and departed.

"I have my mystery, likewise, Ruggieri; and, singularly enough, this Crichton is in some way mixed up with it. For the first time this evening I have discovered that a beauty of the first order has been nurtured within the Louvre, whom no one knows, but with whom Crichton is in love. Scarcely have I recovered from the surprise into which I have been thrown by this incident, when thou comest to tell me that the pretty Italian singing-boy, with whose canzonettas and romances I have been so much delighted, and who has been the life and soul of our comedies, turns out to be a girl in masquerade, who, pursued by an ardent lover, flings herself into Crichton's arms. What am I to think of all this, knowing, as I do, that this very Crichton is the favourite of our sister Marguerite, who for him has abjured all her old amourettes, and who watches over him with a jealous frenzy like a first passion? What am I to think of it, I say?"

"That Venus smiled upon his nativity, sire," replied Ruggieri, with a profound inclination of his head. "Little is due to himself —much to the celestial influences—he is predestined to success. By Nostradamus! 'tis fortunate for your majesty that you are not placed in a similar predicament with our mask. Had your affections been fixed upon the same damsel with Crichton, I fear even your chance, sire, would have been a slight one."

"*Sang-Dieu!*" exclaimed Henri, "they are all of one opinion. These are Chicot's sentiments exactly. Mark me, Ruggieri. As concerns Esclairmonde I have my own designs. In this matter of the Gelosa, thou and thy mask may calculate upon my countenance. In return I shall require thy assistance should any unforeseen obstacles present themselves in my own case. As to Crichton, we will leave him to the vigilance of our sister Marguerite. A hint will suffice with her. She will save us a world of trouble. In affairs of gallantry we shall see whether even the Admirable Crichton can cope with Henri de Valois."

Ruggieri shrugged his shoulders. "'Tis vain to struggle with the stars, sire. *Che sarà, sarà.*

"But the stars say not that Esclairmonde shall be his, eh, Ruggieri?"

"His destiny is a proud one," replied Ruggieri; "that, at least, they have foretold."

At this moment Du Halde approached, announcing Her Majesty Catherine de Medicis, and the Demoiselle Esclairmonde.

Both were unmasked.

CHAPTER II

ESCLAIRMONDE

La Reyne-Mère avoit ordinairement de fort belles et honorables filles avec lesquelles tous les jours en son antichambre on conversoit, on discouroit, on devisoit, tant sagement et tant modestement que l'on n'eust osé faire autrement.—BRANTÔME, *Dames Illustres*, discours ii.

HENRI III., though perfectly heartless, was the politest monarch in the world. With all the refined courtesy of manner, therefore, for which he was so eminently distinguished, he gracefully advanced towards Esclairmonde, and, as she tendered to him her homage, he gallantly raised her hand to his lips, and with his most captivating smile, proceeded to eulogise her beauty in those soft periods of adulation which kings know so well how to turn, and no king better than Henri; exerting himself so well to relieve her embarrassment, that his efforts were not long unsuccessful. To a monarch's attention, indeed, few female hearts are insensible.

Surprised at the sight of Ruggieri, for whose unbidden appearance at the fête she felt unable to account, and who in vain, by sundry significant gestures, sought to convey to her some notion of his errand to the Louvre, Catherine de Medicis, ever suspicious of her confidants, could not, or would not, be made to comprehend his hints; but regarding him with a look of displeasure during the brief ceremonial of presentation, she motioned him aside, so soon as etiquette permitted, and proceeded to question him as to the cause of his presence. Seeing his lynx-eyed mother thus occupied, Henri, not slow to profit by the opportunity which her present distraction afforded him of assailing the heart of her lovely maid of honour, proffered Esclairmonde his hand, and gently drew her towards the deep embrasure of a magnificent window where they might converse unobserved.

Though not habitually sincere in his expressions of admiration, Henri, on this occasion, must be acquitted of any attempt at dissimulation. He was greatly struck, as indeed, he could not fail to be, with the loveliness of Esclairmonde. Accustomed to the blaze of beauty by which his court was encircled; with a heart little susceptible of any new emotion, and with a disposition to judge somewhat too nicely each attribute of female perfection, he could not help admitting that not only were the charms of Esclairmonde without parallel, but that there was no point either of her countenance or person, or what was of equal importance in his eyes, of her attire, which his critical eye did not pronounce to be faultless.

Alas! how inadequate are mere words to convey a notion of the beauty sought to be portrayed. The creation of the poet's fancy fades in the evanescent colouring he is compelled to employ. The pen cannot trace what the pencil is enabled so vividly to depict: it cannot accurately define the exquisite contour of the face, neither can it supply the breathing hues of the cheek, the kindling lustre of the eye, the dewy gloss of the lip, or the sheen of the hair, be it black as the raven's wing, glowing as a sunbeam, or fleecy as a summer cloud. The imagination alone can furnish these details.

Imagine, then, features moulded in the most harmonious form of beauty, and chiselled with a taste at once softened and severe. The eyes of a dark deep blue, swimming with chastened tenderness. An inexpressible charm reigns about the lips; and a slight dimple, in which a thousand Cupids might bask, softly indents the smooth and rounded chin. Raised from the brow so as completely to display its snowy expanse, the rich auburn hair is gathered in plaits at the top of the head, crisped with light curls at the sides, ornamented with a string of pearls, and secured at the back with a knot of ribbons; a style of head-dress introduced by the unfortunate Mary Stuart, from whom it derived its name, and then universally adopted in the French court. The swan-like throat is encircled by a flat collar of starched muslin edged with pointed lace. Rich purple velvet of Florence constitutes the material of the dress, the long and sharp bodice of which attracted Henri's attention to the slender shape and distinctly defined bosom of the lovely demoiselle.

In passing, it may be remarked that the rage for the excessively attenuated waist was then at its highest. Our tight-laced grand-mothers were nothing to the wasp-shaped dames of the court of Catherine de Medicis. Fitting like a cuirass, the corset was tightened around the shape till its fair wearer, if her figure happened to exceed the supposed limits of gracefulness, could scarcely gasp beneath the parasite folds, while the same pre-posterous sleeve which characterised the cavaliers of the period, likewise distinguished the dames. Nor had Esclairmonde neg-lected due observance of this beauty-outraging mode, or despite her personal attractions she would scarcely have found favour in her sovereign's eyes. Those prodigious coverings of the arms were stuffed out, and sustained by a huge pile of wool, and were of such amplitude and width that they would easily have contained three or four of our modern sleeves. Edged with pointed lace, starched like that of the collar, a ruff of muslin completed the gear of the arm. Around her neck was twined a chain of bronze medallions, and a single pear-shaped pearl descended from the acute extremity of her stomacher.

Tall and majestic in figure, the carriage of Esclairmonde was graceful and dignified; and as he contemplated her soft and sunny countenance, Henri thought that, with one solitary exception, he had never beheld an approach to its beauty. That exception was Mary of Scotland, whose charms, at the period when she was united to his elder brother, Francis the Second, had made a lively impression on his youthful heart, some sense of which he still retained, and whose exquisite lineaments those of Esclairmonde so much resembled, as forcibly to recall their remembrance. There was the same sleepy languor of the dark, blue eye—the same ineffable sweetness of smile—the same pearly teeth displayed by the smile—the same *petit nez retroussé* (that prettiest of all feminine features and well meriting La Fontaine's admiration—

> Nez troussé, c'est un charme encor selon mon sens,
> C'en est même un des plus puissans—

though perhaps it may evidence a slight tendency to coquetry on the part of the owner), the same arched and even brow—in short, there were a hundred traits of resemblance which Henri was not slow to discover. In a few minutes he became desperately in love; that is, as much in love as a king could be under the circumstances, and moreover such a *blasé* king as Henri.

"By Cupidon! *belle* Esclairmonde," he said, still retaining possession of her hand, "I am half disposed to charge my mother with *lèse-majesté* in so long denying me the gratification I now experience in welcoming to my masque the loveliest of my guests. *Mort-Dieu!* ardent admirer as she knows I am of beauty, her majesty's omission savours of positive cruelty; nor should I so readily overlook the fault, did not my present satisfaction in some degree reconcile me to the previous disappointment."

"Your majesty attachés more importance to the circumstance than it merits," returned Esclairmonde, gently endeavouring to disengage her hand. "Flattered as I am by your notice, it is an honour to which I had no pretension to aspire."

"In faith, not so, fair demoiselle," replied the king. "Beauty had a claim upon my attention to which all other recommendations are secondary. I were no true Valois were it otherwise. You will not refuse me your hand at the banquet," he added, in a lower tone, and with an *empressement* of manner which could not be mistaken.

The colour mounted to Esclairmonde's cheeks.

"Sire!" she returned, with a thrill of apprehension, "my hand is at your disposal."

"But not your heart?" asked the king, in an impassioned whisper.

Esclairmonde trembled. She saw at once the danger of her position, and summoned all her firmness to her assistance. "Sire!" she replied, with her eyes fixed upon the ground, and in a tone which struggled to be firm, "my heart is not my own. It is devoted to another."

"*Mort-Dieu!*" exclaimed the king, unable to control his displeasure. "You avow it—you love——"

"I said not so, sire."

"How!—and devoted to another?"

"I am betrothed to Heaven; my destiny is the cloister."

"Is that all?" said Henri, recovering his composure. "I half suspected there were other ties that bound you to earth. But a cloister—no, no—this must never be, *mignonne*. No monastery shall entomb so fair a saint, while I can hinder it. Such gifts are not lightly bestowed, nor should they be heedlessly thrown away; and I shall fulfil a duty in preventing such an immolation at the shrine of mistaken zeal, as would be your imprisonment in a cloister. If the resolution proceed from the Queen-Mother, my authority shall be interposed to restrain her intentions, for, by Our Lady! I cannot believe that you, child, have any such dissatisfaction with the world as to wish to withdraw yourself from it, when its gayest prospects are opening before your view; when your path is strewn with flowers, and when all the chivalry of France, with their monarch at their head, are eager to contend for your smiles."

"It is your royal mother's will that I accept it," replied Esclairmonde, timidly glancing at Catherine de Medicis, who, still engaged in deep conference with the astrologer, was too much absorbed to observe her look. "From her majesty's resolves there is no alternative. She will dispose of me as she sees fitting."

"But not without my concurrence," returned the king. "*Mort-Dieu!*—her majesty trifles with the sceptre till she fancies it is her own hand that sways it. I must convince her to the contrary. How she can entertain a notion so absurd as to think of burying one of the loveliest of her attendants within the gloom of a convent, passes our comprehension. Had it been our Queen Madame Louise de Vaudemont, who ever carries a missal within her *gibecière*, I could understand it; but that our mother, who, though zealous as ourselves at her vespers and masses, has no particular fanaticism, should contemplate an act so preposterous, seems unaccountable. *Morbleu!* she must have some motive."

"Her majesty has no motive save zeal in the cause of her religion."

"So it may appear to you, *mignonne*; but our mother's reasons lie not on the surface. Be they what they may, you need no longer apprehend her interference. Unless prompted by your own inclinations, you will never utter the vows which will bind you wholly to Heaven to the neglect of all on earth."

"Upon my knees, sire," replied Esclairmonde, "would I thank you for the precious boon you promise me, would thanks suffice; but I feel they would not. I cannot misunderstand your looks. Gratitude, devotion, loyal affection towards your majesty will ever influence my bosom; but not love, except such as a subject should feel towards her sovereign. My life, my destiny is at your disposal; but seek not my heart, sire, which is neither mine to bestow, nor yours to solicit."

"If not your own," said Henri, somewhat maliciously, "to whose keeping have you entrusted it?"

"The question is ungenerous—unworthy of your majesty."

"You need not answer it, then," returned the king; "the rather," he added, with a meaning smile, "that the secret is mine already. Few whispers breathed within these walls fail to reach my ears; nor were those of the Admirable Crichton so low as to escape our attention. Nay, tremble not, child, I betray no confidences. There is one person, however, against whom I must put you upon your guard. You know her not as well as I do. Fate grant you never may."

"To whom does your majesty allude?" asked Esclairmonde, with an expression of uneasiness.

"Have you no suspicion? Does not your heart prompt you?— I' faith, you are not so much taken with this Crichton as I imagined, or else, which I can scarcely believe, you have little jealousy in your composition."

"Of whom would your majesty have me entertain a feeling of jealousy? Against whom would you put me on my guard?"

"Whom you see yonder—the star queen of the revel, round

whom all the lesser orbs revolve—who attracts all within her
sphere, and who sheds, as such stars generally do, her rays on
all alike?"

"Your majesty's sister, the Queen of Navarre?"

"Precisely; and it is of her I counsel you to beware."

"I do not understand your majesty."

"*Mort-Dieu!* that is strange. You do not mean to say that,
in alluding to Crichton's amourette with the Queen of Navarre,
we tell you anything new. Why, the whole court rings, or did
ring, with it; for, in fact, the scandal is somewhat stale, and no
one now concerns himself about it. Our sister changes her
gallants so often that her constancy is the only thing that
excites a moment's marvel. A short while ago it was Martigues
—then La Mole—then *le beau* Saint-Luc—then Monsieur de
Mayenne, '*bon compagnon, gros et gras,*' as our brother Henri
of Navarre calls him—then Turenne, a caprice—then Bussy
d'Amboise, a real passion. After Bussy, appeared Crichton,
who, having disarmed D'Amboise, till that time deemed invincible, became the reigning favourite—making the grand
corollary to these pleasant premises. So the affair stands at
present. How long it is likely to continue, rests with you to
determine. Marguerite will never brook a rival; and can you
suffer him you love to be the slave—the worshipper of another?"

"I knew it not. And does he—does the Seigneur Crichton—
aspire to *her* affections?"

Henri smiled.

"He has deceived you," said he, after an instant's pause,
during which time he intently watched the workings of her
countenance. "Revenge is in your power. His perfidy demands
it. The game is in your hands—play off a king against his queen."

"Never."

"The cloister, then, awaits you."

"I will die rather. I am of the reformed faith, sire."

"Damnation!" ejaculated Henri, recoiling, telling his beads,
and sprinkling himself with perfume from one of the flacons at
his girdle; "a Huguenot, *Mort-Dieu!*—I shall expire—a heretic
in our presence! It is an affront to our understanding—and the
girl is so pretty, too—*Diable!* 'Indulgentiam, absolutionem et
remissionem peccatorum tribue, Domine!'" he continued,
devoutly crossing himself; "I am stricken with horror—pah!
'Ab omni phantasiâ et nequitiâ vel versutiâ diabolicæ fraudis
libera me, Domine!'" And he recited another paternoster,
performing a fresh aspersion, after which he added with more

composure: "Luckily, no one has overheard us. It is not too late to recant your errors. Recall those silly words, and I will endeavour to forget them."

"Sire," replied Esclairmonde, calmly; "I cannot recall what I have asserted. I am of the faith of which I have already avowed myself a member. I reject all other creeds save that which I believe to be the truth. In that I will live—in that, if need be, die."

"Your words may prove prophetic, demoiselle," returned Henri, with a sneer; "are you aware of the peril in which this mad avowal of your opinions might place you?"

"I am prepared to meet the doom, which in the same cause, made martyrs of my father and all my family."

"Tush! you heretics are ever stubborn. This accounts for your non-compliance with my wishes. However," he muttered, "I shall not give up the point thus readily, nor for a scruple or so in point of conscience, baulk my inclinations. Besides, I remember I have an indulgence from His Holiness, Gregory XIII., providing for a contingency like the present. Let me see, it runs thus: for an affair with a Huguenot, twelve additional masses per week, to be continued for three weeks; item—a rich coffer for the Sacristy of the Innocents; item—a hundred rose-nobles for the Ursulines, and a like sum for the Hieroni-mites; item—a procession with the Flagellants; and then I have the condonation of His Holiness. The penance is light enough, and were it more severe, I would willingly incur it. 'Tis strange —a Huguenot *perdue* in the Louvre—this must be inquired into. Our mother must be in the secret. Her mystery—her caution—proclaim her acquaintance with the fact. I will inquire into it at my leisure, as well as investigate all particulars of this girl's story. A Huguenot! *Mort-Dieu!* From whom," he added, aloud to Esclairmonde, "did you derive these abominable doctrines, demoiselle?"

"Your majesty will excuse my answering that question."

"As you please, *mignonne.* This is neither the time nor the place to enforce a reply. Your story and your conduct alike perplex me—but time will unravel the affair. Now, mark me, demoiselle. As yet I have approached you as a humble suitor, desirous in that capacity to win your regard. I now resume the king, and remind you that your life, your liberty, your person, are at my disposal; nor shall I forget the interests of your soul, in which good office I may call in the assistance of some of my most zealous ecclesiastics. If my measures appear harsh, you may thank your own perversity. My wish is to be lenient. Obedience is all I require. Till midnight, therefore, I give you to reflect. On the one hand, you will weigh my favour, my love —for I still love you; on the other, Crichton's infidelity, a cloister, perchance a darker doom. Make your own election. After the banquet I shall expect an answer."

"My answer will still be the same," returned Esclairmonde.

At this moment a loud clapping of hands was heard at the farther end of the hall, and the music replied to the acclamations in loud and joyous strains. To Esclairmonde the notes sounded wild and dissonant, and the laughing buzz of gaiety pealed like the din of some infernal concourse. The glittering saloon and its gay and ever-changing throng of masks and revellers vanished from her sight, and before her, like a ghastly vision, rose the cowled Inquisitors, the stern and threatening judges, the white-robed sisterhood, in whose presence she seemed to stand with hair unbound, and with a thick black veil thrown over her face! She shrank as for protection, and recovered her senses only to encounter the libertine gaze of Henri.

Again the music sounded joyously, and the torches of the bransle being lighted, the giddy dancers passed them in a whirl of flame.

"*Ma foi*, we lose time here," said the king. "Not a word, demoiselle—as you value your life or his, of our converse, to Crichton—should he still, as is not unlikely, make his appearance at our revel.—Resume your mask and maintain your composure. Soh, 'tis well."

Though scarcely able to command herself, Esclairmonde, in compliance with the king's request, placed her violet-coloured mask upon her face, and yielded, not without a shudder, her hand.

As they issued from the recess in which their conversation had taken place, the jester Chicot advanced towards the monarch.

"What wouldst thou, gossip?" said Henri. "Thy wise countenance is charged with more than its usual meaning."

"A proof I am neither in love nor drunk, *compère*," replied Chicot; "as in either case our family resemblance becomes the stronger, your majesty being always either the one or the other, and not unfrequently both. The superabundance of my meaning, therefore, you will lay to the charge of my sobriety and discretion."

"Bah!—this jesting is ill timed."

"Then it is in keeping with your majesty's love-making."

D 804

"Be silent, sirrah, or say what brings thee hither!"

"What shall be done to the man whom the king delighteth to honour?"

"And who is the man, gossip?"

"He who threatens, more than Henri of Lorraine, or Henri or Navarre, or Philip of Spain, or, despite the Salic law, your royal mother to depose you, sire—see how your loyal subjects quit your side. If your majesty decline the office, permit the Demoiselle Esclairmonde to offer him welcome."

"Ha! I begin to comprehend thee. It is the Admirable Crichton whom thou wouldst announce."

"I took the precaution to warn your majesty of his coming, as I would apprise a friend of a jealous husband's return."

"Crichton!" exclaimed Esclairmonde, roused from her stupor by the mention of the name; "he here! May I crave your permission to rejoin her majesty?"

"By no means, *mignonne*," replied Henri, coldly; "I would not deprive you of the pleasure of witnessing my interview with this phœnix of schoolmen. You will, therefore, remain near me —and neglect not," he added, in a tone only calculated for Esclairmonde's hearing; "the caution I have given you. You shall have proof enough of his inconstancy anon. Messeigneurs," he added aloud, addressing the lords in attendance, "approach. The victor of the university is at hand. It is not often that it falls to a king's lot to number a scholar amongst his courtiers. You may remember, messeigneurs, at our last jousting, I foretold Crichton's distinction, and promised him a boon. To-night I will redeem the royal pledge. Joyeuse, bid Her Majesty of Navarre attend upon me. To her, no doubt, my welcome will possess peculiar interest. Madam, my mother, if your conference be ended with Ruggieri, your presence will lend additional grace to the reception. Be seated, I pray you. I would welcome the Admirable Crichton as a king should welcome him."

Seating himself upon a richly ornamented fauteuil brought by his attendants, Henri was instantly encompassed by his courtiers, who formed a brilliant semicircle around him.

Catherine de Medicis, whose conference with the astrologer had been long since ended, remarked Henri's attention to Esclairmonde with some dissatisfaction. Accustomed, however, rather to encourage her son's wayward inclinations than to check them (and therein lay the secret of her rule), she allowed no expression of displeasure to escape her, but took her seat majestically by his side. Behind Catherine, crouched Ruggieri, uneasily shuffling to and fro, with the glare and the shifting movement of a caged hyæna.

Nearer to the king, and clinging to his throne for support, was placed Esclairmonde, now almost in a state of distraction.

Chicot reclined himself familiarly at Henri's feet, with his marotte in hand, and the monarch's long-eared, large-eyed, favourite on his knee, its long ears sweeping the floor. Poor Chatelard! As the gentle animal submitted to his caress, Henri thought for an instant of her from whom he had received him as a sister's remembrance—he thought of Mary of Scotland—of her captivity—of her charms—and of Esclairmonde's strange resemblance to her—and this brought back the whole tide of passion. "Singular, most singular," he mused; "would she had been a Jewess, or a Pagan! There might then have been some hope of her—but a Huguenot—ouf!"

CHAPTER III

HENRI III.

Don Carlos. A genoux, duc! reçois ce collier—sois fidèle!—
Par Saint Etienne, duc, je te fais chevalier.
VICTOR HUGO, *Hernani*, act iv. scene vi.

CRICHTON'S arrival at the revel had created an extraordinary sensation. His brilliant achievements at the university, which, coupled with his gallant and chivalrous and anything but scholastic character, excited universal astonishment, formed the chief topic of conversation, and everybody expressed surprise as to the time when he acquired the wondrous store of erudition which had confounded all the wisdom of the land. How could he have attained such boundless information? He had been at the chase, the hall of arms, the carousal, the fête—in short, he had been everywhere but where he might be supposed to be—alone and in his study. He had been the life of everything—dashing at all, and succeeding in all; rejecting nothing in the whole round of pleasurable amusement—now swayed by the smile of beauty—now attracted by the beck of the gamester, whose dice seemed obedient to his will—now pledging toast for toast with the votary of Bacchus, whose glowing cups seemed to have for him no inebriation. He had been all this and more; and yet this reckless, heedless voluptuary, who pursued enjoyment with an intensity of zeal unknown even to her most ardent followers, had excelled the learned and laborious denizens of wisdom's chosen retreat.

All was animation on his entrance. The report flew along the saloon on wings, swifter than those of scandal. "He is arrived," was echoed from mouth to mouth. The songsters were deserted, though the band was Catherine's choicest Italian company—the ballet was abandoned, though it had only just commenced—though the *danseuses* were the most graceful imaginable, and *à moitié nues*—the *bransle-des-flambeaux* was neglected, though the perfumed torches had reached the point when their blaze was to make one giddy whirl of many-coloured flame—the stately pavane broke into a quick movement—the grave pazzameno lost all bounds—the commotion became general—the infection irresistible. Eyes, brighter than the jewels of their wearers, rained their influence upon Crichton as he passed, and odorous bouquets fell at his feet as if they had dropped like manna from the skies. Human nature could not resist homage so flattering, and the handsome Scot appeared for an instant almost overpowered by it.

The same richness of taste that characterised Crichton's costume of the morning distinguished his evening attire. He wore no mask—nor, what was then generally adopted, a toque or cap with a panache of gay-coloured feathers—neither had he assumed any fanciful garb. His dress was a rich suit of white satin slashed with azure, the jerkin and hose fitting without a crease to the modelled limbs. Having divested himself of his Spanish cloak and plumed cap in the entrance-hall, nothing interfered with the exact display of his symmetrical person; and as, with a step elastic and buoyant as that of a winged Mercury, he passed through the crowded groups, he appeared like an impersonation of fabulous grace and beauty.

Not a trace of the fatigue which might be supposed incident to his prolonged intellectual conflict was discernible in his proud, steadfast features. High emotions sat upon his lofty brow—his countenance was radiant—and a smile was on his lip. With chivalrous and courteous grace, he returned the congratulations and compliments showered upon him, neither appearing to avoid nor yet court attention, but essaying to pass on to the upper end of the saloon.

Presently Du Halde made his appearance; and, sensible that all eyes were upon him, that mirror of courtliness performed his task to admiration.

When Henri's intimation became known, a new impetus was

given to the assemblage. In vain the almost bewildered Du Halde raised high his fleur-de-lis-covered rod of office. In vain he shrugged his shoulders, and made the most pathetic remonstrances, and to remonstrances added entreaties, and to entreaties, threats. The tide would not be repressed, but, like that of the scholars of the morning, pressed forward quite resolved, it would seem, to be present at Crichton's audience with the king. Deference, however, for the royal presence withheld them from advancing too close. The royal guard of halberdiers, pages and lackeys placed themselves in front, and formed a dense phalanx round the throne.

The clamour subsided, as, preceded and announced by Du Halde, Crichton approached the king, and made a graceful and profound obeisance. The music also ceased, there being no longer any reason for its continuance. The distant minstrel strained his neck to gaze towards the royal circle, and the attendant at the refreshment-table took the opportunity of pledging his companions in a brimmer of Cyprus.

Meanwhile, the royal group had been increased by the arrival of the lovely Marguerite de Valois, and her scarcely less lovely maids of honour, La Torigni, Françoise de Montmorency, surnamed La Belle Fosseuse, and La Rebours, the two latter of whom have been immortalised by Sterne.

The Queen Louise, with her discreet dames, had just withdrawn, it having been whispered to her majesty that her august spouse had betrayed symptoms of a new passion.

Henri was wholly unprepared for, and not altogether pleased by, the rapturous admiration excited by Crichton; but he was too much of an adept in dissimulation to suffer any symptom of displeasure to escape him. On the contrary, he received the laurelled scholar with his blandest and most deceptive smile, graciously according him his hand and, apparently not content with this mark of his friendship, instantly after raising him from his kneeling posture and cordially embracing him.

An irrepressible murmur of applause following this act of gracious condescension showed that Henri had not miscalculated its effect upon the enthusiastic minds of the spectators. In fact, despite his malevolence, he could not be entirely insensible to the influence of the scene and, in common with all present, felt and recognised the majesty and might of mind and its wondrous combination in the present case with personal advantages. He knew he was in the presence of one of the master spirits of the age and for an instant, forgetting Esclairmonde, half persuaded himself he was in reality the gracious monarch he was proclaimed by his courtiers.

There was one, however, who viewed his conduct in a different light, but she was mute.

"*Vive le Roi!—Vive notre bon Henriot!*" cried Chicot, who had withdrawn himself on Crichton's approach, addressing the Vicomte de Joyeuse, who stood near him. "The grande Rue Saint-Jacques appears to be the high-road to his majesty's favour. Henceforth, we shall all become scholars, and I may exchange my fool's bauble for a folio, my cockscomb for the *cappa rotunda,* and my surcoat for the prescribed *tabaldi seu houssiæ longæ* of the College of Navarre. How say you? It is only a year or two since our dear Henriot took to the study of Latin in the grammar of Denon. It is never too late to learn, and if the good Pantagruel propounded nine thousand, seven hundred, sixty-and-four conclusions, as his historian, Maître Alcofribas Nasier, affirmeth, why should not I offer a like number for controversy?"

"Nay, I see no reason to the contrary," replied Joyeuse. "Thy conclusions will, in all probability, be as intelligible and irrefragable as those of the sophists, and, as extremes meet, thou mayst be as near to Crichton as the line of intersection which divides the heights of folly from the depth of wisdom will permit. Meantime, pay attention to thy liege and master, for methinks he is about to bestow a gift on Crichton not unworthy of himself or of the acceptor."

And so it proved. Commanding Crichton to kneel, Henri detached the lesser collar of the Saint-Esprit from his throat, and placing the glittering badge around the scholar's neck, unsheathed his sword from its crimson-velvet scabbard, and touching him thrice with the blade upon the shoulder, added, "In the name of God and of our lord and patron, Saint Denis, we create thee, James Crichton, knight commander of the holy and honourable Order of the Saint-Esprit! We do not say, support its statutes and maintain its splendour without spot. That were needless. The name of Crichton is sufficient to preserve its glory untarnished."

"Your majesty has bestowed upon me a boon which I should have esteemed more than adequate reward for long and zealous service, or for highest desert," replied Crichton, rising. "But as I can call to mind no such service, can discern no such desert, I must esteem myself wholly unworthy of your distinction. This consideration, however, while it annihilates all fancied claim to favour, enhances my gratitude; and we shall see whether that feeling prove not a stronger stimulant than interest or ambition. Devotion is all I can offer your majesty. I have a sword, and I dedicate it to your cause; blood, and it shall flow in your defence; life, and it shall be laid down at your bidding. Emulative of your own great deeds at Jarnac and Moncontour, beneath your banner, sire—beneath the Oriflamme of France, it shall be my aim to make the holy and illustrious Order with which you have invested me, the proudest guerdon of knightly enterprise."

"I accept your devotion, Chevalier Crichton," returned Henri. "I rejoice in your professions, and, by Saint Michael! I am as proud of my knight as my good grandsire, François I., was of his fellowship in arms with the fearless and reproachless Bayard. The ceremonial of your installation shall take place on Friday, within the church of the Augustines, where you will take the oath of the Order, and subscribe to its statutes. After the solemnity, you will dine at the Louvre with the whole assembled fraternity of the knights commanders, and in the meantime, that nothing may be omitted, our treasurer will have it in charge to disburse to your uses our accustomed benefice of eight hundred crowns."

"Sire, your favours overwhelm me."

"Tut!" interrupted Henri, "I would not be outdone by my subjects in the expression of our admiration. Besides," he added, smiling, "my conduct, after all, may not be so disinterested as at first sight it would appear. Under any plea, I am glad to include within my newly instituted and cherished Order such a name as that of the Admirable Crichton—a name which reflects more lustre on us than knighthood can confer upon you. Freely as it was made, I accept your pledge. I may, anon, take you at your word, and require a service at your hands."

"Ask my life—'tis yours, sire."

"Enough. I am well content."

As Henri spoke, a half-stifled sob was heard, proceeding from someone near him. The sound reached Crichton's ears and smote, he knew not why, like a presage of ill upon his heart.

Henri could scarcely conceal his exultation. "I will no longer detain my guests," he said, "this audience must be dull work to them, and, in sooth, I am tired by it myself. Let the ballet proceed."

Accordingly, the king's pleasure being made known, the musicians instantly struck up a lively strain, the maskers dispersed to comment upon the scene they had witnessed, and the ball recommenced with more spirit than before.

CHAPTER IV

CATHERINE DE MEDICIS

Voilà pourquoi j'ai par quelque temps fait conscience d'écrire cet échantillon de la vie et des actions de Catherine de Medicis: pour ce que cette femme est un natif tableau et exemplaire de tyrannie en ses déportemens publics, et de toutes sortes de vices en ses plus privés.

HENRI ETIENNE, *Discours Merveilleux de la Vie de Catherine de Medicis.*

"*Par la Mort-Dieu! mon cher Crichton,*" said Henri in a languid tone, helping himself to some of the perfumed confectionery which he carried in his escarcelle, "I am quite taken with the brilliancy and whiteness of your collar. I thought my Courtray *gauderonneurs* inimitable, but your artist far exceeds those Flemish pretenders. I am critical in such matters, you know— Heaven having endued me with a taste for costume."

"True, gossip," replied Chicot. "It is not for nothing that you have acquired the titles of *Gauderonneur des Collets de votre Femme, et Mercier du Palais.*"

"*Corbleu, messieurs!*" continued Henri, heedless of the interruption, and apparently struck with a bright idea, "I abandon for ever my pet project, the *plat Saint-Jean,* and direct you henceforth to assume the collar *à la Crichton!*"

"Your majesty will then do manifest injustice to your own invention," said Crichton, "by so styling my poor imitation of your own surpassing original, and I pray you not to alter the designation of a vestment which appears to have some importance in your eyes. Let it bear the name of him alone to whom the merit of the conception is due. I can by no means consent to hold honours which do not belong to me, and no one would think for an instant of disputing with your majesty the eminence you have so justly attained."

"You flatter me," replied Henri, smiling; "but still I must retain our opinion. And now a truce to compliment. Do not let me detain you, *mon cher,* nor you, messeigneurs, I know you love the dance. The Navarroise is just struck up. That figure has always attraction for our sister Marguerite. Pray ye, solicit the favour of her hand."

With a smile like a sunbeam, the royal Circe extended her hand to Crichton, as he advanced towards her. That smile went like a dagger to the heart of Esclairmonde.

"An instant, madam," said Crichton. "Ere I quit his majesty's presence I have a suit to prefer."

"Say on," replied Henri.

"Were my intercession in your behalf needful, you should have it," said Marguerite de Valois, "but your interest with the king our brother is greater than my own."

"Still let me have your voice, madam," returned Crichton, "for my solicitation refers to one of your own sex. My life was saved this morning by a disguised Venetian girl, and I have since ascertained that her life is threatened by the traitor Ruggieri."

"Traitor!" echoed Catherine de Medicis, starting to her feet, and fixing a fierce glance upon Crichton—"ha! consider well what you advance, messire—this pertains to me—Ruggieri a traitor!—to whom?"

"To his sovereign, madam—to the king, your son," answered Crichton, resolutely returning Catherine's gaze.

"By Notre Dame! this concerns me, it would seem," said Henri. "Nay, frown not, madam. Since his reported medication of my brother Charles's beverage, I have ever misdoubted your astrologer; and, to speak truth, I wonder not at Crichton's charge, for the countenance of Ruggieri carries treason in every wrinkle. But I will not judge him unheard. But first let us know more of this Venetian girl. How is *she* threatened by Ruggieri?"

"She is his prisoner, sire," replied Crichton, "confined within the turret, belonging to her majesty, near the Hôtel de Soissons. I have myself penetrated the turret, where I heard moans, and saw her through the bars of her cell——"

"And you dared to force your way thither!" exclaimed Catherine—"by my right hand, messire, you shall repent your temerity!"

"The girl risked her life for mine, madam—my head shall be the price of her deliverance."

"I take you at your word, messire. You shall have the girl if you will adventure again within my tower."

"Beware, beware," whispered Marguerite de Valois, pressing Crichton's hand tenderly; "as you value my love, say no more. See you not, she smiles; one step more, and you tread upon your grave."

"It matters not," replied Crichton, withdrawing his hand from the clasp of the Queen of Navarre. "Your majesty's threats," he added, addressing Catherine de Medicis, "will hardly deter me from the execution of an enterprise in which my honour is at stake."

"Ha! braved!" cried Catherine.

"No, no," said Marguerite imploringly. "He does not brave you, mother."

"I only uphold the oppressed," said Crichton. "My head be the penalty of my failure."

"Be it so," answered Catherine, reseating herself.

"And *en attendant*, Chevalier Crichton, you withdraw the charge of treason which you preferred against Ruggieri?" said Henri.

"No, sire," replied Crichton, "I accuse Cosmo Ruggieri, Abbé of Saint-Mahé, of high treason and *lèse-majesté*, and of machinations against the State. These charges I will substantiate against him by proof unquestionable."

"By what proof?" demanded Henri.

"By this scroll, sire, set forth in alchemical characters; unintelligible it may be to your majesty, or to anyone here assembled, but which my acquaintance with its cipher enables me to interpret. This scroll, exhibiting a scheme for the destruction of your life, seized within Ruggieri's retreat, upon his own table, with the traces of his own ink scarce dried upon it, furnishes proof incontrovertible of a dark conspiracy against your safety, of which this accursed astrologer is the chief instrument. Let his person be secured, sire, and, difficult of comprehension as the mystic letters of this document appear, I undertake to make them clear and evident as his guilt is black and damning to the tribunal before which he shall be arraigned."

Henri looked for an instant irresolutely towards his mother. Ruggieri was about to cast himself at the king's feet, but at a gesture from Catherine he remained stationary, regarding Crichton with a scowl of bitterest animosity. "Your boasted powers of logic, Chevalier Crichton," said the Queen-Mother, "might have taught you that from unsound premises false conclusions must come. If you have no further proof against Ruggieri than that adduced from this document, your charge falls to the ground."

"Not so, madam; this cipher implicates a higher power than Ruggieri."

"It does proceed from a higher source than that of Ruggieri," replied Catherine. "That scroll is my contrivance."

"Yours, madam!" exclaimed Henri, in surprise.

"Question me not further, my son," returned Catherine. "Be assured that I watch over your interests with maternal solicitude, and that if I work in darkness, I have only one aim—the maintenance of your glory and power. Hereafter you shall know the real purport of this scroll. Leave the cares of rule to me."

"Puero regnante, fœmina imperante," whispered Chicot.

"This hare-brained youth has marred one of my best-laid plans," continued Catherine, scornfully, "but I pardon his indiscretion, for his zeal in your behalf, Henri. But let him use more caution in future. Zeal over much becomes officiousness, and will as such be punished."

"The zeal you reprobate, madam," replied Crichton, proudly, "prompts me, at the peril perhaps of my life, to tell you, that even *you* are the dupe of Ruggieri. This scroll is not what you suppose it."

"Ha!" exclaimed Catherine.

"From its tenor I am satisfied it is not the document he had your authority to prepare."

"Now, by Our Lady! this insolence passeth all endurance," cried Catherine, furiously. "Henri, your sire would have hewed off his best knight's spurs at the heel ere your mother's word had been doubted!"

"Do not irritate yourself, madam," replied the king, coolly. "The Chevalier Crichton's chief fault in your eyes appears to be his anxiety for my safety, for which I own I find it difficult to blame. With all your subtlety, you are no match for Ruggieri. And I would willingly hear my advocate out ere I relinquish an investigation which appears to involve such important consequences to my safety."

Catherine grew pale, but she spoke with calmness.—"Proceed, sir," she said, addressing Crichton, "the king wishes it. I will answer you."

"To prove to you, madam," said Crichton, "how much you have been deceived, I will ask you whether it was by your authority this image was prepared?" And Crichton drew forth from his pourpoint a small waxen figure representing the king.

"*Par Notre Dame de Bon Secours*," stammered Henri, growing white, in spite of his rouge, with choler and affright, "an image of myself—ha!——"

"Pierced with a poniard to the heart, sire," replied Crichton. —"Behold where the puncture is made!"

"I see it—I see it," ejaculated Henri. "*Ave Maria!*"

"Sire," exclaimed Ruggieri, flinging himself at the king's feet, "hear me—hear me——"

"Away, infidel dog!" cried Henri, spurning Ruggieri from him; "thy touch is pollution."

Exclamations of horror burst from the group immediately around the king. Swords flashed from their scabbards, and had it not been for the interference of Catherine de Medicis, to whose knees the affrighted astrologer clung in mortal terror, he would have been slaughtered on the spot. "Back, messeigneurs!" exclaimed Catherine, rising and spreading her arms over Ruggieri; "strike him not—he is innocent—on your allegiance I charge you, sheathe your swords!"

"Be tranquil, gentlemen," said the king, who had by this time collected himself.—"*Par la Mort-Dieu!* I will deal with this traitor myself. A waxen figure, forsooth! Let me look at it nearer. By my faith! the knave has caught my lineaments far better than my sculptor, Barthélemy Prieur!—a dagger in the heart—I have felt a strange pain in my side these three days. Is this accursed image the handiwork of Ruggieri?"

"Undoubtedly, sire," replied Crichton.

"'Tis false, sire. I had no hand in its manufacture. By my salvation, I swear it," ejaculated the affrighted astrologer.

"Thy salvation!" echoed Chicot, with a scream of derision—"ha! ha! thou hast long since lost all chance of salvation! Rather swear by thy perdition, miscreant abbé."

"I found it within his chamber," said Crichton. "Your majesty will treat the superstitious device with the scorn such a futile attempt against your safety merits. But this consideration will not relieve Ruggieri from the charge of treasonable practices against your life. For like attempts, La Mole and Coconnas were adjudged to the block."

"And on the scaffold he dies," replied the king, "if this offence be proved against him. The question shall enforce the truth. After this, madam," continued Henri, addressing his mother, "I think you will scarcely seek to advocate further the conduct of your astrologer."

"Were I satisfied of his guilt, assuredly not, my son," returned Catherine. "But what proof have we that the whole of this accusation is not a contrivance of this fair-spoken Scot, to rid himself of a foe, for such he confesses Ruggieri to be?"

"You speak the truth, madam," cried the astrologer. "I will satisfy his majesty of my innocence—and of the Seigneur Crichton's motive for this accusation. Grant me but time."

"I have said that a higher power than that of Ruggieri was implicated in this matter," returned Crichton. "That power is——"

"Forbear!" cried the astrologer, "lead me to the rack; but utter not that name; you know not what you would do."

"Villain!" exclaimed Crichton; "you find I am too well acquainted with your crimes. I have read the secrets of your heart. I would confront you with him you have betrayed. Would he were here to confound you with his presence!"

"He *is* here," replied a masked figure, stepping suddenly forward.

"The mask!" exclaimed Crichton.

"As I live, the mask in person!" said Henri. "I begin to have some insight into all this mystery."

A momentary pause succeeded, during which no one spoke. The mask at length broke silence. "The charge you have brought against Ruggieri, Chevalier Crichton," he said, sternly, "is false, unfounded, and malicious; and that you have made it wilfully, and knowing it to be such, I will approve upon you by mortal combat; to which, as Ruggieri's voluntary champion, I here defy you."

"And will you undertake the felon Ruggieri's defence? Will you draw your sword in his behalf?" asked Crichton, with a look of incredulity and surprise.

"King of France," said the mask, dropping upon one knee before Henri, "I beseech your majesty to grant me right of *combat à l'outrance* with all weapons, and without favour against the Chevalier Crichton."

Henri hesitated.

"Nay, my son," replied Catherine, "this is my quarrel—not Ruggieri's. I am glad to find I have one sword ready to start from its scabbard in my behalf. You cannot refuse this appeal."

"You have our permission, then," returned Henri.

"I here, then, repeat my defiance," said the mask, rising haughtily, and hurling his glove to the ground. "I challenge you, Chevalier Crichton, to make good your accusation with your life."

"Enough," returned Crichton, "I accept the challenge, and I counsel you, sir, not to throw aside your mask when you draw your blade in a cause so infamous. I am well content that Ruggieri's fate be left to the decision of my hand. Joyeuse," he continued, "may I calculate upon your services in this matter?"

"Most certainly," replied the vicomte, "but will not your adversary favour us with his name or title? As a commander of the Saint-Esprit you are aware you cannot fight with one of inferior rank?"

"If *I* am satisfied, Monsieur le Vicomte," replied the mask, haughtily, "to waive that consideration, a cadet of fortune like the Chevalier Crichton will have little need to take exceptions. We meet as equals only with our swords."

So saying, the mask disdainfully placed his ungloved hand upon the hilt of his rapier. Crichton regarded him fixedly for a moment.

"Sir mask," he said, at length, in a tone of cold contempt, "whoever you may be, and I have no desire to publish your incognito, whatever blood may flow in your veins, be it derived from prince or peer, I hold it cheap as water in the unworthy cause you have espoused; and were you base-born vassal, as I believe you to be honourable gentleman, and your quarrel the right, it would weigh more with me than noblest lineage, or proudest blazonry. Cadet of fortune I am, no doubt. Nevertheless, even the royal Henri might cross swords with me without degradation. On either side my ancestry is illustrious. My blood is that of the Stuart; my heritage, an untarnished name; my portion, a stainless sword. In God and Saint Andrew I place my trust!"

"Bravely spoken," cried Saint-Luc.

"You are satisfied of your antagonist's rank?" asked Joyeuse of Crichton.

"I will answer for him," said Henri.

The vicomte raised the glove, and thrust it in his girdle.

"Whom may I have the honour of addressing as your second, seigneur?" asked Joyeuse, in a tone of constrained courtesy.

"The Duc de Nevers," replied the mask, haughtily.

"*Vive Dieu!*" exclaimed the vicomte, "this is better than I anticipated. Monsieur le Duc, I shall be delighted to confer with you on this duel."

At the mention of his name, the Duc de Nevers, a grave and stately nobleman, wearing the full insignia of the Order of the Saint-Esprit, stepped forward, in some astonishment, but, after having conversed an instant with the mask, he advanced, and with a formal salutation took Crichton's glove from the hand of the vicomte.

"*Mort-Dieu!* messeigneurs," said Henri, "I had rather the whole science of astrology were exterminated, together with all its idolatrous professors, than that you should battle to each other upon grounds so frivolous, and for a cause so unworthy of your swords. However, since you will have it so, I will not oppose your inclinations. Let the combat take place at noon to-morrow, within the hall of arms. My pleasure, however, is that in lieu of the duel with rapier and dagger—which, remembering the end of Caylus and Maugiron, I interdict—that you break a lance together in the lists. On the issue of the third course, let the astrologer's fate depend. I will not have the life of a valiant cavalier, or of one dear to me, sacrificed in this worthless dispute. Meantime, Ruggieri shall be placed under the safeguard of the walls of the Châtelet, to abide the issue of the encounter, and may God defend the right!"

"I will answer for Ruggieri's attendance," said Catherine de Medicis. "Let him be escorted to my turret. I will place my own guard over him."

"As you please, madam," returned Henri, "but have a care you produce him at the lists."

"Fear me not, my son."

"And now, sir mask," said the king, turning round. "*Mort-Dieu*, vanished!——"

"And now for the Navarroise," said Crichton, taking the hand of Marguerite de Valois.

"I thought you had forgotten it," replied the queen, smiling; "but let us go—I am wearied of this crowd. We shall, at least, be alone in the dance."

And, all eyes following their majestic figures, they swept down the saloon.

While this was passing, Catherine motioned Ruggieri to approach her. The astrologer threw himself at her feet, as if imploring compassion. "I would question thee ere thou depart," she said, aloud, adding in a whisper, "this combat must never take place."

"It must not," returned the astrologer.

"I will find means to prevent it. Give me the phial thou hast ever with thee—the Borgia tincture."

"That were too tardy, madame: this potion you will find more efficacious. It is the same deadly mixture as that prepared, by your majesty's orders, for the Admiral Coligni, which you entrusted to his valet, Dominique d'Albe."

"No more—I will find a surer agent than that timid slave," said Catherine, taking the phial which Ruggieri slipped into her hands; "I must see the mask to-night," she continued. "Give me the key of thine inner chamber in the turret—I will instruct him how to come thither unperceived, by the subterranean passage from the Hôtel de Soissons."

"The key is here, madam," replied the astrologer.

"Let Ruggieri be removed," said Catherine, aloud; "and a triple guard placed at the portal of our *hôtel*. Suffer none to go forth, nor to enter, save at our order."

"Your highness's commands shall be obeyed," said Larchant,

advancing towards Ruggieri, and surrounding him with some half-dozen halberdiers.

"And your devilish schemes circumvented," added Chicot, gliding from the fauteuil of the Queen-Mother, whither he had crept unperceived; "and, now to apprise Crichton of his danger! —*Mort-Dieu!*—I tremble lest our Jezebel should find an opportunity of effecting her accursed designs."

Full of apprehension for Crichton's safety, the jester was about to follow the course taken by the Scot and his illustrious partner, but he found them surrounded by such a crowd of eager spectators, that approach was next to impossible. He was constrained, therefore, to remain stationary. Presently, a lively flourish of music told that the Navarroise had commenced; and all the jester could discern was the tall and majestic figure of Crichton revolving with that of the queen in the rapid circles of the dance. Round after round they whirled—the music each instant increasing the rapidity of its movements, till Chicot's brain began to spin like the giddy measure he witnessed.

Suddenly the strains ceased. "Now is my opportunity," exclaimed the jester, preparing to dart forward.

At that instant he was arrested by a voice behind him. It was that of the king, with the hand of a masked maiden within his own. Henri stood by his side. "Follow me, *compère*," whispered the monarch, "I have need of thy assistance. I shall require a mask and domino, and a hat with plumes, unlike those I am accustomed to wear. Follow me!"

"An instant, sire,——"

"Not a second! Keep near me; I will not have thee quit my sight. Come, demoiselle," added Henri, with a triumphant look at his companion; "you shall now be satisfied of your lover's perfidy."

Chicot did not hear the words; but he saw the lady tremble violently, as the king dragged her on.

"Malediction!" mentally he exclaimed. "Escape is now impossible! Crichton must take his chance."

CHAPTER V

MARGUERITE DE VALOIS

Ah! que le temps est bien changé à celuy que quand on les voyoit danser tous deux en la grande salle du bal, d'une belle accordance, et de bonne volonté. Si l'un avoit belle majesté, l'autre ne l'avoit pas moindre.

BRANTÔME, *Dames Illustres*, discours v.

MARGUERITE DE VALOIS, consort of Henri of Navarre, afterwards Henri IV., was now in the full éclat of her almost unrivalled beauty. Smitten by her nascent charms, Ronsard proclaimed her, in her fifteenth spring, *La belle Charité Pasithée*. Nor was the appellation unmerited. Chiselled by the Apollonian sculptor, Aglaia never rose upon the view more surpassingly lovely. Some of her after-admirers distinguished her by the title of Venus Urania; and we might follow in their steps, had we not been forewarned that such description—high-flown as it appears —was wholly inadequate to her matchless attractions. Hear what the Abbé de Brantôme says on the subject: "Encore croit-on," he writes, "que par l'advis de plusieurs jamais Déesse ne fut veue plus belle, si bien que pour publier ses beautez, ses mérites, et ses vertus, il faudroit que Dieu allongeast le Monde, et haussast le ciel plus qu'il n'est!"—and he concludes his panegyric by averring, that by her side all the goddesses of old, and empresses, such as we see them represented on the ancient medals, however pompously arrayed, would appear little better than chambermaids—(*que chambrières au prix d'elle!*) No wonder when her chronicler sent this *éloge* for Marguerite's inspection, she should return it, saying, "I would have praised you *more*, had you praised me *less*."

But due allowance being made for the worthy abbé's warmth of style, which carried him a little into extremes, no doubt can exist as to Marguerite's eminent personal attractions; and that she ranked as beautiful amongst the beautiful, even in the age that produced Mary Stuart.

Marguerite's eyes were large and dark, liquid, impassioned, voluptuous, with the fire of France, and the tenderness of Italy, in their beams. An anchorite could scarce have resisted their witchery. And then her features! How shall we describe their fascination? It was not their majesty—yet they were majestic as those of her mother—(grace, in fact, is more majestical than majesty's self, and Marguerite was eminently graceful)—it was not their regularity—yet they were regular as the severest judgment might exact—it was not their tint—though Marguerite's skin was dazzlingly fair—but it was that expression which resides not in form, but which, emanating from the soul, imparts, like the sun to the landscape, light, life, and loveliness. This it was that constituted the charm of Marguerite's features.

The Queen of Navarre's figure was full and faultless; or, if it had a fault, it might be deemed by those who think embonpoint incompatible with beauty, a little too redundant. But then if you complained of the Hebe-like proportion of her swelling shoulders, surely the slender waist from which those shoulders sprang would content you. The cestus of Venus would have spanned that waist; and *did* span it for aught we know—Marguerite's fascination, indeed, would almost warrant such a conclusion. Her throat was rounded and whiter than drifted snow—"Jamais n'en fut vue," says her historian, "une si belle, ny si blanche, si pleine, ny si charnue." Her hands—the true Medici's hand—(Ronsard did well to liken them to the fingers of the young Aurora—rose-dyed, dew-steeped)—were the snowiest and smallest ever beheld—her feet were those of a fairy, and the ankles that sustained them fine and fairy-like as the feet.

Of her attire, which was gorgeous as her beauty, we dare scarcely hazard a description. We shrink beneath the perilous weight of its magnificence. Brilliants flamed like stars thick set amidst her dusky tresses. Besprent with pearls, her stomacher resembled a silvery coat of mail. Cloth of gold constituted her dress, the fashion of which was peculiar to herself; for it was remarked of her that she never appeared in the same garb twice; and that the costume in which she was seen last was that which became her most. Be this as it may, upon the present occasion, she had studied to please—and she who pleased without study, could scarce fail to charm when it was her aim to do so. Around her fair throat hung a necklace of cameos, while in one hand *mignonnement engantelé,* as Rabelais hath it, she held a kerchief fringed with golden lace, and in the other a fan of no inconsiderable power of expansion.

In accomplishments, Marguerite might vie with any queen on record. Gifted with the natural eloquence of her grandsire, Francis the First, her own Memoirs amply testify her literary attainments—while her unpremeditated reply, in elegant latinity, to the Bishop of Cracovia, may be brought in evidence of the extent of her classical information, proving her no unworthy descendant, as she was the inheritress of the kingdom and of the name, of the amiable and virtuous Marguerite de Valois, spouse of Henri d'Albert, King of Navarre, and authoress of the *Heptameron*, and of the *Miroir d'une âme pécheresse*, and surnamed La Marguerite des Marguerites—or pearl of pearls. Marguerite was the friend of the arts, and cultivator of poesy; and if her predecessor could boast of the friendship of Melanchthen and Clément Marot, she was not less fortunate in the devotion of Ronsard and Brantôme, besides a host of minor luminaries. But if she had many friends and panegyrists, she had likewise numerous enemies and detractors; and to discover how busy scandal was with her reputation, we have only to turn to the pages of the *Divorce Satirique*, published under the name and with the sanction of her husband, Henri IV.

Her life, a mixture of devotion and levity, presents one of those singular anomalies of which her sex have occasionally furnished examples; and which, without calling her sincerity in question —(for Marguerite, though profligate, was not a dissembler, like the rest of her family)—can only be reconciled upon such grounds as those on which Shelley seeks to harmonise the enormities, and yet continuous prayers and prostrations, of the ruthless Cenci. "Religion," he acutely remarks, "in a Catholic has no connexion with any one virtue. The most atrocious villain may be rigidly devout, and, without any shock to established faith, confess himself to be so. Religion pervades intensely the whole frame of society, and is, according to the temper of the mind which it inhabits, a passion, a persuasion, an excuse, a refuge; never a check." Marguerite, we have observed, was no hypocrite —her undisguised excesses attest the very reverse. With her, religion was a passion. One half of her existence was abandoned to a round of indulgences—the other to exercises of devotion, or to what would bear the name of devotion. She would hear three masses a day—*une haute, les deux autres petites* [1]—would communicate thrice a week, and perform sundry acts of self-inflicted penance; but this inordinate zeal offered no interruption to her irregularities; on the contrary, it appeared to lend piquancy to them. Satiated with amusement, she retired to pray with renovated fervour; and she issued from her oratory with a new appetite for sin.

With her after-sorrows we have no concern; nor with the darker period of her existence, when, in the touching words of the poetical Jesuit, Lemoine, she became—

> Epouse sans époux, et reine sans royaume;
> Vaine ombre du passé, grand et noble fantôme.

[1] Pasquier.

Our business is with the brighter portion of her career—ere care had stricken her, or sorrow robbed her of a charm.

Of the grace and elegance of Marguerite de Valois in the dance, Brantôme has left us the most rapturous particulars. With lover-like enthusiasm he dilates upon her majestic carriage, and indescribable fascinations; and the vivid portrait he has taken of the lovely queen (sketched at some such scene as that we are now attempting to describe) blooms, breathes, and stands before us in all its original beauty and freshness—a splendid "phantom of delight," sparkling within that gallery of high-born dames and gallant cavaliers which he has preserved for the gaze of the world.

With Crichton's supremacy in the somewhat trifling, but then highly estimated art which

Teacheth lavoltas high, and swift corantos,

with his perfect mastership of all its difficulties (for in those days, when Italy, Spain, and Germany, and almost each province of France contributed their quota of figures and national peculiarities, the dance *had* its difficulties), with his unequalled possession of all its graces, the reader, aware of the universal scope of his accomplishments, must be already acquainted. He was accounted the most proficient in the dance at a court, each member of which would probably have been considered in the same important light in any other in Europe. Henri III. was passionately fond of the amusement, and largely indulged in it. In earlier days, Catherine de Medicis had been no less partial to the dance, and Marguerite de Valois, as we know, held it in high esteem. All the courtiers, therefore, emulous of distinction in their sovereign's eyes, bestowed unremitting attention upon this accomplishment, and it was no slight merit to eclipse in skill performers of such consummate ability. As in the hall of arms, the arena of learning, the tourney, the chase, or other exercises in which strength or dexterity is concerned—so in the ball-room Crichton outstripped all competitors. From the inimitable "constitution of his leg," it would seem, "that he was born under the star of a galliard." Terpsichore might have presided at his nativity.

It was Crichton's remarkable spirit, displayed in one of the wild and national dances of his own country, then little known, or regarded as semi-barbarian in the polite court of France, and perhaps seen there for the first time when he undertook it, that first attracted the attention of the Queen of Navarre towards him, and afterwards riveted her regards. With Crichton, it was indeed that poetry of motion, that inspiration of look and gesture (terms idly applied in these later days to the performances of the hired artist), called into play by the agency of the dance, and giving to that light and graceful pastime its highest and most imaginative character. In him, the dance was not a medium for the display of brilliant and faultless execution of paces, and flourishing of limb. His action—his *impersonation,* we might almost say, of the melody by which his movements were guided —was fanciful, inspiriting, harmonious, as the melody itself. We question whether the pyrrhic, or enoplian dance of old, or hyporchematic measure were ever executed with more fervour and inspiration, or produced more thrilling effects upon the beholders than Crichton's performances. The same ease—the same unconscious grace, which accompanied his demeanour on the parade, followed him in the volte, the bransle, or the pazzameno. In each, like mastery was exhibited—in each were the various involutions required preserved; but, change the figure as often as he might, one *expression* pervaded all — in that expression, unattainable by other aspirants, resided his superiority.

Whether upon the present occasion Crichton felt inspired by the presence and acclamations of the vast assemblage—the gaze of which he felt was fixed upon him—or whether he was resolved to show how inexhaustible were his energies, we know not; but he appeared to surpass himself. Such was the springy lightness with which he bounded through the rapid Navarroise (a species of waltz peculiar to the pleasant land from which it derived its name), that his foot scarcely seemed to touch the floor, or if it did alight upon it, it was only as Antæus acquired fresh vigour from his mother earth, to gain elasticity from the momentary contact. A movement so rapid and whirling as to have turned the heads of any less practised than the admirable Scot and his royal partner, brought the dance to a spirited and striking conclusion.

All etiquette was forgotten. An irrepressible excitement took possession of the spectators—*vivats* and *bravos* resounded on all sides—the burnished roof of the grand saloon re-echoed with the plaudits, and the effect produced upon the courtly throng by the brilliant achievements of the distinguished couple, seemed to be precisely similar to that which results from the most electrifying effects of the divinities of the ballet.

Never had Marguerite appeared so animated; even her dames

of honour were surprised at her unusual elation. "*Mon Dieu!* I have never seen her majesty execute that dance with so much spirit since I first beheld it," said La Fosseuse, "when her partner was Henry of Navarre, and the occasion her own espousal."

"Her majesty has all the air of a bride now," returned La Rebours, pensively. This fair demoiselle, whom Marguerite in her Memoirs terms "*une fille malicieuse, qui ne m'aimoit pas,*" became shortly afterwards the chief favourite of Henri of Navarre. It might be presentiment.

"Poh!" replied La Torigni, "I remember the night La Fosseuse speaks of well. By my reputation, I have reason to do so. Henri of Navarre was a mere lump of rusty armour compared with the Chevalier Crichton, who vaults in the dance as if he had stolen the wings of Icarus. Nor does Madame Marguerite appear insensible to the change. *She* look like a bride, *ma foi!* you ought to know better, La Rebours. Even if she have it not, your bride is sure to affect a bashfulness, and you cannot lay any excess of that sort to Madame Marguerite's charge at the present moment."

"Why no," replied La Rebours, "not exactly; but Henry makes a charming partner."

"As to the spirit with which she dances," continued the sprightly Torigni, "her nuptial ball was nothing to it. But what say you? *You* recollect that night, I dare say, Abbé de Brantôme?"

"Perfectly," replied Brantôme, with a significant glance, "*then* it was Mars, *now* Apollo and Venus are in conjunction."

While Marguerite de Valois remained panting within Crichton's arms with one hand retained within his own, and her waist still encircled by the other—with her eyes, to the neglect of all observers, passionately fixed upon his gaze, a masked cavalier, enveloped in a black domino, and wearing a hat surmounted by sable plumes, accompanied by a dame whose features were concealed by a violet-coloured vizard, took up a position opposite to them.

"Do you note their looks? Do you mark their caressing hands?" asked the cavalier of his companion.

"I do—I do!" was her reply.

"Look again."

"My eyes dazzle—I can see no longer."

"You are satisfied, then?"

"Satisfied, oh! my head burns—my heart throbs almost to

bursting—horrible emotions possess me. Heaven give me strength to conquer them—prove—prove him false—prove *that*—and——"

"Have I *not* proved it? No matter; you shall hear him avow his perfidy with his own lips, shall behold him seal it with his kisses. Will that content you?"

The maiden's reply, if her agitation permitted her to make any, was unheard in the din of a fresh burst of music, which struck up in answer to a wave of Du Halde's wand. The grave and somewhat grandiose character of the strain, announced an accompaniment to the *Pavanne d'Espagne,* a dance not inaptly named after the strutting bird of Juno, which had been recently introduced from the court of Madrid into that of Paris, by the ambassador of Philip II., and which, in consequence of the preference entertained for it by Marguerite de Valois, was, notwithstanding that its solemn and stately pace harmonised more completely with the haughty carriage of the grandees of Spain than with the livelier bearing of the French *noblesse,* now greatly in vogue amongst the latter.

La Pavanne d'Espagne, which had some of the stiffness with more than the grace of the old *minuet de la cour,* presented a strong contrast to the national dance that preceded it. In the one all was whirl, velocity, abandonment; in the other, dignity, formality, gravity. The first was calculated to display the spirit and energy of the performers; the second exhibited their grace of person and majesty of deportment.

As, in accordance with the haughty prelude to the figure— a slow martial strain breathing of the proud minstrelsy of Old Castile, interrupted at intervals by the hollow roll of the Moorish atabal—he drew his lofty person to its utmost height, his eyes blazing with chivalrous fire, awakened by the vaunting melody, and his noble features lighted up with a kindred expression, the beholder might have imagined he beheld some glorious descendant of the Cid, or inheritor of the honours of the renowned Pelayo.

Advancing towards the Queen of Navarre with a grave and profound salutation, he appeared to solicit the honour of her hand, to which courteous request Marguerite, who, for the nonce, assumed all the hauteur and august coquetry of an *infanta,* disdainfully answered by conceding him the tips of those lovely fingers which Ronsard had likened to the rosy digits of the daughter of the dawn. Here began that slow and stately procession from which the dance obtained its designation, and in which its chief grace consisted. Hand in hand they sailed down the saloon

Like two companion barks on Cydnus' wave,

a prouder couple never graced those festal halls. With a pace majestic as that of a king about to receive the crown of his ancestry, Crichton pursued his course. Murmurs of admiration marked his steps.

Nor was Marguerite de Valois without her share of admiration, though our gallantry may be called into question, if we confess that the meed of applause was chiefly bestowed on Crichton. With the fair Queen of Navarre, we have observed, this dance was an especial favourite; and justly so, for it was the one in which she most excelled. In its slow measure the spectator had full leisure to contemplate the gorgeous majesty and resplendent loveliness of her person; in its pauses, her surpassing dignity and queenly grace were brought into play; in its gayer passages —for even this grave dance had a pleasant admixture of spirit (the sunshine stolen from its clime)—her animation and fire were shown; while in its haughtier movements was manifested the fine disdain she knew so well how to express.

"By Apollo!" exclaimed Ronsard, as soon as the *vivats* which followed the conclusion of the pavane had died away, "the whole scene we have just witnessed reminds me of one of those old and golden legends wherein we read how valour is assailed by sorcery, and how the good knight is for a time spell-bound by the enthralling enchantress."

"Certes, *la bella* Alcina was but a prototype of Marguerite," said Brantôme.

"And Orlando of Crichton," added La Torigni.

"Or Rinaldo," continued La Fosseuse. "He is the very mirror of chivalry."

"He must have more skill than Ulysses to break the snares of his Circe," whispered Ronsard.

"True," replied Brantôme, in the same tone. "It was not without good reason that Don Juan of Austria said to me when he first beheld her peerless charms: 'Your queen's beauty is more divine than human, but she is the more likely to drag men to perdition than to save them!'"

Turning then to the maids of honour, the abbé added aloud: "The mistake in all matters of enchantment appears to be that your knight-errant should ever desire to burst such agreeable bondage. To me it would be like awakening from a pleasant dream. Ah! were there some good fairy left who would tempt me—you should see whether I would resist or seek to be disenchanted!"

"Well, of all agreeable dances commend me to the bransle," said La Torigni, as that figure was struck up.

"Apropos of temptation, I suppose," said Brantôme; "for *you* never look so captivating as when engaged in it, Signora Torigni. For my part I envy the Chevalier Crichton his success in the dance more than his *bonnes fortunes*. I never could accomplish a *pas*."

"A *faux pas*, I suppose you mean, abbé," whispered Ronsard.

"Indeed!" returned La Torigni. "Suppose you take a lesson now. What say you to a turn in the bransle? That is the easiest figure of all. Our royal mistress has disappeared with her all-accomplished Scot, so my attendance will be dispensed with for the present. We shall be free from interruption. Never mind your being a little lame—the bransle is the best specific in the world for the rheumatism. Come along. Monsieur de Ronsard, your gout I know will not permit you, or I would bid you give your hand to La Fosseuse; but you can at least amuse her with a *mot*, or perhaps improvise a sonnet for her entertainment upon the pretty sight we have just witnessed; and the more you stuff it with loves and doves, kisses and blisses, gods, goddesses and heroes, till like a cup of hydromel it overflow with sweetness, the better she will like it. Your hand, abbé." And, despite his remonstrances, the laughing Florentine dragged the reluctant Brantôme to the bransle.

Slowly, meanwhile, glided along Crichton and the Queen of Navarre. Neither spoke — neither regarded the other — the bosoms of both were too full; Marguerite's of intense passion— Crichton's of very different emotions. He felt the pressure of her arm—the throbbing of her bosom, but he returned not the pressure, neither did his heart respond to those ardent pulsations. A sudden sadness seemed to overspread his features; and thus in silence they wandered along, inhaling new clouds of flattering incense from each worshipping group they passed.

Their steps were followed at a wary distance by three other masks, but this circumstance escaped their notice. Marguerite thought of nothing save her lover, and Crichton's mind was otherwise occupied.

Anon they entered a small ante-chamber opening from the vestibule of the hall of entrance. This room, which was filled with the choicest exotics, and hung around with cages containing squirrels, parrots, and other gaily plumaged birds, was for the moment deserted even of the customary attendants.

Marguerite glanced cautiously around her, and seeing the room vacant, applied a small golden key, which she took from her girdle, to a concealed door, in the side wall. The valve yielded to the touch—thick tapestry then appeared, which being raised, the pair found themselves within a dimly lighted chamber, the atmosphere of which struck upon their senses, as they entered, warmly and odoriferously. A *prie-dieu*, cushioned with velvet, stood at the farther end of the apartment. Before it was placed a golden crucifix. Over the crucifix hung a Madonna by Raphael; the glowing colouring of which admirable picture was scarcely discernible by the faint light of the two perfume-distilling lamps suspended on either side. This room was the oratory of the Queen of Navarre.

Scarcely had the lovers gained this retreat when the valve was opened noiselessly behind them—again as cautiously closed— and three persons who had thus stealthily obtained admission to the chamber, posted themselves in silence behind the tapestry, the folds of which being slightly drawn aside, enabled them to discern whatever might be passing within the oratory.

CHAPTER VI

THE ORATORY

Marie. Tu es jeune, il y a beaucoup de belles femmes qui te regardent fort doucement, je le sais. Enfin, on se lasse d'une reine comme d'une autre.
                                      VICTOR HUGO, *Marie Tudor.*

"CRICHTON, *mon beau chevalier*," exclaimed Marguerite de Valois, raising her beautiful head, and gazing fondly and inquiringly into his face, "why are you thus silent and pre-occupied? Amid the prying assemblage we have quitted—with all eyes upon us and all ears eager to catch our lightest whisper— it were well to observe such caution; but here this reserve is needless. Is it that your quarrel with the queen, my mother, gives you uneasiness? I cautioned you not to arouse her anger, but you were wilful, and would not listen to my entreaties. Catherine de Medicis *is* an enemy to be feared; but you need have no fear of her. Dread not her poniards—her poisons. I will watch over your safety, and arrest the secret steel, should she point it at your breast. I will prove an antidote against the infected chalice, should its venom touch your lips. Be not afraid."

"I am not afraid, Marguerite. I will trust to my own arm for deliverance from your mother's assassins, while, for preservation from her poisons, I am content to rely upon forbearance from her banquets."

"That were a vain precaution. The scarf you wear, the flower you smell, the very atmosphere you breathe, may become the agent of death. Even *I* might be the instrument of her vengeance."

"You, Marguerite!"

"Unconsciously, but you should not fall alone. I will save you, or share your fate."

"How can I repay this devotion?" replied Crichton, in a tone as if he struggled with some deep and suppressed emotion; "I am unworthy of this solicitude. Believe me, I have no fears for my own safety—no dread of poisons, be they subtle as those of Parysatis, or Locusta. I possess an assured safeguard against their baneful effects."

"So thought Bernardo Girolamo, yet he perished by the drugs of Cosmo de Medicis. His was a light offence compared with yours. But a remedy *does* exist—a counter-poison. Henri and I, alone, possess it. I have sworn to use it only for the preservation of my own existence. You are my existence. You shall have the phial."

"You shall not break your vow, my gracious queen. Nay, I am resolute in this. For me, I repeat, your mother's wrath has no terrors. If it be the will of Heaven that I must fall by the assassin's dagger, or by more secret means, I shall not shrink from my fate, but meet it as beseems a brave man. But my destiny, I feel, is not yet fulfilled. Much remains to be accomplished. My aspirations, my energies, all tend towards one great end. Fate may crown me with success, or crush me at the outset of my career. I can have no foreknowledge, though your mother's starry lore would tell you otherwise—nor, it may be, free-agency. No matter! My aim is fixed—and thus much of the future, methinks, I can read—I shall not perish by the hand of Catherine de Medicis."

"Is not your destiny accomplished, Crichton? Are not your brows bound with laurels? Have you not this day achieved more than man ever achieved before you? Are you not girt with honourable knighthood? What more remains to be performed?"

"Much—much——"

"Have you not my love—my devotion—a *queen's* idolatry, Crichton? You are insatiate in your ambition, seigneur."

"I *am* insatiate, or how should my desires extend beyond this moment?"

"Crichton, you no longer love me. Beware—beware; I love you fervently, but I can hate in the same degree. I am by nature jealous. The Medicis' blood within my veins fires me to love with desperation or to resent as strongly. As yet I only love. But if I discover aught to confirm my suspicions—if I find you have breathed words of passion to another, my rival dies, though her destruction cost me my kingdom—that which I hold dearer than my kingdom—yourself. I am a queen, and if I am wronged, will have a queen's revenge."

"Why this sudden frenzy, Marguerite?—whose rivalry do you apprehend?"

"I know not—I would not know. I look around in dread. At the fête I am beset with fears—here I am assailed with new agonies. My life is one long pang of jealousy. Have I a rival, Crichton?—Answer me.—Oh! if I have one, let her avoid my presence."

"Calm yourself, Marguerite.—Banish these idle fancies——"

"*Are* they fancies, Crichton?—*are* they idle? Methinks I feel my rival's presence within this chamber—here—here."

"Shall I chide or smile at your folly, my queen?"

"Again I ask you, are my suspicions groundless? Call to mind your attentions to the Demoiselle Esclairmonde—were they not sufficient to awaken doubts as to your sincerity to me? Oh, Crichton! I have been anxious—miserable since that night; but I am easier now."

"Right—right, sweet Marguerite—but, as you *have* alluded to her, may I, without reviving your apprehensions, inquire whether Esclairmonde is at the fête to-night?"

"She is," replied Marguerite, with a smile.

"I did not observe her," said Crichton, with affected indifference.

"Yet she was at no great distance from you."

"With the queen your mother?"

"With the king my brother."

"With him!" ejaculated Crichton

"She stood by Henri's side when he bestowed this decoration of the Saint-Esprit upon you."

"The violet mask?"

"You have guessed shrewdly."

"And she remained with the king when we quitted the grand saloon?"

Despite his efforts to control himself, Crichton was unable to conceal his emotion. With sarcastic levity Marguerite replied to his question. "Esclairmonde, I must inform you, has, upon her presentation to-night, achieved a conquest no less important than that of his majesty. He is evidently enthralled by her; and (jealousy apart) it must be owned she is sufficiently charming to warrant his sudden fascination. With Henri it was decidedly love at first sight, which, ridicule it as one may, is the only true love after all. Since she tendered her hand to the king, he has never quitted it; and to judge appearances, he has already made no inconsiderable progress in her affections."

"Ha!" ejaculated Crichton.

"She will have the post of honour at the banquet," continued Marguerite, "and will be henceforth the reigning favourite, with power absolute over all the court. To speak truth, I am not sorry for it, as it nips a rival in the bud, though the queen, my mother, who, I suspect, had other intentions with the demoiselle, may not entirely approve of the arrangement."

"Marguerite, I implore you to return to the fête."

"Crichton, you love this girl," cried Marguerite, furiously.

"I would save her from dishonour. Hear me, Marguerite!— Amid the tainted atmosphere of this court, one pure fair flower blooms and is seen for a moment—the next, a rude hand grasps it—scatters its fragrance to the wind, and levels it with the weeds that grow rife around it. Esclairmonde is that flower— save her from the spoiler's hand. Have pity on her youth— her innocence. She is unfriended—alone. Be to her a preserver, my gracious queen. You know what Henri's love is—that he spares naught to gratify his desires. Save her—save her!"

"For you—never——"

"Mistake me not—let not your jealousy confound my apprehension for her safety with other feelings, which, even if I entertained them, would weigh little with me in comparison with my anxiety for her preservation."

"I am sure you love her. Now hear *me*, Crichton. My husband, Henri of Navarre, demands my presence. This morn a messenger arrived from the camp at Pau. My reply depends on you. Will you form one of my escort? Say you will do so, and I will be myself the bearer of my answer."

"Marguerite, to what end should I go thither? I respect the bravery of Henri of Navarre.—I admire his chivalrous character, his bonhomie, his frankness; but having pledged myself to your royal brother's cause, how can I enlist under hostile banners? I cannot quit the court of France."

"Do not equivocate, messire, you cannot quit Esclairmonde —you refuse to accompany me."

"Torture me not thus, Marguerite; for pity's sake, if you will not go with me to the fête, suffer me to return alone."

"Go."

"Marguerite, farewell. I quit you but for an instant."

"For ever."

"For ever! Marguerite, did I hear aright?"

"Stay!" cried the queen, after a momentary but fearful struggle with herself, "stay, I command—entreat you—return not to the fête. Have pity on *me*, Crichton."

"This delay is cruel—even now I may be too late to warn her of her danger. Henri may triumph if I tarry longer. Marguerite, I take my leave."

"It *is* true!" exclaimed Marguerite, with a look of unutterable agony, "my frightful suspicions are confirmed. You have never, never loved me—ingrate—deceiver—never—never——"

Crichton would have spoken. Marguerite, however, impetuously interrupted him. "Do not forswear yourself. You cannot deceive me longer. Ah, Crichton! Is it possible you can have forgotten—or that you are willing to forget—my tenderness? Is it possible? but I will no longer indulge this weakness— leave me—go—go!"

Crichton appeared irresolute. Marguerite continued in the same vehement tone, "But dare not to approach your minion Esclairmonde—dare not, as you value her life, breathe aught of love or counsel within her ear, for, by my hope of Heaven, if you do so, she survives not the night. Now you are at liberty to depart—yet stay, you shall not go hence alone. After what I have said, I shall be curious to see how you will attempt to succour this distressed damsel."

"*Mort-Dieu!* Margot, you shall not go far to witness it," said Henri, thrusting aside the tapestry, and dragging Esclairmonde forward. "Your own appointment, you perceive, has not been without witnesses."

"Henri!" ejaculated Marguerite, sternly, so soon as she recovered her surprise.

"Esclairmonde!" exclaimed Crichton, recoiling in astonishment and displeasure.

A momentary pause ensued, during which each party regarded

the other in doubt and silence. The king alone appeared easy and unconcerned. He was at home in scenes like the present, and hummed laughingly a light air. Crichton at length spoke. .

"Is it customary, sire," he said, in a tone of irony, "with the King of France to play the eavesdropper? I have heard of such practices in Arabian story, but the incident is new to the annals of your realm."

"In love and war all stratagems are fair," replied Henri, gaily, "and I have the sanction of precept and custom, if I cared for either, for my conduct. All that I desired was to satisfy Esclairmonde of your perfidy. Yon arras afforded us an excellent screen—not a word of your *tête-à-tête*, or of our sister's reproaches escaped us. I thank you for your good opinion of myself; I thank you for your kind intentions in respect to Esclairmonde, and I thank you still more for proving yourself so satisfactorily the inconstant she conceived you to be. *Voilà tout, chevalier!*"

"I congratulate your majesty upon your address," returned Crichton. "Few scruples appear to stand in the way of your inclinations."

"*Pardieu! compère,*" exclaimed Chicot, who formed part of the group, and who, with difficulty, had hitherto restrained himself from interference, "our gossip, Henri, is too great a king not to be exempt from vulgar weaknesses. Delicacy has never been classed amongst his foibles."

"And you, Esclairmonde," said Crichton, somewhat reproachfully, "you have condescended to this——"

"Meanness, you would say," interrupted Marguerite, scornfully. "Give her conduct its proper term—none else will suit it. My heart told me she was beside us. The instinct of hate never deceives."

"You have, then, overheard our converse, demoiselle?" said Crichton.

"I have," replied Esclairmonde, blushing deeply.

"And you are aware of the peril in which you stand," added Crichton, looking significantly at Henri as he spoke. "One step more, and all is irretrievable."

"I know it," replied Esclairmonde, distractedly.

"Esclairmonde!" persisted Crichton, "by all that is sacred in your regards, I conjure you listen to my counsels—pause—reflect—or you are lost for ever."

"There is something of the Huguenot about you after all, Crichton," interposed Henri. "You preach in a style worthy of an Anabaptist, or Antinomian, and not like the easy galliard I have hitherto supposed you. Esclairmonde is infinitely indebted to you for your agreeable diatribe; but she has had ample time for reflection behind yon arras, and her choice is made. The demoiselle prefers a royal lover, with a heart, a court, rank, title, power, almost half a throne to offer her, to one who has none of these gifts, not even an undivided heart to bestow. Are you answered, messire?"

"Esclairmonde!" exclaimed Crichton.

"Beware, insensate madman!" cried Marguerite.

"Crichton!" exclaimed Esclairmonde, suddenly extricating herself from the king's grasp, and throwing herself into his arms. "To your protection I commit myself."

"And with my life will I defend you." returned Crichton, clasping her to his bosom.

"I tremble no longer to avow my love: I am yours for ever, I will brave all. We can at least die together!" exclaimed Esclairmonde.

"It were bliss to do so," answered Crichton.

"Confusion!" exclaimed the king, "Chicot, our guard." The jester reluctantly quitted the oratory.

"Be your wish gratified," exclaimed Marguerite, in a tone of bitter derision; "perish together, since you wish it. Henri, I crave a boon from you."

"What is it, Margot?"

"It is this," replied Marguerite, kindling into fury as she spoke: "that the work of vengeance may be entrusted to my hands; that I, who have witnessed their transports, may witness, also, their pangs. I must have blood, Henri—blood—*his* blood! Call in the guard. Leave me alone with them—I will see it done. It will gladden me to see a sword drawn."

"I doubt it not, Margot," replied Henri, who had now resumed all the indifference he had previously exhibited, "as Du Guast's epitaph can testify. I am in no mood for butchery. If I should need an executioner, I will call in your aid. But the sword is scarcely required on this occasion. A word will recall the Chevalier Crichton to his senses."

"Be it as you please," replied Marguerite fiercely. "My own particular wrong shall not pass unavenged."

"Chevalier Crichton," said Henri, advancing toward the Scot, and, fixing a steadfast glance upon him, addressing him at the same time in a tone of high and prince-like courtesy, "need I remind you of your voluntary proffer of obedience to my mandates? The time is arrived when I hold it fitting to claim fulfilment of your pledge."

"What do you demand, sire?"

"Possession of this damsel."

"Crichton!" shrieked Esclairmonde, clinging more closely to her lover, "kill me rather than yield me to him."

"I have his word," said Henri coldly.

"He has!—he has!" exclaimed Crichton, in accents of desperation. "Take back your title—take back your honours, sire, if they are to be bought by this sacrifice. Take my life—my blood —though it flow drop by drop—but do not extort fulfilment of a rash promise which, if you claim, you pronounce a sentence upon two heads far more terrible than death!"

"I am to understand, then, messire," returned Henri, scornfully regarding him, "that your word, rashly plighted, is not held binding on your supple conscience. 'Tis well. I now know how to proceed."

"Would your majesty have me break these clinging arms, and hurl her I love senseless at your feet? Call your guards, sire, and let them unloose her clasp. I will not oppose your mandate."

"'Twere better to do so," said Marguerite, "or I will stab the minion in his arms."

"Peace," cried Henri, "she relents even now."

"Crichton, your word is passed," said Esclairmonde, "you cannot protect me."

"My arm is paralysed," replied her lover, in a tone of anguish.

"When that vow was uttered," continued Esclairmonde, with dreadful calmness, "I shuddered for its consequences. Nor was I deceived. Who would place his dagger in the assassin's hand and hope for mercy? He to whom you pledged your knightly word exacts its fulfilment—and I know he is inexorable. Obedience is all that remains: and that you may, without remorse, obey him, I will voluntarily surrender myself. Think of me no more—you must not think of me, Crichton—and, by the love you have professed for me, I beseech you not to attempt my rescue."

"Did I not say she relented?" exclaimed Henri, triumphantly taking her hand. "As to you, Chevalier Crichton, I am really sorry for your disappointment; but I trust the Order you are graced with will, in some degree, content you for the loss of your mistress."

"Well has it been said—place no faith in princes!" exclaimed Crichton, tearing the jewelled badge of the Saint-Esprit from his neck, and trampling it beneath his feet, "their gifts, like that of Nessus, are bestowed only to destroy. Perish these accursed chains that fetter my soul's freedom, and with them perish all sense of obligation."

"*Grand merci!*" rejoined Henri coldly, "my favours must be of little worth if they can be thus readily set aside, but I shall take no offence at your want of temper, chevalier. A little reflection will make you calmer. You Scots are apt to be hot-headed, I have heard, and I now experience the truth of the assertion. I make all excuses for you. Your situation *is* mortifying, but give yourself no further uneasiness, I will answer for the demoiselle's safety. *Allons!* To the banquet."

So saying, he applied a silver whistle to his lips. At the call, the valve was suddenly thrown open, the tapestry drawn aside, and through the door appeared the ante-chamber full of lights, with a file of valets and halberdiers arranged on either side of the entrance. At the same moment Chicot entered the oratory. A peculiar smile played on Henri's features.

"For what do we tarry?" he asked, glancing exultingly at Crichton.

"For my guidance, I conclude," replied Chicot, stepping forward; "nothing but Folly will serve to direct your majesty's course."

"*Méchant,*" exclaimed Henri. And passing Esclairmonde's arm within his own, he quitted the apartment.

Crichton stood for some moments like one suddenly stunned, with his face buried in his hands. He was aroused by a light touch upon the shoulder.

"Marguerite," he exclaimed, returning the gaze of the Queen of Navarre, with a terrible look, "why do you remain here? Is not your vengeance complete? You have sacrificed virtue, pure affection, at the shrine of depravity—are you not content? Do you remain to taunt me, or do you pant for my blood? Take this dagger and plunge it into my heart."

"No, Crichton," returned Marguerite, "I will have nobler vengeance. I will liberate this maiden from her thraldom."

"Amazement!"

"I will free her from Henri's snares. But if I do this, you must swear by the Virgin who regards us," pointing to the Madonna, "never more to regard her as a lover."

Scarcely were the words uttered, than Chicot appeared.

"His majesty commands your instant presence at the banquet," he said, almost breathless with haste.

"Hence!" exclaimed Marguerite.

"Her majesty, the Queen-Mother——" added the jester, in an undertone.

And as he spoke Catherine de Medicis abruptly entered the oratory.

"Daughter," said Catherine, "I have sought you throughout the grand saloon. Why do I find you here, and thus attended?"

"Madam," interposed Marguerite.

"I would speak with you alone—dismiss this gentleman," continued Catherine, glancing haughtily at Crichton.

"Leave us, Chevalier Crichton," said Marguerite, and she added, in a lower tone, "remember what I have said."

Crichton had scarcely gained the ante-chamber when he perceived Chicot. A few hasty words passed between them.

"And thou apprehendest the abduction of the Gelosa?" said Crichton. "The guard report, thou sayest, that Ruggieri's tower has been invested by an armed band requiring her deliverance to them? Difficulties multiply—no matter. I will be equal to any emergency. Where is the mask?"

"As well might you pick out a domino in carnival time as discern him amidst yon crowd of revellers. No one noted his approach, nor did anyone, that I can learn, witness his departure. For my part," added Chicot, pointing downwards, "I think he disappeared as another black gentleman is said to be in the habit of taking his departure. Were I you, gossip, I would have my sword blessed by some holy priest ere I ventured to engage with him on the morrow, or carry a scapulary, an Agnus Dei, or other sacred relic beneath my pourpoint."

"Pshaw!" exclaimed Crichton. "He is a mere mortal foe. But hence, good gossip—to the banquet-hall—account for my absence in the best way thou canst to his majesty. I will be there anon."

"Make yourself easy on that score, gossip; I will divert his inquiries—but when you *do* appear at the banquet, bear in mind what I said respecting Catherine's kind intentions towards you."

"I shall not fail to do so, and in the meantime am greatly indebted to thy zeal."

And with this he quitted the ante-chamber.

Chicot looked after him an instant, and shook his head. "*Sang de cabres!*" he muttered, "it has turned out precisely as I anticipated. No good ever comes of making love to two women at the same time, especially when one of them has the fortune to be a queen. But, not content with this, this galliard, forsooth, must saddle himself with a third. I wish him well of it! But if he gets clear of all these scrapes, and escape from the poisoned bowl of Queen Catherine, he will richly deserve his title of the Admirable Crichton. *Corbleu!* I have never seen such a picture of jealous rage as our own Queen of Navarre has just exhibited since I beheld the Sieur La Mole devour the plumes of his hat for very fury, and Clermont d'Amboise break a bottle of ink upon his mistress's eyebrow with which she had indited a *billet* to a more favoured lover. After all, her jealousy is absurd. She has already had lovers enough to content an Isabel de Bavière, or a Marguerite de Bourgogne. What says our chronicle?" And Chicot hummed the following ditty:

MARGUERITE [1]

I

Marguerite, with early wiles—
    Marguerite
On light Charins and D'Antragues smiles—[2]
    Margot, Marguerite.
Older grown, she favours then,
Smooth Martigues,[3] and bluff Turenne.
    The latter but a foolish *pas*,
    Margot, Marguerite *en bas*.[4]
But no more these galliards please,
    Marguerite.
Softly sues the gallant Guise,
    Margot, Marguerite.
Guise succeeds, like God of war,
Valiant Henri of Navarre;
    Better stop, than further go,
    Margot, Marguerite *en haut*.

II

Loudly next bewails La Mole,[5]
    Marguerite,
On the block his head must roll,
    Margot, Marguerite.
Soon consoles herself again,
With Brantôme, Bussi,[6] and Mayenne,[7]
    Boon companions *gros et gras*,
    Margot, Marguerite, *en bas*.

[1] A catalogue of Marguerite's various amourettes will be found in the *Divorce Satirique*, published under the auspices of her consort, Henri IV. More than half, however, are, most probably, scandal.
[2] Marguerite was then of the tender age of eleven.
[3] Colonel-General of the French infantry. Brantôme has written his *éloge*.
[4] This refrain is attributed to the Duchesse de Guise.
[5] The Sieur La Mole, surnamed "*Le Baladin de la Cour*;" beheaded by Charles IX., it is said, from jealousy. *Mollis vita, mollior interitus.*
[6] Bussi d'Amboise.—*Formosæ Veneris, furiosi Martis alumnus.*
[7] The Duc de Mayenne, brother to the Duc de Guise.

Who shall next your shrine adore,
Marguerite?
You have but one lover more,
Margot, Marguerite!
Crichton comes—the *preux*, the wise,
You may well your conquest prize;
Beyond *him* you cannot go,
Margot, Marguerite *en haut*.

Chanting these libellous strains as he went, Chicot slowly sought the banquet hall.

Scarcely another moment elapsed when Catherine de Medicis and Marguerite issued from the oratory. The features of the latter were pale as death, and their expression was utterly unlike that which they habitually wore. Catherine was unmoved, majestical, terrible. "Must it indeed be so, mother?" asked Marguerite, in a broken voice.

"It *must*," replied Catherine, with deep emphasis. "Henri will, no doubt, as he is wont, carouse till dawn. By that time the draught will have done its duty. But if he survive, Maurevert and his band will await Crichton's coming forth from the Louvre, and will complete the work. Shrink not from thy task. Our honour is at stake."

They then separated. Catherine rejoined her attendants and took the direction of the hall of entrance. Marguerite almost mechanically returned to the grand saloon.

As Catherine pursued her course, she perceived a masked figure single itself from the crowd at her approach. Its stature was that of Crichton's challenger—the plumes were his—the sable cloak in all respects the same. Catherine paused. The figure paused likewise. "'Tis he!" thought the Queen - Mother, and she dispatched one of her pages to bid him to her presence.

"What would your highness with me?" said the mask, advancing with a profound and courtly salutation, and addressing Catherine in Italian.

"I was not deceived," thought Catherine; "it *is* the voice. I have sent for you, signore," she added, in a bland and gracious tone, and addressing the mask in the same language, "in order to express to you ere I quit the fête, the lively sense of gratitude I entertain for the important service you have rendered me. Assure yourself, your zeal shall not be overlooked. I am neither unwilling nor, Heaven be praised, I am not wholly unable to requite it."

"Were your majesty aware of the nature of the service I have rendered you, you would scarcely deem it deserving of your thanks," replied the mask.

"Do you rate your adversary thus lightly then?" asked Catherine, complaisantly.

"I hold myself assured of conquest," returned the mask.

"The *migniard* Crichton dupes himself with like belief," rejoined the Queen-Mother, "but not with like assurance of success. The God of battles, I trust, will grant you victory, and enable you to overthrow your enemy."

"Amen!" returned the mask.

"Fall back, messieurs," said Catherine to her attendants, "I have much of moment to communicate to you," she added, assuming a more confidential manner.

"Touching the Gelosa?" inquired the mask, anxiously—"speak, madam."

"Not here," replied Catherine, "*non può bene deliberar chi non è libero*—I am about to return to my palace. You must not accompany me, nor quit the revel at the same time. Too much caution cannot be observed. The palaces of princes are all eyes—all ears."

"Your glove, madam," interrupted the mask, stooping to raise the richly embroidered gauntlet, which Catherine let fall as if by accident.

"Keep it," replied the Queen-Mother, smiling, "within its folds you will find a key, the use of which I am about to explain to you. That glove, I may premise, displayed upon your cap, will obtain you admission to the Hôtel de Soissons. Exchange no words with the attendants, but pursue your way alone. Enter the gallery. Within a niche you will observe three statues. The central figure, that of my father, Lorenzo de Medicis, Duke of Urbino, revolves upon a pivot. Touch the spear within its grasp, and you will perceive a subterranean passage leading to my turret of observation. Apply the key I have given you to a door which will impede your further progress, and you will find yourself in Ruggieri's laboratory. An hour hence I shall expect you there."

"And the Gelosa?"

"She is in my charge. Crichton's idle boast I see weighs with you—but trust me neither force nor stratagem will gain him entrance to that tower. *Santa Maria!* so easy do I feel on the score that I will give him the girl if he finds means of reaching her prison."

"Yet he has adventured there already, madam," returned the mask, eagerly, "and should he take you at your word, would you part with your charge upon such easy terms?"

Catherine smiled.

"Your majesty would almost appear to favour your enemy's designs," continued the mask, jestingly.

"*Non per amor ma per vendetta,*" returned Catherine, in the same tone. "Crichton will never more venture there, signore, unless," added she, smiling, "he come thither under *your* guidance. You shall know more of his destiny an hour hence. Meanwhile, I must conclude our interview—we are observed. The banquet, too, awaits you. One caution on parting I bequeath you. His majesty holds his revels late, and it is often his custom to detain his guests. Should he issue his commands to close the doors of the oval chamber, you will find beneath the suit of hangings which represents Diana and her nymphs, a sliding door."

"I understand, your majesty."

"A rivederci, signore."

"I kiss your majesty's hand," replied the mask, with a profound obeisance. The figure then mingled with a group of revellers who approached them, and who were joyously hurrying towards the grand hall of banquet; while Catherine, ushered forth by a concourse of pages and lackeys, entered her sumptuous litter and departed from the Louvre.

CHAPTER VII

THE BEZOAR

Maffio. Oh! l'on conte des choses bien étranges de ces soupers de Borgia!
Ascanio. Ce sont des débauches effrénées, assaisonnées d'empoisonnements.
                        VICTOR HUGO, *Lucrèce Borgia.*

THE thick folds of the magnificent crimson hangings, heightened with arabesques and fleur-de-lis of gold, that served in lieu of folding doors to separate the chief banqueting-hall from the grand saloon, had meanwhile, at a signal from the major-domo, been drawn aside, and the long and glittering board, arrayed with all the costly appliances of the royal feast, was suddenly exhibited to the view of the assemblage.

The *coup d'œil* was charming. Far as the eye could reach appeared walls festooned with flowers fragrant and blooming as if the season had been latest spring. Mirrors, wreathed with Provençal roses, reflected the lustre of a thousand flambeaux and multiplied the gleaming plate and star-like crystal with which the board was loaded. But the object on which the eye

chiefly rested—not merely because it was the principal feature
of attraction to the expectant guests, but by reason of its proud
pre-eminence—was the table itself. It was a fitting place for
the celebration of the combined rites of Ceres and Bacchus.
Reared upon a massive platform—six feet at least above the
floor—approached by a triple flight of steps—covered, both as
to its mimic stairs and summit, with cloths of dazzling whiteness
(*fort mignonement damassé*, as we learn from a contemporary
authority)—this mighty table, extending the whole length of
the vast hall, looked like a mountain of snow, or, perhaps, to
vary the simile, like a prodigious frosted cake baked in the oven
of Gargantua by the skilful *Fouaciers de Lerné*, the culminating
point of which cake or mountain was formed by a cloudy
representation of Olympus, in which Henri and his favourites
figured as presiding divinities.

A nearer approach to the table showed that the surface of
its damask covering was, according to the fashion of the court,
ribbed in fanciful and waving plaits, so as to resemble the
current of a stream crisped by a passing breeze. This stream
bore upon its bosom a proud array of gold and silver vases,
crystal goblets, and cups, all of rarest workmanship, and many
wrought by the hand of the matchless Benvenuto Cellini during
his visit to Francis the First at Fontainebleau. In the words
of brave Ben Jonson, there were

> Dishes of agate set in gold, and studded
> With emeralds, sapphires, hyacinths, and rubies.

Nothing could exceed the magnificence of the repast.

The material of the feast was worthy of Apicius or Lucullus.
Every dainty that the most consummate epicure of the time
could require was to be met with in profusion. Fancy ran
riot amid the countless covers, and the endless varieties of
piquant viands displayed on their removal. Pyramids of confectionery—piles of choicest fruit appeared at intervals; while,
scented from afar like the aromatic groves of Lebanon, appeared
antique-shaped urns steaming with the rich produce of the
grapes of Crete, Cyprus, or Syracuse; wines being then, for the
most part, drunk hot and spiced, or, as we should say, mulled.
Here and there might be seen the ushers and chamberlains
with their fleur-de-lis-covered wands of office—butlers with
embossed flagons and salvers—troops of valets and pages—
and, distributed at certain stations of the board, servitors, each
with a napkin on his shoulder, and an enormous knife in hand,
seemingly impatient for the signal of attack.

Amid loud fanfares of trumpets, blended with the gentler notes of the hautboy and viol, Henri, accompanied by Esclairmonde, led the way to the banquet. The monarch, however, tarried not within the hall we have described. His orgies were held in a smaller and more retired *salle-à-manger,* opening from the grand festal chamber, and separated from it by an arched doorway; within which was placed a line of high gilded railing, an unequivocal evidence of exclusiveness on the part of the monarch that called forth much sarcastic remark from his subjects, and, amongst other pasquinades, gave rise to the following quatrain affixed to the offensive partition:

> Puisqu'Henri, roi des François,
> N'en aime que quatre ou trois,
> Il faut que ses trois ou quatre
> Aillent ses ennemis combattre.

To the king's private table his favourites only, and *their* favourites, were admitted. Ushers of the feast were stationed at the door with a list of the guests expected. No others were allowed to pass. Towards this room Henri now repaired, followed by a jocund troop of dames and revellers. He was in the most buoyant spirits, and descanted with the greatest animation on all that passed. A singular change seemed to have been wrought in the demeanour of Esclairmonde. She replied to Henri's lover-like assiduities with a vivacity bordering almost upon levity, which a nicer observer might have imputed to distraction and despair, but from which Henri drew a favourable augury. Her cheek was flushed, and her eye shone with unwonted lustre. Once only, as she entered the oval chamber, of which some rumours had reached even *her* ears, she started, and a slight shiver ran through her frame. But she instantly recovered herself.

The oval chamber was a retreat fitted for a voluptuary. Heavy with perfume, the atmosphere struck upon the senses of the guests as they entered, producing a soft inebriating effect. Pages, equipped in fanciful attire, sustained torches, the odorous wax of which shed a warm light upon the richly painted arras, charged with the glowing legends of antiquity, in which in the guise of nymphs and goddesses of old, were represented the chief beauties who had bloomed within the atmosphere of the Louvre. In this suite of tapestry the lovely Diane de Poitiers was represented, as the goddess her namesake, disporting after the chase: in that, Venus Anadyomene sparkled from the sea-foam in the shape and lineaments of La Belle Ferronnière—the gallant Francis, blowing his wreathed conch as an attendant

* E 804

Triton. Here the fascinating Françoise de Foix bloomed as Egeria, Francis appearing again as Numa—there the captivating Marie Touchet, whose anagram, "Je charme tout," so well described her, was given as Callirhoë; her lover, Charles IX., being drawn as the hunter Eurimedon; while in the last compartment figured our *bon* Henri, who was represented, strangely enough, as Ulysses surrendering himself to the blandishments of Circe, the features of the enchantress bearing evident resemblance to those of his first mistress, *la belle* Châteauneuf. Upon the frescoed ceiling were depicted the silver fountains and dragon-watched fruit of the Hesperides.

The supper to which Henri sat down was the triumph of his *chef*—the inimitable Berini—a cook, whose name deserves to be associated with that of Luther, Calvin, Knox and other great reformers of the sixteenth century, the spirit of which stirring age he represents as strongly as the great Ude stamped the character of our own time. The signal revolution which took place in the science of cookery at this remarkable epoch may be clearly traced to the unwearying efforts of Berini. Comprehending the growing wants of his species, with the prescience of a true philosopher, he saw that a change must be effected, and he accomplished it. He overthrew many old and tough abuses; and if he increased the demand for good cheer, he did not diminish the supply. To him, amongst a thousand other gifts, mankind is indebted for the *fricandeau*, a discovery which, his biographer judiciously remarks, required *une grande force de tête!* He projected sauces so savoury that terms of alchemy were required to express their stimulative effects upon the system. These sauces, however, we regret to say, modern science has pronounced injurious. And, finally, he trampled down popular prejudices which still remained in favour of the finger, and introduced the fork.

The only stain attached to the memory of Berini is, that he was an instrument of Catherine de Medicis—in other words, that he occasionally mingled other compounds with his sauces than were prescribed by the recipes of his art. For the sake of so great a professor of so great a science we hope this is mere scandal. No wonder, with dishes so exquisite placed before him, that a great man should occasionally die from indigestion; but surely the cook is not to be blamed for an occurrence so very natural. Rather let us look to the goblet as the origin of ill. We have mentioned that the wines were at this time generally drunk mulled and spiced—a practice which, while it presented abundant facilities for the insidious admixture of poisonous drugs, completely baffled all precautions of the drinker. Leaning, therefore, to the side of genius, we are inclined to discredit this charge against the gifted Berini, and impute the criminality of these transactions to Catherine's cup-bearer, whose name is deservedly buried in oblivion.

The repast, we have said, was Berini's triumph. In conception —in execution—it was perfect. The eye of the gourmand Marquis de Villequier glistened as he gazed upon the dainty fare. Ronsard insinuated that with such ragouts before him, it was easy to understand how Vitellius and Heliogabalus exhausted an empire; a remark which, luckily for the poet, did not reach the ears of the king. Henri, in fact, was too much engrossed by Esclairmonde to attend to the pleasantries of his guests. So soon as his majesty and the demoiselle, whom he honoured with his smiles, were served, the monarch graciously expressed his pleasure that the company, whom etiquette had hitherto kept upon their feet, should be seated.

The carouse now began in earnest. The guests were few in number, consisting merely of some half-dozen of Henri's favourites, the dames of honour of Marguerite de Valois, one or two of Catherine's prettiest attendants, the Abbé de Brantôme, and, as we have just hinted, the poet Ronsard. The latter, who was by no means indifferent to good cheer, as his gout testified, was transported into a seventh heaven of delight with a ragout of ortolans with which the considerate abbé had loaded his plate; Villequier had fallen to with equal industry and zeal. Esclairmonde was placed at his majesty's right hand. On his left, two seats remained unoccupied.

Behind the royal chair stood Chicot, and next to him another buffoon, whom we have hitherto omitted to notice: a strange malicious wight, yclept Siblot, infinitely more disliked by the courtiers than his companion in folly, Chicot, inasmuch as his jests were chiefly practical ones, and his *hits* for the most part made with his marotte. In face—in figure, and in agility, he resembled an ape. His head was clothed with sleek, sable, shining hair, like the skin upon a mole's back. His nature was so snarling and malignant that, when seized, he would snap and bite like an enraged cur, and even severest chastisement was found ineffectual to change or restrain his mischievous propensities. Siblot's costume only differed from that of his brother buffoon in its hues. Embroidered on the front and at the back with the royal blazon, the surcoat was of sable, slashed with white: his marotte was of ebony. Siblot was a favourite with Henri, who, being a genuine lover of mischief, was diverted with his monkey-tricks; and he would often laugh till the tears ran down his cheeks at the confusion created by the buffoon amongst the grave ambassadors, the scarlet-capped ecclesiastics, and stately cavaliers, who attended his audiences.

Meanwhile, the feast proceeded. Henri continued unremitting in his attentions to Esclairmonde, who, though she could not be prevailed upon by all his importunities to partake of the banquet, maintained an exterior of perfect calmness and composure. Beneath that mask of smiles was hidden acute suffering. The demoiselle was, however, an object of envy to the other dames of the party, who attributed her indifference to the monarch's gallant regard to mere coquetry.

"By my faith, monsieur le vicomte," said the gay Torigni to Joyeuse, who was placed on her right hand, "the Demoiselle Esclairmonde is a finished coquette. Her coyness is admirably assumed. Where she can have acquired such arts I cannot imagine. But some people are born with a genius for their vocation—and conquest is hers, I suppose. She would have the king believe she has a perfect horror of his freedoms. I need not tell you that I have had some experience in the art of entanglement, and I declare upon my reputation, I could not have played the part better myself."

"I am quite sure of it," replied Joyeuse, "because I think his majesty's attentions are not so perfectly to her taste as you might conceive they would be to yours. Her thoughts, I suspect, are wandering upon Crichton."

"Poh!" rejoined La Torigni, "no such thing. She is not such a simpleton. Why should her love for Crichton prevent her bestowing an occasional smile elsewhere? He is not a mirror of constancy, whatever he may be of chivalry; nor wholly insensible, as you know, to the supreme attractions of our royal mistress. The thing is quite natural."

"Your reasoning is perfectly convincing, demoiselle."

"The Chevalier Crichton is very well in his way—but a king, you know——"

"Is irresistible. You have found it so, demoiselle."

"You are impertinent, monsieur le vicomte."

"*A la bonne heure.* You have prodigiously fine eyes, demoiselle. Italy boasts the darkest eyes in the world—Florence the darkest eyes of Italy, and the lovely Torigni the darkest eyes of Florence. I pledge them in a bumper of Cyprus."

"Your France is a nation of courtiers," replied La Torigni, laughing, "and the Vicomte de Joyeuse the most finished courtier in France. I return your pledge, monseigneur. After all," continued the lively Florentine, in a tone half jest, half earnest, "I should not object to be in Esclairmonde's situation."

"Indeed!" replied Chicot, who happened to overhear this latter exclamation.

At this moment Marguerite de Valois entered the room. Some slight ceremony was observed at her appearance, but the fair queen took her place at Henri's left hand, without attracting his notice.

"Your majesty suffers from some sudden indisposition," observed Brantôme, in a tone of sympathy, remarking the haggard looks of the queen.

"No, no," returned Marguerite, "I am perfectly well, Abbé."

"Will your highness allow me to recommend this *coulis à la cardinal* to your attention," said Villequier. "Ronsard pronounces it thoroughly Catholic, and I were an heretic to doubt him. Suffer me, madam——"

Marguerite declined the tempting offer of the marquis, and suffered her eyes to stray over the company. Crichton was not amongst the number.

"Thank Heaven, he is not here!" exclaimed the queen, giving involuntary utterance to her thoughts, and sighing deeply as if some heavy oppression were removed from her bosom.

"Who is not here?" asked Henri, turning quickly round at the exclamation.

Chicot stepped suddenly forward.

"Methinks," said he, familiarly placing his hand upon the king's shoulder, "methinks, *notre oncle*, you are in need of some excitement, you lack somewhat to give a fillip to your spirits— a spice to your wine—what can we direct you to? Shall it be a song? I have a rare charivari on Madame the Duchesse d'Uzès's third espousals—a Pantagruelian legend on Pope Joan's confinement before the conclave—or a ditty on the devil's exploit, at Pope-Feagueland—at your service. Or if you like not this, shall I bid my gossip Siblot smack the rosy lips of all the coyest dames at table, beginning with the Demoiselle Torigni, and afterwards cut a lavolta on the board itself to the blithe accompaniment of ringing glass? Or if a gayer mood possess you, will it please you to command Maître Samson to bring forth that quaint drinking-cup, the merry devices and playful grotesques whereof are wont to excite so much amusement, and such mirthful exclamations from our dames of honour—and which cup, moreover, is so much to the fancy of our grave and discreet gossip, Pierre de Bourdeille?"

"Cousin of Brantôme," said Henri, smiling; "our jester libels you."

"Nay," replied Brantôme, laughing, "I care not to own that the goblet of which the knave speaks has afforded me amusement, though I must, on the score of propriety, venture to oppose its introduction upon the present occasion."

"Propriety!" echoed Chicot derisively; "propriety sounds well in the lips of the Abbé de Brantôme; ha, ha, which of the three shall it be, gossip—the song, the kiss, or the cup?"

"A song," returned Henri, "and see that thy strains lack not spice, gossip, or look for no hippocras from the hands of Samson as thy meed."

"Spice!" repeated Chicot, with a droll grimace; "my strains shall smack of pimento itself." And assuming the air of an improvisatore, the jester delivered himself as follows:

ALL-SPICE, OR A SPICE OF ALL

The people endure all,
The men-at-arms cure all,
The favourites sway all,
Their reverences flay all,
The citizens pay all,
Our good king affirms all,
The senate confirms all,
The chancellor seals all,
Queen Catherine conceals all,
Queen Louise instructs all,
Queen Margot conducts all,
The Leaguers contrive all,
The Jacobins shrive all,
The Lutherans doubt all,
The Zuinglians scout all,
The Jesuits flout all,
The Sorbonists rout all,
Brother Henri believes all,
Pierre de Gondy [1] receives all,
Ruggieri defiles all,
Mad Siblot reviles all,
The bilboquets please all,
The sarbacanes tease all,
The Duc de Guise tries all,
Rare Crichton outvies all,
Abbé Brantôme retails all,
Bussy d'Amboise assails all,
Old Ronsard recants all,
Young Jodelle enchants all,
Fat Villequier crams all,

[1] Bishop of Paris.

His Holiness damns all,
Esclairmonde bright outshines all
And wisely declines all,
La Rebours will bless all,
La Fosseuse confess all,
La Guyol will fly all,
Torigni deny all,
John Calvin misguide all,
Wise Chicot deride all,
Spanish Philip [1] may crave all,
The Béarnais [2] brave all,
THE DEVIL WILL HAVE ALL!

"Gramercy," said Henri, as Chicot came to a pause; more, it would appear, from want of breath than from lack of material for the continuance of his strains, "thou hast fairly earned thy hippocras, were it only for the justice rendered to the lovely Esclairmonde, who, as thou truly sayest, outshines all. But, by Our Lady, messeigneurs, we must not neglect the service of Bacchus for that of Apollo. Samson, thy choicest Cyprus— a health!"

Every glass was raised—every eye bent upon the king. "To her," continued Henri, draining his goblet, "who in her own person combines all the perfections of her sex—*la belle* Esclairmonde!"

"*La belle Esclairmonde!*" echoed each guest, enthusiastically clashing his glass against that of his neighbour.

Amidst the confusion incident to this ceremony, Crichton entered the room. For an instant his gaze rested upon that of the demoiselle, and, momentary as was that glance, a world of sad and passionate emotion was conveyed to the hearts of both. He then took the seat which had been reserved for him, by the side of Marguerite de Valois. Conversation in the meantime proceeded. "I would fain inquire from your majesty," said Brantôme, in a tone which showed that the Cyprus he had quaffed had not been without its effect upon his brain, "what are the precise notions which you entertain respecting beauty. For, with a due appreciation of diaphanous orbs and hyacinthine tresses, I cannot entirely," and here the abbé cast a look, inebriate as that of Septimius on Acme, upon Marguerite de Valois; "I cannot, I say, admit their supremacy over eyes black as night, and locks dark as the raven's wing. Both styles have merit, no doubt; but surely your majesty cannot be aware of the 'thirty requisites,' or you would never assign the palm of perfect beauty to a blonde."

"Thou art a heretic, cousin," replied Henri, laughing; "but

[1] Philip II.　　　　　[2] Henri of Navarre, afterwards Henri IV.

we plead ignorance as to thy 'thirty requisites.' Let us hear them, we shall then see how far our own opinions correspond with thine."

"I had them from a fair *doña* of Toledo," replied Brantôme, "a city where there are many gracious dames; and though I have never, except in one instance," he added, again glancing at Marguerite, "met with a combination of such excellencies, yet I may fairly enough assert that I have encountered them all in detail."

"The requisites, cousin!" said Henri impatiently.

"Your majesty will excuse my rhymes," replied the abbé, with becoming modesty, "I am no poet, like Ronsard. Thus they run:

THE THIRTY REQUISITES [1]

Thirty points of perfection each judge understands,
The Standard of feminine beauty demands.
Three white:—and, without further prelude, we know
That the skin, hands and teeth should be pearly as snow.
Three black:—and our standard departure forbids
From dark eyes, darksome tresses and darkly fringed lids.
Three red:—and the lover of comeliness seeks
For the hue of the rose in the lips, nails and cheeks.
Three long:—and of this you, no doubt, are aware?
Long the body should be, long the hands, long the hair.
Three short:—and herein nicest beauty appears—
Feet short as a fairy's, short teeth and short ears.
Three large:—and remember this rule as to size,
Embraces the shoulders, the forehead, the eyes.
Three narrow:—a maxim to every man's taste—
Circumference small in mouth, ankle and waist.
Three round:—and in this I see infinite charms—
Rounded fullness apparent in leg, hip and arms.
Three fine:—and can aught the enchantment eclipse,
Of fine tapering fingers, fine hair, and fine lips?
Three small:—and my thirty essentials are told—
Small head, nose and bosom, compact in its mould.
Now the dame who comprises attractions like these,
Will require not the cestus of Venus to please,
While he who has met with an union so rare,
Has had better luck than has fall'n to my share."

Brantôme's song was exceedingly well received, inasmuch as it enabled the gallants to offer various compliments, direct and indirect, to the fascinations of their fair companions. Neither

---

[1] These verses are imitated from a *trentaine* of *beaux Sis*, recorded in the *Dames Galantes*. Brantôme gives them in Spanish prose from the lips of a fair Toledan, mentioned in the text; they are, however, to be met with in an old French work anterior to our chronicler, entitled *De la Louange et Beauté des Dames*. The same maxims have been turned into Latin hexameters by François Corniger (an ominous name for a writer on such a subject), and into Italian verse by Vincentio Calmeta.

did Henri fail to take advantage of the plea it afforded him, of scrutinising the charms of Esclairmonde, as the particular features of beauty passed in review before the abbé.

Crichton looked sternly on. His blood boiled within his veins, and his indignation might have carried him to some extremities, if Esclairmonde's imploring looks had not restrained him.

Amidst the laughter and acclamations of the guests Marguerite's voice sounded hollowly in his ear, "I have watched your glances, Crichton. In your kindling eyes I read your thoughts. Your minion is wholly in Henri's power. You *cannot* deliver her."

Crichton's reply was interrupted by a wild scream of laughter proceeding from the buffoon Siblot, who, regardless of the confusion he created, or the risk which the costly vessels on the board might incur from his antics, suddenly whirled himself into the very centre of the table, taking up a position on the cover of a vase supported on three feet, upon the knob of which he described various rapid circles with the dexterity and ease of the most perfect posture-master. No sooner was this feat accomplished amidst the laughter and astonishment of the guests, than bounding—without injury to the economy of the banquet—over enamelled dish and plate, with a velocity which left little time for consideration, he brushed with his shaggy beard the fair cheeks of every dame he passed, not excepting even Marguerite de Valois, and only paused when he arrived at last before Esclairmonde. He then chuckled and nodded at Henri, as if consulting his inclinations, as to whether the demoiselle should be submitted to the same disgusting ordeal as the others, but receiving no signs of encouragement from the monarch, he retreated to his vase, where, like a priestess of Apollo upon her tripod, after a brief prelude of gyrations, with a rapidity of utterance almost as bewildering as his antic mazes, and an infinitude of grotesque gesticulations, he burst into the following amphigouri:

THE TEMPTATION OF ST. ANTHONY [1]

I

Saint Anthony weary
Of hermit cell dreary,
Of penance, and praying,
Of orison saying,

[1] See Callot's magnificent piece of *diablerie* upon this subject, and the less extravagant, but not less admirable, picture of Teniers; and what will well bear comparison with either, Retzch's illustration of the Walpurgis Night Revels of Goethe.

Of mortification,
And fleshly vexation,
By good sprites forsaken,
By sin overtaken,
On flinty couch lying,
For death, like Job, crying,
Was suddenly shrouded
By thick mists, that clouded
All objects with vapour,
And through them, like taper,
A single star shimmered,
And with blue flame glimmered.

II

What spell then was muttered
May never be uttered;
Saint Anthony prayed not—
Saint Anthony stayed not—
But down—down descending
Through caverns unending,
Whose labyrinths travel
May never unravel,
By thundering torrent,
By toppling crag horrent,
All perils unheeding,
As levin swift speeding,
Habakkuk out-vying
On seraph-wing flying,
Was borne on fiend's pinion
To Hell's dark dominion.

III

Oh! rare is the revelry
Of Tartarus' devilry!
Above him—around him—
On all sides surround him—
With wildest grimaces
Fantastical faces!
Here huge bats are twittering,
Strange winged mice flittering,
Great horned owls hooting,
Pale hissing stars shooting,
Red fire-drakes careering
With harpies are fleering.
Shapes whizzing and whirling,
Weird Sabbath-dance twirling,
Round bearded goat scowling,
Their wild refrain howling—
"Alegremonos alegremos
Que gente nueva tenemos." [1]

---

[1] According to Delancre, the usual *refrain* of the Sorcerers' Sabbath-song. See his "Description of the Inconstancy of Evil Angels and Demons." "Delancre's Description of the Witches' Sabbath," observes the amusing author of *Monsieur Oufle*, "is so very ample and particular, that I don't believe I should be better informed concerning it if I had been there myself."

IV

Here Lemures, Lares,
Trolls, foliots, fairies,
Nymph, gnome, salamander,
In frolic groups wander.
Fearful shapes there are rising,
Of aspect surprising,
Phantasmata Stygia,
Spectra, Prodigia!
Of aspect horrific,
Of gesture terrific.
Where cauldrons are seething,
Lithe serpents are wreathing,
And wizards are gloating
On pois'nous scum floating,
While skull and bone placed out
In circle are traced out.
Here witches air-gliding
On broomsticks are riding.
A hag a fawn chases,
A nun Pan embraces.
Here mimic fights waging,
Hell's warriors are raging;
Each legion commanding
A chief is seen standing.
Beelzebub gleaming,
Like Gentile god seeming—
Proud Belial advancing,
With awful ire glancing;
Asmodeus the cunning,
Abaddon, light shunning,
Dark Moloch deceiving,
His subtle webs weaving;
Meressin air-dwelling,
Red Mammon gold-telling.

V

The Fiend, then dissembling,
Addressed the saint trembling:
"These are thine if down bowing,
Unto me thy soul vowing,
Thy worship thou'lt offer."

"Back, Tempter, thy proffer
With scorn is rejected."

"Unto me thou'rt subjected,
For thy doubts, by the Eternal!"
Laughed the Spirit Infernal.

At his word then compelling,
Forth rushed from her dwelling
A shape so inviting,
Enticing, delighting,
With lips of such witchery,
Tongue of such treachery
(That sin-luring smile is
The torment of Lilis),

Like Eve in her Eden,
Our father misleading,
With locks so wide-flowing,
Limbs so bright-glowing,
That Hell hath bewrayed him,
If Heaven do not aid him.

"Her charms are surrendered
If worship is rendered."

"Sathan, get thee behind me!
My sins no more blind me—
By Jesu's temptation!
By lost man's salvation!
Be this vision banished!"

And straight Hell evanished.

And suiting the action to the phrase, at the conclusion of his song, Siblot threw himself head over heels from the table, and vanished likewise. Acclamations were heard on all sides. Whatever the festive assemblage might think of the jester's song, they were infinitely amused by his summersault. By this time, too, the generous wines, with which each goblet was constantly replenished, had begun to do their duty. Every eye grew bright —every tongue loud, and a greater degree of licence reigned throughout. Crichton alone partook not of the festivities.

"*Par la Mort-Dieu, mon brave Ecossois,*" said Henri, with a smile of exultation, "you are not in your usual spirits to-night. You have not a smile for a fair dame—you do but indifferent justice to Berini's supper (and Villequier, or your brother bard, Ronsard, will tell you it has merit)—and you wholly neglect Samson's goblets, though this Syracuse hath potency enough to turn the blood to flame. Try it, I pray of you. Your thoughtful visage assorts ill with our sprightly associates. Let your spirits sparkle like our wine, like the eyes around us, and drown your despondency in the flowing bowl."

"An excellent proposal, sire," said D'Epernon; "Crichton is either in love or jealous—perhaps both—he eats not, talks not, drinks not—signs infallible."

"Pshaw," replied Joyeuse, "he has lost a favourite hawk, or a horse, or a thousand pistoles at play, or——"

"He thinks of his duel with the mask," added Saint-Luc; "he has confessed and received the Holy Communion, and the priest has enjoined a night of fasting and repentance."

"He has lost a supper, then, which, like Brantôme's beauty, has every requisite," said Villequier, with his mouth full of marchpane. "I pity him."

"Or his appetite," said Ronsard, "without which even a supper at the Louvre would be thrown away."

"Or a rhyme," said Torigni; "a loss to make a bard look sad, eh, Monsieur Ronsard?"

"Or a sarbacane," said Chicot.

"Or a bilboquet," said Siblot.

"Or a toy of less moment than either," hiccupped Brantôme—"a mistress."

Here a loud laugh was raised. "A truce to raillery," said Henri, laughing with the rest; "Crichton is a little out of sorts—fatigued, naturally enough, with his disputation of the morning, and his exertions in the ball-room—however, I trust he has not entirely lost his voice, but that he will favour us with one of those exquisite *chansons-à-boire*, with which of old he was wont to enliven our wassailry!"

"A song!—a song!" echoed all the symposiacs, laughing louder than ever.

"My strains will scarcely harmonise with your revel, sire," replied Crichton, gloomily; "my livelier thoughts desert me."

"No matter," replied Henri, "be they sad as those of Erebus —'twill give a sharper edge to our festivity."

In a voice then which, as he proceeded, gradually hushed all disposition to mirth, Crichton sang:

THE THREE ORGIES

I

In banquet-hall, beside the king,
Sat proud Thyestes revelling.
The festal board was covered fair,
The festal meats were rich and rare;
Thyestes ate full daintily,
Thyestes laughed full lustily;
But soon his haughty visage fell—
A dish was brought—and, woe to tell!
A gory head that charger bore!
An infant's look the features wore!
Thyestes shrieked—King Atreus smiled—
The father had devoured his child!
  Fill the goblet—fill it high—
  To Thyestes' revelry.
  Of blood-red wines the brightest choose,
  The glorious grape of Syracuse!

II

For a victory obtained
O'er the savage Getæ chained,
In his grand Cæsarean hall
Domitian holds high festival.
To a solemn feast besought

Thither are the senate brought.
As he joins the stately crowd,
Smiles each pleased patrician proud.
One by one each guest is led
Where Domitian's feast is spread;
Each, recoiling, stares aghast
At the ominous repast:
Round abacus of blackest shade
Black triclinia are laid,
Sable vases deck the board
With dark-coloured viands stored;
Shaped like tombs, on either hand,
Rows of dusky pillars stand;
O'er each pillar in a line,
Pale sepulchral lychni shine;
Cinerary urns are seen,
Carved each with a name, I ween,
By the sickly radiance shown
Every guest may read his own!
Forth then issue swarthy slaves,
Each a torch and dagger waves;
Some like Manes habited,
Figures ghastly as the dead!
Some as Lemures attired,
Larvæ some, with vengeance fired.
See, the throat of every guest
By a murderous gripe is prest!
While the wretch, with horror dumb
Thinks his latest hour is come!
Loud then laugh'd Domitian,
Thus his solemn feast began.
 Fill the goblet—fill it high—
 To Domitian's revelry.
 Let our glowing goblet be,
 Crown'd with wine of Sicily.

III

Borgia [1] holds a papal fête,
And Zizime, with heart elate,
With his chiefs barbarian
Seeks the gorgeous Vatican.
'Tis a wondrous sight to see
In Christian hall that company!
But the Othman warriors soon
Scout the precepts of Mahoun.
Wines of Sicily and Spain,
Joyously those paynims drain;
While Borgia's words their laughter stir.
"Bibimus Papaliter!"
At a signal—pages three,
With gold goblets, bend the knee:

[1] Pope Alexander VI., of the family of Lenzuoli, but who assumed previous to his pontificate the name of Borgia, a name rendered infamous, as well by his own crimes and vices, as by those of the monster offspring Cæsar and Lucrezia, whom he had by the courtesan Vanozza, was, according to Gordon, instigated to the murder of Zizime or Djem, son of Mahomet II., by a reward of 300,000 ducats, promised by Bajazet, brother to the ill-fated Othman prince.

Borgia pours the purple stream
Till beads upon its surface gleam.
"Do us reason, noble guest,"
Thus Zizime, the pontiff pressed:
"By our triple-crown there lies,
In that wine-cup Paradise!"
High Zizime the goblet raised—
Loud Zizime the Cyprus praised—
To each guest in order slow,
Next the felon pages go.
Each in turn the Cyprus quaffs,
Like Zizime, each wildly laughs,—
Laughter horrible and strange!
Quick ensues, a fearful change,
Stifled soon is every cry,
Azrael is standing by.
Glared Zizime—but spake no more:
Borgia's fatal feast was o'er!
    Fill the goblet—fill it high—
    With the wines of Italy;
    Borgia's words our laughter stir—
    Bibimus Papaliter!

"*Bibimus regaliter!*" exclaimed Henri, as Crichton's song concluded. "*Dieu merci!* we have no dread of such a consummation at our orgies. A reveller might well stand in awe of the bowl, if after his nocturnal banquet he should awaken in Elysium. You must now perforce pledge us, *mon Ecossois,* or we shall think you hold our feasts in the same horror as those of Borgia—a cup of Cyprus—you will not refuse us?"

"He will not refuse *me,*" said Marguerite de Valois. "Give me a goblet, Loisel."

A page approached with a flagon of gold. "Fill for me," said the queen. And the wine was poured out. "To our reunion," whispered she, drinking. "*La forza d' amore non risguarda al delitto.*"

"I pledge you, madam," answered Crichton, raising the goblet.

Marguerite's eyes were fixed upon him. All trace of colour had deserted her cheeks. "How is this?" exclaimed Crichton, laying down the goblet untasted. "Poison! Do Borgia's drugs find entrance here?"

"Poison!" echoed all, rising in astonishment and dismay.

"Ay—poison!" reiterated Crichton. "See the ruddy bezoar in this ring has become pale as opal. This wine is poisoned!"

"*I* have drunk of it," said Marguerite, with a withering look. "Your own faint heart misgives you."

"Some poisons have their antidotes, madam," observed Crichton, sternly. "The knife of Parysatis was anointed on one side only."

"Bring Venetian glass," cried Henri, "that will remove or

confirm your suspicions. *Sang-Dieu!* Chevalier Crichton, if this interruption be groundless, you shall bitterly repent it."

"Give me the Venice glass," said Crichton, "I will abide the issue."

A glass was brought, bell-shaped, light, clear as crystal. Crichton took it and poured within it the contents of his own goblet.

For a second no change was observed. The wine then suddenly hissed and foamed. The glass shivered into a thousand pieces.

All eyes were now turned on the Queen of Navarre. She had fainted.

"Let her be cared for," said Henri, affecting indifference; "Miron must attend her—he will understand——" and the king whispered a few words to Du Halde. "Fair dames, and you, messeigneurs," added he to the guests, who looked on aghast, "this incident must not interrupt our revel. Samson, we appoint thee our taster—wine—wine."

CHAPTER VIII

THE JESTER

Le Marchant. Vous estes, ce croy-je, le joyeulx du Roy?
Panurge. Voire.
Le Marchant. Fourchez là.
                                    RABELAIS, *Pantagruel*, liv. iv. chap. vi.

THE effect of the occurrence, just detailed, was visible in the altered complexion and demeanour of the dames, and it required all the gallantry and attention of the cavaliers, in any degree to restore their gaiety. Conversation, however, soon became more free and discursive. Each galliard boasted, in his turn, of his prowess in arms—of his dexterity in horsemanship—of his unerring aim with the pistol—of his fatal stroke with the poniard—of his ability with the rapier—in short, of his perfect acquaintance with the whole "theoric and practic" of the duello —a subject which necessarily involved the discussion of Crichton's approaching combat. The discourse began to take a very animated turn, many speculations being hazarded as to the rank and name of the challenger, a subject upon which the dames appeared singularly curious, and even Esclairmonde manifested anxiety, when, as if brought thither to gratify their wishes, the sable mask suddenly presented himself at the entrance of the banquet-chamber.

Henri instantly commanded admittance to be given to him,

and the mask was, in consequence, ushered to the seat which Marguerite de Valois had abandoned, thus bringing him into immediate contact with his adversary Crichton. Their situation appeared to be agreeable to neither party; but it was now too late to remedy the mistake, and Henri laughed it off in the best way he could.

"Nothing can be farther from my intention than to interrupt the harmony of your majesty's table," said the mask, in reply to the king's apology, "and, I trust, I shall not incur the censure of your brave gentlemen, by offering a second offence to one, whom I have already defied to the combat. I am no faith-breaker, sire. But I crave your pardon for trespassing on your patience. I came not hither to join your revels.

"'Fore Heaven, then, *mon cousin!*" replied Henri, regarding the mask with some astonishment, "if not to festivity, unto what hath your visit relation?"

The mask looked with some anxiety towards Crichton. The Scot instantly rose.

"I am in the way, sire," he said. "Your councils will be more securely carried on if I quit the banquet."

"No, by Our Lady!" cried Henri, rising, and with great courtesy motioning Crichton to resume his seat—"this shall never be. If anyone *must* suffer inconvenience, it shall be ourself. I am at your service, *mon cousin*, though I must need say you have chosen a strange season for an audience."

So saying, the monarch reluctantly led the way towards an embrasure.

"Chicot," he said, in an undertone as he passed, "do thou assume our seat for the nonce. We must not attend to the interests of others to the entire exclusion of our own—and hark ye, gossip, as you value your ears, suffer not a syllable to pass between Crichton and our *mignonne*, Esclairmonde—you understand."

With a mock dignity, infinitely diverting to the guests, Chicot instantly installed himself in Henri's vacant chair, his first proceeding being to place his marotte between the lovers, which he laughing termed "his ambassador's sword, whereby they were to understand they could only speak by proxy." His next, was to call upon Ronsard for a song. The bard would willingly have declined the jester's invitation, but the voices of the revellers were against him, and he was necessitated to promise compliance.

"Fool," muttered Crichton, sternly, who had already taken advantage of the king's absence to hazard a whisper to

Esclairmonde, "wilt thou mar this opportunity afforded us, by chance, of devising means for her escape? Why should she not fly now? I alone will withstand every attempt at pursuit."

"And who will then be the fool?" replied Chicot. "No—no, my addle pate hath hatched a scheme worth two of yours. Set yourself at ease. Borrow a sarbacane from the Vicomte de Joyeuse, and meanwhile suffer the 'law-giver of Parnassus,' as his flatterers term him, to proceed with his roundelay. See you not that it diverts the attention of the guests and leaves us at liberty.—Fool, quotha!—recant that appellation, brother."

"I cry thee mercy, gossip," rejoined Crichton, "thou art, indeed, a very miracle of wit. Joyeuse," he added, addressing the vicomte, "I prithee, lend me thy sarbacane."

"To dispatch a billet to some distant fair one in the outer banquet-hall; ah! galliard; here 'tis." And with this, Joyeuse sent his page with the long tube of chased silver resting by his side, to the Scot.

Ronsard, meanwhile, commenced his song, which, if it should not be found to equal in merit some better known lyrics of the bard, "*qui, en François, parla Grec et Latin,*" its failure must be attributed to the supper he had eaten, and the Cyprus he had swallowed (both, according to his former patron, Charles IX., unfavourable to the Muse), and, in some degree, to the quaintness of the measure he selected.

THE LEGEND OF VALDEZ

I

'Tis night!—forth Valdez, in disguise,
Hies;
And his visage, as he glides,
Hides.
Goes he to yon church to pray?
Eh!
No, that fane a secret path
Hath,
Leading to a neighbouring pile's
Aisles;
Where nuns lurk—by priests cajoled
Old.
Thither doth Don Valdez go—
Oh!
Thither vestal lips to taste
Haste.

II

'Neath yon arch, why doth he stand?
And
Haps it that he lingers now
How?

Suddenly cowl'd priests appear
            Here.
Voices chant a dirge-like dim
            Hymn:
Mutes a sable coffin drear
            Rear;
Where a monument doth lie
            High
'Scutcheons proud Death's dark parade
            Aid.
Valdez sees, with fresh alarms,
            Arms,
Which his own—(gules cross and star!)
            Are.

III

An hour—and yet he hath not gone
            On;
Neither can he strength to speak
            Eke.
Hark! he cries, in fear and doubt,
            Out,
"Whom inter ye in that tomb?
            Whom?—''
"Valdez!—He'll be, ere twelve hours,
            Ours!—
Wait we for his funeral
            All!"

IV

"Monk! thou bringst, if this be truth,
            Ruth!"
Valdez his own fate with dread
            Read.
Question none he uttered more;—
            O'er
'Twas; and he doth peacefully
            Lie
In the tomb he saw, thus crazed
            Raised

L'ENVOY

Memento mori—Life's a stale
            Tale.

During the progress of Ronsard's song, the jester had not remained idle. Amidst a thousand absurd grimaces, intended for the amusement of the company, he had contrived in various ways to make known the nature of his intentions respecting Esclairmonde's deliverance to Crichton, and the latter, struck, apparently, with the feasibility of his plan, traced a hurried line on the paper-covering of a dragée, which he took from a pile of confectionery before him, and then applying the sarbacane to his lips, winged with dexterous aim, the sugared missive into the lap of the Demoiselle Torigni. This incident, if it attracted any notice at all, passed for a mere piece of gallantry, a supposition abundantly confirmed by the conduct of the fair Florentine, whose sparkling eyes and throbbing bosom, as she perused the paper, as well as her nod of acquiescence, while she finally crushed it within her hands, sufficiently attested the nature of her feelings. Brantôme, who was her neighbour, hemmed significantly. Torigni crimsoned to the temples; but nothing more passed upon the matter.

"Bravo!" exclaimed Crichton, who, flushed with the anticipated success of his scheme, had now entirely recovered his spirits, and joined enthusiastically in the applauses bestowed upon Ronsard's performance; though it may be suspected, from the warmth of his praises, that not a word of the song had reached his ears. "Bravo!" he cried, with well-feigned rapture; "the strains we have listened to are worthy of him who has won for himself the proud title of the 'Poète François, par excellence'; of him who will enjoy a kindred immortality with the Teian and Mæonian bards; of him whom beauty has worshipped, and sages honoured; and to whom one fairer than the fairest nymph of antiquity—the loveliest pearl of Scotia's diadem—hath inscribed her priceless gift.

A Ronsard l'Apollon de la source des Muses.

Happy bard! upon whom such a queen hath smiled. Not Alain Chartier, upon whose melodious lips, when closed in sleep, Margaret of Scotland impressed a burning kiss; not Clément Marot, the aspiring lover of Diane de Poitiers, and of the royal Marguerite, was so much to be envied. Happy!—happy bard! upon whom all lovely things smile."

"Except the lovely Torigni," interrupted Chicot, "and she alone, who smiles on all, frowns upon him. For my part, I have the bad taste to prefer my own verses, or those of Mellin de Saint-Gelais, our 'French Ovid,' or the elegies of my cousin, Philippe Desportes (our 'Tibullus,' if Ronsard is to be our 'Anacreon'—bah!)—*his* sonnets are worth all the erotic poesy indited

By Ronsard on these ladies three,
Cassandra, Helen, or Marie."

"Peace!" said the Scot, "and to confound thee and all such unbelievers, I will, if my memory serves me, recite an ode recently written by the bard thou hast traduced, worthy to be classed with the most fervid strains ever poured out by him who sang of old, of love and of the vine. Attend!" And addressing the poet, whose handsome countenance glowed with satisfaction, and who acknowledged the compliment (for your bard is never insensible to flattery) by kissing his wine-cup, Crichton, with the grace and fervour of an Alcibiades, delivered himself of the following ode:

ANACREONTIC [1]

I

When Bacchus' gift assails my brain,
Care flies, and all her gloomy train;
My pulses throb, my youth returns,
With its old fire my bosom burns;
Before my kindling vision rise
A thousand glorious phantasies!
Sudden my empty coffers swell,
With riches inconsumable;
And mightier treasures 'round me spring
Than Crœsus owned, or Phrygia's king.

II

Naught seek I in that frenzied hour,
Save love's intoxicating power;
An arm to guide me in the dance,
An eye to thrill me with its glance,
A lip impassioned words to breathe,
A hand my temples to enwreathe:
Rank, honour, wealth and worldly weal,
Scornful, I crush beneath my heel.

III

Then fill the chalice till it shine
Bright as a gem incarnadine!
Fill!—till its fumes have freed me wholly
From the black phantom—Melancholy!
Better inebriate 'tis to lie,
And dying live, than living die!

"*Trinquons, mon cher,*" cried Ronsard, holding out his goblet as Crichton concluded; "my verses acquire a grace from you, such as they never possessed before."

"Forget not the rhymes of the good Pantagruel," said Chicot:

"Et veu qu'il est de cerveau phanaticque,
Ce me seroit acte de trop picqueur,
Penser mocquer ung si noble trincqueur."

At this moment the Vicomte de Joyeuse slightly coughed,

[1] Paraphrased from Ronsard's Ode—*Lorsque Bacchus entre chez moi*, etc

and directing a glance of intelligence at Crichton, volunteered and executed, with much vivacity and spirit, the following:

DIRGE OF BOURBON

I

When the good Count of Nassau
Saw Bourbon lie dead,
"By Saint Barbe and Saint Nicholas!
Forward!" he said.

II

"Mutter never prayer o'er him,
For litter ne'er halt;
But sound loud the trumpet—
Sound, sound to assault!

III

"Bring engine—bring ladder,
Yon old walls to scale;
All Rome, by Saint Peter!
For Bourbon shall wail."

And now, to follow the king and the mask.

"We would willingly serve you in this *enlèvement* of the Gelosa," said Henri, continuing a conversation with the unknown, the earlier part of which it is not necessary to repeat; "willingly —but shall I own to you a weakness!—I have apprehensions——"

"Of Crichton?" asked the mask, scarcely able to repress his scorn.

"Of my mother, *caro mio*. I hold it a rule never to interfere with *her* plans, unless they interfere with my own, and in this instance I see not how our interests can be mixed up with your wishes. Besides, to speak plainly, I have an affair on hand at this moment which may not improbably excite her displeasure; and I am unwilling to hazard aught that may occasion serious grounds of difference between us. Why not tarry till to-morrow?"

"Because—but I have already stated my reasons for this urgency—it *must* be to-night——"

"You have as little reliance on Ruggieri as I have, *mon cousin*," laughed the king.

"I am as little accustomed to baulk my inclinations as your majesty," replied the mask, impatiently—"the prey is stricken. Shall I hesitate to seize it? By Saint Paul, no. I detain you, sire. Suffer me to quit the presence. Since you decline giving me your authority, I will act upon my own responsibility."

"Stay," replied the king, vacillating between the awe in which he stood of Catherine's resentment, and his anxiety to serve the mask, "the guard stationed round the Hôtel de Soissons refused you admittance, you say. This ring will obtain it for you. Take it, and take the girl, and Ruggieri, too, if you list. So that you rid us and our good city of Paris of him and his accursed waxen images, I care not. If you encounter the Queen-Mother I leave you to make your own excuses. Take care not to compromise me in the matter. You need fear no interruption on the part of Crichton. He is safe within this chamber, and I will give instant orders that the doors of the Louvre be closed till dawn."

"In an hour that caution will be needless," exclaimed the mask, triumphantly. "Ere that space be past, my views will be accomplished."

And with a haughty salutation the unknown departed.

The king remained an instant in conference with Du Halde. Chicot, who, upon the departure of the mask, had vacated his seat, approached them. Our jester had a strong penchant for eavesdropping.

"Let the portals of the Louvre be instantly closed," said Henri; "not a guest must go forth till dawn—above all, the Chevalier Crichton."

The chief valet bowed.

"I have further commands for thee," continued the king, lowering his tone—"at my wonted signal thou wilt extinguish the lights."

A scarcely perceptible smile played upon Du Halde's courtier-like countenance.

"Ha! runs it so?" said Chicot, drawing nearer to the group. And here we leave him to return to the lovers.

"Esclairmonde," whispered the Scot, as the buffoon quitted the table, "place your trust unhesitatingly in that man. He is your safeguard. Confide in him, and fear nothing."

"I do not fear, Chevalier Crichton," replied the demoiselle, in the same low tone. "In my extremity I have one friend who will not fail me—the good Florentin Chrétien."

"You have one who will perish *for* you, or *with* you," returned Crichton. "We shall meet again?"

"Perhaps," answered Esclairmonde; "and yet I know not—the future is a gulf into which I dare not gaze. If possible I will quit this palace—this city—on the morrow. One tie alone can detain me, if I am free from this hateful bondage."

"And that is——?"

"Henri de Valois," rejoined a voice.

CHAPTER IX

THE SARBACANE

Je dis, et je le sçai que le Roy ayant pris une merveilleuse frayeur de ces choses, dès le tems de la Sarbacane, devint enfin si peureux qu'il trembloit à la vûe du moindre éclair.—*Confession de Sancy.*

THE king, whose quick ear caught the last words of their conversation, had approached the lovers unperceived. In vain did the jester attempt to warn them by slightly coughing. Henri was too rapid in his movements to allow him to proceed, and he was fearful of awakening suspicion by any overt display of his sympathy with their situation.

"Chevalier Crichton," said the monarch, angrily regarding the Scot, "I would not have to remind you a second time of your plighted word. Take heed how you rouse my choler. I have something of the Medicis in my composition, though it may not often manifest itself."

"And I," returned the Scot, fiercely——

"Le monde est un bouffon, l'homme une comédie,
L'un porte la marotte, et l'autre est la folie,"

chanted Chicot, adding in a whisper to Crichton, "Your intemperate Scotch blood will ruin all—bethink you what you do."

"You talk boldly, chevalier," said Henri, "and I trust you will demean yourself as stoutly on the morrow with your sword. Your adversary of the mask threatens to rob you of your laurels, and to put a stain upon the spotless Order, with which I have invested you."

"The modest precepts of chivalry teach us, sire," replied Crichton, "that to vaunt is not to vanquish.

Un chevalier, n'en doutez pas,
Doit férir haut, et parler bas.

I shall abide the issue—content to rely upon a sword which has never yet failed me, and a cause which I maintain to be the right."

"Enough," replied Henri, whose petulance was readily dissipated. "I have bidden Du Halde give orders for the proclamation of the jousts at noon upon the morrow, within the lesser gardens of the Louvre, and I bid ye all, fair dames and puissant knights, to grace it with your presence.

Servans d'amours, regardez doulcement
Aux eschaffaux anges de Paradis:
Lors jousterez fort et joyeusement
Et vous serez honorez et chéris."

As Henri sung this refrain of an old ballad of the tourney by

Eustache Deschamps, with much taste and some feeling, his features assumed, for a moment, the expression which might have animated them, when, flushed with the promise of a glorious manhood, his youthful valour had achieved the victory of Moncontour.

"Ah, Crichton!" he sighed, as he concluded, "the days of Tannegui, Duchâtel, and Gaston de Foix are past. With my brave father, Henri de Valois, chivalry expired!"

"Say not so, sire," replied Crichton, "while yourself can yet wield a lance, and while a Joyeuse, a D'Epernon, and a Saint-Luc, yet live to raise their banners."

"To say nothing of a Crichton," interrupted Henri, "whose name will gild our reign hereafter, when others are forgotten.— With the Béarnais in the field—the Balafré coquetting with my crown, and my brother of Anjou in open revolt against me, I have need of loyal hearts and true. Joyeuse, *mon enfant*, I heard thy voice just now—hast thou not some stirring strain of knightly days to chime with the chord which chance has struck within my breast?"

"If such be your pleasure, my gracious liege," replied Joyeuse, "you shall have the lay of the truest knight that ever served monarch of your realm—the valiant constable, Bertrand du Guesclin."

With a fire and spirit which evinced how completely the glorious prowess of the warrior, whose brave deeds he celebrated, was in unison with his own ardent aspirations after chivalrous renown, Joyeuse then sang, in a rich melodious voice, the following:

DITTY OF DU GUESCLIN [1]

I

A silver shield the squire did wield, charged with an eagle black,
With talon red, and two-fold head, who followed on the track
Of the best knight that ere in fight hurled mace, or couched the lance,
Du Guesclin named, who truncheon claimed as Constable of France.

[1] A free version of an "olde gentil" Breton lay of the age of Charles V. of France, a stanza is subjoined, that the reader may have a taste of its freshness and simplicity. The ballad, it may be observed, has remained wholly unedited, until the publication by M. Crapelet, of the golden manuscript of the *Combat des Trente*, extracted from the *Bibliothèque du Roi*.

LE DISTIC DE MONS. BERTRAN DE GLASGUIN
Lescu dargent a . I . egle de sable
A . ij . testes et . I , roge baston
Pourtoist li preux le vallant connestable
Qui de Glasguin Bertran auoist a nom
A bron fu nes le chevalier breton
Preux et hardi courageux come . I . tor
Qui tant serui de louial cuer et de bon
Lescu dazur a . iij . flours de lis dor.

II

In Brittany, where Rennes [1] doth lie, Du Guesclin first drew breath;
Born for emprize—in counsel wise, brave, loyal unto death.
With hand and sword, with heart and word, served well this baron bold
The azure scutcheon that displayed three fleurs-de-lis of gold. [2]

III

Like Guesclin bold of warriors old in prowess there was none,
'Mid peers that stood 'round Arthur good, Baldwin or brave Bouillon;
Nor, as I ween, hath knighthood seen a chief more puissantly
With staff advance the flower of France 'gainst hostile chivalry.

IV

—Guesclin is dead! and with him fled the bravest and the best,
That ever yet, by foe beset, maintained fair Gallia's crest!
His soul God shrive!—were he alive, his spear were couched again
To guard the three gold lilies from the white cross of Lorrain! [3]

"Heaven rest the soul of the valiant constable!" sighed
Henri, as Joyeuse brought his ballad to a close. "Would he were
living now!—but wherefore," he added, glancing affectionately
at the vicomte, "should I indulge the wish while thou, my
gallant D'Arques, remainest to me?—With thee by my side,"
he continued, smiling, "I need have little anticipation of the
third crown which the Duchesse de Montpensier promises me—
Poland's diadem I have already borne—that of France I now
possess—but the monk's tonsure——"

"Will become her brother, the Balafré, better than you, my
gracious liege," interrupted Joyeuse. "To Tartarus with the felon
cross of Lorrain and its supporters."

"Ah! Joyeuse—my brother," said Henri, smiling affectionately,
"thou art, indeed, as brave as Du Guesclin, as loyal as Bayard."

"Bayard!" exclaimed Crichton, "my heart leaps up at that
name, as at the clarion's call. Would that my life might be like
Bayard's, and," he added, fervently; "my life's close likewise!"

"To that prayer, I cry 'amen' with my whole soul," said
Joyeuse. "But while our hearts are warmed with the thoughts
kindled by such glorious recollections, prithee, Crichton, clothe
somewhat of their gallant deeds in thine inspiring verse. Thou

---

[1] The Château de la Motte-Broon, near Rennes.
[2] The royal arms of France.
[3] The cognisance of the house of Guise. The double Cross of Lorraine
was adopted as an ensign by the Leaguers, of whom the Duke of Guise
was the prime mover:—a circumstance which gave rise to the following
sarcastic and somewhat irreverent quatrain, quite in the spirit of the times:

"Mais, dites moi, que signifie
Que les Ligueurs ont double croix?—
C'est qu'en la Ligue on crucifie
Jésus-Christ encore une fois."

art a minstrel worthy of Bayard. Even my friend, Philippe Desportes, must yield the palm of song to thee."

"Joyeuse is in the right," said Henri. "A nobler subject for the bard could not be found, nor better bard to rehearse such subject. Three well-beneficed abbeys were the meed of as many sonnets from Desportes. I know not how I shall requite your performance, *mon cher*."

"Bestow not such unmerited praise on me, I beseech your majesty," replied Crichton, "or I shall scarce adventure my lay on a theme I cannot dwell upon without deepest emotion."

"First let us pledge the memory of the reproachless chevalier," said Henri, "and then embalm his deeds in song."

The goblets were filled—and drained. Crichton pronounced his pledge with devotion, and quaffed the sparkling contents of his wine-cup to the dregs.

In a tone, then, which showed how deeply his own sympathy was enlisted in the subject-matter of his strains—with an unstudied simplicity of manner perfectly in unison with the minstrel measure he had chosen, and with much knightly fervour—he sang the following ballad:

THE SWORD OF BAYARD

I

"A boon I crave, my Bayard brave":—'twas thus King Francis spoke;
"The field is won, the battle done,[1] yet deal one other stroke.
For by this light, to dub us knight, none worthy is as thou,
Whom nor reproach, nor fear approach, of prince or peer we trow."

II

"Sire!" said the knight, "you judge not right, who owns a kingdom fair,
'Neath his command all knights do stand—no service can he share."
"Nay! by our fay!" the king did say, "lo! at thy feet we kneel,
Let silken rules sway tiltyard schools, *our* laws are here of steel."

III

With gracious mien did Bayard then, his sword draw from his side;
"By God! Saint Michael! and Saint George! I dub thee knight!" he cried.
"Arise, good king! weal may this bring—such grace on thee confer,
As erst from blow of Charles did flow, Roland or Oliver!"

IV

With belted blade, the king arrayed—the knight the spur applied,
And then his neck with chain did deck—and accolade supplied—
"Do thy devoir at ghostly choir—maintain high courtesie,
And from the fray in war's array, God grant thou never flee!"

[1] The famous engagement with the Swiss, near Milan, in which Francis the First came off victorious. Fleuranges places the ceremony of the king's knighthood *before* the battle. The *Loyal Servant*, however, states that it occurred, as is most probable, after the conflict.

V

"Certes, good blade," [1] then Bayard said, his own sword waving high,
"Thou shalt, perdie, as relic be preserved full carefully!
Right fortunate art thou, good sword, a king so brave to knight!
And with strong love, all arms above, rest honoured in my sight.

VI

"And never more, as heretofore, by Christian chivalry,
My trenchant blade, shalt thou be rayed, or e'er endangered be!
For Paynim foes reserve thy blows—the Saracen and Moor
Thine edge shall smite in bitter fight, or merciless estour!" [2]

VII

Years, since that day, have rolled away, and Bayard hurt to death,
'Neath grey Rebecco's walls outstretch'd, exhales his latest breath.
On Heaven he cried, or e'er he died—but cross had none, I wist,
Save that good sword-hilt cruciform, which with pale lips he kissed. [3]

VIII

Knight! whom reproach could ne'er approach, no name like unto thine,
With honour bright, unsullied, white, on Fame's proud scroll shall shine!
But were it not to mortal lot denied by grace divine,
Should Bayard's life, and Bayard's death, and his good sword be mine.

"Bravo!" exclaimed Joyeuse, "may the same spirit which animated Bayard animate you on the morrow!

A bien jouster gardez votre querelle
Et vous serez honorez et chéris,

as runs the old refrain. 'Souviens toi,' as the poursuivants-at-arms are wont to cheer us at the tourney, 'de qui tu es fils, et ne forligne pas!'"

"My father's sword will, I trust, be grasped by no degenerate hand," replied Crichton, smiling, "and prove as fortunate to me as Orlando's resistless blade Durandal, or thy namesake Joyeuse, the trenchant weapon of Charlemagne. I shall neither forget of what worthy gentleman I am the son, nor," he added, glancing at Esclairmonde, "of what fair dame I am the servant."

"Will not the dame you serve," asked the vicomte, smiling,

[1] "Tu es bien heureuse d'avoir aujourdhui, à un si beau et si puissant roi, donné l'ordre de chevalerie. Certes, ma bonne épée, vous serez comme reliques gardée, et sur tout autre honoré!"—*Précis de la Chevalerie.*

[2] Estour—a grand mêlée.

[3] This sword has been lost. Charles Emanuel, Duke of Savoy, requested it of Bayard's heirs. One of them, Charles du Motet, Lord of Chichiliane, sent him, in default of it, the battle-axe of which Bayard made use. The duke told the Dauphinese gentleman, when he wrote to thank him for the present, "That in the midst of the pleasure he felt at beholding this weapon placed in the worthiest part of his gallery, he could scarce choose, but regret that it was not in such good hands as of its original owner."—CHAMPIER. See also the account of Bayard's death in the *Chronicle of the Loyal Servant.*

"in accordance with the good old practice of chivalry, too much neglected, I grieve to say, nowadays, bestow some token or favour upon you? The dame De Fluxas gave her sleeve to Bayard, when he gained the prize of the tourney at Carignan."

"I have no other token but this to bestow," said Esclairmonde, blushing, and detaching a knot of ribbons from her hair, "which I now give to the Chevalier Crichton, and pray him to wear for my sake."

Crichton took the gage, and pressing it to his lips, exclaimed with fervour:

"I will bear it upon my lance; and if my adversary boast like token of his lady's favour, I trust to lay it as an offering at your feet."

"No more," interrupted Henri, impatiently. "I, myself, will break a lance in your behoof, *belle* Esclairmonde, and here appoint you Queen of the Lists. Remember, messeigneurs, the heralds will proclaim the joust to-morrow. I, myself, will enter the barriers, which I have appointed with more than usual magnificence. Thus much I owe to the combatants. Do thou, Joyeuse, array fourteen of thy followers in white scarves, and thou, D'Epernon, the like number of thy *Quarante-Cinq*, in yellow. I will have the courses, *à la foule*, take place by torchlight, as was the custom of my chivalrous father—at which time, also, I will make trial of my Spanish jennets in the new Ballet des Chevaux, devised by my chief equerry. *Par la Mort-Dieu!* if my reign be remembered for nothing else, it shall be referred to for its ceaseless festivities."

"And now," he added, gallantly, "that we have listened to the lay of *preux chevalier*, I trust the response of gentle dame will not be denied us. The fair Torigni, I know, hath a witching skill upon the lyre, but the voice I chiefly desire to hear is that of my lovely neighbour. Nay, fair demoiselle, I am peremptory, and will take no refusal. She whose lightest tones are music, cannot be held excused on plea of want of skill. You need but to link your voice with the words of some simple legend, and I will engage that your performance shall exceed in attraction the most finished effort of the choicest Italian cantatrice, even though your opponent should be"—with a glance at Crichton— "the divine Gelosa herself, whose notes attracted all our good citizens to the Hôtel de Bourbon."

Aware that remonstrance would be unavailing, with the best grace she could assume, and in a voice, the tones of which, as Henri justly remarked, were perfectly musical, Esclairmonde, without hesitation, complied with the king's request, and with much natural and touching pathos, executed the following Spanish romance:

YUSEF AND ZORAYDA [1]

I

Through the Vega of Granada, where the silver Darro glides—
From his tower within the Alpuxar—swift—swift Prince Yusef rides.
To her who holds his heart in thrall—a captive Christian maid—
On wings of fear and doubt he flies, of sore mischance afraid.
For ah! full well doth Yusef know with what relentless ire,
His love for one of adverse faith is noted by his sire:
"Zorayda mine," he cries aloud—on—on—his courser strains—
"Zorayda mine!—thine Yusef comes!"—the Alhambra walls he gains.

II

Through the marble Court of Lions—through the stately Tocador—
To Lindaraxa's bowers he goes—the queen he stands before;
Her maidens round his mother group—but not a word she speaks.
In vain amid that lovely throng, one lovelier form he seeks;
In vain he tries 'mid orient eyes, orbs darker far to meet;
No form so light, no eyes so bright, as hers his vision greet,
"Zorayda mine—Zorayda mine! ah whither art thou fled?"
A low, low wail returns his cry—a wail as for the dead.

III

No answer made his mother, but her hand gave to her son—
To the garden of the Generalif together are they gone;
Where gushing fountains cool the air—where scents the citron pale,
Where nightingales in concert fond rehearse their love-lorn tale,
Where roses link'd with myrtles make green woof against the sky,
Half hidden by their verdant screen a sepulchre doth lie;
"Zorayda mine—Zorayda mine!—ah! wherefore art thou flown,
To gather flowers in Yemen's bowers while I am left alone!"

IV

Upon the ground kneels Yusef—his heart is like to break;
In vain the queen would comfort him—no comfort will he take.
His blinded gaze he turns upon that sculptured marble fair,
Embossed with gems, and glistening with coloured pebbles rare;
Red stones of Ind—black, vermeil, green, their mingled hues combine,
With jacinth, sapphire, amethyst, and diamond of the mine.
"Zorayda mine—Zorayda mine!"—thus ran sad Yusef's cry,
"Zorayda mine, within this tomb, ah! sweet one! dost thou lie?"

V

Upon that costly sepulchre, two radiant forms are seen,
In sparkling alabaster carved like crystal in its sheen;
The one as Yusef fashioned, a golden crescent bears,
The other, as Zorayda wrought, a silver crosslet wears.

[1] The incidents of this ballad are, with some slight variation, derived from those of the exquisite French romance, *Flore et Blancheflor*, the date of which may be referred to the thirteenth century, and which unquestionably, as its recent editor, M. Paulin, Paris, supposes, is of Spanish or Moorish origin.

And ever, as soft zephyr sighs, the pair his breath obey,
And meet within each other's arms like infants in their play.[1]
"Zorayda fair—Zorayda fair"—thus golden letters tell
"A Christian maid lies buried here—by Moslem loved too well."

VI

Three times those golden letters with grief sad Yusef reads,
To tears and frantic agony a fearful calm succeeds—
"Ah! woe is me! Zorayda mine—ah! would the self-same blow
That laid thee 'neath this mocking tomb, had laid thy lover low;
Two faithful hearts, like ours, in vain stern death may strive to sever—
A moment more, the pang is o'er, the grave unites us ever,
Zorayda mine—Zorayda mine—this dagger sets me free—
Zorayda mine—look down—look down—thus—thus I come to thee!"

VII

"Hold! Yusef, hold!" a voice exclaims, "thy loved Zorayda lives—
Thy constancy is well approved—thy sire his son forgives.
Thine ardent passion doubting long—thy truth I thus have tried,
Behold her whom thy faith hath won—receive her as thy bride!"
In Yusef's arms—to Yusef's heart, Zorayda close is press'd,
Half stifled by a flood of joy, these words escape his breast:—
"Zorayda mine—Zorayda mine!—ah! doubly dear thou art.
Uninterrupted bliss be ours, whom death has failed to part!"

The monarch's loud applauses at the close of the song were
reiterated to the echo by the assemblage. Crimsoning with shame,
Esclairmonde ventured a glance towards her lover, whose silent
admiration was of more value in her eyes than the courtly compliments which were so freely lavished upon her efforts.

"And now for the lay of the *belle* Torigni," said Henri; "her
songs are wont to be of a more sprightly description—ah!
Signorina mia! Shall we sue in vain?"

Torigni needed little pressing; but with much archness and
spirit, complied with the king's request in the following ballad:

YOLANDE [2]

I

A golden flower embroidering,
A lay of love low murmuring;
Secluded in the eastern tower
Sits fair Yolande within her bower:
    Fair—fair Yolande!

[1] This circumstance is thus depicted in the French romance:

> "En la tombe et quartre tuiaus
> Aus quartre cors bien fait et biaus.
> Es quiex li quartre vent féroient
> Chascuns, ainsi com'il ventoient.
> Quant li vens los enfans tochoit,
> L'un beisoit l'autre et accoloit;
> Si disoient, par nigromance
> De tout lor bon, de lor enfance."—*Flore et Blancheflor.*

[2] A very free adaptation of a sparkling little romance by Audefroy-le
Bastard, to be found in the *Romancero François*, entitled *Bele Yolans.*
Much liberty has been taken with the concluding stanza—indeed, the song
altogether bears but slight resemblance to its original.

Suddenly a voice austere,
With sharp reproof breaks on her ear:—
Her mother 'tis who silently
Has stolen upon her privacy—
. Ah! fair Yolande!

"Mother! why that angry look?
Mother! why that sharp rebuke?
Is it that I while away
My solitude with amorous lay?
Or, is it that my thread of gold
Idly I weave, that thus you scold
Your own Yolande—Your own Yolande?"

II

"It is not that you while away
Your solitude with amorous lay,
It is not that your thread of gold
Idly you weave that thus I scold
My fair Yolande!

Your want of caution 'tis I chide:—
The Baron fancies that you hide
Beneath the cushion on your knee,
A letter from the Count Mahi:—
Ah! fair Yolande!

Busy tongues have filled his brain
With jealousy and frantic pain;
Hither hastes he with his train!—
And *if* a letter there should be
Concealed 'neath your embroidery?
Say no more. But give it me,
My own Yolande—my own Yolande."

"By Our Lady!" exclaimed Henri, laughing, "that ditty likes me well. Samson, a cup of Syracuse—messeigneurs, I pledge our fair minstrels.—Ah!—*par la Mort-Dieu!*—I have a feeling of such unwonted exhilaration in my heart, that I must perforce give vent to it in song. My Hippocrene is this fiery wine—my inspiration the lovely Esclairmonde."

This gracious intimation on the part of his majesty was received, as might be anticipated, coming from such a quarter, with acclamations.

"Henri is certainly drunk, abbé," observed Joyeuse.

"Beyond a doubt," returned Brantôme, shaking his head, and perfectly unconscious of his own condition, "wine speedily assaults *his* brain—ha ha! But do you not perceive, my dear vicomte, that the banquet draws to a close?"

"Do you think so?" asked Torigni—"my heart flutters very unaccountably. Monsieur le vicomte, bid your page give me the least possible drop of Cyprus. I have not entirely recovered the shock Her Majesty of Navarre gave me."

"Or the effects of Crichton's billet," returned Brantôme, hemming significantly.

"His majesty's song," interposed Joyeuse.

With a taste and skill that showed how highly cultivated had been the musical talent he possessed, Henri then gave the following rondel:

ESCLAIRMONDE

I

The crown is proud
That decks our brow;
The laugh is loud—
That glads us now.
The sounds that fall
Around—above
Are laden all
With love—with love—
With love—with love.

II

Heaven cannot show,
'Mid all its sheen
Orbs of such glow
As here are seen.
And monarch ne'er
Exulting own'd,
Queen might compare
With Esclairmonde—
With Esclairmonde.

III

From Bacchus' fount,
Deep draughts we drain;
Their spirits mount,
And fire our brain;
But in our heart
Of hearts enthroned,
From all apart,
Rests Esclairmonde—
Rests Esclairmonde.

"Perfect!" exclaimed Ronsard.

"Perfect!" repeated every voice.

"His late majesty Charles IX. never improvised strains more delightful," continued the bard.

"Never," replied Chicot, "Charles's unpremeditated strains being generally understood to be *your* composition, Monsieur de Ronsard. I think nothing of them. Mediocrity is the prerogative of royalty. A good king must be a bad poet. But you have all praised his majesty's performance, now listen to the moral of the story—though morality I must own is a little out

* F 804

of fashion in the Louvre." And mimicking, so far as he dared, the looks and tones of the king, the jester commenced his parody as follows:

> The crown is proud,
>   But brings it peace?
> The laugh is loud—
>   Full soon 'twill cease.
> The sounds that fall
>   From lightest breath,
> Are laden all
>   With death—with death.
>   With death—with death.

"Enough, and too much," interrupted Henri, "we will not have our flow of spirits checked by thy raven croaking. Be prepared," he whispered, "with the signal; and now, messeigneurs," he continued aloud, "the night wears, the music sounds again, the new masque of 'Circe and her Nymphs' awaits you. Nay, *mignonne*," he added, in a low impassioned tone, and forcibly detaining Esclairmonde, "you must remain with me."

At this hint from the monarch the guests arose, and each gallant taking a dame under his arm, left the banquet-hall. Crichton and Torigni were the last to quit the room. A significant look passed between the Scot and Chicot, as he lingered for an instant at the doorway, the meaning of which the latter appeared clearly to comprehend, for waving his hand, as if in obedience to the royal command, the perfumed torches were suddenly extinguished. Page, valet, usher and buffoon disappeared; the tapestry was swiftly drawn together; the valves were closed, and Henri was left in darkness with the demoiselle.

All this was the work of a moment. The king was taken a little by surprise. Chicot had given the signal sooner than he intended.

Concluding himself alone with Esclairmonde, Henri addressed a passionate exclamation to her, at the same time endeavouring to obtain possession of her hand. The demoiselle, however, with a cry of terror, eluded his grasp, and fled, so far as she was able to determine in the obscurity in which all was wrapped, towards the door.

"Ah, ah, fair bird! you cannot escape me now," exclaimed Henri, exultingly, following in pursuit.

And as he spoke, with outstretched hands he grasped at something which, in the darkness, appeared to be the flying figure of the damsel. The sudden prostration of his royal person, and the subsequent loud jingle of falling glass, mixed with the clatter of plate, soon, however, convinced him of his error;

while a stifled laugh, proceeding, as he concluded, from the demoiselle, completed his mortification.

The king arose, but said nothing and, suspending his own respiration, listened intently. For a moment not a sound was heard. Henri then thought he detected a light step stealing towards the other side of the room, and directed his attention to that quarter. A noise, as of arras being raised, followed by a faint creak, such as might be produced by a sliding panel, was just audible. "*Diable!* the secret door—can she have discovered it?" ejaculated Henri, rushing in the direction of the sound. "She may elude me after all."

A light laugh, however, issuing from a different part of the chamber, and which, questionless, originated with his inamorata, satisfied him that she was still in the room. Gliding noiselessly forward, guided by the sound, ere another instant he had grasped a small soft hand, which he covered with a thousand kisses, and which, strange to say, palpably returned his pressure.

Henri was in positive raptures.

"How much one may be deceived!" exclaimed the enamoured monarch; "this delightful gloom makes all the difference in the world. I was quite right to have the torches extinguished. You, fair Esclairmonde, who, a few minutes ago, were all coyness and reserve—a very *belle dame sans merci*—are as amiable and complaisant as—(whom shall I say?)—as the obliging Torigni."

"Ah, sire!" murmured a low voice.

"I' faith, fair demoiselle," continued the delighted Henri, "so charming do I find you, that I am half tempted to become a heretic myself. On these lips I could embrace any faith proposed to us——"

At this moment, a hollow voice breathed in the very portals of his ear these words: "VILAIN HERODES"—an anagram framed by the Jacobins upon his own name—Henri de Valois.

The king started and trembled.

It has already been stated that Henri was bigoted and superstitious to the last degree. His hand now shook so much that he could scarcely retain the fair fingers he held within his grasp.

"Did *you* speak, demoiselle?" he asked, after an instant's pause.

"No, sire," replied his companion.

"Your voice appears strangely altered," returned Henri, "I scarcely recognise its tones as those of Esclairmonde."

"Your majesty's hearing deceives you," returned the lady.

"So much so," replied Henri, "that I could almost fancy

I had heard your voice under similar circumstances before. This shows how one may be mistaken."

"It does, indeed," replied the lady; "but perhaps your majesty found the voice to which you allude more agreeable than mine."

"By no means," replied Henri.

"You would not then change me for any other?" asked the lady timidly.

"Not for my kingdom," exclaimed Henri, "would I have any one else in your place! She of whom I spoke was very different from you, *ma mie*."

"Are you quite sure of that, sire?"

"As of my salvation," replied Henri passionately.

"Of which thou art by no means assured," breathed the deep sepulchral voice in his ears.

"There—again—did you hear nothing, demoiselle?" asked the king in new alarm.

"Nothing whatever," rejoined the lady. "What odd fancies you have, sire!"

"Odd, indeed!" answered Henri, trembling. "I begin to think I acted wrongly in loving a Huguenot.—*Par la Saint-Barthélemy!* you must reform your faith, demoiselle."

"'Tis thou, Henri de Valois, who must reform," returned the sepulchral voice, "or thy days are numbered."

"Averte faciem tuam à peccatis meis!" exclaimed the terrified king, dropping on his knees, "et omnes iniquitates meas dele!"

"What ails your majesty?" asked his companion.

"Hence—hence—fair delusion!" exclaimed Henri—"avoid thee!—*Docebo iniquos vias tuas, Domine!*"

"Trouble not the virtuous Huguenot," continued the voice.

"In peccatis concepit me mater," continued Henri.

"True," replied the voice, "or the memory of Fernelius hath been scandalously calumniated."

"Fernelius!" echoed Henri, scarcely comprehending what was said to him, and fancying in his terror that the voice had acknowledged itself to belong to the shade of his mother's departed physician. "Art thou the spirit of Fernelius arisen from purgatory to torment me?"

"Even so," was the response, which seemed mingled with diabolical laughter.

"I will have nightly masses said for the repose of thy soul, unhappy Fernelius," continued the king, "so thou wilt no more perplex me. *In Paradisum deducant te Angeli! Suscipiant Martyres!*"

"Thou must do more," returned the voice.

"I will do anything—everything you enjoin, gracious Fernelius," said the king.

"Cherish thy jester Chicot," continued the voice.

"As my brother," answered the king.

"Not as thy brother—but as thyself," returned the shade of Fernelius.

"I will—I will," replied Henri. "What more?"

"Abandon this vain quest of the virtuous Esclairmonde, and return to her whom thou hast abandoned."

"Whom mean you?" asked the king, somewhat perplexed—"to whom have your words especial reference, most excellent Fernelius—to my Queen Louise?"

"To the Demoiselle Torigni," rejoined the voice.

"Torigni!" echoed Henri, despairingly—"any of my former lovers were preferable to *her*. Is there no other alternative?"

"None whatever," sternly answered the spectre.

"Sooner then," replied Henri, "will I incur—ha!—*diable!*—a ghost indulge in merriment—this is some trick," he exclaimed, suddenly recovering his confidence, and starting to his feet, while, with his right hand, he grasped at some object near him. "We have traitors here," he continued, as steps were heard retreating. "This is no ghost—no Fernelius——"

"What in the name of wonder has your majesty been talking about all this time?" asked the lady with affected astonishment.

"You shall hear anon. 'Fore Heaven, demoiselle, you will have reason to repent this conduct—and your accomplice likewise will rue his rashness. We can readily divine who is the author of this mistaken pleasantry. What ho! lights! lights!" And applying a whistle to his lips, the doors were instantly thrown open, and the attendants rushed in with flambeaux.

The torchlight fell upon the monarch and his companion. Abashed probably at the presence of so many spectators, the lady covered her face with her hands.

"Look up, demoiselle!" ejaculated Henri, angrily. "Nay, I will not spare your blushes, depend upon it. Our whole court shall learn the trick you would have put upon your sovereign: our whole court shall witness your exposure. Look up, I say—if your effrontery could carry you thus far, it may bear you still farther. A few moments back the laugh was on *your* side, it is now on *ours*—ah!—ah!—*Par Dieu!*—I would not spare you this infliction for our best barony. Look up—look up, Demoiselle Esclairmonde——"

And forcibly withdrawing the hands of the lady, her features were revealed to the general gaze.

They were those of Torigni!

Despite the presence in which they stood, the courtiers found it impossible to repress a titter. *"Diantre!"* exclaimed Henri, pettishly.—"Duped!—deceived!—what—what has become of Esclairmonde?"

At this moment the crowd respectfully drew aside, and the Queen Louise stepped forward.

"The Demoiselle Esclairmonde has placed herself under my protection," she said, approaching his majesty.

"Under your protection, Louise!" said the monarch, in amazement. "Do you afford sanctuary to a Huguenot? By the four Evangelists! madam, we esteemed you too good a Catholic to hazard even the chance contamination of a heretic's presence."

"I trust I may sympathise with the distress of those whose opinions differ from my own without offence to Him who is in Himself all charity," replied Louise mildly; "and in this case, where innocence and purity have sought refuge with me, I could lay little claim to the first of Christian virtues—Mercy—had I refused it. I have passed my word for her safety."

"You have done wisely—very wisely—I must say, madam," exclaimed Henri, contemptuously, "and, no doubt, your father confessor will concur with your sentiments. We shall see. I shall not argue the point now. There is one person, however, with whom we can deal. Where is the demoiselle's loyal servant? Where is Crichton? *He* has not taken shelter under your wing likewise. Your word, we conclude, is not passed for *him*."

"The Chevalier Crichton has quitted the Louvre, Henri," replied Louise.

"Impossible!" exclaimed the king; "the gates are closed by an express order."

"He is gone, nevertheless," rejoined Torigni.

"Gone!" echoed Henri. "By your contrivance, madam," he added, looking angrily at the queen.

"No, Henri," replied Louise, gently; "neither had he a hand in Esclairmonde's liberation. The demoiselle sought me alone."

"How, then, did he contrive his flight?" demanded the king, turning to Torigni.

The demoiselle glanced towards the secret panel and nodded. Henri understood her.

"Enough," he said; "I see it all, but where is your accomplice —the spectre?"

"Here—sire—here," cried Siblot, dragging forth Chicot, whose feet he had detected peeping from under the table, "here is——"

"The Doctor Fernelius," replied Chicot, with a look of droll contrition; "pardon—pardon, sire."

"Thou Fernelius!" exclaimed Henri, who, notwithstanding his displeasure, could scarcely forbear laughing at Chicot's grimaces. "How didst thou produce those awful sounds, thou treacherous knave?"

"By this tube," replied Chicot, holding up the sarbacane of the Vicomte de Joyeuse. "You must own I played my part with *spirit.*"

"A sarbacane!" exclaimed Henri—"henceforth I banish all tubes of this description from the Louvre, and thou mayst thank our clemency, deceitful varlet, that I do not banish thee with them."

"Surely your majesty would not pass a sentence of self-exile," returned the jester. "Sire, you promised the worthy Fernelius to cherish me as yourself."

"*Coquin,*" cried Henri, "I am half disposed to send thee to keep Fernelius company. But enough of this, Joyeuse," he added, "go with thy followers to the Hôtel de Soissons, and if thou encounterest this wayward Crichton or the mask within its walls place both under arrest till to-morrow. Lose not a moment on the way. Madam, I attend you."

CHAPTER X

THE HÔTEL DE SOISSONS

Voilà donc son exécrable palais! palais de la luxure, palais de la trahison, palais de tous les crimes!—VICTOR HUGO.

QUITTING the Louvre, its festivities and its enraged and discontented monarch, and descending into the gardens of the palace, we shall now pursue the footsteps of a masked cavalier, who, wrapped in the folds of a sable domino, took his hasty way through its embowered walks and trim arcades.

The whole of the space, at this time crowded by the courts and other buildings forming the offices of the Louvre, was, at the period of our narrative, disposed in noble alleys bordered with exquisite shrubs—shadowed by tall trees—with here and there terraces and patches of the smoothest verdure—balustred with marble steps and low pillars—and watered by gushing fountains of the clearest crystal; anon diverging into labyrinths and bowers, in which gleamed Faunus or Diana, or haply some "nymph to the bath addressed," and displaying throughout the luxury and magnificence of the monarch (Francis I.), by whom the plaisance had been laid out.

The moon shone clear and cold in the highest heavens as the cavalier hurried swiftly through this region of beauty. For one instant he paused to gaze at the wing of the Louvre fronting the spot on which he stood. The casements were brightly illuminated with the torches of the fête—the music resounded blithely from afar—but the masker's eye rested not upon the festive lights, nor did he listen to the gay symphonies. His eye was fixed upon a lamp shining like a star from one of the higher towers of the period of Philip Augustus that flanked the palace, and his ear was strained to catch the faint sound produced by the closing of a lattice. He then plunged into a dark avenue formed by two rows of clipped yews before him.

The gardens of the Louvre were bordered on the one hand by the waters of the Seine, across which river-chains were drawn so as to cut off all approach in this quarter, while on the other, they were defended by a turreted wall and external moat, which separated it from the encroaching buildings of the Rue de Coq. Emerging suddenly from the alley in which he had disappeared, the cavalier stood beneath the shade of a spreading elm, whose branches overtopped the wall upon which he gazed.

The figure of a sentinel, with harquebus in hand, was seen slowly parading the rampart-walk, his steel cap and habergeon gleaming in the pale moonlight. To divest himself of his domino, underneath which appeared a rich satin ball-room costume— to swathe the folds of the cloak around his left arm, and with his right hand pluck his poniard from its sheath, and strike it deeply into the bark of the tree, by which means he rapidly climbed it—to pass along its branches—to drop within a few paces of the astonished sentinel—and swift as thought to place the weapon at his throat, was with the cavalier little more than the work of a moment.

So unexpected had been the assault, that the sentinel scarcely attempted any resistance, and was so closely gripped as to be unable to raise a cry; his harquebus was wrested from his hold, and hurled into the foss; while his antagonist, having apparently accomplished his purpose in disarming him, bounded over the parapet of the wall and, clinging to the rough side of a buttress, descended with the utmost velocity and certainty to the very edge of the water, where, taking advantage of a projecting stone, he contrived to bring both feet together, and with a single spring, cleared the wide deep moat, and alighted in safety on the other side—disappearing instantly afterwards in the far-cast shadows of the gloomy Rue du Coq—and accomplishing what appeared in the eyes of the sentinel, who had watched his efforts from above, a marvellous and almost superhuman feat.

"*Mille tonnerres!*" exclaimed the sentinel, who had made sure that the cavalier would have fallen midway into the moat, rubbing his eyes in astonishment as he beheld him arrive on the opposite bank, "it must be the fiend in person!" whereupon he devoutly crossed himself, adding, "No man of mortal mould, save one, perchance, could have taken that leap, and he who might have done it, the Scottish galliard Crichton, people say, *is* something more than mortal. I recollect seeing him leap five-and-twenty feet in the hall-of-arms, but that was nothing to this moat, which, if it be an inch, must span nine yards, with scarcely a resting-place for the point of a toe to spring from—to say nothing of a run. *Tu-Dieu!*—if it *be* the Chevalier Crichton, and *he* be not the devil, he has had a narrow escape of it to-night, in more ways than one; for had he passed through any gate of the Louvre, instead of down that break-neck wall, he had encountered the dagger of Maurevert, or some of Madame Catherine's mouchards. *Notre-Dame!* if it be Crichton, I am not sorry he has escaped, as we shall have the combat to-morrow in that case. But *peste!* why did he throw away my harquebus?"

With his vain lamentation, and his vain search for his gun, we shall leave the sentinel, and once more track the steps of the cavalier, who had no sooner gained the shelter of the houses, than he resumed his domino. Swiftly shaping his course through the deserted streets, he glided along like a phantom, without encountering so much as a stray sergeant of the *guet royal,* some of whom were, for the most part, to be met with at all hours in this frequented quarter, when, at the very moment he passed it, the door of a small tavern, the "Falcon," situate where the Rue Pélican turns from the Rue Saint-Honoré, was suddenly thrown open, and forth issued two roystering blades, members of the university it would seem from their scholastic caps and gards, who had evidently been indulging in copious libations, and were now, in all probability, retreating to their place of rest for the night.

In figure, the one was tall, light, and not without a certain air of dignity in his deportment. Despite its uncertainty, his step was light and agile as that of a mountaineer, and about his shoulders light, long, yellow hair depended in great profusion. The second scholar was more squarely and stoutly built, and moved forward as if urged into his present quick movement by the energy of his companion. A small square cap surmounted a head of rough brown curling hair, shading an open manly countenance, lighted up by a keen grey eye, sparkling at this moment with unwonted fire. His whole appearance, while it betokened the possession of great personal strength, showed also that his vigour was united with a sluggish temperament. With a step almost as heavy as that of his master, a huge dog plodded at his heels, bearing undoubted marks of his English origin. And if any doubts could be entertained as to what country either dog or master might belong, the student settled that question by roaring at the top of a strenuous voice the following chant, in a tongue which requires no translation on our part to place it before the reader:

ALE AND SACK

I

Your Gaul may tipple his thin, thin wine,
And prate of its hue, and its fragrance fine,
Shall never a drop pass throat of mine
                Again—again!

His claret is meagre (but let that pass),
I can't say much for his hippocrass,
And never more will I fill my glass
                With cold champagne.

II

But froth me a flagon of English ale,
Stout, and old, and as amber pale,
Which heart and head will alike assail—
                Ale—ale be mine!

Or brew me a pottle of sturdy sack,
Sherris and spice, with a toast to its back,
And need shall be none to bid me attack
                That drink divine!

The reader will have been at no loss to discover in these students his somewhat neglected friends Ogilvy and Blount. To the cavalier also they would appear to be equally well known, for he instantly joined them, addressing the former by his name.

Ogilvy at once came to a halt, uttering an exclamation of

delight and astonishment. "You are fortunately encountered, Jasper," said the cavalier; "you can serve me."

"Show me but how!" exclaimed Ogilvy—"my arm shall second your wishes."

"If your head have discretion enough to guide it, I am assured it will," returned the cavalier; "but the enterprise on which I am bent requires coolness as well as courage, and you were better able to assist me had your libations been poured from the fountain rather than from the wine-flask."

"Our libations have been poured forth in honour of the victor of the University of Paris—of the admirable Crichton," returned Ogilvy, somewhat reproachfully, "and if blame is to be attached to our carouse, he who is the cause of it must be content to bear the burden. My pulse beats quick, 'tis true, but my brain is calm enough—and if need be, I will plunge into the first well we encounter on our road."

"And I," said Blount, "have little to observe, noble sir, except that I will follow you wherever you list to lead me. The wines I have swallowed—as sour as Flemish beer, with (Heaven save the mark!) your honoured name upon my lips—and the stupefying *herbe à la reine*, as these Frenchmen call their tobacco leaves, which I have puffed away, may have muddled my intellects, but they have not extinguished my courage. I can, if need be, put some guard upon my tongue, having no great fancy for talking at any time. And I can still (I would fain hope) wield staff or sword, as occasion may require, to some purpose. But if I should fail in my devoir, there is a follower at my heels, whose brain is at all seasons as bright as my own; who is no toper, and who will serve you loyally tooth and nail. What ho, Druid!"

A deep-toned growl from the dog answered his master's call.

"Brave dog," said the cavalier, patting the animal's leathern side, "would thou couldst go with me!"

"By Saint Dunstan! he *shall* go with you if you desire it, worthy sir," rejoined Blount.

"Will he leave, then, his master," asked the cavalier incredulously.

"He will do aught I bid him," answered Blount. "Here, sirrah," and stooping for an instant, he muttered somewhat in Druid's ear, accompanying his intimation with an emphatic gesture, perfectly intelligible, it would seem, to the dog, who instantly quitted his side, and attached himself to that of the cavalier. "He will not quit you now till I recall him," said

Blount. "Druid knows his duty as well as the most trusty retainer."

"His sagacity is indeed wonderful," said the cavalier, "and I thank you for your confidence in trusting me with so valued a friend. But I pray you to recall your boon. The risk I run is imminent."

"I have given you my dog as a gage, noble sir," returned Blount, firmly, "and I may as well throw my own life into the bargain, seeing I would almost as soon part with one as the other. I give you both, therefore, freely. Be the result of this adventure—whither tending, to what concerning I know not—what it may, it matters not; my prayers are soon said; my tenure to this world is but slight, and I have never yet heard of the danger I would not confront. In which respect I am somewhat of honest Druid's opinion, who holds all antagonists unworthy of his teeth who will not rouse his ire; and who will not turn his back on any beast that ever walked. Lead on, sir, I have that within me that prompts me to be doing."

"And you, Jasper Ogilvy——?"

A tight grasp of the cavalier's hand was all Ogilvy's answer.

"Enough!" said the leader, hastening forward.

And as they proceeded with the same rapid pace as heretofore, the mask briefly developed his project. "And so the Geloso, whom that assassin Spaniard stabbed, turns out to be a girl after all," said Ogilvy.—"By Saint Andrew, the interest I felt in her behalf is not so unaccountable as I conceived it to be. Right gladly will I lend a hand to her deliverance from this cursed astrologer's roost, and from her persecutor. I marvelled as much to see you in that mask and guise, but now 'tis all explained. You are in the right to undertake her rescue; and were none other to be found, I would alone attempt it. A maiden—by my troth 'tis passing strange."

"Not so strange, friend Jasper," remarked the Englishman, laughing, "as the change which this metamorphosis, in point of sex, appears to have wrought in thy sentiments. This morning thou hadst a holy horror, worthy of John Knox himself, of everything savouring of a player. Now, when a pair of bright eyes stare thee in the face, thou carest not to avow thine errors. Ah! I fear thou art fallen into the wiles of the enemy. Those dark looks and dark eyes are but snares, Jasper, and her calling is a vain one."

"Tush," returned Ogilvy, "my abomination of her calling is not a whit diminished. And if I have expressed any concern respecting her, it is because——"

"She finds favour in thine eyes—I am at no loss to perceive it," rejoined the Englishman.

"No such thing," answered Ogilvy sharply, "and if you repeat that assertion, Master Blount, I shall think you desire to put an affront upon me. I repeat I care not for the girl. Of a verity she *hath* charms. But what of that? Marian Graham, to whom I plighted my troth, hath a far sweeter smile, though her eyes may not be so bright, or her tresses so near rival to the raven's wing. I care not for her—nay, now I bethink me of her calling, were it not the pleasure of my patron and friend that I should accompany him upon this adventure, she might even tarry with Ruggieri in his tower, for any effort I would make to release her."

"Your want of interest in her occasions some slight discrepancy in your sentiments, Jasper," returned Blount, laughing; "but since you find the matter irksome, leave it to us, and return to the Ecossois. We will accomplish the adventure alone, I warrant you."

"No!" exclaimed Ogilvy impatiently; "it shall never be said——" And he was proceeding with some warmth, when his speech was cut short by the cavalier, who addressed him with some coolness: "It was not without reason, Jasper, that I told thee thy tongue was scarcely under the control of thy reason. I may not accept of thy assistance, if I am to purchase it at the hazard of failure."

Thus rebuked, the choleric Scot held his peace, and the party moved on for some moments in silence.

Arrived within the Rue des Deux-Ecus, at that time shadowed by the tall trees which formed the avenues and groves of Catherine's stately gardens, the cavalier, pointing out the high Belvedere of the vast Palladian structure, constituting the Hôtel de la Reine, now distinctly defined against the fleecy clouds of the moonlit sky, exclaimed, "You now behold the castle of the enchantress. I have not disguised the peril you will incur by entering it. Will you go on?"

Both answered in the affirmative. The party, therefore, turned the corner of the palace, and entering the adjoining Rue du Four, along one side of which its lofty walls ran, the principal front of the magnificent building, and its grand portal, erected by Bullan upon the model of the Farnese Palace at Caprarola (upon which an immense shield of marble displayed the blazon and cipher of the Queen-Mother), were at once brought into view. In that still hour, and in that mysterious light, there was something ominous in the appearance of the gigantic building which stood before them. Perhaps, in no instance, was the superstition of Catherine's character more strongly evidenced than in the construction of this proud but needless palace—needless, we say, because she had already expended vast sums upon the erection of the Tuileries, having after her husband's death abandoned the Tournelles, when terrified by the predictions of her astrologers, who foretold that she would perish in some place bearing the name of Saint-Germain; and the Tuileries unfortunately happening to be in the parish of Saint-Germain-l'Auxerrois—for this idle reason only did she abandon the glorious edifice of her own construction, and at an infinitude of trouble, accompanied by prodigious outlays, required when her exhausted funds could ill brook such wanton expenditure, together with the secularisation of an abbey and the overturning of a nunnery (Les Filles Pénitentes), for which purposes she had to procure bulls from the Pope; on this account alone, we say, did she proceed to cumber the ground with this huge structure—not a stone of which is now left standing, with the exception of the column or observatory attached to its courts, toward which building we are shortly about to repair, and shall then more particularly describe. It may not, perhaps, be here altogether out of place to mention, as a sequel to the story, a circumstance which has been much dwelt upon by the supporters of judicial astrology, and which would almost seem to verify the prophecy of her soothsayer: namely that Catherine, notwithstanding all her precautions, eventually expired in the arms of Saint-Germain Favyn, Bishop of Nazareth, chief confessor to her son, Henri III.

The party now approached the grand portal, before which was arrayed a guard of some half-dozen musketeers with their sergeant at their head—the royal blazon upon their doublets glimmering in the moonlight—who placed their long musketoons in the rests, and blew their lighted tow-matches as they drew nigh, while the sergeant, in a loud tone, commanded a halt.

A brief parley ensued. But, perceiving the queen's glove displayed upon the cap of the cavalier, the sergeant immediately drew his men aside and suffered them to pass. The gate was unbarred at their summons, and as the porter somewhat slowly performed his office, the following remarks from the sergeant reached the ears of the cavalier and his companions:

"*Ventrebleu!* Chopin—we have a strange night of it. We are set here to prevent Ruggieri's escape, and it seems as if

he had called all the fiends in Tartarus to his aid. First comes
that mask and seeks admittance: we refuse him. Anon he comes
again with a crowd of imps blacker than himself, demanding
the deliverance of a player-girl. Then, for a third time, he appears,
with the king's signet, which we dare not disobey, and gains
admission with his comrades. Well! no sooner do we think we
are rid of him, than, by Proteus! here he is again, with a couple
of familiars in the shape of scholars, and a dog the like of which
I never saw before. *Diable m'emporte!* if I can understand it.
One thing is clear, he has got the queen's licence, and so we
must not say him nay, but he must have the devil's watchword
if he would return again, for, by holy Peter! he comes not
forth without a bullet to try the proof of his pourpoint."

"Heard you not that?" whispered the cavalier; "our foe is
beforehand with us. Not a moment is to be lost."

The porter started, as he beheld the mask, and involuntarily
placed his hand before his eyes to ascertain whether or not his
vision deceived him. He bowed, however, to the ground as he
recognised the ensign of the Queen-Mother, and the next
moment the party found themselves within the courtyard of
the palace.

Before them stretched a smooth parterre, in the midst of
which, bathed in the moonlight, glimmered a lovely statue of
the Queen of Love, the workmanship of the famous sculptor
Jean Goujon, the restorer of the art in his own country, and
surnamed the Phidias of France, who perished by the hands of
Charles IX., at the massacre of Saint-Barthélemy. But it was
not to gaze on this miracle of art that the cavalier now paused.
Neither was it to admire the gorgeous and illuminated windows
of Catherine's embowered chapel—the then wonder of Paris—
to listen to the choral hymn resounding from its shrines, and
breaking the midnight stillness around them—nor to note the
majestic towers of Saint-Eustache, which commanded the spot
whereon they stood. Pointing out a tall column which might
be discerned spiring from out a grove that skirted an extensive
esplanade, and indicating the path that led to it through the
gardens of the palace, the cavalier was about to quit his companions, when Ogilvy's quick eye detected figures gliding at
some distance from them amongst the trees. "They are yonder,
by Saint Andrew!" exclaimed the Scot, "there is yet time."

Scarcely had the words escaped him ere the cavalier disappeared, and the two scholars instantly commenced a pursuit
of the figures they had descried. Druid regarded his master

wistfully for a moment, but receiving a fresh command from him to that effect, put himself upon the track of the cavalier.

The doors of the hôtel were opened to the cavalier's summons. Not a word was exchanged between him and the ushers, from one of whom he received a torch. Alone he passed through a magnificent hall, the ceiling of which was decorated with exquisite frescoes—ascended a vast staircase of carved oak, and entered a long and glorious gallery crowded with trophies and panoplies collected by the chivalrous Henri II., and streaming with painted glass, "blushing with blood of queens and kings." This gallery he swiftly traversed, and finally reached a recess, within which, as Catherine had informed him, were placed three bronze statues. Touching the spear of the central figure, it yielded to his pressure, disclosing a dark and tortuous passage, into which the cavalier unhesitatingly plunged.

CHAPTER XI

THE LABORATORY

Foresight. But I have travelled in the celestial spheres, know the signs, and planets, and their names—can judge of motions direct and retrograde; of sextiles, quadrates, trines and oppositions, fiery trigons and aquatical trigons.—CONGREVE, *Love for Love.*

LEAVING the cavalier to pursue his subterranean path alone, we shall endeavour, in the meantime, to give the reader some idea of the singular scene that awaited his arrival in the laboratory of the astrologer.

Let him picture to himself a high vaulted chamber, cylindrical in shape, massive in construction, dungeon-like in aspect. Let him darken its grey granite walls with smoke—erect within it four pilasters, and decorate the fluted shafts of each with crowns, fleurs-de-lis, broken mirrors, horns of abundance, and with the letters ℂ. and ℏ. interlaced and surrounded with love-knots, devices emblematic of the widowhood and queenly state of the builder of the turret. Let him next place within each subdivision of the wall, created by these pillars, talismanic effigies of superstitious import, and lest his fancy should not be wild or extravagant enough to supply sculpture sufficiently grotesque, we will endeavour to give some direction to it. In the first compartment, then, let him imagine "a kingly and crowned shape" seated astride upon an eagle, grasping in one hand a thunderbolt, and in the other a sceptre, while a female figure, beaked like the Ibis, holds to his gaze an enchanted mirror. Let him surround this group with hieroglyphics and cabalistic characters, and engrave beneath it the word **Bagiel:** the intelligence of Satan. In the next compartment let him place another female shape of rare beauty, with dishevelled hair, grasping in the right hand a serpent, and in the left a singularly formed knife—let him encircle this medallion with Hebrew and Chaldaic sentences, and inscribe at the head **Redemel**—the spirit of Venus; and at the feet **Asmodel**—one of the twelve angelic governors of the celestial signs. We may add, also, that these talismans, esteemed of sovereign virtue, and of power to aid in the acquisition of mystical lore, were composed of divers metals, molten when the constellations presiding over the nativity of the queen, by whose command they were fabricated, held sway, and were soldered together with human gore, and the blood of goats. The third compartment is occupied by a group yet more fantastical. Here may be seen an altar of ivory, against which is placed a crimson cushion sustaining a huge crucifix of silver, enclosing a lesser cross of ebony. On either side stands a satyr, wrought in bronze, supporting his rugged person with a club, and bearing upon his shoulder a vase of pure and shining crystal, containing certain unknown drugs, destined, it would appear, for some impious oblation to the Evil One at the celebration of the Sorcerers' Sabbath.

Within the fourth and last compartment some mystery is evidently shrouded beneath the close-drawn folds of a thick and gloomy curtain.

Ruggieri's laboratory would have been incomplete had it wanted what, in the jargon of hermetic philosophy, would be termed the keeper of secrets, the producer of immortal fire, the athanor, or furnace. Behold it!—In shape round, as directed by the formula of the science, capped and winged on either side with a thin tube, with door and window, brazen plate, matrass, and cucurbite complete. Upon the furnace door, this profane application of the sacred text has been made: "Quærite, quærite et invenietis, pulsate et aperietur vobis." Around the square pane of the little window is traced the following enigmatical inscription, the solution of which must be left to the reader's ingenuity:

Nunc dimittis Super fundamenta
Fundamenta Super verba mea
Verba mea Super diligam te
Diligam te Super attendite.

Upon the furnace is placed a gourd-shaped, bolt-headed glass vessel, hermetically sealed, and filled with a red fluid, the label of which purports to be *lac virginis*. Next to this stands another cucurbite plunged *in balneo,* containing a specific prepared according to the recipes of Flamel, Artephius, Pontanus and Zacharius, for the cure of all astral diseases. Affixed to the copper vessel, denominated Saint Mary's Bath, in which this bolt-head is deposited, is the following inscription:

> Maria mira sonat
> Quæ nobis talia donat
> Gummis cum binis
> Fugitivum fugit in imis
> Horis in trinis,
> Tria vinclat fortia finis
> Filia Plutonis
> Consortia jungit amoris.

On the floor near to the furnace is strewn all the heterogeneous lumber proper to the retreat of an adept: to wit, earths, metals, "vitriol, sal-tartar, argaile, alkali," gums, oils, retorts, alembics, "crosslets, crucibles and cucurbites." Nor must we omit a slab of black marble, on which are deposited certain drugs and small phials, together with a vizard of glass, a circumstance sufficiently attesting the subtle and deadly nature of the tinctures sometimes extracted by the inmate of the chamber.

Having thus put the reader in possession of the features of the room, we shall now place before him its occupants.

At a table, quaint and grotesque in its character as the rest of the furniture, lighted by the dull red flame of a silver lamp, furnished with an hour-glass and a skull, with a mystical scroll stretched out before him, and apparently buried in deep calculations in a high-backed oaken chair, wrought with the same bizarre devices as the table, sat an old man in a black velvet garb with flowing sleeves—whose livid countenance and bald furrowed brow, clothed with a velvet skull-cap, proclaimed him to be the presiding influence of this weird abode. Beside Ruggieri sat another stately figure, in whose haughty, imperious demeanour and proud brow the reader, we apprehend, will have no difficulty in recognising the Queen-Mother.

Underneath the table, and almost appearing with his broad, hunched shoulders to lend it support, glared the dwarf, Elberich, his red luminous eyes sparkling like phosphoric coruscations in the gloom. Nothing of the manikin's swart and shapeless figure could be discerned in the obscurity, beyond the outline, which resembled that of a grisly bear. But his hand would seem to grasp the wheel of some hidden machinery, serving to raise a trap-door, carefully contrived within the floor of the turret. At the dwarf's feet was rolled what appeared to be a round furry ball, but which, in reality, was a small black cat, of the civet species: an animal held in great request by the ancient necromancers for the confection and perfection of various charms, a certain pebble lodged beneath its tongue being supposed to confer the gift of vaticination.

At the moment when we raise the curtain of this picture for the reader's inspection, the group we have portrayed was silent and motionless. Ruggieri pursued his calculations with earnest zeal, and the progress of his studies was watched with intense interest by the Queen-Mother. The dwarf remained immovable as an ebon image. Nothing but the flashing of his eyeballs betokened animation.

Suddenly a sharp musical ring was heard vibrating in the air, like the sound produced by a glass vessel accidentally stricken. The Queen-Mother raised her eyes, and fixed them upon a curiously constructed astrological instrument, placed on a stand in her immediate vicinity. Framed according to the instructions delivered by the star-wise seers of antiquity, this machine represented seven figures symbolical of the planets (whom Mercurius Trismegistus calls the seven Governors of the World)—wrought with infinite labour and cost when each orb was in ascendance, of the most precious stones, earths and metals supposed to be under its especial influence. The figure upon which Catherine's gaze now turned was that of an armed man of ruddy brass, mounted upon a lion of the same metal, grasping in his right hand a naked sword, and in his left a trunk-less head, carved in a blood-stone. Upon the helm of this martial image flamed a beryl, and in its slow ascent, the weapon within its grasp coming in contact with a bell-shaped glass above it, had given the alarm.

"The mask comes not," exclaimed Catherine, regarding the image with some dismay. "Bright Jove hath no more dominion, we are now under the rule of fiery Mavors—a planet of malignant aspect towards us."

"True, my daughter," returned the astrologer. "And see the red orb ascends within the second face of Aries. Would he had arrived ere this conjunction had occurred! Our scheme will scarcely prosper."

"Say not so, father," replied Catherine confidently: "If Crichton perish we shall have achieved much towards its accomplishment. And when did thy tinctures, or Maurevert's poniard fail us?"

"If the blow be dealt, or the potion swallowed, never, my daughter, but——"

"But what, father? Why these misgivings?"

"The heavenly configurations presage danger to the Scot, not death," answered the astrologer, gravely. "For, though in his horoscope the giver of life meets with the interficient at this hour; though the lord of the fourth house is in conjunction with the lord of the ascendant in Aries, within the orbs of a square of Saturn; and Capricorn descends upon the cusp of the eighth; yet there are other strong and countervailing signs. He may escape us, daughter."

"Ha!" exclaimed Catherine.

"Methinks I see his star still shining in the heavens," continued Ruggieri, "majestic and serene it traverses the skies. A halo of glory surrounds it. Malignant and cross aspects dart their baneful rays athwart its track. In vain they scowl. It pursues its course in splendour undisturbed."

"Does thine art tell thee this?" demanded Catherine impatiently.

"My silent and unerring counsellors thus admonish me, my daughter," replied the astrologer, "I am but their interpreter."

"Say on, then," continued Catherine coldly.

"The star has become a meteor," returned Ruggieri. "Its lustre is blinding."

"What more?"

"I gaze again. The heavens are void and dark: the meteor that dazzled me has sunk—the star of Crichton has set for ever."

"And when will this occur?"

"Ere half a lustre shall have elapsed, my daughter."

"So long! and how will this doom be accomplished?"

"The sign is fiery, and Saturn the afflicting planet," returned the astrologer. "Within his leaden sphere Hylech is cadent. The native will perish by the edge of the sword."

"And if the unerring counsellors tell thee thus much concerning this Scot, what import do they bring touching thine own fate?"

"Shall I erect a scheme, my daughter?"

"It were needless," returned the Queen-Mother sternly, "I will read it for thee. Thy destiny is linked with that of Crichton. Or he or thou wilt perish. If he survives the night, the stake will be thy portion on the morrow; I will stretch not forth my hand, as heretofore, to redeem thee from the wheel."

"My gracious mistress!——"

"If the heavenly influences fail thee, wrest aid from darker powers. Summon to thy assistance by potent spells, such as thou boastest to have won from thy magical lore, a demon, like that which served the wise Cardan, and bid him smite thine enemy. For, by my soul, if Crichton live to annihilate my projects, thy ashes shall be strewn by the winds over the Place de Grève, ere night once again draw her veil over the city!"

"The gnome who served the wise physician you have named," replied Ruggieri firmly, "had not power over life. Jerôme Cardan could foresee, but not avert, and yet he was well versed in the language of the stars. When he foretold that your august spouse, Henri II., was menaced with a fearful and sudden death, he could not unfold the means of its avoidance; neither could his art turn aside the fatal lance of Montgomery. The end of the illustrious monarch was decreed on high. And when my long communing with the celestial intelligences informs me that your own great career will close within the limits of Saint-Germain, I can do no more than point to the term of destiny. It is not enough that your majesty has abandoned the Tournelles and Tuileries; nor that you abstain from setting foot within the district bearing that name; your destiny will infallibly be accomplished, despite your precautions. I have promised you length of days, power and dominion, and my prognostications will be fulfilled. But the means of their fulfilment rests with myself. I have shown you how your dominion may be maintained, your power extended, and by what means length of days may be ensured. If I perish, your honours, your rule, your sway over the king, your power will depart from you, and moulder like a worm-eaten truncheon into dust. Deliver me to my enemies, and ere a week have elapsed, I predict that Louise de Vaudemont will have absolute sway over her husband's affections. Joyeuse will be in power, the League destroyed, Guise and his partisans, who indirectly aid your schemes, crushed; Henri of Navarre and the Huguenots will regain their strength in Paris, and your majesty will be without a party, and perchance in exile with your son the Duc d'Alençon. These results, which I foresee, my skill enables me to avert; and when my dust whitens the pavement of the Place de Grève, and your foes exult in your downfall, you will then call to mind my warning."

Catherine uttered a single exclamation of displeasure, but she offered no interruption to the astrologer.

"To summon a spirit of darkness were matter of little difficulty," continued Ruggieri, who had entirely regained his confidence, "to him who possesses the treasured hieroglyphics of Nicholas Flamel—who can draw the names of the evil angels from Holy Writ, as did the learned Hebrew Mecubals—who can search the ancient Chaldean sages for a genius in the rays of Sol or Luna—who understands the characters and seals of spirits, the kingly writing of the Malachim, that which is termed by the soothsayers of the East 'the passing of the river,' and the Notariacon of the Cabalists. But a spirit invoked without due preparation, like the extraction by yon athanor of the *argent-vif*, in which strange colours, called out of season, endanger the magisterium, may, in lieu of assistance, bring destruction. Nevertheless, if your majesty desires it, I will prepare to raise a phantasm, proceeding according to the directions of Apollonius, Triphonius, Albertus and Raimundus Lullius, and shall make use of the signs given by the wise Porphyrius in his occult treatise *De Responsis*."

"I do not desire such evidence of thy skill," returned Catherine coldly. "Choose some more convenient season for thy consultations with the powers of darkness. I would not have my own soul placed in jeopardy by such unhallowed intercourse. But if thou hast, in truth, a familiar spirit who serves thee, he should have guarded thee against thine enemy. Crichton should never have found entrance here."

"Crichton obtained admittance by stratagem, gracious madam. I was at the moment engaged in tending the wounds of the Gelosa, and Elberich for the first time neglected his trust. The Scot had seized the image and the scroll ere I could prevent him or destroy them."

"And by his acquaintance with the character of that scroll, he is master of all our intrigues with the Guise and the Bourbon —of our communication with his holiness, and above all, of the hidden purport of our mission to Mantua——"

"He is, madam?"

"And he is aware of this mask's connection with our plot —of the part which he was destined to play in aiding our son, the Duc d'Alençon, to the throne of his brother Henri—all this thou hadst set down in thy accursed document."

"It were vain to attempt to disguise my inadvertence from your majesty.—I had done so."

"And, by consequence, he is acquainted with the name and rank of this mask."

"Unquestionably, madam."

"And does my name—mark me, Ruggieri—answer, and equivocate not—does my name, I say, appear in connection with that of the Duc d'Alençon in the plot for Henri's dethronement?"

"No, madam," returned Ruggieri boldly.

"Art thou sure of this?"

"As of my existence."

"Cosmo Ruggieri, thou hast sealed thine own fate."

"How, madam?"

"The king requires a victim. I must make a virtue of necessity. Justice must take its course upon the morrow."

"And your majesty will surrender me to the tribunal?"

"If Henri demand it, I cannot offer resistance."

"Have you reflected on the consequences of such a step, madam?" returned Ruggieri, with sullen audacity.

"The consequences—ha!"

"The question may enforce strange truths from me."

"Who will credit an accusation from *thee*—and against *me*—if written proof exist not?"

The furrows upon Ruggieri's sallow brow were wrinkled into a bitter smile.

"But if written proof *should* exist, madam—if I can produce your own dispatches—subscribed with your own hand, sealed with your own signet?"

"Ha!"

"If I can exhibit your own confessions that you have poisoned two of your sons, and are now conspiring to dethrone a third — what appearance will the charge assume then, madam?"

"Hast thou not destroyed my letters?" demanded Catherine, trembling with wrath—"but no—no—'tis false—thou triflest with me."

"Behold them!" cried Ruggieri, drawing a packet from his bosom.

"Traitor!" exclaimed Catherine, "thou hast preserved those papers to betray me."

"No, madam," replied Ruggieri—"but to protect myself. I have served your majesty faithfully. I have betrayed no trust confided in me; and the rack shall tear me limb from limb ere it shall wrest word from me to your dishonour. Deliver me to Henri's tribunal. Surrender me to the Chambre Ardente —and do so fearlessly. Here are your papers."

"I was indeed mistaken in thee, Ruggieri," rejoined the Queen-Mother, moved. "While aught of power remains to me, not a hair of thy head shall be injured."

"I have ever found you a noble and generous mistress," cried the crafty astrologer, respectfully kissing the hand which Catherine extended to him.

"Commit this packet to the flames, my loyal servant," said Catherine; "it may fall into other and less loyal hands than thine."

"Before I do so, will it please your majesty to examine its contents?" returned Ruggieri. "There are certain papers which you may not choose to have destroyed."

"I know of nothing I should care to preserve," said Catherine, musing. "Speak if there be aught I call not to mind, good father."

"Amongst other matters, that packet contains the proofs of Esclairmonde's birth, which may be needful, should your majesty ever reinstate the fortunes of her house—or use her as a hostage against the Huguenot party——"

"True—true," replied Catherine, "give them to me—these proofs are needed now. I must lay them before Henri. I must reveal to him the secret of her birth. I observed to-night that he looked with eyes of devotion upon the demoiselle. Thy enchantments have wrought upon him in a quarter least expected. I must caution him against further advances."

"Ahreman grant your caution come not too late, madam," said Ruggieri; "his majesty is greatly enamoured, and he hath a rival, moreover, to give a spur to his passion."

"Indeed!" exclaimed the Queen-Mother, "who has dared to approach my protégée in the character of a lover?"

"He who dares everything."

"Thou canst not allude to Crichton?"

"I have his majesty's assurance that the accursed Scot is her favoured suitor," returned Ruggieri.

"Insolent!" exclaimed Catherine; "and yet I might have guessed as much from Marguerite's vindictive ravings, with which I thought Esclairmonde's name was strangely coupled."

"His majesty has, no doubt, carried his design into execution and roused the suspicions of the Queen of Navarre," returned the astrologer; "he threatened as much in my hearing."

"Doubtless he hath done so," answered Catherine, "and if jealousy befriend us with Marguerite, little more is to be feared from Crichton. On that score we need entertain no further apprehension. Thy phial was entrusted to her——"

"To Marguerite?" exclaimed Ruggieri uneasily.

"Upon a solemn pledge, which she dares not disobey. Be tranquil—Crichton will trouble us no more."

"A woman's will may waver," muttered Ruggieri; "of all your sex, your majesty is the only one I have met with possessing inflexibility of purpose."

At this instant a sound was heard within the wall of the apartment, as if a key were turned within the wards of a lock.

"He comes!" ejaculated Catherine joyfully—"all is well."

And the next moment a door, so carefully concealed within the masonry of the turret as to be wholly undistinguishable, was thrown open, and the masked cavalier stood before them. Druid followed at his heels.

CHAPTER XII

THE INCANTATION

Voulez-vous en être convaincu tout à l'heure (reprit le Comte) sans tant de façons! Je m'en vas faire venir les Sylphes de Cardan, vous entendrez de leur propre bouche ce qu'ils sont, et ce que je vous en ay appris.
Le Comte de Gabalis, Quatrième Entretien.

A COURTEOUS greeting passed between the cavalier and the Queen-Mother; but unequivocal symptoms of dissatisfaction were exhibited by the dwarf and his feline companion at Druid's intrusion into their domain. Bristling, spitting and erecting her back, the cat, like an enraged virago, seemed prepared to attack the stranger with tooth and talon, while the dwarf, no less offended, searched about for some more formidable weapon of offence. Druid, however, taking up his position at the feet of his new master, treated these hostile demonstrations with disdain, keeping his glowing eyes fixed upon the movements of the astrologer, in whom he appeared to recognise an enemy.

Catherine's first inquiries from the cavalier were, whether he had been present at the royal supper, and receiving a reply in the affirmative, she continued her interrogations; "and your adversary was there likewise," she asked, "was he not?"

"He was, madam," answered the mask.

"Did he occupy the seat wont to be reserved for him by our daughter Marguerite?" demanded Catherine eagerly.

"The Chevalier Crichton was placed next to the Queen of Navarre," returned the mask.

"And she—she pledged him—did you observe so much, signor?"

"I saw the wine poured out. I heard your daughter's whispered pledge. Crichton raised the cup to his lips——"

"Now the Virgin be praised," exclaimed Catherine triumphantly; "that draught has rendered him immortal. Ruggieri, the stars have deceived thee. Thine horoscope was false. Thy potion hath been swallowed. Our enemy is removed. You are right welcome, signor. You bring us glad tidings. I promised you you should learn more of Crichton's fate when you came hither. That cup——"

"Was poisoned," rejoined the mask; "I know it, madam."

"Ha!—was its effect so sudden?—Is he then dead?"

"He lives."

"Lives!"

"A jewel within his ring gave him timely warning of his danger. The deadly potion did not pass his lips."

"Confusion!" exclaimed Catherine. "But though the poison has failed, twenty poniards invest the Louvre—he cannot avoid them all."

"Crichton *has* quitted the Louvre, and is yet in safety," returned the mask; "he has baffled the vigilance of your spies."

"My horoscope deceived me not, you find, good daughter," said Ruggieri, who, despite the ill success of their schemes, could not repress his exultation at this testimony to his astrological skill.—"My apprehensions were not groundless."

"Peace!" cried the Queen-Mother, "when I requested your attendance here, signor, it was to confer on matters of more moment than this Scot's escape, and I crave your pardon if I dwell too much upon it. I am not accustomed to defeat. Mother of Heaven! it would not now surprise me if this minion of fortune, deeming himself invincible, and puffed up by his success, should adventure hither and attempt the rescue of the Gelosa—as he vaunted he would do, in the presence of my son's assembled court. Heaven grant he may carry his boast into execution. But no, even *his* audacity hath its limits."

"Your desires may be gratified, madam. Crichton, I doubt not, will fulfil his word. Are you sure he is not here already?"

"Signor!"

"Nay, madam, the question is not irrelevant. He is aware of

your appointment with myself—he quitted the Louvre in a disguise in all respects like my own—he has escaped your guard—he has vowed to attempt the Gelosa's rescue—why should not I look for him here?"

"You forget, signor, that you alone possess our glove. Your enemy may have the same masquerade attire in all respects; but, without that passport, he could not gain entrance to our palace."

"My enemy possesses the king's signet, madam," returned the mask, "which even *your* guard must respect."

"Ha! doth he so?" exclaimed Catherine; "this is news, indeed. Ruggieri, who waits without?"

"Some half-dozen trusty blades, with a Spaniard, and a son of Anak, whom I have taken this night into your majesty's service. Knaves who fear not to use the stiletto; and who have, moreover, a wrong to avenge upon this Scot, being somewhile students of the university."

"Enough—summon them to my presence."

Ruggieri stamped upon the floor.

"Madam," said the mask sternly, "I am accustomed to meet my adversaries in the field—sword to sword. I cannot sit by and see murder done."

"Murder!" laughed Catherine derisively; "that phrase suits not with the justice of a queen. What ho! Ruggieri, come they not?"

The words had scarcely escaped her lips, when several dark figures ascended from the trap-door, the bolts of which were withdrawn by the dwarf, and arranged themselves in silence before the queen. Amongst them were the Spanish student Caravaja, and the giant Loupgarou. These desperadoes appeared to be now in their native element, and their fierce and reckless countenances well assorted with the nature of the occupation for which they were now apparently destined.

"Get behind yon carvings," said Catherine, motioning to the darkling group; "yet stay—let him who has the surest dagger remain behind."

"*Por la vida del Rey!* I claim that honour from your majesty," said Caravaja; "my dagger hath never failed me."

"Let thy blow be dealt with more certainty, braggart, than was his, who this morn aimed at the same breast—that of the Chevalier Crichton."

"*Por la alma de mi madre!*" ejaculated the Spaniard; "is it Crichton whom your majesty——?"

"Ha! dost parley with us, knave? Take thy place above the
trap-door—strike as he ascends."

Carajava drew his dagger, and took the position indicated
by the queen.

"He will not escape us now, methinks," exclaimed Catherine
triumphantly.

"Is it possible, madam, you can witness this slaughterous
deed unmoved?"

"You shall behold my calmness. You know me not, signor."

"I hear a footstep," exclaimed Ruggieri; "he comes."

"Art ready?" asked the queen of the Spaniard.

"My dagger thirsts for his blood," returned Caravaja; "I see
the waving of a domino within the vaulted passage below; it is
a masked figure, your majesty—not Crichton."

"Be silent, fool, 'tis he."

"Madam," exclaimed the mask firmly, "this must not be.
No assassin's blow shall be struck while I stand by."

"Would you assist your enemy?" said Catherine scornfully:
"an Italian, and forgive!"

"I do not ask Crichton's life of your majesty; I see well you
are relentless. I entreat you only to delay the stroke till you
have confronted him with me. Seize him, and stay his speech.
But strike him not till I withdraw my mask."

A terrible smile played upon Catherine's features.

"Though you begged this boon upon your bended knee,"
said she; "though my own soul were set upon the issue, I would
not delay my vengeance one second. Are you answered, signor?"

"I am," replied the mask sternly, and laying his hand upon
his sword.

A profound silence ensued. Not a breath was drawn. There
was something so appalling in this momently anticipated
assassination that the hearts of the spectators grew chill with
horror, and even Ruggieri's livid cheek took a more ghastly
hue. Catherine alone was superior to this weakness of humanity.
Her countenance was lighted with a glance of triumph—and
she listened intently for the approaching footsteps. The sounds
drew nearer, and the points of a sable feather could now be
discovered, emerging from the trap-door.

Catherine motioned to Caravaja: the latter raised his dagger
and drew back to give more certainty to the stroke. The new-
comer slowly ascended, uttering an exclamation as his eye
rested upon the queen and her companions. At this moment
the Spaniard's weapon gleamed in the lamp-light; but he struck

not—his arm was disabled and pinioned by the teeth of Druid, and his poniard rolled upon the floor. The new-comer, whose attire and mask in all respects resembled that of the sable cavalier, started and looked round irresolutely.

"Hence!" exclaimed the cavalier, "your plans are foiled—your stratagem is discovered—your life endangered—hence!"

"My followers are within hearing," returned the mask, raising a call to his lips.

But ere sound could be emitted, the trap-door closed with a hollow clangor beneath his feet: the machinery having been suddenly turned and the bolts shot into their sockets by the dwarf.

Catherine arose and fixed her piercing eyes upon the cavalier.

"A moment ago I told you, signor, that you knew me not. Take heed you purchase not that knowledge too dearly. I forgive this indiscretion on the score of your youth—but beware how you incur my displeasure a second time. The proverb would tell you that the offender writes in sand—the offended in marble. My wrong is engraven in adamant. This man hath defied me, and by my father's head, he shall die the death."

"What am I to understand from this, madam?" inquired the mask, in a voice so exactly resembling that of the cavalier, that the nicest ear could not detect a shade of difference in the intonation, and even Catherine started at the sound.

"Now, by Our Lady of Good Succour," cried the queen, addressing the cavalier, "were I not assured of your identity, signor, I should almost doubt the evidence of my senses—the delusion is wonderful."

"No delusion is practised on my part," returned the mask, haughtily. "Your majesty is the dupe of other artifice."

"You bear yourself boldly, messire," returned Catherine, "but your confidence will not long avail you. Tear off his mask!"

At this command of the queen the men-at-arms, headed by Loupgarou, sprang from their concealment.

"Ha!—Saint Anthony to the rescue!—off!" cried the mask, fiercely, putting himself in a posture of defence. "He dies, who first advances."

"Soh!—you refuse to remove your vizard," said the queen; "you are self-convicted, messire."

"To you, madam, I should not hesitate to reveal my features," replied the mask, "but before these rude assailants—never. You forget to whom you offer this indignity."

"By my soul, no—I forget it not," returned Catherine, scornfully; "I offer it to one who hath openly defied my power—who threatened to snatch a captive maiden from my grasp, and who volunteered his own head as the price of his failure. He *has* failed, and think not I will omit the penalty."

"Those were Crichton's words, madam."

"And Crichton's are the features I would unmask."

"Then let your attendants tear off *his* vizard who stands beside you."

"Insolent!" exclaimed the queen, "I trifle—upon him, varlets—strike first—I shall have leisure to peruse his lineaments afterwards."

"Hold, miscreants," cried the cavalier, drawing his sword, and placing himself between the mask and the assailants—"hold, or——"

"Your blood be upon your own head," ejaculated Catherine, impatiently. "I have already warned you."

"On one condition, madam, I will sheathe my sword," said the cavalier.

"If that condition be the life of Crichton, you will in vain propose it," returned Catherine.

"I do not ask Crichton's life," rejoined the cavalier; "I ask you only to defer your vengeance. Grant me a few minutes conference with your majesty, and let the removal of my mask be the signal to your executioners to assail their victim."

"Be it so," replied Catherine.

And, at a gesture from the queen, ere he could offer any effectual resistance, the mask was disarmed and secured by Loupgarou and his crew, and his arms bound together by the leathern girdle of one of the men-at-arms. Caravaja by this time, not without the loss of much of his raiment, and somewhat of his skin, had liberated himself from Druid's teeth, and muttering deep execrations, retired crestfallen amongst his comrades.

"*Por la oreja sagrada de Malchos!*" growled he to Loupgarou; "that hound must certainly be a wizard. I may say, with old Cornelius Agrippa, 'Abi, perdita bestia, quæ me totum perdidisti.'"

"Hear *me*, madam!" exclaimed the mask furiously, as soon as his choler allowed him utterance. "I repeat, you are the dupe of artifice. Let both vizards be removed, and you will then judge between us."

"I shall exercise my own pleasure upon that head, messire," returned Catherine; "away with him, varlets, to the guard-room. See that the doors are barred against his followers, and if rescue be attempted, tarry not for further orders."

"We understand your majesty," replied Loupgarou, in a hoarse tone, inclining his enormous person towards the queen in such manner as a tall cedar might be bent by the desert blast towards some tree of meaner growth—the giant, we may remark, had been incontinently chosen (such is the reverence in which brute force and stature are held by the vulgar) to the command of this bravo troop. "Have you any further commands, madam?" asked the Titan, with a second obeisance.

The cavalier again interposed.

"Your majesty will, I trust," he said, "issue your commands—that your captive be treated with the courtesy and respect to which his condition entitles him. I have your promise that he shall receive no injury till I withdraw my mask. But I will rather remove it now, and bring his fate to an instant issue, than expose a gentleman to the debasing taunts of a felon band like this, whose insults, were I in his place, it would be more difficult to brook than their daggers' points."

"I see not wherefore we should respect *his* honour who regarded not mine, signor," returned Catherine, sarcastically—"but be it as you desire. Remove the captive," she continued, addressing Loupgarou. "Treat him with all consideration consistent with his safe custody. It were well if he bestowed the few minutes of grace left him, in preparation for the eternity he will so soon enter upon. Look to him well—the lives of all shall answer for his life."

"Madam!" exclaimed the mask, "by my soul, you are deceived."

"Away!" cried the queen. And without allowing him time for further speech, the mask was hurried down the trap-door, and the iron valve instantly closed over him.

The dwarf expressed his satisfaction at his disappearance by a multitude of elfin gambols. Catherine clapped her hands—her custom when greatly pleased—and turning to the cavalier, said, with a benignant smile:

"I will now come to the subject nearest your heart, signor, and speak of her whose deliverance this luckless Crichton was to have effected—the Gelosa. You may desire to behold her."

"I came hither for that purpose, madam," replied the cavalier.

The queen motioned to Ruggieri. Followed by the dwarf, the astrologer withdrew to that side of the chamber across which the curtains were drawn, and busied himself in describing

certain lines with his Jacob's staff upon the floor, while his
companion proceeded to set fire to various spicy woods in a
brazier, in which from time to time he cast other odoriferous
ingredients, presently filling the chamber with a cloud of
vapour.

"Hath a magical ceremonial to be performed previous to
her appearance?" asked the cavalier, in a tone of impatience.

"Said I not there was sorcery in the case?" returned Ruggieri.
"The girl is under the dominion of invisible but powerful
essences, over whom these spells have control. You shall not
only behold her in person, but learn by what charms she has
so long held your soul in subjugation."

"It needs no conjuration to discover the nature of those
allurements," returned the cavalier impatiently. "She whose
eyes shame the star Aldebaran in lustre, and whose form rivals
that of the sylph Agla in lightness, need not resort to enchantment to hold her lover's heart in thraldom. I can divine whence
her fascination arises without thine aid, good father."

"Can you likewise divine whence arises her repugnance
towards your suit, noble signor? Can you tell by what power
she is enabled to resist your passionate suit?"

"By that power, over which no art or enticement, human or
superhuman, can prevail—that of virtue," returned the cavalier.

"Pish!" exclaimed Ruggieri, scornfully shrugging his shoulders; "the honour of man and the faith of woman, like trinkets
used to decorate apparel, are excellent embellishments to
discourse, but of little real utility to the possessor. I understand
not the advantage of such ornamental qualities, and have no
strong belief in their existence. Virtue, however, has little to
do with this girl's repugnance to you, signor. She prefers another,
and has been, moreover, in possession of a charm which, as I told
you, I removed this morning from her neck. Take this key,
signor, I have plunged it into a collyrium of such efficacy that
it cannot fail to draw her love towards him who wears it. Her
heart will no longer dwell upon Crichton, but upon you."

The cavalier took the key and examined its curious workmanship attentively. Ruggieri withdrew to continue his mysterious
rites.

"While the astrologer is occupied with his suffumigation,"
said Catherine, assuming a confidential tone, "you shall learn
the secret I have to disclose to you—a secret which, as I have
already observed, nearly concerns yourself."

"A secret which concerns *me*, madam?" said the cavalier,

whose eye was still fixed upon the golden key he held; "does it relate in any way to the Gelosa?"

"By Our Lady!" exclaimed Catherine scornfully, "Ruggieri was not far from the truth when he said you were bewitched by this girl. Your thoughts run on naught else. But do you imagine, fair sir, I am equally the subject of her fascinations, that I should trouble myself with the affairs of a minstrel?"

"Your pardon, madam. But I thought you had made some discovery touching the condition of this girl. There is an inscription graven upon this key, from which I gather somewhat of her history."

"Indeed!" said Catherine, "what imports it?"

"That she is the daughter of a dame of Mantua, of rank; her name Ginevra."

"How learn you this, noble signor?" asked the astrologer, anxiously returning towards him.

"From the handle of this key, upon which these characters, revealed by the powerful acid thou hast applied, have become apparent—'Ginevra, daughter of Ginevra Malatesta—Mantua.'"

"Taphthartharath!" exclaimed the astrologer, shaking as if a vision had passed before him.

"What ails you, father?" inquired the queen.

"Nothing, madam—nothing," stammered Ruggieri, desirous, it would seem, to conceal the interest he took in the cavalier's discovery; "but there is more, is there not, noble signor? Give me that key—why did I part with it from mine own keeping?"

"Of what avail had it been to thee?" said Catherine scornfully; "thy boasted art could not enable thee to detect those hidden characters. But what mean those mystic letters and that figure? Can you unravel this further mystery, signor?"

"The figure is that of the planet Saturn, under whose dominion the metal of which this key is wrought is placed by the disciples of occult philosophy. The letters are cabalistic characters, referring by numbers to those of the Hebrew alphabet, and forming, when placed together, a legend in that tongue, which may be thus interpreted:

> Gold! who wert a father's bane,
> Gold! who wert a mother's stain,
> Gold! be thou a daughter's chain
>   Of purity.
> Shield her breast from sword and fire,
> From intemperate desire;
> From a heaven-abandon'd sire,
>   In charity!

"A singular inscription!" exclaimed Catherine, "and by my faith, signor, you have shown no little ingenuity in its elucidation. I question whether my captive Crichton, who is said to be as well versed in the mysteries of the Cabala as Pico di Mirandola, could have rendered it more felicitously. But love is quick-sighted."

"Suffer me to behold that inscription, noble signor," said Ruggieri, trembling with agitation. "I would fain examine those characters with mine own eyes."

"Not now—not now, good father," interrupted Catherine peremptorily; "this bauble has already offered too much interruption to my conference. What matters it to thee who was the sire, or who the mother of this girl?"

"Everything!" exclaimed the astrologer eagerly, but correcting himself, he added, "that is, my charm would be more perfect if I possessed the talisman."

"'Tis plain thou didst not understand its use or virtue," returned the queen. "To thy task without more delay."

And Ruggieri, seeing opposition was useless, slowly withdrew, casting a lingering, longing glance upon the amulet which he had so heedlessly abandoned to another, and which (now that he had parted with it) appeared to assume infinitely more importance in his eyes than it had done while it continued in his own possession.

"Your majesty had a disclosure to make to me?" said the cavalier, as soon as the astrologer had retired—"may I venture to recall your attention to the subject?"

"I have a secret to communicate not less singular than that you have just chanced upon," said the queen; "but before I unfold my mystery, I must inquire from you whether amongst the beauties who thronged the Louvre to-night, you noticed one who held the chief place among our dames of honour, and who was for some time the favoured object of the king, our son's regard?"

"Your majesty cannot mean the Demoiselle Esclairmonde?" returned the cavalier, starting. "Is it possible your communications can have reference to her?"

"My disclosure *has* reference to Esclairmonde, signor," rejoined the queen. "You have heard, perhaps, that there is a mystery attached to her birth."

"I have heard, madam, the court rumour, which runs that she is an orphan, the daughter of a Huguenot gentleman of distinction, but that her real name is carefully concealed even from her own knowledge by your commands."

"The tale whispered abroad by my orders has reached your ears, I find," replied Catherine, "nor is it altogether wide of the truth. She *is* the daughter of a Huguenot leader—but that leader was Louis I. de Bourbon, Prince de Condé."

For a moment the cavalier appeared to be lost in astonishment. Uttering a single exclamation of surprise, he maintained a perfect silence, as if overwhelmed by the queen's intelligence. Catherine regarded him fixedly.

"My news," she said, "excites your admiration. You deemed not that in my unknown attendant, Esclairmonde, you beheld the daughter of a house illustrious as your own."

"I am indeed filled with wonder, madam," faltered the cavalier—"Esclairmonde a Princess of Condé!—can it be?"

"Look at these papers which authenticate her birth," returned Catherine, placing the packet given her by Ruggieri before the cavalier. "Read that dispatch from Tavannes, the captor of the infant princess—read those instructions from the Cardinal of Lorraine—that memorial of the guard who seized her—this credential of her attendant, and my own letters of authority written at the period. Let your own eye glance over these documents, and you will at once satisfy yourself of the truth of what I have asserted."

With a hand trembling with eagerness, the cavalier took the packet. His eye wandered rapidly over its contents.

"I am satisfied, madam," replied he, as his hasty scrutiny concluded. "And the secret of Esclairmonde's birth is, of course, wholly unknown to the prince her brother?"

"Henri de Bourbon believes that his sister perished in her infancy," returned the queen. "I will briefly relate to you how she fell into my hands, and you will then perceive his grounds for that supposition. During Louis de Bourbon's flight from Noyers to Rochelle, an ambuscade, placed by my directions in the mountain passes near Sancerre for the purpose of intercepting the fugitives, surprised and attacked the litter in which the princess and her infant charge were conveyed. By miracle she and her son escaped: but a fair child—a babe—scarce weaned, was borne off in triumph by the assailants. Condé, at the head of his ritters, vainly sought to recover his treasure. His efforts were so desperate that a stratagem was resorted to, to baffle his fury. A child snatched from one of his household was hurled beneath his horse's feet, and deceived by the outcry of his opponents—thinking that he had unwittingly contributed to the destruction of his own offspring—the prince in despair directed his attention to the preservation of his distracted consort, with whom, and with his son, he succeeded in effecting a secure retreat. From that day to the hour when his blood dyed the battle-field of Jarnac, Condé continued in ignorance of his child's existence. She was to him as she had been no more."

A deep sigh burst from the cavalier's breast as Catherine paused for a moment to ascertain the impression she had produced. Apparently satisfied, she proceeded with her narrative.

"A month after the event I have described," continued the queen, "a fair-haired infant was brought to me at the Louvre, by a faithful emissary of Tavannes. 'The fawn is netted,' wrote the maréchal in the letter now lying before you, 'the deer hath escaped our toils.' By the advice of the Cardinal of Lorraine, the wisest and most prescient of counsellors, the princess was reared in entire seclusion and in ignorance of her rank—and by the cardinal's advice also, the motives of which you will find there developed, she was secretly suffered to imbibe the Calvinistic principles of her family. Of late, in order the more effectually to mask my designs, I have given it out that I intend her for the cloister, and I have noted with satisfaction the effect which this announcement of my will has produced upon her. The period which the sage cardinal foresaw is arrived. Anjou's plot is ripe. The Huguenots must be gained. With Esclairmonde I have the means of winning over their leader. With her I have an earnest of Condé's fidelity, should he league his arms with ours—with her I can paralyse his efforts should he declare against us."

"A refined and subtle scheme, madam," replied the cavalier, who had with difficulty repressed his indignation during the latter part of the queen's recital, and whose vizard alone prevented the wrathful expression of his countenance from being perceived, "and worthy of a disciple of Niccolo Machiavelli, such as the Cardinal of Lorraine was known to be. But may I venture to ask, madam, whether you now propose to restore the princess to her brother? And, furthermore, what may be your majesty's motive in making me the depository of so important a State secret as the mystery of her birth?"

"Your questions are somewhat abrupt, signor," replied Catherine, with a slight expression of displeasure; "nevertheless, I will answer them as freely as they are put. Your alliance with Anjou—your devotion towards myself—entitle you to my confidence. Why I have entrusted you with a secret so dear to me as that of Esclairmonde's birth will presently appear. Meantime I will answer your first inquiry at once, by saying that I do *not* propose to restore the princess to her brother, till the full object of her detention shall be accomplished. I have other and more extended views respecting her. In a word, I have yet to dispose of her hand in marriage."

The cavalier started.

"How?" he exclaimed, with some impatience. "Will your majesty exercise the power which you have acquired over the destiny of this princess to give away her hand without the consent—without the knowledge—of her brother, Henri de Bourbon?"

"Without his consent—without her own," returned Catherine. "Think you the Prince de Condé's approval will be needed to ratify an alliance proposed and sanctioned by Catherine de Medicis? I shall bestow her upon him who serves me best, not on him who may please her fancy most, or that of Henri de Bourbon. The choice of the one might fall upon some hostile leader of the Huguenot party—the election of the other, were she consulted, might be declared in favour of some such arrogant adventurer as the young Scot, whose life now hangs upon my breath, and who, as I learn from Ruggieri, hath already dared to offer his suit to her."

"It was in ignorance of her rank that he did so," returned the cavalier, "for whatever opinion I may entertain of the scope and aim of Crichton's ambition, I cannot think that, had he been acquainted with Esclairmonde's exalted birth, he would have ventured to aspire to her hand."

"He has already aspired to the favours of my daughter, Marguerite de Valois," returned Catherine, frowning, "and he who will dare to soar so high in gallantry, will scarce content himself with a lowly flight in honest love. You are mistaken in your estimate of the Scot's character, signor. I read it more clearly than you do. His ruling passion is ambition. He aims at distinction in all things, and were I to free him from his fetters, and to entrust him with the secret I have just now communicated to you, the first use he would make of his liberty would be to renew his suit with redoubled ardour to the princess."

"There, I am assured you wrong him, madam."

"No matter," cried Catherine, "I shall not afford him the opportunity. Crichton is of an order of men who must be crushed ere thay attain dangerous eminence. To elevate him would be to endanger our own power. Henri is ruled, as you well know, by his minions—the minions are ruled by Crichton.

His mental acquirements—his bravery, and his various and unequalled accomplishments have already obtained complete ascendancy over a court, which of all others is most easily dazzled by such qualities."

"And are these the only faults you can lay to Crichton's charge, madam?" asked the cavalier.

"No," replied Catherine, "he has yet a greater fault."

"Beseech your majesty name it."

"He is of incorruptible honesty," rejoined Catherine; "had he been otherwise, he had been the fittest instrument I could have chosen for my purposes; as it is, he is only an obstacle——"

"Which will speedily be removed," supplied the cavalier, gravely. "Suffer me to change the subject, and to return to that from which we have wandered?"

"The Princess of Condé—true," replied Catherine; "you beheld her at the Louvre to-night, signor. I would gladly learn what is your opinion of her attractions! Is her beauty equal to that of our dames, think you?"

"It is without a peer in the world," sighed the cavalier.

Catherine smiled complacently.

"Mary Stuart," she said, "in the zenith of her youth and loveliness—when the walls of the Louvre resounded with the sighs of her thousand worshippers—and when the whole chivalry of Europe flocked to the court of France to bask in her smiles— was not so beautiful."

"I can well believe it, madam," returned the cavalier, in a tone of deep despondency; "I have myself seen the unfortunate Queen of Scots, and her charms of person, wondrous as they still are, cannot, I think, have equalled the matchless perfections of Esclairmonde."

Catherine again smiled, and it was with some playfulness of manner that she now continued the conversation.

"She is indeed most lovely—so lovely that, I think, if Anjou's suit fail, as it is not unlikely, with that experienced coquette our sister (as her years as well as her regal dignity entitle her to be termed), Elizabeth of England, I shall console him for his disappointment with the hand of the fairest princess of her time. What he loses in power he will gain in beauty. How say you, signor? Does this alliance meet with your approval?"

"Beseech you, madam, press not that question upon me," replied the cavalier, in a troubled tone, "and to be frank with you, let me confess at once, that if the object of your conference be the consideration of an alliance between the Duc d'Anjou and Esclairmonde, I am myself far too deeply interested in the fate of the fair princess, to be able to offer an impartial opinion upon the policy or impolicy of the proposed union, and must, therefore, with your majesty's permission, decline its further discussion. Esclairmonde's charms would alone entitle her to the hand of the proudest prince in Europe, who might deem himself supremely blest in their possession."

"Say you so, signor?" returned Catherine gaily. "What if I change the title and designation of the bridegroom? What, if for François de Valois, Duc d'Anjou, I substitute that of Vincenzo di Gonzaga, Prince of Mantua—will that alliance please you better?"

"Madam!" faltered the cavalier.

"Have I not read your heart aright? Do you not love this maiden?"

"More than my life."

"She is yours, then—I give her to you—and moreover, I will enrich her with a dowry from my coffers, such as neither the D'Este nor the Farnese could bestow."

A deep-drawn sigh was the only response made by the cavalier. Putting her own construction upon his silence, the queen continued: "Lend your aid with arm and counsel to place Anjou upon his brother's throne and Esclairmonde is your reward."

"And is the best blood of France," returned the cavalier, with bitterness, "to be bartered for treason?"

"These are strange words from you, prince," rejoined Catherine; "can I have been mistaken in you? Have I fostered a secret foe—are your own dispatches—are those letters delusive? Answer me, Vincenzo. Do I address an ally of Anjou, or a secret foe of Henri—the friend of an aspiring prince, or the tool of a falling monarch?"

"You speak to one who thinks, acts and speaks freely and fearlessly, madam; who aspires to honour by honourable means —and who would hurl from his grasp the sceptre of France, could it be attained only by treachery. Your plot against Henri, phrase it how you may, is treasonable."

"I will not quarrel with your terms, prince," replied Catherine coldly. "Words are to us the cloak 'neath which the sword is hidden, and the more honestly they sound the less suspicion they are likely to awaken. You are welcome, therefore, to call our plot rebellious, so long as you can enact the part of an arch-rebel yourself. But enough of this. You say you love the

Princess of Condé. Assist Anjou in his (if you so please to phrase them) treasonable designs. Place him upon the throne, and she shall be the meed of your services."

Catherine paused and fixed her eagle glance upon the cavalier, awaiting his reply. But he spoke not. Contending emotions seemed to agitate his bosom.

"What means this?" exclaimed the queen, rising in displeasure. "Do you reject my offer?"

"A fatal bar exists against its acceptance."

"Your passion for this girl—this Gelosa—is it so? By Our Lady! there must be witchcraft in the case. Ruggieri, proceed with thine enchantments—we must dissolve the spell. Prince," she continued in a stern deep tone, "reflect upon my offer. I shall expect your answer on the morrow. Meanwhile, bury the secret I have committed to your keeping within the inmost recesses of your heart. Breathe it not even to your confessor. You can now conjecture why I desired this interview with you—why I selected you as the depository of the secret of Esclairmonde's birth. You have perused those evidences of her illustrious origin. You have satisfied yourself she is the daughter of Henri de Bourbon. I will now commit those documents to the secure custody of this coffer." Saying which, Catherine extended her hand to receive back the packet.

"An instant, madam, I beseech you," returned the cavalier, still detaining the papers, while his eyes appeared eagerly to scan their contents.

"You will have more leisure for their perusal on the morrow," replied the queen; "in the meantime turn your thoughts to her who more immediately claims your attention."

At this juncture, and ere Catherine could possess herself of the packet, the chamber was plunged in darkness. Unobserved, during their conference, the dwarf had silently crawled near the speakers and, at a signal from Ruggieri, suddenly extinguished the lamp which hung above their heads.

"The letters," demanded Catherine hastily. And as she spoke, what she conceived to be the packet was placed in her hands.

Suddenly a low and plaintive strain of music—whence proceeding it was impossible to determine—was heard, and at the same moment a cool and refreshing odour addressed itself to the senses of the cavalier. The effect of this subtle spirit, combined with the rich and fragrant exhalations of the chafing-dish, induced an agreeable languor, against the overpowering influence of which it was vain to contend. It disposed the mind unresistingly to surrender itself to the delusions about to be practised by the sorcerer. Through the dense cloud of vapour that now filled the apartment, nothing could be seen but the dull red fire of the brazier, and the symphony became each instant more faint, until it gradually died away. The voice of the astrologer was then heard chanting the following strains:

INCANTATION

Lovely spirit, who dost dwell
In the bowers invisible,
By undying Hermes reared;
By Stagyric sage revered;
Where the silver fountains wander;
Where the golden streams meander:
Where the dragon vigil keeps
Over mighty treasure heaps;
Where the mystery is known,
Of the wonder-working Stone;
Where the quintessence is gained
And immortal life attained—
Spirit!—by this spell of power,
I call thee from thy viewless bower.

The footstep of the astrologer was now heard to approach the brazier. A hissing noise, as of some fluid cast upon the fiery coals, succeeded. Fresh volumes of smoke ascended to the ceiling, emitting vivid sparks as they arose, and Ruggieri, muttering some unintelligible sounds, continued his spell.

The charm is wrought—the word is spoken,
And the sealed vial broken!
Element with element
Is incorporate and blent;
Fire with water—air with earth.
As before creation's birth;
Matter gross is purified,
Matter humid rarefied;
Matter volatile is fixed,
The spirit with the clay commixed.
Laton is by azoth purged,
And the *argent-vif* disgorged;
And the black crow's head is ground,
And the magistery found;
And with broad empurpled wing
Springs to light the blood-red king.
By this fiery assation—
By this wondrous permutation,
Spirit, from thy burning sphere
Float to earth—appear—appear!

For an instant all became dark. Even the dull glare of the chafing-dish was obscured. A fresh strain of music more soft, more plaintive than the preceding melody, was heard. A dazzling stream of light was seen to cut swiftly through the air, and to settle near the astrologer.

CHAPTER XIII

THE MAGIC RING

It was then perceived that the brilliant flame flowed from a sword held by a female shape, robed in shining attire of almost gossamer texture. This sylph-like figure, so far as it could be discerned through the vapour, appeared of rare and almost unearthly loveliness. In her right hand the spirit bore a flaming brand; in her left a small vase of crystal, while in a thrilling voice she warbled the following strains:

SONG OF THE SPIRIT

I

Within the golden portal
  Of the garden of the wise,
Watching by the seven-spray'd fountain,
  The Hesperian Dragon lies.[1]
Like the ever-burning branches
  In the dream of holy seer;
Like the types of Asia's churches
  Those glorious jets appear.
Three times the magic waters
  Must the Winged Dragon drain;
Then his scales shall burst asunder,
  And his heart be reft in twain.
Forth shall flow an emanation,
  Forth shall spring a shape divine,
And if Sol and Cynthia aid thee,
  Shall the Charmed Key be thine.

[1] The above lines are little more than a versification of some of the celebrated President d'Espagnet's hermetic canons, with which the English adept must be familiar in the translation of Elias Ashmole. D'Espagnet's *Arcanum Philosophiæ Hermeticæ* has attained a classical celebrity among his disciples, who were at one period sufficiently numerous. The subjoined interpretation of this philosophical allegory may save the uninitiated reader some speculation. "La *Fontaine* que l'on trouve à l'entrée du *Jardin* est le Mercure des Sages, qui sort des sept sources, parce qu'il est le principe des sept métaux, et qu'il est formé par les sept planètes, quoique le soleil seul soit appelé son père et la lune seule sa mère. Le *Dragon* qu'on y fait boire est la putréfaction qui survient à la matière qu'ils ont appelée *Dragon*, à cause de sa couleur noire, et de sa puanteur. Ce dragon quitte ses vêtemens, lorsque la couleur grise succède à la noire. Vous ne réussirez point si Vénus et Diane ne vous sont favorables, c'est à dire, si par la régime de feu, vous ne parvenez à blanchir la matière qu'il appelle dans cet état de blancheur le règne de la lune."—*Dictionnaire Mytho-Hermétique.* The mysterious influence of the number *Seven* and its relations with the planets is too well known to need explanation here. Jacques Bohom has noticed it in the enigma contained in his *Aquarium Sapientium* beginning:

"Septem sunt urbes, septem pro more metalla,
  Suntque dies septem, septimus est numerus."

κ. τ. λ.

II

In the solemn groves of Wisdom,
  Where black pines their shadows fling
Near the haunted cell of Hermes,
  Three lovely flow'rets spring:
The violet damask-tinted,
  In scent all flowers above;
The milk-white vestal lily,
  And the purple flower of love.
Red Sol a sign shall give thee
  Where the sapphire violets gleam,
Watered by the rills that wander
  From the viewless golden stream,
One violet shalt thou gather—
  But ah!—beware, beware!—
The lily and the amaranth
  Demand thy chiefest care.[1]

III

Within the lake of crystal,[2]
  Roseate as the sun's first ray,
With eyes of diamond lustre,[3]
  A thousand fishes play.
A net within that water,
  A net with web of gold,
If cast where air-bells glitter,
  One shining fish shall hold.

IV

Amid the oldest mountains,[4]
  Whose tops are next the sun,
The everlasting rivers
  Through glowing channels run.
Those mountains are of silver,
  Those channels are of gold;
And thence the countless treasures
  Of the kings of earth are roll'd;
But far—far must he wander
  O'er realms and seas unknown,
Who seeks the ancient mountains,
  Where shines the WONDROUS STONE!

As the spirit concluded her song she presented the crystal
vial to the astrologer, exclaiming:

In that mystic vase doth lie
Life and immortality.

[1] Vous ne séparerez point ces fleurs de leur racines—c'est à dire, qu'il ne
faut rien ôter du vase. Par ce moyen on aura d'abord des violettes de
couleur de saphire foncé, ensuite de lys, et enfin l'amaranthe, ou la couleur
de pourpre, qui est l'indice de la perfection du soufre aurifique.—*Dictionnaire Mytho-Hermétique.*

[2] Les philosophes ont souvent donné le nom du *Lac* à leur vase, et au
mercure, qui y est renfermé.—*Dictionnaire Mytho-Hermétique.*

[3] Lorsque la matière est parvenue à un certain degré de cuisson, il se
forme sur sa superficie de petites boules qui ressemblent aux yeux des
poissons.—*Dictionnaire Mytho-Hermétique.*

[4] Quelquefois les Alchimistes ont entendu par le terme de *Montagne*
leur vase, leur fourneau, et toute matière métallique.—*Dictionnaire
Mytho-Hermétique.*

Life to him who droops in death,
To the gasping bosom breath.
Immortality alone
To him to whom the "Word" is known.
Take it—'tis a precious boon,
Vouchsafed by Hermes to his son.

Ruggieri reverently received the gift. And, as if extinguished
at a breath, the blue flame playing upon the edge of the sword
expired and the phantom vanished. The brazier once more
became visible, and the magician resumed the performance of
his mysterious rites. At a gesture from his master, Elberich
brought a pannier filled with sundry magical ingredients, together
with a ponderous volume fastened with brass clasps, and clothed
in black vellum. From time to time Ruggieri took some herb or
root from the basket and cast it into the brazier, when it crackled
and fumed, and eventually burst into flame. Nothing was wanting
to add to the effect of the ceremonial. The dwarf gibbered, the
cat hissed, Druid uttered a deep and prolonged howl. The
suffumigation mounted in clouds—and the voice of Ruggieri,
hoarse and broken, and half choked by the vapour he inhaled,
arose above the clamour. Thus ran his invocation:

On the smouldering fire is thrown
Tooth of fox and weasel's bone,
Eye of cat and skull of rat,
And the hooked wing of bat,
Mandrake root and murderer's gore,
Henbane, hemlock, hellebore,
Stibium, storax, bdellion, borax,
Ink of cuttle-fish, and feather
Of the screech-owl, smoke together.

With his Jacob's staff, the astrologer then proceeded to trace
certain figures upon the floor, and taking the black book from
the dwarf, read aloud a mystical sentence, after which he closed
the volume and resumed his spell:

On the ground is a circle traced;
On that circle a seal is placed;
On that seal is a symbol graven;
On that symbol an orb of heaven;
By that orb is a figure shown;
By that figure a name is known:
Wandering witch, it is thine own!—
But thy name must not be named,
Nor to mortal ears proclaimed.
Shut are the leaves of the Grimoire dread;
The spell is muttered—the word is said,
And that word, in a whisper drowned,
Shall to thee like a whirlwind sound.
Swift through the shivering air it flies—
Swiftly it traverses earth and skies;—

Wherever thou art—above—below—
Thither that terrible word shall go.
Art thou on the waste alone,
To the white moon making moan?
Art thou, human eye eschewing,
In some cavern philters brewing?
By familiar swart attended—
By a triple charm defended—
Gatherest thou the grass that waves
O'er dank pestilential graves?—
Or on broom or goat astride,
To thy Sabbath dost thou ride?
Or with sooty imp doth match thee?
From his arms my spell shall snatch thee.
Shall it seek thee—and find thee,
And with a chain bind thee;—
And through the air whirl thee,
And at my feet hurl thee!
By the word thou dreadst to hear!
Nameless witch!—appear—appear!

Scarcely were the words pronounced, when a rushing sound
was heard, and the figure of a hideous hag suddenly stood before the astrologer. About her withered neck and shoulders the
witch's wintry locks hung in wild disorder; her apparel was
loathly and forbidding as her features. For a moment she
remained with one arm leaning upon a staff, and with the other,
smeared, it would seem, with blood, stretched out towards
Ruggieri.

"Whence comest thou?" demanded he.

"From my Sabbath-revel at Montfaucon," replied the hag.
"Wouldst hear how we have passed the night? Wouldst learn
the pranks we have played beneath the moon—how Satan hath
piped for us—how the dead have danced with us—how we have
boiled infants' flesh—brewed philters—and confected poisons—
ha ha!—attend!"

And in a harsh discordant tone the hag sang the following
wild rhymes.

THE SORCERERS' SABBATH [1]

I

Around Montfaucon's mouldering stones,
    The wizard crew is flitting:
And 'neath a Jew's unhallowed bones,
    Man's enemy is sitting.

[1] Le Loyer observes that the *Saboe, evohe,* sung at the *orgia,* or *Baccha-
nalia,* agree with the exclamations of the conjurors and witches—"*Her
Sabat—Sabat*"; and that Bacchus, who was only a devil in disguise, was
named *Sabassus,* from the Sabbath of the Bacchanals. The accustomed
form of their initiation was expressed in these words: "I have drunk of

Terrible it is to see
Such fantastic revelry!
Terrible it is to hear
Sounds that shake the soul with fear
Like the chariot wheels of Night
   Swiftly round about they go;
Scarce the eye can track their flight,
   As the mazy measures flow.
Now they form a ring of fire;
Now a spiral, funeral pyre:—
Mounting now, and now descending,
In a circle never ending.
As the clouds the storm-blast scatters—
As the oak the thunder scatters—
As scared fowl in wintry weather—
They huddle, groan, and scream together.
Strains unearthly and forlorn
Issue from yon wrinkled horn,
By the bearded demon blown,
Sitting on that great grey stone.
   Round with whistle and with whoop,
   Sweep the ever-whirling troop :
   Streams of light their footsteps trail,
   Forked as a comet's tail.
   "Her Sabat!—Sabat!—" they cry—
   An abbess joins their company.

II

Sullenly resounds the roof,
With the tramp of horned hoof:—
Rings each iron-girdled rafter
With intolerable laughter:
Shaken by the stunning peal,
The chain-hung corses swing and reel.
From its perch on a dead-man's bone,
Wild with fright, hath the raven flown:
Fled from its feast hath the flesh-gorged rat;
Gone from its roost is the vampire-bat;
Stareth and screameth the screech-owl old,
As he wheeleth his flight through the moonlit wold;
Bays the garbage-glutted hound,
Quakes the blind mole underground.
Hissing, glides the speckled snake;
Loathliest things their meal forsake.
From their holes beneath the wall,
Newt, and toad and adder crawl—
In the Sabbath-dance to sprawl!
   Round with whistle and with whoop,
   Sweep the ever-whirling troop ;

the drum, and eaten of the cymbal"; and am become a proficient"; which
Le Loyer explains in the following manner: By the *cymbal* is meant the
cauldron used by the modern conjurers to boil those infants they intend
to eat; and by the *drum* the goat's skin, blown up, whence they extract
its moisture, boil it up fit to drink, and by that means are admitted to
participate in the ceremonies of Bacchus. It is also alleged the name *Sabbath*
is given to these assemblies of conjurers, because they are generally held
on *Saturdays.*—MONSIEUR OUFLE, *Description of the Sabbath.*

Louder grows their frantic glee—
Wilder yet their revelry,
"Her Sabat!—Sabat!—" they cry—
A young girl joins their company.

III

See that dark-hair'd girl advances—
In her hand a poniard glances;
On her bosom, white and bare,
Rests an infant passing fair:
Like a thing from heavenly region,
'Mid that diabolic legion.
Lovelier maid was never seen
Than that ruthless one, I ween.
Shape of symmetry hath she,
And a step as wild-doe free.
Her jetty hair is all unbound,
And its long locks sweep the ground.
Hushed in sleep her infant lies—
"Perish! child of sin," she cries,
"To fiends thy frame I immolate—
To fiends thy soul I dedicate!
Unbaptised, unwept, unknown—
In hell thy sire may claim his own."
From her dark eyes fury flashes—
From her breast her babe she dashes.
Gleams the knife—her brow is wrinkled—
With warm blood her hand is sprinkled!
Without a gasp—without a groan,
Her slumbering infant's soul hath flown.
At Sathan's feet the corse is laid—
To Sathan's view the knife display'd.[1]
A roar of laughter shakes the pile—
A mocking voice exclaims the while:—
"By this covenant—by this sign,
False wife! false mother! thou art mine!
Weal or woe, whate'er betide,
Thy doom is sealed, infanticide!
Shall nor sire's, nor brother's wrath,
Nor husband's vengeance cross thy path;
And on *him*, thy blight, thy bane,
Hell's consuming fire shall rain!"
Round with whistle and with whoop,
Sweep the ever-whirling troop;
In the cauldron bubbling fast,
The babe is by its mother cast!
"Eman hetan!" shout the crew,
And their frenzied dance renew.

IV

The fiend's wild strains are heard no more—
Dabbled in her infant's gore,
The new-made witch the cauldron stirs—
Howl the demon-worshippers.

---

[1] Sathan will have an ointment composed of the flesh of unbaptised children, that these innocents being deprived of their lives by these wicked witches, their poor little souls may be deprived of the glories of Paradise.—DE LANCRE.

Now begin the Sabbath rites—
Sathan marks his proselytes; [1]
And each wrinkled hag anoints
With unguents rank her withered joints.
Unimaginable creeds—
Unimaginable deeds—
Foul, idolatrous, malicious,
Baleful, black and superstitious,
Every holy form profaning,
Every sacred symbol staining,
Each enacts, fulfils, observes,
At the feet of him he serves.
——Here a goat is canonised,
Here a bloated toad baptised;
Bells around its neck are hung,
Velvet on its back is flung;
Mystic words are o'er it said,
Poison on its brow is shed. [2]
Here a cock of snowy plume,
Flutters o'er the cauldron's fume;
By a Hebrew Moohel slain,
Muttering spells of power amain. [3]
——There within the ground is laid
An image that a foe may fade,
Priest unholy, chanting faintly
Masses weird with visage saintly;
While respond the howling choir
Antiphons from dark grimoire, [4]
Clouds from out the cauldron rise,
Shrouding fast the star-lit skies.
Like ribs of mammoth through the gloom,
Hoar Montfaucon's pillars loom;
Wave its dead—a grisly row—
In the night-breeze to and fro,
At a beck from Sathan's hand,
Drop to earth that charnel band,—
Clattering as they touch the ground
With a harsh and jarring sound.
Their fluttering rags, by vulture rent,

[1] The devil marks the sorcerers in a place which he renders insensible. And this mark is, in some, the figure of a hare; in others, of a toad's foot, or a black cat.—DELRIO, *Disquisitiones Magicæ.*

[2] As the sabbath toads are baptised, and dressed in red or black velvet, with a bell at their neck, and another at each foot, the male sponsor holds their head, the female their feet.—DE LANCRE.

[3] The sacrifice of a snow-white cock is offered by the Jews at the feast of the reconciliation. This was one of the charges brought against the Maréchale D'Ancre, condemned under Louis XIII. for sorcery and Judaism. Another absurd accusation, to which she pleaded guilty, was the eating of rams' kidneys! Those kidneys, however, we are bound to state, had been blessed as well as devilled. From Cornelius Agrippa we learn that the blood of a white cock is a proper suffumigation to the sun; and that if pulled in pieces, while living, by two men, according to the ancient and approved practice of the Methanenses, the *disjecta membra* of the unfortunate bird will repel all unfavourable breezes. The reader of Rabelais will also call to mind what is said respecting *le cocq blanc* in the chapter of *Gargantua* treating "de ce qu'est signifié par les couleurs blanc et bleu."

[4] The "Black Book."

A ghastly spectacle present:
Flakes of flesh of livid hue,
With the white bones peeping through.
Blue phosphoric lights are seen
In the holes where eyes have been:
Shining through each hollow skull,
Like the gleam of lantern dull!
——Hark! they shake their manacles—
Hark! each hag responsive yells!
And her freely-yielded waist
Is by fleshless arms embraced,
Once again begins the dance—
How they foot it—how they prance!
Round the gibbet-cirque careering,
On their grinning partners fleering,
While, as first amid their ranks,
The new-made witch with Sathan pranks.
——Furious grows their revelry—
But see!—within the eastern sky,
A bar of gold proclaims the sun—
Hark! the cock crows—all is done!
With a whistle and a whoop,
Vanish straight the wizard troop;
On the bare and blasted ground,
Horned hoofs no more resound:
Cauldron, goat and broom are flown,
And Montfaucon claims its own.

"Thou hast sent for me," said the hag, as she concluded her song; "what wouldst thou? Be brief. Ashtaroth hath called me twice; the third summons I must obey. There are mortals here whose presence frets me? They are not marked with the sign, or baptised with the baptism of hell. Besides, I am in haste to rejoin the revel I have quitted. My aching bones are unanointed, and the cauldron boils over. Speak, and let me go."

"Daughter of darkness; foul hag that thou art," cried Ruggieri, in a voice of thunder, "was it to hear thine accursed strains that I summoned thee hither? No, thy master may call thee, but I will detain thee at my pleasure." So saying, he sprinkled some liquid upon her face. "Now," he continued, as the witch howled with pain, "art thou content to tarry?"

"What wouldst thou?" demanded the hag fiercely.

"I would have the potion which thou alone of all thy brood of Tartarus canst prepare," returned the astrologer; "the draught which will turn love to hate, and hate to love. Hast thou that philter by thee? If so, give it to me, and thou art free to depart."

"I have that will serve thy purpose better," responded the hag, drawing from her girdle a silver ring fashioned like a wreathed serpent; "this enchanted hoop—thou shalt have it

—but take heed upon whom thou bestowest it; thy boon may prove unlucky to thyself, for

> Little thrift
> Hath the witch's gift.

Ha ha!"

"Leave that to me," cried Ruggieri impatiently.

"Ah! there again," exclaimed the witch, "Ashtaroth calls, his tone is wrathful. A moment, master, a moment, and I come. The wizards are shrieking, the fiend is piping, the unguent is seething! Well, well, I will be there anon. Take it—take it,

> With a blight and with a ban
> On love of maid, and faith of man—

Take it with the witch's benison, or malison, which you will, and listen to me—

> When the moon was in her trine,
> And the star of love benign;
> When a purple gleam was sent
> From red Mars beneficent;
> And one ray from Saturn flowing,
> Struck the cusp of Scorpio glowing;
> Was this wizard ring confected,
> And the potent charm perfected.
> Gathered at propitious hour
> Stone and herb of sovereign power,
> Grey ætites, coral white,
> Jasper green, and chrysolite;
> Vervain, violet and myrrh,
> And all flowers that frenzy stir,
> Through this ring were swiftly passed,
> And in heaps around it cast.
> And the fragrant pile was lighted,
> And a magic verse recited,
> And the starry signs were sought,
> And their mystic symbols wrought.
> Bound with spell—inscribed with sign—
> Take this charmed ring—'tis thine;
> He who wears it need not woo,
> Woman's will 'twill swift subdue."

And with a wild scream of laughter the witch vanished.

The cavalier, meantime, had witnessed Ruggieri's magical ceremonials with impatience, somewhat curbed by astonishment. Prepared to treat the whole performance as the juggling exhibition of a charlatan, he was, nevertheless, greatly struck by the extreme ingenuity displayed by the astrologer in his contrivances—nor less surprised at the extent of his resources and the nature of the confederacy required to give due effect to his impostures. But when he reflected upon the length of time which Ruggieri had supported the character of a magician, and that the turret he inhabited had been erected under his own direction, his wonder at his skill diminished, and his impatience to bring the scene to a close returned with greater vehemence than ever. The delay which occurred was, in one respect, accordant with his wishes, as it enabled him to revolve over some means of extricating himself from the perilous situation in which he was placed or, at least, of accomplishing the purpose now dearest to his heart—that of communicating to Esclairmonde the secret of her birth. For some time he was lost in painful speculation. Suddenly a plan occurred to him— the expedient was hazardous—but it was the only one which could be adopted with any probability of success. Taking a packet from his bosom, he unfastened his scarf, in the folds of which he placed the letters, together with the knot of ribbons given to him by Esclairmonde, and then calling Druid towards him, contrived in the gloom, unperceived, to swathe the bandage firmly round the body of the dog. This done, with heart elate, he arose, and advanced towards the astrologer. At this juncture it was that the witch disappeared. Ruggieri heard his step and, in a voice in which rage struggled with terror, exclaimed:

"Retire—retire—signor—back, or you endanger soul and body—tread not within that magic circle—the girl is yours— be patient an instant. Take this ring—the witch's gift—it will render your suit resistless—and withdraw, or by Orimasis, I will exert my art to enforce compliance with my injunctions."

So saying, Ruggieri thrust the ring upon the cavalier's finger, and stamped upon the floor. The latter uttered an exclamation of impatience, but at that moment his mantle was seized behind with such unlooked-for energy, that he was involuntarily dragged several paces backwards. Placing his hand upon his poniard, the cavalier was about to free himself from his assailant, who, he doubted not, was the dwarf, but his design was checked by the relinquishment of the grasp, and by the sudden opening of a curtain disclosing to his view, within a small recess, the sleeping figure of the Gelosa.

CHAPTER XIV

THE TWO MASKS

One of these men is genius to the other—
————— Which is the natural man,
And which the spirit?—Who shall decipher them?
Comedy of Errors.

SUSPENDED over the pallet upon which she lay, a lamp threw a faint light upon the features of the unfortunate singer. Her countenance was deathly pale, and though her slumber was calm, it was evidently not the repose induced by "Nature's best nurse," but the torpor occasioned by some medicated potion. Escaped from their confinement, her raven tresses wandered over her person, still clothed in the boyish garb of the morning, and their dusky hue contrasted strikingly with the exceeding fairness of her neck and throat, now partially exposed by the disorder of her habiliments. Something there was in her situation so touching as powerfully to enlist the sympathies of the cavalier in her behalf, and (shall we injure him in the esteem of our fair readers if we confess so much?) something so resistless in her beauty as to awaken in his bosom a momentary emotion more akin to love than to pity. In palliation of this brief disloyalty, we may add that Catherine de Medicis, hitherto a stranger to the attractions of the Gelosa, as she regarded her features with some attention, was so struck with her beauty that she no longer felt any surprise at the extravagant passion with which she had inspired her illustrious admirer.

"By Our Lady!" she exclaimed, "the girl is fairer than I thought her. Is it possible that that lovely creature can be lowly born?"

"It would seem not from the amulet I hold," replied the cavalier.

"Permit me to examine that key more narrowly, signor," said Ruggieri, advancing towards them. "I may be able to resolve her majesty's question. Meantime, I pray you take this phial. The damsel sleeps, as you perceive, but let her breathe from this flagon, and her slumbers will at once be dissipated."

"'Twere better she should awake no more than to dishonour," murmured the cavalier, as he took the phial and restored the golden key to Ruggieri. "Poor girl!" he mentally ejaculated as he approached the couch, "my chance of rescuing thee from persecution, and from what is worse than death, is now slight indeed. But the attempt shall be made. I have vowed to accomplish thy rescue, and I *will* accomplish it or perish in the effort!"

And with these musings he employed the phial as directed by Ruggieri, nor had he to wait long for the result of his application. The Gelosa started and unclosed her eyes; but as her gaze fell upon the cavalier's sable mask, with a scream of terror she hastily averted her head.

"He here again!" she shrieked. "Mother of mercy, shield me from this demon!"

The cavalier bent his head over the shrinking maiden, and in a low tone breathed in her ear her name—"Ginevra."

Not more suddenly does the falcon turn her wing at her master's call than did the Gelosa start at the cavalier's voice. Trembling from head to foot, she raised herself upon the couch —she bent her gaze upon his figure—she peered into the holes of his mask as if to seek some further confirmation of her hopes —she dashed aside her blinding tresses, passed her fingers rapidly across her brow, as if to collect her scattered senses, and in a low tone exclaimed: "That voice—do I still dream? —that voice coupled with that hideous phantom—methinks I heard my own name pronounced by tones, so loved, so tender; but it must have been a dream—how should he know my name? Oh! I am very faint." And she again sank backwards."

The cavalier regarded her with deep commiseration, but scarcely knowing how far in her present state of excitement it would be prudent to trust her with a knowledge of his plans, he deemed it advisable to resume the disguised tone of voice he had adopted in his conference with Catherine. "For whom do you take me, Ginevra?" he asked.

"For whom?" exclaimed the maiden. "I took you for an angel of light, but I find you are a spirit of darkness. Hence and leave me. Torture me no longer with your presence. Have I not already endured agony at your hands? Must dishonour likewise be my portion?—Never. I have resisted all your efforts —your blandishments—your entreaties—your force—and I will continue to resist you. I can yet defy your power, as I defied you in your palace at Mantua. Woman's love may be fickle, but her hate is constant. I hate you, prince, and I will die a thousand deaths rather than yield me to your embraces."

As Ginevra spoke, she became, for the first time, aware of the disordered state of her apparel. If her complexion had been heretofore as white as that of the mountain snow, its hue was

as suddenly changed as that of the same snow when it is tinge
by the purpling sunset. Neck, cheek and throat were turned t
crimson by the hot and blushing tide, while shame, mingle
with resentment, was vividly depicted upon her glowin
countenance.

"Ah! false and felon knight," she cried bitterly, "thou has
done well to steal upon a maiden's privacy—upon her slumber
—but get hence, or by the Virgin I will tear off this bandag
from my wound and breathe out my life before thine eyes
Ah! why was not that blow more surely aimed—why did I no
perish in saving Crichton!"

"And do you love Crichton thus devotedly?" asked th
cavalier.

"Do I love him?" repeated Ginevra—"do I love Heaven—
adore its saints—hate *thee?*—Love *him!*" she continued pas
sionately—"he is to me life—nay, more than life. Understan
me—thou whose dark heart can only couple love with desir
—the affection which I bear to Crichton is that of the devote
for the saint. He is my heart's idol, its divinity. I aspire not t
his love. I ask for no return. I am content to love without hope
It were happiness too much to die for him: but having faile
in that, think not I will live for another."

"Then live for him!" said the cavalier in an undertone, an
resuming his natural voice.

To describe the effect produced upon the Gelosa by thes
words, and by the sudden change of tone, were impossible. Sh
passed her hand across her brow; she gazed upon her maske
companion in doubt and amazement, and then exclaime
under her breath, and with a look, as if her life hung upon th
issue of her inquiry, "Is it?"

"It *is,*" returned the cavalier. And her head declined upo
his shoulder.

Catherine was not more surprised at this sudden change i
the Gelosa's manner than the astrologer.

"Thy spell begins to work, good father," she said; "the gi
relents."

"*Maledizione!*" returned Ruggieri furiously.

"How!—art thou not satisfied with thine own handiwork?'
demanded Catherine in surprise; "thou art distraught."

"'Tis because it *is* mine own handiwork that I am distraught,'
returned the astrologer. "My gracious mistress," he continued
throwing himself at the queen's feet, who viewed his conduc
with increased astonishment, "I have served you faithfully——'

"Go to—what wouldst thou?"

"I ask a boon in requital of my long services—a light request, madam."

"Name it."

"Suffer not yon girl to quit the chamber to-night. Or, if she must go hence, let me accompany her."

Catherine returned no answer, but clapping her hands together, the dwarf, in obedience to her signal, rushed to the trap-door.

To return to the cavalier. His efforts, seconded by his kindly words, speedily restored the Gelosa to consciousness. Gently disengaging herself from his embrace, and casting down her large eyes, as if fearing to meet his gaze, she thus, in a low tone, addressed him: "Pardon me, noble signor, my late freedom of speech. My lips have betrayed the secret of my heart, but on my soul I would not so have spoken had I deemed that my words would ever have reached your ears."

"I need not that assurance, fair Ginevra," returned the cavalier, "and it pains me to think that your love is fixed upon one who can only requite your devotion with a brother's tenderness. But listen to me. With this key you will pass, by a subterranean outlet, to the Hôtel de Soissons. Escape will then be easy. Tarry without its walls, on the quarter nigh the church of Saint-Eustache, for an hour. If in that space I join you not, depart, and go upon the morrow to the Louvre. Seek out the Demoiselle Esclairmonde—do you mind that name, Ginevra?"

"I do——" gasped the Gelosa.

"You will find her amongst the attendants of the Queen Louise. Bear to her this paper."

"'Tis stained with blood," cried Ginevra, as she received the letter.

"'Tis traced with my dagger's point," rejoined the cavalier. "Will you convey it to her?"

"I will."

"And now," continued the cavalier, "collect all your energies, fair maiden. You must leave this chamber alone."

"And you——?"

"Heed me not; a fate dearer than mine hangs upon that paper—upon your safety. You have said you love me. You have approved your devotion. But I claim a further proof. Whatever you may hear or see, tarry not. When I bid you, go. You have a poniard—ha?"

"What Italian woman is without one?"

"It is well. You who dread not to die, need fear nothing. Your hand. I am once more the mask. Be firm—ha—it is too late."

The latter exclamation was uttered as the cavalier perceived the trap-door open and Catherine's guard ascend. One by one the dark figures stepped upon the floor. At last the mask appeared bound, and conducted by Loupgarou and Caravaja.

"What means this?" inquired the affrighted Gelosa.

"Ask not, but follow me," replied the cavalier, advancing quickly towards the queen.

"Madam," he exclaimed, "before this execution takes place, I pray you suffer this maiden to withdraw. Let her await our coming forth within the corridor of your palace."

"Be it so," returned Catherine.

"Go," whispered the cavalier to Ginevra—"you have the key—there is the masked door."

"She stirs not hence," said Ruggieri, seizing the maiden's arm.

"What mean'st thou, old man," cried the cavalier. "What right hast thou to oppose her departure?"

"A father's right," returned Ruggieri—"she is my child."

"Thy child!" screamed the Gelosa, recoiling. "Oh no—no—not thy child."

"Thou art the daughter of Ginevra Malatesta—thou art likewise my daughter."

"Believe him not, dear signor," cried the Gelosa, clinging to the cavalier—"he raves—I am *not* his daughter."

"By my soul I speak the truth," ejaculated Ruggieri.

"My patience is exhausted," exclaimed the queen; "let the girl tarry where she is. I have not done with her. Crichton's execution shall no longer be delayed."

"*His* execution!" cried the Gelosa, with a thrilling scream. "Is it Crichton whom you would put to death?"

"Be calm," whispered the cavalier. "Heed not me, but in the confusion make good your own escape."

"Thou hast said it, maiden," returned Catherine, sternly smiling—"that mask conceals thy lover's features——"

"That mask!—ha!"

At this moment Catherine again clapped her hands. There was an instant movement amongst the men-at-arms. Quick as thought the mask was dragged forwards. A block of wood was placed upon the ground by Caravaja. The sword of Loupgarou gleamed in the air.

The cavalier placed himself between Catherine and the executioners. His hand was laid upon his vizard.

"You have said the withdrawal of your mask should be the signal of Crichton's doom," cried the queen, addressing the cavalier, "are you prepared, signor?"

"I *am* prepared, madam," replied the cavalier calmly, "to meet my own fate. Not against yon mask, but against me, must your vengeance be directed."

And as he spoke, he withdrew his vizard.

"Malediction!" exclaimed Catherine, as she beheld the features of the Scot, "traitor!—have we, then, been thy dupe all this while—have I been betrayed into the avowal of my most secret schemes—into the commission of a grievous and scarce pardonable indignity to my nearest and dearest ally? Have I—but thy cunning shall avail thee little. *Dieu merci!*—thou art still in my power. Don Vincenzo," she continued, turning to the mask, whose vizard, having been in the confusion hastily removed by Caravaja, discovered dark and haughty lineaments, inflamed with choler, but strongly impressed with the lofty and peculiar character proper to the southern noble—(a character which the reader will at once understand if he will call to mind the grave and majestic Venetian faces of Titian) —"Don Vincenzo," said Catherine, addressing the prince, who still remained surrounded by the guard—"What reparation can I offer you for the affront I have thus unintentionally put upon you?"

"One only reparation will I accept," cried Vincenzo, proudly shaking off the grasp of Loupgarou, and advancing towards the queen.

"Give me to understand your wishes," returned Catherine.

"I claim the life of my adversary," returned Gonzaga.

"Now, by my soul, prince," said Catherine, in a deep whisper, "you have asked a boon I cannot grant. Crichton's life is necessary to *my* safety—to *your* safety. He must die."

"He *shall* die, madam, upon the morrow," returned Vincenzo, in the same tone; "but the blazon of Gonzaga were for ever stained, my honour as a knight for ever spotted, if he, whom I have defied to mortal combat, should be assassinated in my presence. He must be set free."

"Never," replied Catherine; "his death will lie at my door. He is in possession of my schemes—of Anjou's plot—and of a secret of vital import, which I deemed I had communicated to yourself; no, he must die."

"I had rather perish upon the block, by the hands of those miscreants, than suffer my honour to be thus sullied," exclaimed Gonzaga. "Hear me, madam," he cried aloud. "Suffer him to depart, and I will gage my princely faith that the Chevalier Crichton betrays no secret—reveals no plot. The laws of honour, imperative on me, are not less binding upon him. Let him depart without fear and entrust the work of vengeance to me. To-morrow we meet as mortal enemies—to-night we part as fair foemen."

"Gage not your faith for me, prince," said Crichton, who with sword and dagger fiercely confronted his assailants; "I can neither accept life nor freedom upon the terms you propose. If I depart hence, the secret I have obtained will be revealed —nay, if my voice be silenced in death, my last gasp will be cheered with the conviction that other tongues than mine will breathe it for me."

"Ha!" exclaimed Catherine.

"*My* vengeance will survive me, madam," continued the Scot; "you may float this chamber with my blood—may hew me limb from limb—but that secret will escape you—nay, it *has* already escaped you. I may never behold her more, may never exchange word with her again, but, ere to-morrow's sun shall set, the proof of her birth will be laid before the Princess of Condé."

"Thou liest!" cried Catherine.

"Where are the dispatches of Tavannes, the letters of the Cardinal of Lorraine, your own written authority?" demanded Crichton.

"Ha!" exclaimed Catherine, hastily glancing at the packet she held within her hand. "Traitor! where are they?"

"On their way to the Louvre," replied Crichton.

"Impossible!"

"I have found a faithful messenger——"

"*En verdad, su magestad,* this braggart's only messenger can have been the great dog who accompanied him," exclaimed Caravaja. "The accursed brute dashed down the trap-door as we ascended, and I remarked that he had a scarf twisted round his throat."

"That scarf contained the letters," said Crichton, with a smile of triumph.

"And the hound escaped you?" demanded Catherine, of the Spaniard.

"It is no dog, but a fiend in bestial shape," replied Caravaja; "the phantasm was out of sight in a moment."

"Chevalier Crichton," said Catherine, advancing towards him, and speaking in an undertone, "those papers are of more value to me than your life. I will capitulate with you. Upon the conditions offered to you by the Prince of Mantua, you may depart freely."

"I have said that I reject them, madam. Bid your assassins advance. To Heaven and Saint Andrew I commit my cause."

"I will die with you," murmured Ginevra.

"Rash girl, thou hast no part in this fray," cried Ruggieri; "hence with thy father."

"Never," shrieked the Gelosa, "I will never quit the Signor Crichton's side—the blow which is his death shall be mine likewise. Let me go, I say. I am not thy child. Thou hast invented this story to betray me."

"Hear me, Ginevra. I have proofs——"

"No, I will not listen to thee. Thou wouldst have bartered my honour for the Prince of Mantua's gold. Was that a father's love? But if thou *art* my father, leave me, and draw not my blood, as well as that of my mother, upon thy head, for, by Our Lady of Pity! I will plunge this steel to my heart rather than yield to thy licentious master."

"Ginevra, I would free thee from him. In mercy listen to me." But ere he could proceed, the fiery girl drew her stiletto, and extricating herself from his grasp, once more took refuge by the side of Crichton.

Catherine, meantime, despite the indignant remonstrances of Gonzaga, who, being unarmed, could take no part in the conflict, had commanded the men-at-arms to assault the Scot.

"Upon him, knaves," she cried; "what do you fear? He is but one—strike! and spare not."

Crichton breasted their fury, as the rock resists and hurls back the breakers. The gleam of their swords flashed in the eyes of the Gelosa, the clash of steel resounded in her ears. The strife was terrific. But amidst it all the Scot remained uninjured; not a thrust could reach him, while several desperate wounds were received by his antagonists. The vociferations, the clamour, the trampling of feet were deafening. Suddenly the noise ceased. Catherine looked to see if her enemy had fallen, but she beheld him in an attitude of defence, calmly regarding his antagonists, who had drawn back to take breath and consider upon some new plan of attack. Mortified and dismayed, the queen began to apprehend the issue of the combat might yet determine in favour of Crichton, when she beheld a dark figure stealing behind him.

It was the dwarf. With stealthy steps she saw him approach the Scot. He bounded forward—a dagger was in his grasp—when at that moment he was felled by the stiletto of the Gelosa. Catherine could not restrain an exclamation of displeasure.

"Cravens," she cried, "ye lack the nerves of men. Give me a sword, and I will show you how to wield it."

Thus exhorted, the ruffian band renewed the conflict, and with better success than before. A few blows only had been exchanged, when Crichton's sword, a light rapier, intended more for ornament than use, was shivered, and with the exception of his poniard—a feeble defence against six trenchant blades—he lay at their mercy. A savage yell was raised by his opponents. A few moments more they saw would now decide the fight. Resolved, however, to sell his life dearly, Crichton darted forward, and seizing the foremost of the crew by the throat, plunged his dagger into his breast. The wretch fell with a deep groan. His comrades pressed on to avenge him. With his cloak twisted round his arm, Crichton contrived for some moments to ward off their blows and rid himself of another foe. But it was evident what must be the result of a contest so unequal: nevertheless, the Scot's defence was so gallant as still to leave his enemies in doubt, when, as he seconded a feint with a thrust at Loupgarou, his foot slipped upon the floor, now floating in blood, and he stumbled. Swifter than thought Ginevra interposed her own person between Loupgarou and Crichton, and the blow intended for him must have transfixed her, had not a loud cry from Ruggieri arrested the hand of the giant.

"Spare my child!—spare her! my gracious mistress!" ejaculated the distracted astrologer.

But Catherine was deaf to his entreaties.

"Spare neither," she said sternly.

Crichton, however, had recovered his feet. A word even in that brief interval had passed between him and the Gelosa. Ere his intention could be divined, he had flown, together with the maid, to the recess, and the curtains falling at the same moment to the ground, concealed them from view. An instant afterwards, when these hangings were withdrawn by Caravaja and Loupgarou, they had disappeared. A masked door within the wall, half open, showed the means by which their flight had been effected. "*Sangre de Dios!*" cried Caravaja, as this door was suddenly closed, and a bar, as was evident from the sound, drawn across it on the other side, "our purpose is frustrated."

"*Cap-dé-Diou!*" ejaculated Loupgarou, "whither doth that outlet lead?"

As he spoke, the giant felt his leg suddenly compressed by a nervous grip, while, at the same time, a noise like the hissing of a serpent sounded in his ears. Starting at the touch, Loupgarou beheld the red orbs of Elberich fixed upon him. The unfortunate manikin, mortally wounded, had contrived to crawl towards him. The stream of life, flowing in thick and inky drops from his side, was ebbing fast—-but the desire of vengeance lent him strength. Directing the giant's attention towards a particular part of the wall, he touched a spring and another but a smaller door flew open. Through this aperture the dwarf crept, beckoning Loupgarou, who with Caravaja and his two remaining followers instantly went after him.

Scarcely had the party disappeared, when the door through which Crichton had approached the turret from the queen's palace, revolved upon its hinges, and the Vicomte de Joyeuse, accompanied by Chicot, and attended by an armed retinue, entered the chamber. He cast a quick glance round the room, and his countenance fell as he beheld the bloody testimonials of the recent fray.

"Monseigneur," he said, advancing towards Gonzaga, who remained motionless with his arms folded on his breast, "I have it in his majesty's commands to assure myself of your person till the morrow."

"A prisoner!" exclaimed Gonzaga, his hand vainly searching for his sword. "Know you whom you thus address?"

"I know only that I address one whom I hold to be a loyal cavalier," returned Joyeuse quickly; "but when I gaze around this chamber and behold these marks of butchery, doubts arise in my mind which I would fain have removed. Whom have I the honour to place under arrest?"

"The Prince of Mantua," replied Catherine; "the king's arrest cannot attach to him."

"*Vive Dieu!*" exclaimed the vicomte. "I am indeed much honoured. But you are mistaken, madam—his majesty's arrest does attach to the prince. Messieurs, to your charge I commit his highness. My duty, however, is only half fulfilled. May I crave to know where I shall meet with the Chevalier Crichton, if he be, as I conjecture, within this turret?"

"You will scarce need to assure yourself of *his* person, monseigneur," replied Catherine smiling; "my attendants have already saved you that trouble."

"How, madam?" exclaimed Joyeuse, starting.

"Outcries and footsteps resound from this doorway," ejaculated Chicot. "Methinks I hear the voice of Crichton— there again—to the rescue, Monsieur le Vicomte."

"Prince," cried Joyeuse, "you shall answer to me for the life of the Chevalier Crichton. In his quarrel with you I was chosen his *parrain*, and by Saint Paul, if he have perished by assassination in your presence, I will proclaim you felon and craven, throughout every court in Christendom."

"Monsieur le Vicomte, you do well to threaten a prisoner," replied Gonzaga haughtily. "But a season will arrive when you shall answer to *me* for these doubts."

"And to *me* likewise," added Catherine haughtily. "Monsieur le Vicomte, I command you and your followers to withdraw, on pain of incurring my deadliest resentment."

"I am his majesty's representative, madam," returned Joyeuse proudly, "and invested with his authority to seek out and detain a noble cavalier, somewhile distinguished as 'the mask,' together with the Chevalier Crichton, during his sovereign pleasure. You are best aware what account you will render of the latter to his majesty."

"To the rescue! to the rescue! monseigneur," screamed Chicot, "I hear a female voice."

"My daughter! my daughter!" ejaculated Ruggieri.

"Some of you take charge of yon caitiff," exclaimed Joyeuse, pointing with his sword to the astrologer; "he is concerned, I doubt not, in this foul transaction—and now follow me who may? Montjoie! Saint Denis!—on!——"

So saying, he dashed through the narrow portal, and sprang swiftly up a dark and winding staircase, down which the echoes of oaths and other vociferations now distinctly resounded.

CHAPTER XV

THE COLUMN OF CATHERINE DE MEDICIS

On luy attachoit ung cable en quelque haute tour pendant en terre: par icelluy avecques deux mains montoit, puis devaloit si roidement, et si asseurément, que plus ne pourriez parmy ung pré bien egallé.
RABELAIS, *Gargantua*, liv. i. chap. xxiii.

OPPOSITE the Rue de Viarmes, and reared against the circular walls of the Halle-au-Blé—with its base washed by a fountain— its shaft encircled by a cylindrical dial, and huge gnomonic projection, and its summit surmounted by a strange spherical cage of iron—stands, at this day, a tall, fluted, richly decorated Doric column; bearing upon its aspect the reverend impress of antiquity. The fountain and dial are of modern construction; the spherical crest is ancient. Tradition assigns this observatory, for such it is, to Catherine de Medicis. From hence she is said to have nightly perused, within the starry scroll of heaven, the destinies of the great city stretched out at her feet—while, from the same situation, Ruggieri is reported to have gathered the lore by which he was enabled to avert the stroke of danger, and strengthen and consolidate his mistress's power.

The iron cage alluded to, and which is supposed to have some recondite allusion to the mysteries of astrology, was, in all probability, contrived by the Florentine seer. Its form has given rise to much speculation. Consisting of a circular framework of iron, crossed by other circles, and supported by a larger hemisphere of iron bars — "des cercles et des demicercles entrelacés," says M. Pingré—the object of which it is difficult to conceive, unless they were intended as types of the science, to the uses of which the structure was devoted; and erected after the designs of the celebrated Jean Bullan, this pillar situated, at the period under consideration, in the angle of a lateral court of the Hôtel de Soissons, is the sole remnant now existing of that vast and magnificent edifice. Its history is remarkable, but it may suffice to say that it was preserved from the general demolition of Catherine's palace by the generosity of a private individual, Le Sieur Petit de Bachaumont, by whom it was redeemed at the price of 1500 livres. The effect of the observatory is materially injured by its contiguity to the Halle-au-Blé, and its symmetry destroyed by an horologiographical contrivance, as well as by a tasteless tablet placed above its plinth; but notwithstanding these drawbacks—viewed either in connection with its historical associations, or with the mysterious and exploded science of which it is a relic—the column of Catherine de Medicis can scarcely be regarded with indifference. Within its deeply cut chamfering, now almost effaced by time, are still to be traced emblematic devices, similar to those heretofore mentioned as adorning the walls of Ruggieri's laboratory. The elevation of the pillar from the ground is nearly a hundred feet, and its diameter somewhat more than nine feet.

When Crichton and the Gelosa disappeared through the recess, their course was for a few moments shaped along a low, narrow passage, evidently contrived within the thickness of the wall, which, after a brief but toilsome ascent, conducted them to what appeared, from the increased height of the roof and greater space between the walls, to be a sort of landing-place. Whether there was any further outlet from this spot, the profound darkness in which all was involved left them no means of ascertaining; but as they tarried for an instant to recover breath, Crichton took advantage of the occasion warmly to express his thanks to his fair companion for the succour she had so opportunely afforded him.

"But for you," he said, "fair Ginevra, I had perished beneath the daggers of Catherine's assassins. To you I owe my life a second time—how—how shall I requite your devotion?"

"By suffering me to be your slave," cried the impassioned girl, bathing his hand with tears—"to remain ever near you."

"You shall never leave me," returned the Scot kindly, carrying his gratitude to a scarce allowable length, for as he spoke, his lips sought the burning mouth of the Geloso, while his arms pressed her closely to his bosom.

"*Santa Madonna!*" exclaimed Ginevra, hastily drawing back her head, deeply abashed at the impulse to which she had yielded, "our pursuers are at hand."

At the same moment, also, Crichton became aware of the sound of hoarse voices, and approaching footsteps.

"There is—there must be a farther outlet—this chamber communicates with the queen's observatory," cried the Gelosa, "I remember I was dragged to some such place as this, by him who falsely calls himself my father, a few hours ago. Each wall in this frightful turret is perforated, like a State dungeon, with secret passages. Step forward, sweet signor, and you will find the outlet."

With outstretched hand Crichton guided himself rapidly along the wall. The aperture was instantly discovered. His foot was on the flight of steps.

"Follow me, Ginevra," he cried, extending his hand in the direction of the damsel. But a grasp was laid upon her, from which she could not extricate herself. At the same moment a hissing laugh proclaimed her captor to be the vindictive dwarf. With supernatural force the manikin twined himself round her person. The maiden felt herself sinking. His hot breath was upon her face—his horrible mouth approached her throat. She experienced a sharp and sudden thrill of pain. The vampire, having no other weapon, sought to fix his teeth in her neck. In this extremity, as she gave herself up for lost, Elberich's grasp relaxed, and the monster sank, an inert mass, to the earth. Crichton's poniard had freed her from her foe, while his arm bore her up the spiral stairs, just as Loupgarou and his crew reached the landing-place. The giant heard the struggle between Ginevra and Elberich—he heard also the fall of the latter, and with a bound sprang forward. He was too late to secure his prey, and stumbling over the prostrate body of the dwarf, impeded with his huge person the further advance of his followers. Muttering deep execrations, he then arose and began to ascend the column. After mounting some forty or fifty steps, a dull light, admitted through a narrow slit in the pillar, cheered his progress.

"By my fay," cried Loupgarou, as he gazed through this loophole upon the gardens of the Hôtel de Soissons, just visible by the uncertain light of a clouded moon, "we are within her majesty's observatory—those are the royal gardens—and yonder are the old towers of Saint-Eustache."

"*En verdad, compañero,*" replied Caravaja, thrusting forward his visage, and surveying in his turn the scene, "thou hast said it. It must be the structure I have so often gazed at from the Rue des Etuves, with the cage in which folks say Ruggieri keeps Señor Sathanas confined. Many a time have I seen that sooty imp, whose carcass we have left in the room below, practise a thousand fantastic trickeries upon those iron bars. There used to be a rope from which he would fling himself head-long from the summit, and swing backwards and forwards like an ape or a juggler, to the terror of all pious observers.—Ha!— What means that clamour and clashing of swords? There are others at work besides ourselves. *Vamos, camarada!*"

"Softly," replied the lethargic giant, pausing to take breath —"we do not need hurry ourselves, *quo magis properare studeo, eo me impedio magis*—as we say in the schools! We are certain our Scot is in this turret—we are certain, moreover, that he cannot descend without passing us—we are furthermore certain that we are four and that he is but one; *ergo* we may safely reckon upon his head—and upon our reward."

"*Concedo consequentiam,*" returned Caravaja, "but proceed, most redoubted Goliath, or this puissant David may prove too much for thee after all. Ha! hear you that shot? Someone has discovered him from below—mount!—dispatch!"

Thus urged, Loupgarou recommenced the ascent. Another and another loophole showed him the elevation he had attained, and at length his mighty head came in contact with a plate of iron, which proved to be a trap-door opening upon the summit of the column, but which was now fastened on the other side. Here was an unexpected difficulty thrown in their path, not entirely, however, to the dissatisfaction of the giant who, despite his bulk and sinew, like all other men of vast proportions, was of a somewhat craven nature at bottom, and regarded the approaching struggle with considerable misgiving. He deemed it necessary, however, to conceal his gratification under a mask of oath and bluster, and seconding his words with a show of resolution, applied his shoulder to the trap-door with so much good will that, to his astonishment, it at once yielded to his efforts. To recede was now impossible. Caravaja and his comrades were swearing in the rear, so putting a bold face upon the matter, he warily emerged. What was his surprise, and we may say delight, to find the roof deserted. In proportion to his security his choler increased.

"Hola!—my masters," he roared, "we are tricked—duped—deceived. This Crichton is in league with the fiend. He has made himself a pair of wings and flown away with the girl upon his back.—*Cap-dé-Diou!* we are robbed of our reward."

"*San diablo!*" exclaimed Caravaja, as he also emerged from the trap-door. "Gone!—ha—*higados!*—I perceive the device."

To return to the Scot and his fair charge. Sustaining the terrified girl, who was so much exhausted as to be wholly unable to assist herself, within his arms, Crichton rapidly threaded the steps of the column. Arrived at the summit, he gently deposited Ginevra upon the roof, and stood with his dagger in hand prepared to strike down the first of his assailants who should appear at the mouth of the staircase. The cold fresh air now playing upon her cheek in some degree revived the Gelosa. She endeavoured to raise herself, but her strength was unequal to the effort. At this moment an outcry was heard below. It was the voice of Blount calling to his dog. Crichton uttered an exclamation of delight. The packet had reached its destination —it would be delivered to Esclairmonde. Scarcely had this thought passed through his mind, when the sudden report of an harquebus was heard, succeeded by a deep howl. Blount's shouts, mingled with those of Ogilvy, arose loud and stunning. The clash of swords succeeded. Crichton could no longer resist the impulse that prompted him to glance at the combatants. He leaned over the edge of the pillar, but all that he could discern was the Englishman engaged in sharp conflict with several armed figures partially concealed from his view by the intervening shrubs of the garden. Druid was by his side, foaming, furious, and with his teeth fastened upon one of his master's assailants. The scarf was gone. But whether or not it was in Blount's possession, he was unable to ascertain. As he turned in doubt and some dejection towards the trap-door, his eye chanced upon a coil of rope attached to one of the links constituting the larger hemisphere of iron bars by which he was surrounded. A means of escape at once presented itself to his imagination. Swift as thought he tried the durability of the cord. It was of strength sufficient to sustain his weight, and of more than sufficient extent to enable him to reach the ground. He uttered an exclamation of joy, but he suddenly checked himself. The plan was relinquished as soon as formed. He could not abandon the Gelosa.

Ginevra divined his intentions. Collecting all her energies, she threw herself at his feet, beseeching him to avail himself of the opportunity that presented itself of safety by flight.

"And leave you here to fall into the hands of your pursuers —of Gonzaga—never!" replied Crichton.

"Heed me not — heed me not — noble and dear signor," replied the Gelosa. "I have *my* means of escape likewise—go— go—I implore of you. What is my life to yours? By the Virgin!" she continued, with passionate earnestness, "if you do not obey me, I will fling myself headlong from this pillar and free you from restraint, and myself from persecution."

So saying, she advanced to the brink of the column, as if resolved upon putting her threat into instant execution.

"Hold, hold, Ginevra," exclaimed Crichton, "we may both avoid our foes. Give me thy hand, rash girl." And ere she could advance another footstep, the Scot detained her with a powerful grasp. Ginevra sank unresistingly into his arms. Crichton's next proceeding was to make fast the trap-door, the bolt of which presented such feeble resistance to the Herculean shoulders of Loupgarou. He then threw the cord over the edge of the column, and advanced to the brink to see that it had fallen to the ground. As he did so, he was perceived and recognised by Ogilvy, who hailed him with a loud shout, but as that doughty Scot was engaged hand to hand with a couple of assailants, he was not in a condition to render his patron any efficient assistance. Having ascertained that the cord had dropped in the way he thought desirable, Crichton again assured himself of the firmness of the knot, and placing his dagger between his teeth, to be ready for instant service on reaching the ground, and twining his left arm securely round the person of the Gelosa, whose supplications to be abandoned to her fate were unheeded, he grasped the rope tightly with his right hand, and leaning over the entablature of the column, pushed himself deliberately over its ledge.

For a moment the rope vibrated with the shock, and as she found herself thus swinging to and fro in mid-air, Ginevra could scarcely repress a scream. Her brain reeled as she gazed dizzily downwards, and perceived the space intervening between her and the earth. Her head involuntarily sank over her shoulder, and she closed her eyes. Had her safety depended on her own powers of tenacity, she had certainly fallen.

The rope, meanwhile, continued its oscillations. With one arm only disengaged, and the other encumbered by his fair burden, it was almost impossible for Crichton to steady it. The architrave and frieze crowning the capital projected nearly two feet beyond the body of the shaft. For some time he could neither reach the sides of the pillar so as to steady his course by its fluted channels, nor venture to trust himself to the guidance of the shifting cord. His peril appeared imminent. The strain upon the muscles was too great to be long endured. But Crichton's energies were inexhaustible, and his grip continued unrelaxing. At length, after various ineffectual efforts he succeeded in twining his legs securely round the rope, and was about to descend, when an incident occurred that rendered his situation yet more perilous.

Filled with astonishment at the daring attempt they witnessed, as Crichton launched himself from the column, the combatants beneath—friend and foe, as if by mutual consent —suspended hostilities. It was a feat of such hairbreadth risk, that all gave him up for lost. But, when he had made good his hold, their admiration knew no bounds. Blount loudly hurrahed, and threw his cap into the air. Even the adverse party uttered a murmur of applause. Ogilvy rushed forward to seize and secure the rope—and all had been well, but at the same moment he was grappled by one of his antagonists, and in the struggle that ensued the cord was so violently shaken that Crichton had need of all his vigour to maintain his position. The rope whirled round and round, but contriving, amid the gyrations, to insert the point of his foot in the fluting of the pillar, he once more regained his equilibrium.

"Villain," cried Ogilvy, as he threw his enemy to the earth, and plunged his dirk within his bosom, "thou, at least, shall reap the reward of thy treachery. Ah, what is this?" he cried, as from the folds of a scarf, which had dropped from the man's grasp, a packet of letters met his view. He was about to pick them up, when his attention was diverted by a loud cry from Blount.

"Ha! have a care, noble Crichton!" shouted the Englishman; "have a care, I say! Saint Dunstan and Saint Thomas, and all other good saints protect thee!—Desist, craven hound, what wouldst thou do? The curse of Saint Withold upon thee!" The latter part of Blount's ejaculation was addressed to Loupgarou, whose huge person might now be discovered leaning over the architrave of the pillar, and who was preparing to hew the rope asunder with his sword. "Oh, for a sling!" roared Blount, "to smite that accursed Philistine betwixt the temples."

Directed by these outcries and, at the same time, perceiving the effect of a blow upon the rope, Crichton looked upwards. He beheld the malignant and exulting aspect of Loupgarou, who, it is needless to say, through the agency of Caravaja, had discovered the mode of flight adopted by the Scot, and instantly resolved upon the only revenge in his power. It was evident from his gestures and ferocious laughter that the giant had resolved to exercise his utmost ingenuity in torturing his enemy. Before he attempted to sever the cord he shook it with all his force, jerking it vehemently, first on the right hand, and then on the left; but, finding he could not succeed in dislodging the tenacious Scot, he had recourse to another expedient. Taking firmly hold of the iron bar, by dint of great exertion he contrived to pull the cord up several feet. Uttering a loud yell, he let it suddenly drop. Still Crichton, though greatly shaken, maintained his hold. Loupgarou then proceeded slowly to saw the cord with his sword. Crichton gazed downwards. He was still more than sixty feet from the ground.

"Ho, ho!" bellowed Loupgarou, "not so fast, fair sir—*qui vult perire pereat*—ho, ho! You shall reach the ground without further efforts of your own, and somewhat more expeditiously —*sternitur exanimisque tremens procumbit humi*—ho, ho!——"

"That fate shall be thy own, huge ox," screamed the shrill voice of Chicot in his rear; "ho, ho!" laughed the jester, as the giant, whom he pushed forward with all his might, rolled heavily over the entablature; "not so fast, not so fast, my Titan."

"*Quién adelante no mira, atrás se queda,*" exclaimed Caravaja, springing upon the jester with the intent of throwing him after

the giant, "thou shalt reverse the proverb; look first and leap
after." The words, however, were scarcely out of his mouth,
when he found himself seized by the Vicomte de Joyeuse, who
suddenly appeared on the roof of the column.

Loupgarou made an effort to grasp at the architrave of the
pillar as he was precipitated over it, and then at the rope, but
he missed both. His great weight accelerated his fall. He
descended head foremost. His skull came in contact with the
sharp, projecting edge of the plinth, which shattered it at
once, and his huge frame lay without sense upon the pavement
of the court just as Crichton and his now senseless burden
alighted in safety upon the ground.

"By my bauble!" cried Chicot, as he hailed Crichton from
the summit of the column, "the great gymnastic feats of
Gargantua equal not your achievements, *compère*."

But Crichton was too much occupied to attend to the jester.
He had now to defend himself against the assault of Gonzaga's
followers, whose object was to possess themselves of the Gelosa.

At this moment the call of a trumpet sounded from the
summit of the pillar, and the next instant some dozen men
in arms, in the livery of the Vicomte de Joyeuse, made their
appearance at its base.

"Down with your swords, in the king's name," cried the
sergeant of the guard. "Chevalier Crichton, in the name of
his most Catholic majesty, Henri III., you are our prisoner."

"Where is your leader?" demanded Crichton sternly; "to
him alone will I yield myself."

"He is here, *mon cher*," cried Joyeuse, from the top of the
pillar, "and rejoices to find you in safety. I will join you, and
render all needful explanations. Meantime, you must, perforce,
continue my prisoner. Your adversary, Prince Vincenzo, hath
yielded himself without demur."

"'Tis well," replied Crichton, throwing down his poniard.

It is needless to describe the rapturous congratulations of
Ogilvy and Blount. The former appeared so anxious to relieve
his patron from the burden of the fair singer that he at length
committed her to his care. The disciple of Knox gazed at her
with admiration, and his bosom heaved with strange but
inexpressible emotions as he held the lovely player-girl in
his arms.

"Ha!" exclaimed Crichton, turning hastily to Blount, "thy
dog—hath he reached thee?"

"He is here," replied Blount, patting Druid; "he has been

slightly hurt in this fray, poor fellow; the ball of an harquebus hath grazed his side——"

"There was a scarf twined around him—thou hast it?" demanded Crichton.

"I saw nothing," answered Blount, staring in astonishment at the question.

"A scarf," ejaculated Ogilvy; "did it contain a packet?"

"It did," rejoined Crichton. "Have you seen it?"

"'Tis here," answered Ogilvy, springing forward, and once more committing the Gelosa to his patron. "Ha! here is the sash," he cried, "and a knot of ribbons—but the packet is gone."

"Search!" said Crichton—"it may have escaped thy regards."

"It is nowhere to be found," replied Ogilvy, after a vain quest.

"Ah!" exclaimed Crichton, in a tone of anguish, "all my exertions, then, are fruitless. The prize is lost as soon as obtained."

BOOK III

CHAPTER I

HIC BIBITUR

Or, dist Pantagruel, faisons ung transon de bonne chiere, et beuvons, je vous en prie, enfans — car il faict beau boire tout ce mois.

RABELAIS, *Gargantua*, liv. ii. chap. xxx.

ON the day succeeding the events previously related, and about two hours before noon, the interior of the "Falcon" in the Rue Pélican presented a scene of much bustle and animation. The tables were covered with viands, the benches with guests. The former consisting of every variety of refection—liquid and solid —proper to a substantial Parisian breakfast of the sixteenth century; from the well-smoked ham of Bayonne and savoury sausage of Bologna, to the mild *potage de lièvre*, and unctuous *soupe de prime*. The latter exhibiting every shade of character, from the roystering student (your scholars have always been great tavern haunters) and sottish clerk of the Basoche, to the buff-jerkined musketeer and strapping sergeant of the Swiss Guard.

The walls resounded with the mingled clatter of the trencher, the flagon and the dice-box—with the shouts of laughter, and vociferations of the company, and with the rapid responses of the servitors. The air reeked with the fumes of tobacco or, as it was then called, *herbe à la reine*, pimento and garlic. Pots of hydromel, hippocras and wine served to allay the thirst which the salt meats (*compulsoir de beuvettes*, according to Rabelais) very naturally provoked, and many a deep draught was that morning drained to the health of Dame Fredegonde, the presiding divinity of the "Falcon."

In saying that the wines of Dame Fredegonde were generally approved, we merely repeated the opinion of every member of the University of Paris, whose pockets were not utterly exhausted of the necessary *métal ferruginé*, and in averring that her charms were the universal theme of admiration, we reiterated the sentiments of every jolly lansquenet, or Gascon captain of D'Epernon's *Quarante-Cinq*, whose pike had at any time been deposited at her threshold, or whose spurs jingled upon her hearth.

Attracted by the report of her comeliness, half the drinking world of Paris flocked to the "Falcon." It was the haunt of all lovers of good cheer, and a buxom hostess.

> Ah! comme en entrait
> Boire à son cabaret!

Some women there are who look old in their youth, and grow young again as they advance in life: and of these was Dame Fredegonde. At eighteen she did not appear so young, or so inviting, as at eight-and-thirty. Her person might be somewhat enlarged — what of that? Many of her admirers thought her very *embonpoint* an improvement. Her sleek black tresses, gathered in a knot at the back of her head—her smooth brow, which set care and time, and their furrows, at defiance —her soft dimpled chin—her dark laughing eyes, and her teeth, white as a casket of pearls, left nothing to be desired. You could hardly distinguish between the ring of your silver real upon her board, and the laughter with which she received it. To sum up her perfections in a word—she was a widow. As Dame Fredegonde, notwithstanding her plumpness, had a very small waist, and particularly neat ankles, she wore an extremely tight bodice, and a particularly short vertugardin; and as she was more than suspected of favouring the persecuted Huguenot party, she endeavoured to remove the impression by wearing at her girdle a long rosary of beads terminated by the white double cross of the League.

Among her guests, upon the morning in question, Dame Fredegonde numbered the Sorbonist, the Bernardin, the disciples of Harcourt and Montaigu, and one or two more of the brawling and disputatious fraternity, whose companionship we have for some time abandoned. These students were regaling themselves upon a Gargantuan gammon of ham, and a flask of malvoisie. At some distance from this party sat Blount, together with his faithful attendant Druid, who, with his enormous paws placed upon his master's knees, and his nose familiarly thrust upon the board, received no small portion of the huge chine of beef destined for the Englishman's repast. Next to Blount appeared Ogilvy, and next to the Scot, but as far removed from his propinquity as the limits of the bench would permit, sat a youth whose features were concealed from view by a broad hat, and who seemed, from his general restlessness and

impatience of manner, to be ill at ease in the society in which
accident, rather than his own choice, had thrown him.

Passing over the remainder of the company, we shall come
at once to a man-at-arms of a very prepossessing exterior,
who had established himself in close juxtaposition with the
buxom hostess. There was nothing very remarkable in the
costume of this hero. A stout buff jerkin, a coarse brown serge
cloak, a pointed felt hat with a single green feather, a long
estoc, and buff boots with great spurs—this was the sum total
of it. But there was an ease and grace in his deportment, a fire
in his eye, and a tone in his voice, that seemed scarcely to belong
to the mere common soldier, whose garb he wore. His limbs
were well proportioned—his figure tall and manly—his complexion ruddy and sunburnt—his bearing easy and unrestrained,
and his look that of one more accustomed to command than
serve. He had immense moustaches—a pointed beard—a large
nose slightly hooked, and eyes of a very amorous expression,
and taken altogether, he had the air of a person born for conquest, whether of the fair sex or of kingdoms. His way of making
love was of that hearty straightforward kind which carries all
before it. Assured of success, he was, as a matter of course,
assuredly successful. Dame Fredegonde found him perfectly
irresistible. Her last lover, the strapping Swiss sergeant, who
saw himself thus suddenly supplanted, was half frantic with
jealousy, and twisting his fingers in the long black beard that
descended to his belt, appeared to meditate with his falchion
the destruction of his fortunate rival.

So far as splendour of accoutrements went, the Swiss had
decidedly the advantage. No magpie was ever finer. His casaque,
which gave additional width to his shoulders, already broad
enough, was slashed with red and blue stripes, and girded with
a broad red band, tied in a knot and hanging down in points.
One of his stockings was red, the other white. A red garter
crossed his knee. His barret cap had a projecting steel neb like
that of a modern chasseur, with a tuft of scarlet-dyed horsehair
dangling behind. Around his throat he wore a huge ruff, down
which his beard flowed like a dark river. His sword resembled
a Moorish scimitar, while against the table by his side rested a
halberd with a double-axe head. But neither his parti-coloured
raiments, his beard, nor his gestures could draw from Dame
Fredegonde a single smile of encouragement. She was completely
monopolised by the invincible owner of the buff jerkin.

Meanwhile, the scholars had finished their malvoisie, and were calling loudly for a fresh supply. "*Hola! pulchra tabernaria*—queen of the cellar!" shouted the Sorbonist, drumming on the table to attract Dame Fredegonde's attention. "More wine here—Bordeaux, I say—*extemplo!* Leave off love-making for awhile—tear yourself from the arms of that jolly gendarme, if you can, like Helen from the embraces of Paris, *et nobis pronâ funde Falerna manû.* To the cellar, good dame—*sine Cerere et Baccho*—you know the rest; *et amphoram capacem fer cito.* Draw it neat and stint not: *respice personam, pone pro duo ; bus non est in usu,* as the good Grandgousier saith. We are in a great hurry, and as thirsty as sand-beds. *Sang de cabres! compaings,* our hostess is deaf. The combat we came to see will be over before we have done breakfast. Hola!—hola—ho!"

"And we shall look as foolish as we did yesterday," added the Bernardin, thumping upon the board with all his might, "when we found ourselves on the wrong side of the gate of the College of Navarre, during Crichton's disputation. Body of Bacchus! I faint like a traveller in Arabia the Stony. Have compassion, *speciosissima Fredegonda*—your cups are as far apart as the trieteric orgies. The tourney was proclaimed by the heralds to take place at noon, and it is now nine o' the clock. By the love you bear the Béjaunes of the university, use some dispatch, or surrender to us the key of the cellar."

"The scaffoldings are erected, and the barriers raised," cried Harcourt. "I saw the carpenters and tapestry-makers at work; the whole façade of the Louvre looking towards the gardens blazes with silk and scutcheons. Cavaliers and pages are thronging thither in all directions. 'Twill be a glorious sight! I would not miss it for my bachelor's gown."

"Nor I," rejoined Montaigu—"*Mordieu!* we shall see how Crichton comports himself to-day. It is one thing to war with words, and another with swords. He may find the brave Prince of Mantua a better match for him than our sophisters."

"He has only to deal with Gonzaga as he dealt with some dozen of your classes yesterday," observed Ogilvy, in a scornful tone, "to ensure himself as cheap a victory as he then obtained."

"Ah!—are *you* there, *mon brave Ecossois,*" cried the Sorbonist —"I did not notice you before. But one has only to whisper the name of their patron saint, Crichton, and up starts a Scot, when one least expects such an apparition. However, I am glad to see you, Sieur Ogilvy—we have an account to settle together."

"The sooner we arrange it then, the better," cried Ogilvy, drawing his dagger, and springing across the bench. "I thought

you and your rascal rout had met with your deserts at the
scourge of the hangman of the Petit Châtelet, but I care not
if your chastisement be reserved for my hands. Defend
yourself, villain."

"Not till I have eaten my breakfast," replied the Sorbonist
with considerable phlegm. "As soon as I have finished my
meal, I will assuredly do you the honour of cutting your throat.
Sede interim, quæso. We are not now in the Rue de Feurre, or
the Pré-aux-Clercs, but in the jurisdiction of the Provost of
Paris—and under the noses of the watch. I have no intention
of balking your humour, Messire Ecossois, but I have no fancy
for exhibiting myself in the Pilori des Halles to please you."

"Dastard," cried Ogilvy, "will not a blow move you?" And
he was about to deal the Sorbonist a buffet, when Dame Fredegonde, who had witnessed this altercation with some alarm,
suddenly flung herself between the disputants.

"Holy Saint Eloi!" she cried in a loud tone, "a brawl at
this time of the day—and in my reputable house too. I can
scarcely credit my senses. Put up your swords instantly, messires,
or I will summon the watch, and give you all into its charge.
Ah! you think I only threaten—you shall see. Maître Jacques,"
she added, addressing the Swiss sergeant, "this is your business.
Let tranquillity be restored."

Maître Jacques, somewhat gratified to be at length called
into notice by his inconstant mistress, stretched out his hand,
and without altering his position, dragged Ogilvy towards him,
and instantly disarmed him with as much ease apparently as
another would have taken a stick from a child, or removed its
sting from a wasp. Blount, who was a great admirer of feats
of strength, could not refuse a murmur of approbation at the
sergeant's singular exhibition of vigour.

"You shall have your sword again when you have recovered
your temper," said Maître Jacques. "By my beard," he added,
scowling at the scholars, "I will brain with my halberd the first
of you who draws his sword."

Ogilvy regarded the athletic Swiss for an instant, with eyes
glowing with indignation, and as if meditating a reprisal. But
a gentle voice from the bench recalled him to his seat, and
tranquillity was once more restored.

The soldier, who had watched the dispute and its issue with
much nonchalance, now addressed Dame Fredegonde, as she
returned to his vicinity.

"What tourney is this, *ma mie,*" he said, "of which these

brave scholars have just now spoken? You know I am only just arrived in Paris with the King of Navarre's envoy, and know nothing of court news. Who is this Crichton? What doth the Prince of Mantua, if I have heard yon student aright, in Paris? And, above all, what are the grounds of quarrel between the combatants?"

"Do you expect me to answer all those inquiries in a breath, messire?" replied Dame Fredegonde, laughing. "You need not assure me you are a stranger in Paris, since you question me about the Seigneur Crichton. Who is he? He is handsome enough to be a prince. But I believe he is only a Scottish gentleman. He is, however, the finest gentleman eyes were ever set upon. The Seigneurs Joyeuse, D'Epernon and Saint-Luc, and others of his majesty's favourites, are not to be compared with him. He is as witty as he is handsome, and as wise as he is witty. Yesterday he had a great disputation with the heads of the university, and they have not had a word to say for themselves since. To-day he jousts with the Prince of Mantua in the gardens of the Louvre at noon, and I warrant me, he will come off victorious. In short, he has but to speak and you are dumbfounded—to draw his sword, and his enemy drops at his feet—to look at a lady, and straightway she falls into his arms."

"Of a verity, a most accomplished cavalier," said the soldier, with a smile, "but you have not yet told me the occasion of his difference with the young Prince of Mantua. What is their cause of quarrel, sweetheart? Tell me that?"

"No one can tell to a certainty," replied Dame Fredegonde, mysteriously; "but the challenge was given last night at the Louvre. Some say it is about an Italian mistress"—(here the youth near Ogilvy was observed to start)—"some that the Seigneur Crichton has discovered a plot against the king's life, in which Cosmo Ruggieri and a great lady—whom nobody dares to name—together with this prince are concerned, and that in consequence the Prince of Mantua, Vincenzo, who has been for some time at the court in disguise, has defied him to mortal combat. Certes, there were strange doings at the Hôtel de Soissons last night, as the Chevalier du Guet informed me when he made his rounds. But that's no business of mine. They *do* say, also, that the Seigneur Crichton's life was twice endangered—first at the banquet by the jealousy of another great lady who is in love with him, and who poured a dose of poison into his wine."

"What great lady do you mean, *ma mie*? Surely not the Queen-Mother!"

"Holy Virgin! no," cried Fredegonde, with a scream of laughter; "the Seigneur Crichton is hardly likely to be in love with *her*."

"Who then?"

"You are very inquisitive, messire. How can it concern you to know in what way queens and other great dames revenge themselves on their lovers' infidelities?"

"*Ventre-saint-gris!* It may concern me more nearly than you imagine. You know I am from the court at Pau—from Henri of Navarre. You do not mean *his* queen?"

"I do not mean the Queen Louise, and you may, therefore, form a shrewd guess whom I *do* mean," replied Dame Fredegonde significantly. "There you will have a pretty piece of scandal to take back to your monarch. And, as I live, he could not look more blank than you do at the intelligence—ha, ha, ha!"

"*Peste!*" exclaimed the soldier, biting his lip. "And it is for this adventurer that Marguerite refuses to leave her brother's court, and to rejoin her husband."

"To be sure!—she would find your psalm-singing Béarnais rather dull after the gay galliard Crichton. But you look serious, messire?"

"Your sex is enough to make one so," replied the soldier, forcing a laugh.

> "Femmes sont secretes
> En amour discretes
> Doulces mygnonnettes
> Et tant bien parlantes,
> Mal sont profitables,
> Et fort variables
> Y sont tous les diables.

Our good Henri will care no more about the matter than i do. And hark!—those scholars are still clamorous for wine. Allow me to attend you to the cellar. You will want some help to carry that mighty flagon."

To return to Ogilvy and his companions. Blount continued sedulous in his attentions to the chine; but the Scot's appetite was gone. He swallowed a deep draught of wine, and began to hack the table with a knife. To a casual remark, addressed to him by the Englishman, he returned a sullen response. It was evident he was deeply offended. But Blount did not take his petulance in umbrage, but continued his repast in silence, ever and anon bestowing a morsel of fat upon his dog. The

Gelosa now drew nearer to the wrathful Scot, and laid her hand gently upon his arm. Ogilvy turned his inflamed cheek towards her——

"What would you?" he asked.

"I would quit this place," said Ginevra, "a presentiment of misfortune, which I cannot shake off, oppresses me. The clamour distracts me, and I am fearful those reckless scholars may recognise me. Besides," she added, with somewhat of reproach in her accent, "you but ill fulfil your patron's injunctions—you were to protect me—not to endanger my safety by provoking hostilities."

"Pardon my rashness, fair maiden," replied Ogilvy, with some confusion; "I was wrong in giving way to this foolish display of passion, but where the honour of Crichton is concerned, my feelings are irrepressible."

"I honour you for your devotion," returned the Gelosa; "and let not any thought of risk to me deter you from its manifestation. Conduct me hence, and return, if you see fitting, to avenge yourself upon yon insolent scholar."

"Impossible!" replied Ogilvy, "the escort from the Vicomte de Joyeuse which is to conduct you beyond the gates of Paris, and place you on the route to the frontiers of Italy, is not yet arrived. We must await its coming. It was the Chevalier Crichton's desire that we should do so. Fear nothing, fair maiden. I will defend you with the last drop of my blood; nor shall you again have to reproach my intemperate zeal in my patron's behalf."

"My heart misgives me," replied Ginevra, "but since it was his wish, I will remain here. I feel as if I were not yet out of the power of that terrible Gonzaga. And then," she added timidly, and blushing deeply as she spoke, "shall I confess to you, signor, that I would willingly hazard my safety by remaining in Paris—nay, within the precincts of the Louvre, to witness this tourney. If Vincenzo fall, I have nothing to fear."

"But from Ruggieri—from Catherine you may still apprehend peril," returned Ogilvy; "besides know you not that the king has commanded a combat à *plaisance* and not à *outrance*? The prince may be worsted, therefore—but not slain. Your danger will not be diminished by the result of this conflict."

A burst of noisy merriment from the scholars here broke upon them, and the following irreverent Bacchanalian lay was chanted at the top of his voice by the Sorbonist, the other students joining in chorus:

VENITE POTEMUS [1]

I

Venite, jovial sons of Hesper,
Who from matin unto vesper,
  Roam abroad *sub Domino*;
Benedictine, Carmelite,
Quaff we many a flask to-night
  Salutari nostro.
If the wine be, as I think,
Fit for reverend lips to drink
  Jubilemus ei.
Ecce bonum vinum, venite potemus!

II

Hodie, when cups are full,
Not a thought or care should dull
  Corda vestra—
Eat your fill—the goblet quaff,
Sufficient is the wine thereof
  Secundum diem:—
What care I—if huge in size
My paunch should wax?—it testifies
  Opera mea.
Venite potemus!

III

Quadraginta years and more
I've seen; and jolly souls some score
  Proximus fui;
And life throughout, have ever thought,
That they, who tipple ale that's naught,
  Errant corde:
Yea, in my choler waxing hot,
I sware sour beer should enter not
  In requiem meam.
Ecce bonum vinum, venite potemus!

The reappearance of Dame Fredegonde and the soldier bearing a capacious stoup of claret had given rise to this effusion of the Sorbonist, and as each goblet was now filled to the brim, after having been previously emptied, general hilarity prevailed among the thirsty scions of the university. The Bernardin insisted upon the soldier taking a seat beside him, and the Sorbonist deemed it incumbent upon him to present a flagon of the ruby fluid to Maître Jacques, who drained it in a breath.

"*Lans tringue!*" cried the scholar of Harcourt, slapping the soldier on the shoulder, "I drink to thee. Thou hast given us good measure and good wine, i'faith. May our buxom hostess

[1] Adapted from an old French *Imitatoyre Bachique.*

never want such a cellarist—nor ourselves such a drawer—
ha, ha!

Remplis ton verre vuide,
Vuide ton verre plein."

"I will not refuse thy pledge, comrade," replied the soldier,
"though my brain will not brook many such strong assaults so
early in the morning. Here is to thy election to the dignity of
chaplain at the next *Fête de Fous.*"

"Jest not with me, *compaing,* but drink," retorted Harcourt,
angrily, "it were thy safer course. Ah! thou refusest. I discern
something of the Huguenot about thee. I heard thee tell our
hostess just now thou wert from the head-quarters of the
Béarnais. One might guess as much from thy neglect of the
flask and devotion to the petticoats—*dignum patella operculum.*
Ah! if it were ever to occur that thy master should be king of
France, a pretty time we should have of it! The good old days
of François I. would be revived with a vengeance. Not a husband
in Paris could rest in his bed. The saints defend us from such a
consummation. Well, I bear him no ill-will—here's to Alcandre."

"*Maranatha!*" exclaimed the Sorbonist, "that must not pass.
We will be Catholic even in our cups. Thy pledge is heretical
and schismatic. Rather let us drink confusion to the Béarnais,
the Reform, and the Church of Geneva, and success to the
League, the true Church and the brave Balafré!"

"To the Holy Union!" cried the Bernardin.

"To the Pope!" shouted Montaigu.

"To Beelzebub!" roared Harcourt. "I will hurl my wine-cup
in his face who refuses my pledge—Henri of Navarre, and the
Huguenot cause!"

"By the mass, I scent heresy in thy pledge, and refuse it,"
returned the Sorbonist. The words were scarcely out of his
mouth when he received the contents of the scholar of Harcourt's
flagon in his face.

In an instant all was confusion. Swords were drawn and
crossed, and the table nearly upset in the confusion that ensued,
but, by the united efforts of Blount, who had now formed one
of the party, and the Swiss sergeant, the combatants were
separated, and tranquillity for the second time restored. The
cause of the disturbance, meantime, our nonchalant soldier,
so far from taking any share in the struggle, leaned back in
his chair, and indulged in an immoderate fit of laughter.

"How now, thou insensible varlet!" cried Harcourt, whose
furious countenance and ruffled demeanour presented a singular

contrast to his companion's apathy, "hast thou never a sword to draw in thy sovereign's behalf, or grace enough to thank him who is ready to fight thy battles for thee? By my soul, I was wrong. Brother of the Sorbonne, thy hand. Thou wert in the right to object to my rascal pledge. *Ventre-Saint-Quintin!* from a Huguenot one gets neither aid nor acknowledgment."

"The quarrel was of thine own seeking, comrade," returned the soldier, with increased merriment; "I pressed thee not into my service—the good cause of the Reformed Faith needs no such blustering advocate as thou, and the Béarnais will not laugh a whit the less loudly because one sot drinks to his success, and another to his confusion."

"Fairly spoken," cried Montaigu, "for a Huguenot our reformado hath the air of an honest fellow. A truce to raillery, comrades! *Favete linguis.* These brawls interfere with drinking. Let us have a song to restore us to harmony. *Chantons, beuvons ung motet,* as glorious old Rabelais hath it."

"*Entonnons*," cried the others, laughing.

"What shall it be?" asked the soldier.

> "Le chanson de la Peronelle,
> La vie de Monsieur Saint Françoys,
> La Confiteor des Angloys,

or the merry burden of some farce, sotie, or joyous discourse?"

"*La Réformeresse*, for instance," retorted Montaigu, vociferating at the top of his voice:

> "To Paris, that good city,
>   Navarre's young king is come,
> And flock forth the damsels pretty,
>   At the beating of his drum.
> But the fairest 'mid the crowd, sirs,
>   The loveliest of the lot,
> Is a nymph, who cries aloud, sirs,
> To the church, sire, you go not,
>   *Huguenot!*

"E'en give us what thou wilt, my puissant Hector: so thy strains savour not of the nasal melodies of Théodore Beza, or the canticles of Clément Marot, they will be right welcome."

"Lend me your voices in full chorus, then," replied the soldier, "and respond to my litany." And, in a deep tone, he sang as follows:

> From all men, who, counsel scorning,
> To the tavern hie at morning
> With Latin base their talk adorning,
>   *Libera nos, Domine.*

> From all those, who night and day,
> Cards and raiment cast away,
> At cards and dice and other play,
> *Libera nos, Domine.*

"*Satis superque,*" shouted Montaigu, "thy rogation toucheth me too nearly, as testifieth the tattered state of my *exponibles,* to be altogether satisfactory—*Hei mihi!*

> *Alea, vina, Venus, tribus his sum factus egenus.*

Sed parum est. I have still a few liards left, and when my pouch is utterly evacuate, I can turn Huguenot or hang myself—it matters little which. In the meantime——" and here the reckless youth once more broke into song:

SONG OF THE SCHOLAR [1]

I

> A jolly life enough I lead—that is *semper quam possum;*
> When mine host inviteth me, I answer *ecce assum!*
> Women, wine and wassailry *lubens libenter colo,*
> And after meals to pass the time *chartis ludisque volo,*
> Unluckily these games are not *omnino sine dolo.*

II

> Wine to tipple I conceive *quod fui generatus,*
> Treasure to amass, indeed, I doubt if I was *natus,*
> Never yet with coin enough was I *locupletatus,*
> Or, with a superfluity, *vehementer excitatus—*
> *Despice divitias si vis animo esse beatus.*

III

> Whither are my raiments fled? *amice mi!—si quæris,*
> Quaffed they were in flowing cups *in tempore (heu!) veris;*
> Thus am I obliged to roam *subhorridus per vicos,*
> Herding amidst truand rogues *et alios iniquos:*
> *Cum fueris felix multos numerabis amicos!*

"*Bellissime!*" cried the soldier. "Thy case is a hard one, I must needs admit, comrade. But thou art a likely lad, and I promise thee, if thou wilt accompany me to the King of Navarre's camp, whither I set out this morning, and wilt forswear thy roystering habits, and embrace the true doctrine, I will put thee in a way of lining thy pouch with weightier pieces than any it now holds, and of replacing thy threadbare apparel with the hacquetoon and habergeon of the Bourbon."

"Weighty blows are said to abound more than weighty pieces

[1] An adaptation of a few verses of a Macaronic poem of little merit, entitled *Des fames, des dez, et de la taverne,* appended to the last edition of the *Fabliaux et Contes des Poètes François.*

in thy king's psalm-singing camp," returned Montaigu, "and
I must be bribed by present payment if I vend my soul to
Messire Sathanas. But come," he added, filling his goblet, "let
us drink between our songs, and sing between our draughts.
Ædepol! my jolly missioner *ad partes infidelium,* thou hast the
throat of a nightingale, and warblest a song divinely, and as
thou art chary of the flask, wilt have the more leisure to divert
us with another stave."

"*Ventre-saint-gris,*" muttered the soldier, smiling to himself;
"could my faithful Rosni have foreseen, that, during his absence,
I should play the lover to a buxom *aubergiste,* the buffoon to
a pack of losel scholars, and the rebel to myself, I had not
escaped a lecture as long as ever John Calvin pronounced from
his pulpit at Geneva. No matter: the monotony of life must
be relieved, and he is a wise man who makes the most of the
passing moment."

With this philosophical reflection, he yielded to the scholar's
importunities. It has been observed before, that his countenance
was remarkable for its frankness and cordiality. It had, besides,
an indescribable expression of comic humour, which broadened
and brightened as he proceeded with his vocal performance,
into a glow of such irresistible drollery, that his auditors were
almost convulsed with laughter, and, as real mirth is always
contagious, the infection was speedily communicated to every
guest of the "Falcon," the pensive and dolorous Ogilvy not
excepted.

THE CHRONICLE OF GARGANTUA:

Showing how he took away the Great Bells of Notre-Dame

I

Grandgousier was a toper boon, as Rabelais will tell ye,
Who, once upon a time, got drunk with his old wife Gargamelly:
Right royally the bout began (no queen was more punctilious
Than Gargamelle) on chitterlings, botargos, godebillios! [1]
   Sing, *Carimari, carimara! golynoly, golynolo!*

II

They licked their lips, they cut their quips—a flask then each selected;
And with good Greek, as satin sleek, their gullets they humected.
Rang stave and jest, the flask they pressed—but ere away the wine went,
Occurred most unexpectedly Queen Gargamelle's confinement!
   Sing, *Carimari, carimara! golynoly, golynolo!*

[1] Gaudebillaux sont grasses trippes de coiraux. Coiraux sont bœufz
engresses à la creche, et prés guimaulx. Prés guimaulx sont qui portent
herbe deux foys l'an.—*Gargantua,* liv. i. chap. iv.

III

No sooner was GARGANTUA born, than from his infant throttle,
Arose a most melodious cry to his nurse to bring the bottle!
Whereat Grandgousier much rejoiced—as it seemed, unto his thinking,
A certain sign of a humour fine for most immoderate drinking!
    Sing, *Carimari, carimara! golynoly, golynolo!*

IV

Gargantua shot up, like a tower some city looking over!
His full-moon visage in the clouds, leagues off, ye might discover!
His gracious person he arrayed—I do not mean to laugh at ye—
With a suit of clothes, and great trunk hose, of a thousand ells of taffety.
    Sing, *Carimari, carimara! golynoly, golynolo!*

V

Around his waist Gargantua braced a belt of silk bespangled,
And from his hat, as a platter flat, a long blue feather dangled;
And down his hip, like the mast of ship, a rapier huge descended,
With a dagger keen, stuck his sash between, all for ornament intended.
    Sing, *Carimari, carimara! golynoly, golynolo!*

VI

So learned did Gargantua grow, that he talked like one whose turn is
For logic, with a sophister, hight Tubal Holofernes.
In Latin, too, he lessons took from a tutor old and seedy,
Who taught the "*Quid Est,*" and the "*Pars,*"—one Jobelin de Bridé!
    Sing, *Carimari, carimara! golynoly, golynolo!*

VII

A monstrous mare Gargantua rode—a black Numidian courser—
A beast so droll, of filly or foal, was never seen before, sir!
Great elephants looked small as ants, by her side—her hoofs were cloven!
Her tail was like the spire at Langes—her mane like goat-beards woven!
    Sing, *Carimari, carimara! golynoly, golynolo!*

VIII

Upon this mare Gargantua rode until he came to Paris,
Which, from Utopia's capital, as we all know, rather far is—
The thundering bells of Notre-Dame, he took from out the steeple,
And he hung them round his great mare's neck in the sight of all the people!
    Sing, *Carimari, carimara! golynoly, golynolo!*

IX

Now, what Gargantua did beside, I shall pass by without notice,
As well as the absurd harangue of that wiseacre Janotus;
But the legend tells that the thundering bells Bragmardo brought away, sir,
And that in the towers of Notre-Dame they are swinging to this day, sir!
    Sing, *Carimari, carimara! golynoly, golynolo!*

X

Now the great deeds of Gargantua—how his father's foes he followed—
How pilgrims six, with their staves and scrips, in a lettuce leaf he
    swallowed—
How he got blind drunk with a worthy monk, Friar Johnny of the Funnels—
And made huge cheer, till the wine and beer flew about his camp in runnels—
    Sing, *Carimari, carimara! golynoly, golynolo!*

XI

How he took to wife, to cheer his life, fat Badebec the moper;
And by her begat a lusty brat, Pantagruel the toper!
And did other things, as the story sings, too long to find a place here,
Are they not writ, with matchless wit, by Alcofribas Nasier? [1]
      Sing, *Carimæri, carimara! golynoly, golynolo!*

As the soldier brought his song to a close, amid the thundering
applause and inextinguishable laughter of the scholars, his own
exhilaration was considerably damped by the sudden appearance
of two new-comers, who had entered the cabaret, unobserved,
during his performance, and with looks sufficiently expressive
of their disapprobation of his conduct, held themselves aloof
until the termination of his strains, when they slowly approached
the table.

The foremost of these personages was a man of middle age
and severe aspect, fully equipped in the accoutrements of a
military leader of the period; but his breastplate, though of
the brightest Milan steel, was wholly destitute of ornament,
and resembled rather, in its heavy and cumbrous form, an
antique cuirass of the age of Bayard and Gaston de Foix, than
the lacquered and embossed armour worn by the knighthood
of the court of France. A tall plume nodded upon his morion,
and a long two-handed sword, called in the language of the
tilt-yard a *gagne-pain*, was girded to his thigh. The hand, able
to wield such a blade with ease, could not, it was evident, be
deficient in energy. From his right hip hung the long and
trenchant dagger, termed, from its use in combat, a *miséricorde.*
His companion was habited in the black Geneva cloak and band,
constituting the attire of a preacher of the Reformed Faith. He
was a venerable man, with silver hair streaming upon his
shoulders from beneath his black silk calotte. His figure was
bent by age and infirmities, and his steps needed the support
of a staff, but the fire which yet blazed in his deep-seated grey
eye, showed that the ardour and enthusiasm of his youthful
spirit was still unextinguished.

"*Diable!*" mentally exclaimed the soldier, pushing aside his
seat and rising to greet the strangers. "Rosni here—and my old
preceptor Doctor Florent Chrétien. *Parbleu!* Their arrival at
this juncture is unlucky. But I must put the best face I can
upon the matter." And, as these thoughts passed rapidly
through his mind, he reverently saluted the minister, and
exchanging a significant look with the knight, the party ad-
journed to a more retired part of the cabaret.

      [1] The anagram of François Rabelais.

"I did not expect to find your majesty thus occupied," observed Rosni, in a tone of reproach, as soon as they were out of hearing of the company. "Methinks the wise and valiant Henri of Navarre might have more profitably as well as worthily employed his leisure, than by administering to the amusements, and sharing in the pastimes of these unlicensed and idolatrous brawlers."

"Tush, Rosni," replied Henri of Bourbon, "I am *not* a monarch with these revellers, and were I to vouch any explanation to thee, with whom I *am* a king, I could offer such reasons for my conduct as would convince thee, that what I have done has been without impeachment of my 'valour and wisdom,' and was merely undertaken to sustain my character as a soldier."

"Your character as a soldier would have been better sustained by repressing licence than abetting it, sire," returned Rosni, bluntly. "Had I been in your majesty's place, and these riotous Edomites had pressed me to make music for them, I would have treated them to a psalm, such as our pious Calvin hath himself appointed for the recreation of the faithful, or to one of those mournful ballads so displeasing to the enemies of our religion, wherein their own sanguinary atrocities are sternly set forth, and the sufferings of our martyrs painfully recorded."

"And have been laughed at for thy pains," said Henri. "Trust me, my expedient was the wiser one."

At this moment the voice of the scholars again rose loud in song, and the following chorus reached the ears of the King of Navarre and his companions:

> A merry company are we
> Who spend our lives in revelry,
> Self-nicknamed *Enfans-sans-souci!*
> *Cric, croc, cric, croc, la, la!*

"*Ohé!* soldier of the true faith," shouted Montaigu, "another song before we start for the tourney! Heed not thy captain's reprimand. We will bear thee harmless."

"Thou hearest," said Henri, smiling, "those *enfans-sans-souci*, as they not inaptly term themselves, are clamorous for my return. *Ventre-saint-gris!* Rosni, I am half disposed to send thee to them as my substitute. I would gladly see what effect one of thy doleful ditties would have upon their high-flown spirits. Wilt take my seat at yon table?"

"I will obey your majesty's behests," replied Rosni gravely ‑‑"but I wash my hands of the consequences."

"Go, then," replied Henri, laughing; "thou deservest some

punishment for thy imprudence. What, in the devil's name, induced thee to bring old Chrétien to this 'meeting of the mockers,' and 'seat of the scornful,' as he would call it? Thy former experience might have led thee to expect some such untoward accident as the present, and it should be rather thy business to draw a veil over thy sovereign's foibles than to betray them."

"I shall observe more caution in future," returned Rosni, in a tone of irony, "but after his own involuntary promise of amendment, it ill became me to doubt my sovereign's maintenance of his word. Doctor Florent Chrétien, whom I chanced upon at the Protestant consistory in the Faubourg Saint-Germain, this morning, hath a matter of importance to communicate to your majesty's private ear, and to that end I ventured to bring him hither."

"Thou hast done well, Rosni," replied the king; "nevertheless, I cannot pretermit the punishment I have imposed on thee. Hark! my comrades call thee—go and join them."

Again the chorus of the scholars arose above the general clamour, and the Sorbonist was heard vociferating the following verses:

SONG OF THE SORBONIST

Death to the Huguenot! faggot and flame!
Death to the Huguenot! torture and shame!
                            Death! Death!

Heretics' lips sue for mercy in vain,
Drown their loud cries in the waters of Seine!
                            Drown! Drown!

Hew down, consume them with fire and with sword!
A good work ye do in the sight of the Lord!
                            Kill! Kill!

Hurl down their temples! their ministers slay!
Let them bleed as they bled on Barthélemy's day!
                            Slay! Slay!

A roar of insolent laughter followed this effusion. Henri of Navarre bit his lips.

"Go," he said, frowning, "leave me with Chrétien."

"By the holy evangel! I will make these accursed mass-mongers such sport as Samson showed the Philistines," returned Rosni. "But before I quit your presence, sire, I must acquaint you that your escort is in readiness at the Porte Montmartre, and that two of my followers with your steed await your coming forth at the door of this cabaret."

"Let them wait," answered the king, sharply. "I shall not set out upon my journey till the evening."

"How, sire?" asked Rosni.

"It is my intention to attend the jousts held this morning at the Louvre."

"But your majesty——"

"Is resolved to have my own way—so thou mayest spare me further remonstrances on that head, Rosni. Not only will I witness this tourney, but break a lance at it myself in honour of the queen my spouse; though I freely confess she deserves no such attention at my hands, after her refusal to join me where she deems I now am, at my court at Pau. But let that pass. There is a Scottish cavalier, who hath boasted, as it seems to me, somewhat indiscreetly, of Marguerite's favours towards him, whether truly or not signifies little, as I hold secrecy to be the first duty of a gallant. I have a fancy for lowering this prattling mignon's crest, the rather that he is reputed an expert tilter, and as such not unworthy of my lance. And it may chance if Marguerite sees her favourite laid low, she may change her mind as to returning with me. At all events I shall attend this tourney in the quality of a knight-adventurer. Thou shalt ride forth with me anon, and procure me suitable equipments. My own steed will bear me bravely through the day."

"Your majesty shall commit no such folly," replied Rosni, bluntly.

"Baron de Rosni," exclaimed Henri haughtily, "we have honoured thee thus far with our friendship—but there are limits to our good nature which even *you* shall not exceed."

"Pardon my bluntness, sire," returned Rosni, "but at the hazard of forfeiting your favour I would step between you and the peril to which you expose yourself thus rashly. When your faithful counsellors reluctantly consented to your coming hither on this fruitless embassy to a queen who loves you not, but who partakes of the perfidious and inconstant nature of her family —when, I say, they consented to your accompanying your own messengers, in disguise, my life was pledged for your safe return. That life is nothing. But upon your security, sire, hangs the fate of a kingdom, and the prosperity of a pure and holy faith of which you are the defender and champion. Bethink you of the cause in which you have embarked—of your zealous followers —of the whole Protestant world, whose eyes are fixed upon you —bethink you also of the risk you run—of the inevitable consequences attendant upon a discovery of your presence—of your long captivity in the walls of the Louvre from which you have so recently escaped. Think of all this, and blame (if you can) the zeal which prompts me to speak thus boldly."

"Leave me, sir," replied Henri, "I would speak with my old preceptor. You shall know my determination anon."

Rosni bowed and took the place assigned to him by the monarch at the table of the revellers. His arrival was greeted with loud laughter, and many muttered allusions from the reckless crew to his Huguenot principles.

"Hark ye, messires," said Rosni, "you have prevailed upon one of my troop to sing for you, and in return have favoured us with one of those ferocious melodies which your brethren howled to the thundering tocsin of the bloody day of Saint-Barthélemy. Ye shall now have my response. But first I charge ye let your goblets be filled to the brim, and drink the pledge I shall propose to you: 'The downfall of Antichrist, the extermination of the League, and the universal establishment of the True Faith.' Ha! you hesitate. By the evangel! messires, I will thrust my poniard into his throat who refuses my pledge." So saying he drew his dagger and glanced fiercely round the group.

A stern silence succeeded this speech. The mirth of the scholars was suddenly checked. Each one glanced at his neighbour, as if he expected he would resent the insult. But no one dared to do so openly.

"I am with you, Sir Knight," exclaimed Blount. "I will see that all obey you."

"The pledge!" said Rosni, seizing the scholar of Harcourt by the throat, and forcing him to pronounce the hateful words, and afterwards to wash them down with a deep draught of wine.

"By Saint Thomas, thou escapest not," cried Blount, grappling with the Sorbonist.

"Not one shall escape me," said Rosni; "he shall drink it, or die the death."

Accordingly, seeing resistance was in vain against armed force like that of the knight, the scholars sullenly complied.

"I have not yet done with you, messires," said Rosni, in a tone of mockery; "I will not insult the religion I profess, by allowing blasphemers like yourselves to take part in its holy psalms, but as you have rung in my ears the death-knell of our slaughtered saints, ye shall listen to the judgment called down from on high for that offence upon the head of the late treacherous and bloodthirsty sovereign, Charles IX. Stir not, neither offer any interruption, as ye would avoid a sudden and speedy doom."

"Lend me your dagger, Sir Knight," said Ogilvy, unable to control his choler, and springing towards the table, "and I will compel as attentive audience to your strains as ever was accorded to the sermons of our pious Knox."

"And as willing," said the Bernardin with a sneer.

"Take that in earnest of the chastisement I will inflict upon him who shall disobey the knight's commands." said Ogilvy, bestowing a sounding buffet upon the scholar's cheek, adding fiercely, as he received the *miséricorde* from Rosni, "the first of you who speaketh a word of offence breathes his last."

Amid the glances of defiance and suppressed rage cast upon him by the scholars, the knight, in a deep stern tone, sang the following ballad:

CHARLES IX. AT MONTFAUCON

I

"To horse—to horse!" thus spake King Charles, "to horse, my lords, with me!
Unto Montfaucon will we ride—a sight you there shall see."
"Montfaucon, sire!" said his esquire—"what sight, my liege, how mean ye?"
"The carcass stark of the traitor dark, and heretic Coligni."

II

The trumpets bray, their chargers neigh a loud and glad réveillé—
And plaudits ring, as the haughty king from the Louvre issues gaily:
On his right hand rides his mother, with her dames—a gorgeous train—
On his left careers his brother, with the proud Duke of Lorraine.

III

Behind is seen his youthful queen—the meek Elizabeth [1]—
With her damsels bright, whose talk is light of the sad, sad show of death:—
Ah, lovely ones!—ah, gentle ones! from the scoffer's judgment screen ye!—
Mock not the dust of the martyr'd just, for of such was good Coligni.

IV

By foot up-hung, to flesh-hook strung, is now revealed to all,
Mouldering and shrunk, the headless trunk of the good old admiral:

[1] Elizabeth of Austria, daughter of the Emperor Maximilian, an amiable and excellent princess, whose genuine piety presented a striking contrast to the sanguinary fanaticism of her tyrannical and neglectful spouse. "O mon Dieu!" she cried, on the day of the massacre, of which she had been kept in ignorance; "quels conseillers sont ceux-là, qui ont donné le roi tel avis? Mon Dieu! je te supplie, et je requiers de lui pardonner, car si tu n'en as pitié j'ai grand peur que cette offense ne lui soit pas pardonnée."

Gash-visaged Guise the sight doth please — fierce lord, was naught
    between ye?
In felon blow of base Poltrot [1] no share had brave Coligni.

V

"Now, by God's death!" the monarch saith, with inauspicious smile,
As laughing, group the reckless troop round grey Montfaucon's pile;
"From off that hook its founder shook—Enguerrand de Marigni—[2]
But gibbet chain did ne'er sustain such burden as Coligni."

VI

"Back! back! my liege," exclaimed a page, "with death the air is tainted,
The sun grows hot, and see you not, good sire, the queen has fainted."
"Let those retire," quoth Charles in ire, "who think they stand too nigh ;
To us no scent yields such content as a dead enemy." [3]

VII

As thus he spake the king did quake—he heard a dismal moan—
A wounded wretch had crept to stretch his bones beneath that stone:—
"Of dying man," groaned he, "the ban, the Lord's anointed dread,
My curse shall cling to thee, O king!—much righteous blood thou'st shed."

VIII

"Now by Christ's blood!—by holy Rood!" cried Charles, impatiently;
"With sword and pike—strike, liegemen, strike!—God's death! this man
    shall die."
Straight halberd crashed, and matchlock flashed—but ere a shot was fired—
With laugh of scorn that wight forlorn had suddenly expired.

IX

From the Louvre gate, with heart elate, King Charles that morn did ride
With aspect dern did he return, quenched was his glance of pride:—
Remorse and ruth, with serpent tooth, thenceforth seized on his breast—
With bloody tide his couch was dyed—pale visions broke his rest! [4]

[1] Jean Poltrot de Méré, the assassin of François de Guise, father of the
Balafré, probably, in order to screen himself, accused Coligni and Beza
of being the instigators of his offence. His flesh was afterwards torn from
his bones by red-hot pincers, but Henri of Lorraine never considered his
father's death fully avenged until the massacre of the admiral. Coligni's
head was sent by Catherine de Medicis to Rome as an offering to
Gregory XIII. Upon this occasion the Pope had a medal struck off,
stamped with an exterminating angel and subscribed *Ugonotorum Strages.*

[2] *Pereat suâ arte Perillus.* Enguerrand de Marigni, Grand Chamberlain
of France during the reign of Philippe-le-Bel, constructed the famous
gibbet of Montfaucon, and was himself among the first to glut its horrible
fourches patibulaires, whence originated the ancient adage, "Plus mal-
heureux que le bois dont on fait le gibet."

[3] Ensuite Coligni fut traîné aux fourches patibularies de Montfaucon.
Le Roi vint jouir de ce spectacle, et s'en montra insatiable. On ne concevait
pas qu'il pût résister à une telle odeur; on le pressait de se retirer. *Non,*
dit-il, *le cadavre d'un ennemi sent toujours bon!*—LACRETELLE.

[4] La maladie de Charles IX. était accompagnée de symptômes plus
violens qu'on n'en remarque dans les maladies de langueur; sa poitrine
était particulièrement affectée; mais son sang coulait par tous les pores;
d'affreux souvenirs persécutaient sa pensée dans un lit toujours
baigné de sang; il voulait et ne pouvait pas s'arracher de cette place.—
LACRETELLE, *Histoire de France pendant les Guerres de Religion.*

As the Baron de Rosni concluded his song, a sullen murmur arose amongst the scholars, deepening as it proceeded, until it took the character of an angry groan.

"*Par la Porte d'Enfer*, which once conducted the neophyte to our halls," muttered Harcourt. "I would as soon die with the Confession of Augsburg upon my lips as listen to such another ditty. Coligni's own epitaph would make a sprightlier lay:

> Cy gist, mais c'est mal entendu,
> Ce mot pour luy est trop honneste,
> Icy l'Admiral est pendu
> Par les pieds à faute de teste!"

"Par les pieds à faute de tête!" chorused the others, with a roar of derisive laughter.

"Peace, on your lives," cried Ogilvy, with a threatening gesture.

"By the memory of the good Thomas Crucé, who slaughtered eighty of these schismatics with his proper hand," whispered the Sorbonist to the scholar of Harcourt, "I will wash out the affront put upon us, in the blood of that accursed Scot—*offensam ense vindicabo*."

"My blade shall second you," returned Harcourt in the same tone.

CHAPTER II

THE HUGUENOT

> Chaque mot qu'il disait était un trait de flamme,
> Qui pénétrait Henri jusqu'au fond de son âme.
> Il quitte avec regret ce vieillard vertueux;
> Des pleurs en l'embrassant coulèrent de ses yeux.
> VOLTAIRE, *Henriade*, chant 1.

No sooner had Rosni quitted his sovereign's presence than the venerable Florent Chrétien, approaching Henri, took his hand and pressed it fervently to his lips. As the king withdrew his fingers from the old man's grasp, he perceived they were wet with his tears.

"Nay, by my faith, my excellent friend," he said, in a tone of great kindness, "this must not be. Tears from such eyes as yours are reproaches too cutting for endurance. I had rather you would chide me in the harshest terms you could employ, than assail me with the only weapons against which I am not proof. What would you have me do?"

"Does not your own great and generous heart, my liege,"

returned the minister, "which prompts you to interpret the overflowing of an anxious breast into rebuke, tell you what course you ought to pursue? Does it not point out to you that your life, precious in itself—but oh! of inestimable value to all members of our pure religion, to whom you are as Joshua or Maccabæus, may not be lightly imperilled by your own act without manifest departure from that high course, which the King of kings hath appointed you to run, and which in due season, if you remain true to yourself, and to your cause, you will doubtless gloriously accomplish. Well and truly hath your faithful follower the Baron de Rosni spoken, when he averred that on your safety depends that of the true Church of Christ; and not in vain will my tears have been shed, if they avail to turn you from these vanities, and recall your nobler nature. Better I should lament than your enemies rejoice. Better one should blush in secret than a whole kingdom be turned to shame for its sovereign's defection. Cast off this slavery of the senses. Yield not to the devices and snares of the Prince of Darkness. You are our guardian, our bulwark, our tower of strength. Pause ere you wantonly expose our decimated flocks to the further ravages of these devouring wolves."

As he spoke, the old man's eyes glistened, and his looks kindled till his glowing countenance wore an air of apostolic fervour that produced, more than his words, a strong impression upon the king.

"Rest assured, my good friend," replied Henri, "I will in no way compromise my own security, or that of the Church over whose welfare I watch, and in whose behalf I have raised my banner. I have other and stronger motives than the mere love of such a pageant which attract me to these jousts, but I give you my word as a king, that I will place neither my life nor my personal safety in needless jeopardy. And now," he added, with a smile, "thanking you for your admonitory counsels, which, as you well know, are seldom pleasant in royal ears, and having scarce leisure for a longer homily, or even for further conference at this moment, let us turn to your own peculiar concerns. If you have any communication to make, delay it not. I am impatient to know how I can serve you."

"It is not in my own behalf that I would claim your majesty's services," rejoined the preacher, "but in that of one in whom you yourself are nearly interested. Know, sire, that a sister of the Prince of Condé is at this moment a captive in the hands of the bloody Jezebel of France. It is for her deliverance from thraldom and oppression that I solicit your aid; and if you *are* resolved to expose yourself to needless risk, let it be to effect the liberation of a princess of your own royal blood, a zealous believer in our creed, and in the eyes of a searcher of knightly adventure, for as such I must regard your majesty, a distressed and forlorn damsel."

"If this, indeed, were as you represent it, my good friend," replied Henri, "you should have my instant aid, even though it were needful to bear her from the Louvre with my handful of men. But you have been deceived by some false statement. Our cousin of Condé has no sister at the court of France."

"The prince believes she perished in her infancy, sire," returned the preacher, "but her preservation from the sword of those fierce Amalekites, who beset the good Louis de Bourbon on his flight to Rochelle was little less than miraculous, as you will find when I relate to you the history of this unfortunate princess, as it was delivered to me by one of the attendants of the Queen-Mother, who hath recently become a convert to our faith."

"Your information is derived from a suspicious quarter, messire," returned the king with a smile of incredulity. "Catherine's *cameriere* are as deceitful to the full as the daughters of the Philistines. I know them of old. Your proselyte may prove a Delilah after all, and her specious story only a snare laid to entrap you. Our uncle, Louis de Bourbon, it is true, hath often spoken of the hapless fate of his infant daughter in the mountain defiles near Sancerre, but he believed, nay, was assured, that she perished."

"Credit me, sire, she lives," replied Chrétien. And he then succinctly detailed such particulars of Esclairmonde's story as are already familiar to the reader—adding that the princess had been hitherto kept in ignorance of her illustrious origin from a fear lest some inadvertence, not unnatural on the part of one so young and inexperienced, should betray her consciousness of her real rank and condition to the suspicions of Catherine, and militate against any plans formed for her deliverance. The preacher likewise stated that he had been summoned at an early hour on that morning to the Louvre by Annunziata (the attendant from whom he had obtained his knowledge of this important secret) to visit Esclairmonde—that she had revealed to him, without reserve, the events of the preceding night—imploring him to free her from the persecution of her royal lover, who, it appeared, had dispatched a *billet*, stating that if she offered further opposition to his passion he would denounce her as a heretic to the inquisition of the Catholic priesthood. "She was bathed in tears when I entered the chamber," said Chrétien, "and at first refused to be comforted, but deeming the proper period arrived for its disclosure, I acquainted her with the illustrious stock from which she sprang, and besought her to comport herself like a descendant of that royal house."

"Ha! *Corbleu!* how received she the intelligence?"

"Like a daughter of the race of Bourbon," replied Chrétien. "Her grief was at once checked, and she conferred calmly and deliberately with me upon the means of her evasion. One circumstance alone appeared to give her uneasiness—but I doubt whether I am at liberty to mention it to your majesty."

"Do not mention it, then, my good friend," returned the king, "if it is aught the princess would not wish to be divulged to me."

"It is, however, desirable, I think, that your majesty should be acquainted with the state of her heart, the rather that you may form a judgment——"

"Whether the alliance be suitable, ha! messire. What cavalier has been so fortunate as to ingratiate himself into the good opinion of this captive princess?"

"A Scottish gentleman, my liege, who hath greatly distinguished himself at the court of your royal brother of France— the Chevalier Crichton."

"*Mort de ma vie!*" exclaimed Henri, angrily, "doth *he* aspire to her hand?"

"Your majesty forgets that he knew her only as one of Queen Catherine's maids of honour."

"True," replied the king sternly, "but she is now our cousin, and as such no mate for an adventurer."

"It was her sense of this change in her condition, my liege, and of the impassable bar placed between her and her lover that gave her so much pain: nor was her uneasiness diminished, when she learnt, as she shortly afterwards did, from a missive conveyed to her from the Chevalier Crichton, that he had by accident made the discovery of her exalted origin, and at the peril of his life wrested the proofs of it from Catherine's own hands, but in his endeavour to transmit the packet to her, while he was yet in the power of the Queen-Mother, it had been irrecoverably lost."

"*Ventre-saint-gris!*" exclaimed Henri. "Were there such proofs?"

"The Chevalier Crichton affirmed that the packet contained letters from the Queen-Mother, the Maréchal de Tavannes, and the Cardinal of Lorraine."

"*Diable!*" cried the king, with vivacity. "Those letters were well worth the risk of a life, and would have obviated the necessity of bringing forward the scarce credible statement of your proselyte Annunziata. Heaven grant they have not fallen again into Catherine's clutches! It was a bold deed to tear her prey from the lioness, and this Crichton hath proved himself a cavalier of no mean prowess. One question more, good Chrétien; did not this Scottish knight promise to finish his adventure by delivering our captive cousin?"

"Of a verity, my liege, he did so," returned the preacher with some reluctance.

"I knew as much," said Henri, smiling; "Esclairmonde is now at the Louvre?—ha!"

"In the train of Queen Louise, whom she accompanies at noon to the lists, where, by his majesty's commands, she presides as sovereign arbitress. To-night there is a new fête and masque . at the Louvre. Before that time she must be delivered from thraldom, or her fate is sealed."

"Before that hour she *shall* be delivered," replied the king, "or I will myself proclaim her rank before Henri and his assembled court. But time presses, good Chrétien, and I must to the tilt-yard."

"Your majesty——"

"Is peremptory—headstrong—what you will? But waste no more words upon me. Tarry here till the jousts are over, and I will rejoin you."

As he spoke, the king made a sign to the Baron de Rosni, who, with a glance of ineffable disdain at the menacing gestures of the scholars, instantly rejoined him, and after a little further conversation with the preacher, and a valediction, which greatly scandalised the good old man, proffered to his buxom hostess, Henri and his follower quitted the cabaret.

They were about to mount the steeds awaiting their coming forth at the door of the tavern when a band of equerries, pages, and gentlemen-ushers in superb liveries of crimson velvet, slashed with yellow satin, accompanied by a crowd of trumpeters and hautboy-players blowing loud flourishes, rode furiously down the Rue Pélican, shouting as they passed, "Make way for the Queen-Mother—stand back—stand back." Henri drew his cap closely over his brow at this intimation, and

* I 804

appeared to busy himself about the saddle of his charger. Presently Catherine appeared mounted upon a beautiful Spanish jennet, and attended by her *petite bande des dames*, all on horseback, on their way to the Louvre. It was impossible to conceive a gayer or more attractive sight than this brilliant troop of youthful dames, each attended by a page habited in her colours, presented. All were masked in demi-vizards of various dyes, and the beholder therefore could do little more than guess at the loveliness of their lineaments. But the brightness of the orbs flashing through the apertures of those witching *tourets de nez*—the splendour of their attire—the grace they displayed on their steeds—the waving of their silken tresses—the elegance and lightness of their figures, left him in little incertitude as to the charms of feature thus enviously concealed from view. In spite of the risk incurred by such a proceeding, Henri could not resist the temptation of stealing a glance at the fair equestrians as they passed in review before him, and as the person of one, who seemed to be more exquisitely proportioned than her companions, attracted his ardent gaze, the damsel (it was La Rebours) remarked to her companion, "*Sainte Marie!* La Fosseuse, only see how much that soldier resembles the King of Navarre!"

"*Nenni!*" returned La Fosseuse pertly. "I discover no likeness—or if there is any, the soldier has decidedly the advantage over the monarch—his shoulders are broader."

"Perhaps so," sighed La Rebours, "but the resemblance is very remarkable." And as she turned her head to satisfy herself of the fact, the king had disappeared. "How very singular!" she thought, musing on the circumstance as she rode along.

We will now return to the cabaret and inquire after the Gelosa. With difficulty the unhappy maiden mastered her terror when she perceived Ogilvy engaged in a second brawl with the scholars, and found herself deserted by both her protectors; but her alarm was greatly increased, when after the departure of the Baron de Rosni, the menaces of the scholars assumed a more determinately hostile shape, and the Scot was loudly threatened with death on all sides. Neither could the strong arms of Blount and the Swiss sergeant, nor the peaceful interposition of the preacher, avail to allay the storm. They cried out loudly for his blood, and swords and daggers were drawn—tables and benches overturned—glasses broken—deep and vindictive oaths uttered, and a sanguinary conflict must

have ensued, had not the Chevalier du Guet and his two
lieutenants armed with partisans, and accompanied by several
other personages in sable dresses, whose sallow countenances
as well as certain peculiarities in their costume, proclaimed
them to be Italians, suddenly entered the tavern. The chief of
the watch commanded peace in the king's name, and apprehensive of the consequences of a refusal to obey his order, the
combatants were compelled to sheath their blades. But in the
meantime another event occurred, which gave a new turn to
the affair, and served to reawaken their suspended animosity.
As her eye rested upon the new-comers, Ginevra could not
repress a faint scream and, attracted by the sound, one of the
foremost of their number instantly rushed towards her, and ere
the hapless maiden could offer any resistance, she found herself
in the power of the followers of Gonzaga. To rush to her assistance, to extricate her from the grasp of her assailant, was with
Ogilvy the work of a moment. But his assistance was ineffectual.
Ginevra only escaped from one hand to be retaken by the other.
The Sorbonist twined his arms round the form of the flying girl
and bore her back to her captors. Ogilvy meanwhile had not
relinquished the grasp he had fixed upon the Italian. In the
struggle that succeeded, a packet fell from the doublet of the
latter. The Scot recognised it at once.

"Ah!" he exclaimed, setting his foot upon the papers, "to
the rescue, Blount—to the rescue—there is the object of our
patron Crichton's search—the documents establishing the Princess Esclairmonde's birth—to the rescue—to the rescue!"

"Gracious Heaven!" exclaimed the preacher, "to his aid,
young man. I would fain wield a sword in such a cause myself
—help!—help!"

Blount needed not this incitement to draw sword. He threw
himself resolutely upon the Italians, whose weapons were all
directed against Ogilvy's breast, and struck the foremost of
them to the ground. But his purpose was checked by a sudden
and fatal issue being put to the combat. One of the followers of
Gonzaga, watching his opportunity, plunged his stiletto deeply
into Ogilvy's breast. Without a groan, though he felt himself
mortally wounded, the Scot now stooped down, and receiving,
as he did, numberless wounds from his adversaries, obtained
possession of the packet.

"Take it," he said, as with a dying effort he reached the
Englishman's side, "you know its destination—heed me not—
away—my strength will not avail me to fly, but my heart

goes with you and to my patron—tell him—but I cannot speak—go—go."

Uttering these words, he committed the packet to Blount's custody, and suddenly turning, confronted his adversaries with a look so fierce and desperate, that the boldest of them shrank back appalled.

"Follow me, messire," whispered Dame Fredegonde, who, under cover of the protecting arm of the Swiss sergeant, had ventured to approach the combatants; "follow me," she said, plucking Blount's sleeve, "and you, too, worthy sir," addressing the preacher, "you can render little assistance to that dying man, and your presence will only incite these murderous students to further acts of violence. Holy Virgin!—blessed Luther, I mean—but I scarcely know what I am saying—that such a fray as this should dishonour my dwelling. Maître Jacques, look to their swords—mercy upon us!—ward them off—I will find means to requite your valour—come along, messires—quick —quick, this way—this way."

Blount looked irresolute.

"By Saint Ben'et," he said, "I never yet turned my back upon an enemy, and I see not why I should fly for the first time when I have a friend to avenge."

"If thou wouldst indeed avenge me, tarry not," cried Ogilvy. And as he spoke, the sword of one of his antagonists was thrust through his body, and the Scot fell to the earth.

"Let them not wholly triumph," gasped the dying man. "Ah! he escapes," he cried, turning his glazing eyes in the direction of Blount, who defended by the nervous arm and huge falchion of the Swiss, as well as by the dreaded fangs of his dog Druid, and guided by the friendly hostess, speedily effected his retreat, together with the preacher, through a small doorway, not hitherto observed by the guests. As this door was closed and barricaded by the stalwart person of Maître Jacques, a smile of exultation lighted up Ogilvy's features. "I die content," he murmured.

At this moment a piercing shriek rent the air. It proceeded from the Gelosa. Her captors were about to bear her off, but finding her outcries continued, one of them twisted a scarf round her throat in such a manner that it was impossible for the wretched maiden to utter further sound. This done, regarding neither the entreaties of Dame Fredegonde, nor the impotent threats of Ogilvy, they disappeared with their prey. At the same time the Chevalier du Guet and his attendants quitted the tavern.

"Recreants," cried the Scot, who had raised himself upon one arm. "Will none lend a hand to the rescue?—will none help her?—That youth, as you deem him, is a maiden in disguise—will ye stand by and see wrong done to a woman—to the rescue if ye be men!"

"Think you we will defend thy leman, fool," said the Sorbonist, with a derisive laughter, as he passed him; "our vengeance is now fully complete—thou art robbed of life and thy mistress—ha, ha!—Come, comrades, let us to the lists. This augurs well. This Scot's countryman may chance to meet a like downfall. We shall see. And hark ye, messires, if we can lay hands upon that heretic preacher, we will see if there is a faggot to be found in the Pré-aux-Clercs:

> Death to the Huguenot!—fagot and flame!
> Death to the Huguenot!—torture and shame!
> Death!—Death!"

And all joining in this menacing chorus, the scholars quitted the cabaret.

Scarcely had the reckless troop gained the street, when a band of men, wearing the livery of the Vicomte de Joyeuse, entered the chamber.

"Where is the youth whom we are to conduct from Paris?" asked their leader, glancing around in astonishment and alarm.

"In the hands of——," gasped Ogilvy.

But ere he could complete the sentence, the brave Scot became for ever silent.

CHAPTER III

THE PROCESSION

Genets, coursiers, riches bardes, houssures,
Plumars remplis d'orphaveries fines,
Chamfrains dorés à grans entrelassures,
Armets luysans, bicquoquets, capelines,
Bucques de pris, tres riches mantelines—
ANDRÉ DE LA VIGNE, *Le Vergier d'Honneur.*

As the hour for opening the lists drew nigh, all the avenues and approaches of the Louvre were thronged with eager and curious crowds hurrying from each quarter to behold the chivalrous pageant. This concourse consisted of every class of society to be found in the vast and miscellaneous population of Paris, from the sedate citizen and his demure spouse, to be distinguished by propriety of gear (costume being then regulated by sumptuary laws), down to the rough half-clothed boatmen who plied upon the Seine and the sturdy artisan who haunted its banks. Nor must we omit a host of Jews, beggars, *truands* and other non-descript vagabonds who usually formed the mass of a Parisian crowd at the period of our narrative. Amongst these the magistrates of the city, the provosts of the merchants, the *échevins* and their followers, in bipartite robes of crimson, and tawny-coloured stuffs embroidered with a silver ship (the civic cognisance), the sergeants, archers, cross-bowmen and harquebusiers of the town-guard cut a conspicuous figure. As usually happens, however, where a crowd is collected, the softer sex predominated. For one steel or felt cap there were ten coifs of silk or linen. Nor were the members of the various religious fraternities wanting: the grey or russet frock—the cowl, or shaven head —and the long staff—might be detected amid the dense assemblage. Cordeliers, Carmelites and Minims were mingled with the higher dignitaries of the Church. The students of the university, ever on the alert when a spectacle was about to take place, herded thither in vast bands. Here came a courtly abbé—it was our acquaintance, Pierre de Bourdeille—upon a mule with its superb housings, followed by a train of richly-clad lackeys.

The mob doffed their caps as Brantôme ambled on. Next appeared what in our own time would be regarded with much merriment, but which was then a matter of too frequent occurrence to excite either surprise or ridicule, a couple of gaily-attired youths mounted upon the same steed—then a cavalier and dame, likewise on horseback, the latter seated on a velvet pillion, her features concealed, as was the universal mode with the ladies when out of doors, by a demi-mask. The housings of the charger were unusually superb, his broad martingale and wide-reined bridle being of crimson leather richly ornamented with gold. Next followed a company of singly mounted cavaliers, with a host of valets and attendants arrayed in the extremity of the court fashion, with nodding feathers and fluttering mantles; the curvetting of their coursers and the blows of their *houssines*, as they dashed recklessly onwards, occasioned considerable confusion amongst the foot-passengers; and the smiles and compliments they lavished upon the fair *citoyennes* and their daughters, hardly compensated with the bluff burgesses for their own sprained shoulders and broken heads. Nevertheless, in spite of the jostling and hustling, the striving, straining and squeezing, the utmost good humour prevailed; but this, indeed, might be attributed to the presence of so many armed authorities.

Loud shouts were now raised, and the multitude was pushed backwards and driven into more compact masses as the magnificent litter of the Queen of Navarre was borne along to the Louvre. In vain did the spectators endeavour to catch a glimpse of the features or person of the lovely Marguerite. A mask defied their scrutiny, and she leaned back in her carriage as if anxious to elude observation. Not so her attendant, Torigni. The swan-like throat of the sprightly Florentine might be observed above the sides of the vehicle, and her snowy hand, divested of its glove and covered with rings, negligently arranged a raven ringlet. Marguerite's litter swept by, and was followed by the *huissiers* and guard of the Governor of Paris. René de Villequier boasted the most magnificent caroche in Paris, and the vehicle which, upon this occasion, conveyed the portly person of the marquis, was little inferior in decoration and gilding, though somewhat different in construction, from our own Lord Mayor's State equipage.

Then came the trampling of hoofs, and the loud fanfares of trumpets, and the superbly accoutred band of Gascon gentlemen—forty-five in number, whence their designation—commanded by the Baron d'Epernon, wheeled into sight, the sunbeams brightly glancing upon their corslets and upon the tips of their lances. The last fourteen of this gallant company were sheathed in complete steel, with yellow scarves crossing their burnished cuirasses. Two pages succeeded in the violet-coloured livery of the baron, with his blazon displayed upon their sleeves and doublets. Then came his esquires sustaining his shield, charged likewise with his cognisance; and, lastly, appeared D'Epernon himself, in a costly suit of russet armour, enriched with chiselled arabesques and deep reliefs of gold.

Scarcely had the admiration excited by the baron's retinue subsided, ere the spectators were attracted towards a further display of knightly splendour. A flourish of trumpets blown by six mounted men-at-arms, whose clarions were ornamented with silken bandrols fringed with gold, displaying the princely escutcheon of the family of Gonzaga, announced the approach of the Duc de Nevers. The duke rode a noble Arabian courser, and proceeded at a slow and stately pace. His valets and pages were more numerous than those of the Baron d'Epernon, and he was attended by four gentlemen ushers, who walked by his side bareheaded, with wands in their hands. He was fully armed in a suit of Milan steel, of the finest workmanship. His breast-plate was brighter than silver, and reflected the rays of the sun as from a dazzling mirror. His burgonet and his corslet were crusted with gold and pearls, and from his neck, suspended to a chain of the same metal, hung the Order of the Saint-Esprit. A plume of white ostrich-feathers nodded on his crest.

His demeanour was so dignified, and his train so sumptuous, that his appearance was greeted by the assemblage with deafening acclamations—acknowledged by the proud duke with a haughty inclination of the head. Nor was the popularity of the wily Italian diminished, as his attendants showered amongst the mob broad silver pieces, for which they fought and scrambled. By his side, in full ecclesiastical costume of scarlet silk simar with lawn sleeves and snowy rochet, and upon a sleek, well-fed mule, led by two attendants, each of whom had a hand upon the bridle, rode Pierre de Gondi, Bishop of Paris; a prelate in high favour with the Queen-Mother, to whom, indeed, he owed his elevation. There was something sinister in the dark and shifting glance of this Florentine churchman, which seemed to confirm the horrible reports that prevailed as to the motives of Catherine's predilection for him. But be this as it may, the hypocritical smile which now lit up his sallow features was construed by the observers into an expression of infinite benevolence, the rather that his almoner, who followed closely at his heels, distributed a dole with no sparing hand.

Immediately behind the suite of the Duc de Nevers came an esquire of Vincenzo de Gonzaga, bearing a small triangular shield, painted white, on which appeared the device of a sable mask, inscribed with the motto *Vendetta*. This esquire wore the livery of the prince (the combined hues of red and yellow) displayed in the flowing satin housings of his steed, traversed with broad cross-bars of orange and crimson, in his slashed velvet doublet, *haut-de-chausses* of different dyes, and particoloured plumes. Next advanced a band of youthful pages magnificently attired, and mounted on coursers caparisoned in cloth of gold, barred like the housings of the esquire, the stripes being described upon their gorgeous trappings by alternate lines of frieze-wrought and smooth-beaten tissue. Upon the silken *just-au-corps* of each page was embroidered in golden thread the ducal badge of Mantua and Montferrat. So gorgeous were their appointments in detail, that their bonnets, shoes, saddles, bridles, and even the scabbards of their rapiers blushed with crimson velvet.

Then followed a host of lackeys on foot, similarly, though less splendidly arrayed; then another esquire sustaining the tricoloured lance of the prince, decorated with silken pennoncel; then two foot-pages attired in habiliments of cloth of gold and silk, leading his steed—a mighty Allemayne charger with eyes of flame, expanded nostrils, and pawing hoofs—furnished for Gonzaga's use by the provident Duc de Nevers. Thick crimson velvet housing, enwoven with the ducal cognisance, covered this noble animal, and descended almost to his pastern joints; the saddle was of velvet of the same hue as the rest of the harness —the chamfrin, or headpiece, was of gilded mail, with a short projecting steel pike, and tufts of scarlet and saffron-stained plumes adorned his front and croup.

Lastly, armed cap-à-pie, in a suit of black mail embossed with gold and precious stones, rode the Prince Vincenzo. A *garde-bras*, or *haute-pièce*, as it was subsequently termed, covered the front of his cuirass, and defended his throat and left arm, so far as the gauntlet; but being of a single piece, and introduced in those later days of chivalry, for the better security of the jousters, the posture assumed by the knight, who adopted this safeguard in the combat, became fixed and unalterable as that of a statue, his right arm alone being left at liberty. A tall egret of sable feathers shadowed his helm, and with his vizor closed, and maintaining, of necessity, a stern and moveless attitude, Gonzaga passed slowly onwards. His cortège was completed by another band of gaudy valets and the minstrels, who enlivened the procession with the tambour, the cornet and the clarion.

A fresh clangor of trumpets admonished the spectators that other comers were at hand; and the announcement was speedily followed by the brilliant retinue of the Vicomte de Joyeuse, which, if it could not vie with that of Gonzaga in magnificence, surpassed it in number and consequence, consisting of a throng of lordlings and youthful gentlemen of the best families of France, who were eager upon this occasion to array themselves under the banner of their monarch's chief favourite, and to distinguish themselves with the snowy scarf which he had adopted as his ensign. It was true the same prodigality of cloth of gold and velvet was not here exhibited, as in the preceding cavalcade:

> Mais de harnois, ne d'armure de jouste,
> Ne leur failloit une petite pièce.

There was no lack of "tilting furniture, emblazoned shields." A gayer troop was never seen. Nor could a greater contrast have been found to that which preceded it. The vivacity of their hilarious leader seemed to have diffused itself throughout his company. Success appeared to be written in their beaming features. Nothing was heard but shouts of laughter, and the jingling of arms; nothing seen but the waving of plumes and banners, the glitter of helm and spear, and caracoling of coursers.

Completely armed in a suit of polished steel, Joyeuse rode a charger barded with *ung bel et grand couvrechief* of silver tissue, edged with azure fringe, and wore a scarf of white silk, richly embroidered, thrown across his left shoulder. From his morion floated a lambrequin of slashed satin, and his surcoat was decorated with his armorial bearings. His handsome countenance was radiant with gaiety, and he conversed in an animated manner with a knight, who careered by his side, and upon whom, even more than the vicomte, the attention of the gazers was fixed. Nor was the appearance of this cavalier undeserving the admiration he excited. He seemed the very mirror of chivalry. The experienced horseman applauded the consummate grace with which he sat his courser (a powerful and beautifully formed bay, whose skin shone almost as brightly as his rider's coat of mail), and the ease with which he ever and anon compelled him to perform the balotades, croupades, and other graces of the high *manège*, alluded to in the following alliterative verses:

> Vite virade,
> Pompante pannade,
> Saut soulevant,
> Prompte petarrade,

while the female portion of the assemblage marvelled at the exceeding beauty of feature, disclosed by the open vizor of his casque, and the manly symmetry of the limbs, defined by his light and curiously fashioned breast-plate, "brassards, cuissards, jamb and solleret." The housings of his steed were of white damask, diapered with gold, and bordered with minever. His chamfrin was decorated like that of Gonzaga, with a superb *houppe de plumes*, and similarly accoutred. From the crest of the knight depended a lambrequin of slashed silk, and his surcoat was woven with his blazon, a lion rampant azure, armed, and langued gules.

Following this *preux chevalier* rode two esquires, in liveries of azure and white: the one carrying his painted lance, on the coronel of which was fastened a knot of ribbons, the gage, doubtless, of the dame in whose honour he was about to run a course; the other bearing a silver shield with the device of a dragon vert, spouting out fire, and the motto *Loyal au mort*, inscribed in blue characters upon a scroll.

When it became known to the assemblage that this knight, in whom all felt so much interest, was no other than the Admirable Crichton, the adversary of the Prince of Mantua, their acclamations were so loud and deafening, and the efforts of those in the rear so strenuous to obtain a nearer view of his person and features, that it required the application of both partisan and sword on part of the attendants to keep back the rabble; while the object of their curiosity, apprehensive of some such tumult taking place, as occurred on the preceding day at the university, was fain to set spurs to his charger, and to urge his companions into a quicker movement, in order to escape from observation.

"By my halidom!" exclaimed Joyeuse, as they reached the grand portal of the Louvre, and found the space before it invested with a gay confusion of litters, caroches, steeds, lackeys and pages in various and resplendent liveries. "To judge from this rout we shall have a goodly attendance at our jousting. You must do your devoir gallantly, *mon cher*, for you will have the eyes of all the chivalry and beauty of France upon you. There is not a magnate of our court whose colours I do not discern amidst yon rout of servitors. But we are late. Those knaves in the slashed doublets form part of the train of our challenger's *padrino*. Gonzaga is already in the *steccato*."

"Better be the last to enter the field than the first to quit it," replied Crichton, smiling. "But whom have we here? By Saint Andrew! my gossip, Chicot. So ho! Bayard," he cried, patting the neck of his charger, who, obedient to his voice, instantly stood still, but evinced his impatience by arching his neck, champing at the bit, snorting and pawing the ground. "What wouldst thou?" demanded the Scot, as the jester approached him with an odd serio-comic look.

"I am the bearer of a cartel to thee," replied the jester, in a tone of mock defiance.

"Gramercy — gossip — a challenge!" ejaculated Crichton; "from thy brother, Siblot, to shiver a marotte against his cock's-comb? Ha! But knowst thou not, that by the laws of honour, I am restrained from entering into a second quarrel until my first be disposed of?"

"I know it, answered Chicot in an undertone. "But you must offer some response, yea or nay, to my appeal. Here is the missive," he added, delivering a perfumed note, sealed and secured with a silken thread, to the Scot; "peruse it, and deliver me your answer without wrong or supersticerie."

"The cipher of the Queen of Navarre," exclaimed Crichton as he regarded the billet. "Nay, then, it is indeed a *combat à outrance.*"

"I would advise you to decline the encounter, or rather peaceably to arrange it," returned the jester; "but in the meantime will it please you to read the cartel and furnish me with some token of your intentions to convey to my royal mistress."

Crichton hastily broke open the seal, and as his eye glanced over the contents of the note, a slight flush of anger rose upon his cheek.

"I will rather perish than accept the terms she proposes," he murmured, tearing it in pieces, and scattering the fragments to the breezes.

"Hold, gossip," cried Chicot; "reserve that thread of gold; I am to take that to her majesty as a sign of your acquiescence."

"Never," answered Crichton sternly. "Tell her I have burst her chains. She would have some token—'tis well," he added, withdrawing his gauntlet from his hand, and giving the bezoar-ring to the jester; "let this gem be a proof to her that I neither fear her threats, nor will accept of her tenderness."

"*Par Sainct Fiacre en Brie!*" cried Chicot, looking after him with a smile of derision, as he dashed swiftly through the gate-way; "I will prove a better friend to thee than thou deservest. This ring will well beseem my own finger, while this thread," he added, picking up the fastening of the billet, "will perfectly content her jealous majesty of Navarre. For what saith the good Pantagruel:

> Paternostres et oraisons
> Sont pour ceux-là qui les retiennent:
> Ung fiffre allant en fenaisons,
> Est plus fort que deux qui en viennent."

And chanting this wholesome advice "de la marraine de mon grand-père," he entered the lofty portal of the Louvre.

CHAPTER IV

THE LISTS

Ce jour de may en beau barnois de guerre,
Nous joustames assez doucettement,
Et de noz fais qui en voudroit enquerre
Icy n'en fais mencion autrement.

LOUIS DE BEAUVEAU, *Le Pas de la Bergière.*

ACCOMPANIED by the Vicomte de Joyeuse, Crichton now rode into the *champ clos* appointed for the combat. Erected within a court, at the back of the Louvre, the lists were elevated to the height of the thigh-piece of the jousters and extended to the length of sixty yards, while the space within the barriers, being carefully sanded and cleared of all impediments, offered a very advantageous arena for the exhibition of knightly prowess.

Along the façade of the palace, on a level with the windows now thrown open, for the convenience of the spectators, was raised a temporary balcony, descending in wide steps, and hung with magnificent tapestry. Divided, at certain distances, into open canopies, fashioned of the richest brocade, decorated with fleur-de-lis ciphers and escutcheons, and fluttering with silken streamers, this balcony occupied one side of the quadrangular court. At the farther extremity of the lists stood a grand roofed gallery, supported by heavy pillars, destined for the reception of the three queens, their attendants and dames of honour. The curtains and hangings of this splendid structure were of gridelin velvet, flowered with ciphers of silver, displaying in the centre a vast argent shield, emblazoned with the royal escutcheon of France. At the right of the tilt-yard was placed a scaffold, with palisades reserved for Montjoie, the king-at-arms, the marshals and judges of the field; and next to it, under a canopy fretted with gold, ran a line of tabourets, set apart for the favourites of Henri III., in the centre of which was a raised velvet fauteuil for his majesty's own occupation. At either end stood two pavilions of striped silk for the use of the esquires, armourers, and other attendants of the combatants. Upon a low scaffold to the left of the grand gallery, guarded by four officials, disguised in the ghastly leaden-coloured hood called the chaperon, and surrounded by a band of halberdiers, stood Ruggieri, with his hands folded upon his bosom, and his eyes fixed upon the ground.

Indicating to his retinue the position they were to occupy,

Joyeuse rode through the entrance of the lists and joined the marshals of the field. Crichton followed more slowly. The breast of the Scot beat high as he gazed on the inspiring scene. The morning was bright and beautiful; the sunbeams glanced on casque and corslet, and on the thousand dyes of banner and blazon; the soft breeze, tempered by the genial warmth of approaching spring, served with its freshening breath to give enthusiasm to the heart, and vigour to the frame, and so fully did Crichton feel the influence of these stirring thoughts, that spurring his charger, he compelled him to perform a demi-volte in the air, and then to career round the arena. All was animation and excitement. The rustle of silks, the pleasant sound of gentle voices, the flash of brilliants from above, announced the arrival of the *anges de paradis* (as they were rapturously termed by the minstrels) in the balconies. Each casement of the Louvre poured forth its stream of beauty, and as the Scot gazed upon those lovely and high-born dames, whose natural charms were heightened to the utmost by the aid of costliest ornament and dress, he felt his bosom beat with redoubled ardour. Reining his steed, he paused to look around. On all sides were ranged dense masses of spectators, over whose uncovered heads bristled the glancing pikes and halberds of the sergeants. On the right of the royal gallery were arrayed the fourteen followers of D'Epernon, glistening in steel, and headed by the baron himself: on the left, behind the scaffold of the astrologer, stood the sumptuous retinue of the Duc de Nevers. Bands of cavaliers, who, on the appearance of the dames on the balcony, regardless of the interdiction of the heralds, had dashed into the course, were now seen extending their lances towards its sides, whence fell a shower of wreaths, bracelets and scarves, which were speedily attached to salade and spear. Much occupation was thus given to the king-at-arms and the marshals, whose province was to maintain a clear field, and the champions, waving their hands to the mistresses of their hearts, quitted the ring. Amid the subordinate officers of the tilt-yard must be enumerated the pursuivants, the trumpeters with their clarions dressed with silken flags, and troops of minstrels stationed at each outlet.

A shout was now raised by the crowd, and the Scot's attention was directed towards the grand gallery, in which the Queen Louise and her demoiselles made their appearance. Amid the latter Crichton at once distinguished Esclairmonde. The Princess of Condé was perfectly pale, but her want of bloom in nowise detracted from her loveliness. On the contrary, she had never before appeared so eminently beautiful in the eyes of her lover, nor had he heretofore, as he thought, remarked so much dignity and self-possession in her demeanour. In fact, the events of the last night, and the knowledge so recently and mysteriously acquired of her exalted origin, had worked a sudden but entire change in Esclairmonde's character. She was no longer an orphan maiden without name, and without family. She now felt a pride, of which she had been hitherto unconscious, kindled within her bosom, and a resolution, as yet wholly unknown to her, animate and sustain her spirits against the perils and difficulties to which she was exposed. This new-sprung courage was the more fully proved in the ordeal to which she was shortly afterwards subjected in an interview with Catherine de Medicis and Marguerite de Valois, both of whom, with their attendants, now entered the gallery. But her firmness did not fail her in this trial, and she returned the scrutinising look of the Queen-Mother with a glance as lofty as her own. Marguerite was all smiles and courtesy: but the smile of a rival is little to be trusted, and Crichton, who was well acquainted with Marguerite's talent for dissimulation, read in her professions of friendship, and winning attentions, the deadliest treachery. These greetings concluded, Esclairmonde, at the request of Queen Louise, took the throne appointed for her as sovereign arbitress of the tourney—a chair placed a little in advance of the royal seats, and so situated as to make her the principal object of attraction to the spectators. Her costume was a robe of white damask, flowered with silver, with sleeves of snowy silk of the ample mode of the period, embroidered with roseate and green pearls. Never had Queen of the Lists appeared so attractive, and a murmur of admiration arose from the multitude as she became more fully revealed to their view.

At this moment the gaze of the princess fell upon the knightly figure of her lover, who, bending to his saddle-bow, gracefully tendered his homage. As she returned the salutation, Esclairmonde trembled, and her courage entirely forsook her. Crichton perceived the change in her deportment, and anxious, if possible, to dissipate her anxiety, compelled his steed into its liveliest caracoles, and was about to quit the field, when his progress was arrested by loud cries of "Noel! Noel!—vive le roi!—vive le roi!" Fanfares of trumpets and the clash of cymbals succeeded, and Henri, fully and magnificently armed, entered into the arena. He was attended by the Marquis de Villequier, Saint-

Luc, and a courtly throng. The royal charger (a snowy Arabian)
was caparisoned with sweeping bardes of crimson velvet,

Toutes chargées de riche orphaverie,

and figured with golden fleurs-de-lis. Courteously saluting the
Scot, and bidding him prepare for the signal of the combat,
which would be shortly given, Henri directed his course towards
the grand gallery, and addressing Esclairmonde, solicited a
favour at her hands, that he might break a lance in her behalf.
Unable to refuse his request, Esclairmonde took a string of
pearls from her rich auburn tresses, and dispatched it to the
monarch by a page. Acknowledging the boon with a smile of
gratification, and passing many well-turned compliments upon
her charms, Henri proceeded to hold a brief conference with
the Duc de Nevers.

Crichton, meantime, rode into the pavilion appropriated to
his attendants, the hangings of which were closely drawn after
him. Dismounting from his steed, he was presently joined by
the Vicomte de Joyeuse, Montjoie, and Pierre de Gondi, by the
latter of whom the customary oaths of the combat were adminis-
tered. Kissing the crucifix and the *Te igitur*, the Scot next submitted himself to his armourer, who riveted upon his cuirass
a placcate of shining steel, similar to that borne by Gonzaga.
Being thus fully equipped for the fight, notwithstanding the
increased weight of his armour, he vaulted into the saddle
without the aid of the stirrup; and taking his lance from his
esquire, awaited the signal for the combat.

Henri having by this time taken his seat beneath the canopy,
gave with his baton a signal to Montjoie, the king-at-arms, who,
attended by two heralds, advanced, amidst a flourish of clarions
and hautboys, towards the centre of the arena and, commanding
silence, proclaimed in a loud voice the names and titles of the
appellant and the defendant, together with their cause of
quarrel, prohibiting all persons whatsoever from offering interruption, by word or sign, to the combat. Fresh fanfares of
trumpets succeeded this ceremonial, during which all eyes had
been fixed upon Ruggieri, who, though pale as death, maintained
a composed and resolute demeanour, ever and anon stealing a
glance towards the gallery, in which sat the Queen-Mother.
Silence being once more restored, Montjoie cried aloud, "Faites
vos devoirs, chevaliers."

On the third call, the curtains of the pavilions were swiftly
drawn aside, and both knights issued forth, each taking up a

position at the right of the barriers. Esclairmonde's bosom palpitated with emotion as she beheld the stately figure of her lover cased in steel thus suddenly set before her, and recognised her own gage upon his lance's point. Any fears she might have entertained for his safety vanished in his presence, and with a heart throbbing with expectation, she heard the first blast of the clarion sound for the hostile career. A profound hush now reigned throughout the assemblage. Even the royal tenants of the gallery rose and advanced towards its edge, and Marguerite de Valois, disregarding Montjoie's injunction, leaned over the side of the balcony and waved her hand. Crichton perceived the action and, unable otherwise to account for it, attributed it to some return of tenderness on the part of the impassioned queen. Again the trumpet sounded, and as the blast was blown, Crichton struck his spurs into his steed, executing a demi-volte to the right, while he slightly raised his lance in the air, bringing the truncheon within a few inches of his thigh, in readiness for the career. In this action were displayed the unequalled grace and dexterity in the management of his steed, for which the Scot was so eminently distinguished. The martial notes of the clarion now resounded for the third time, and hurling a gauntlet to the ground, Montjoie shouted in a voice of thunder, "Laissez-les aller—laissez-les aller."

Swift as bolt from cloud, Crichton, at this signal, speeded from his post. As the steed started on his rapid career, the Scot, quick as thought, raised the truncheon of his lance to a level with his line of vision, and then firmly fixing it in its rest, declined its point towards the left ear of his charger as he approached within some half-dozen paces of his adversary, and directed his aim against the upper part of his helm. Both lances were shivered as the champions met in mid-career. Gonzaga's mark had been the same as that of his antagonist, but the point of his lance glanced from the sharp gorget of the plastron, while the blow of Crichton, taking place upon the crest of the prince, carried off the panache with which it was surmounted, and scattered the plumes far and wide over the field. Neither, however, had been dismounted, and as each knight gracefully brought his steed to a rest, and hurled away the truncheon of his broken lance, he opened his gauntlet to show that he had sustained no injury from the encounter.

Snatching fresh lances from the attendants, the combatants again started on a new career. In this second attaint, the advantage was decidedly in favour of the Scot, his lance striking his adversary's vizor, and staggering him so much, that he could with difficulty rein in his charger. Notwithstanding the shock he had sustained, the prince seized a sharp-pointed lance from his esquire, and bidding a pursuivant communicate his intentions to his opponent, prepared for the final course.

The excitement of the spectators was now raised to the highest pitch. On the issue of this trial depended the fate of the accused, and the movements of the combatants were watched with intense interest. For the third time they started upon their career. Upon this occasion the steel edge of Gonzaga's lance drew sparkles from the beaver of the Scot, as it came in contact with his helm, but the blow, though well directed, could not shake the firm horseman in his saddle. Not so was it with Gonzaga. The stroke of Crichton, into which he had thrown all his force, was dealt with such resolution upon the vizor of Vincenzo, that, unable to resist its violence, and still maintaining his hold of the bridle, horse and rider were hurled backwards upon the dust.

Instantly recovering his feet, and unclasping his vizor, with a countenance flushed with shame and fury, the prince walked across the lists to the tribunal of the judges, and claimed, in a haughty tone, to be allowed the privilege of the combat with the sword. This request was peremptorily refused, but Crichton, riding up at the same moment, generously seconded his adversary's request, and refusing to consider the triumph he had obtained as decisive. Montjoie's objections were overruled, and the combatants retired to renew their conflict with different weapons. The cheers, meanwhile, from the lookers-on, were almost stunning, and the courtesy of the Scot was on all hands loudly applauded.

Crichton now withdrew to the pavilion, where his armourer unbraced his *haute-pièce*, and furnished him with another and lighter morion of Damascus steel, crested with a tall cluster of white feathers. A long estoc was girt to his side, and to the pommel of his saddle was fastened a keen, well-tempered *miséricorde*. Thus accoutred, he mounted a light agile barb, sent to him by the Vicomte de Joyeuse, as being fitter for the rapid and furious passages he would now have to perform, than his own charger, and returned to the lists "bien gentement férant de l'esperon."

Meanwhile, the barriers traversing the arena had been removed, and the space was left vacant for the combat. As the Scot passed through the outer pales, his visor was raised, and he cast a look towards the gallery in which Esclairmonde was seated. The princess rose as he appeared and gracefully saluted him. Crichton returned her greeting, and unsheathing his sword, kissed the hilt as if vowing to draw it in her name. The action was not unobserved by Marguerite de Valois, over whose countenance came a sudden and fearful change. The Vicomte de Joyeuse on the one hand, and the Duc de Nevers on the other, had in the interim marked out upon the sand of the tilt-yard a circular space, within the limits of which it was necessary that the combatants should keep. Armed in all respects like his antagonist, and similarly mounted, Gonzaga now rode into the lists. Making a motion to the Duc de Nevers that he desired an instant's speech of the Chevalier Crichton, apart from their *parrains*, he rode towards the Scot, who sheathed his sword as he drew nigh, and advanced to meet him. This proceeding on the part of the prince was watched with great anxiety by the spectators, who were apprehensive lest they should lose the most interesting part of the anticipated spectacle. Their doubts, however, were quickly relieved on noting the imperious gestures of Gonzaga, and the corresponding haughtiness with which they were received by his adversary.

"Chevalier Crichton," said the prince, in a deep, low tone, "I am aware that by the laws of arms I am already vanquished, and not more so by your address than by your generosity. So much am I beholden to you for the opportunity you have afforded me of redeeming my honour, that I would evince my sense of your high and chivalrous conduct by the proffer of my friendship, if you will accept it in lieu of doing battle upon a quarrel which, methinks, might be easily adjusted."

"Prince of Mantua," replied Crichton courteously, "I should be proud to accept your friendship if I could do so without impeachment of my honour. But it may not be. I have denounced Ruggieri as false and perjured, an enemy of God, and a traitor to his king. You have falsified my charge, and I must make good the accusation with my sword."

"Enough," replied the prince haughtily; "once and again, I thank you. You have now liberated me from the weight of obligation under which my spirit laboured. The combat which ensues must be a duel to the death. Your generosity might have restrained my arm. It is now free to strike—and, by Saint Paul, I charge you to look well to yourself."

"To your post, then, prince," replied Crichton sternly, "and by the aid of God, Our Lady and Saint Andrew the good knight,

I will approve with my body against your body the justice of
my quarrel."

So saying, with a proud salutation, he closed the vizor of his
helm, and backed his charger till he brought him in a line with
the Vicomte de Joyeuse, while Gonzaga, turning his horse's
head, rejoined his sponsor and second, the Duc de Nevers.

After some little further delay, the combatants, placed about
forty paces asunder, awaited with rapier drawn and beaver up
the fulfilment of the trumpeter's devoir. As the third charge
was sounded, grasping the rein firmly with his left hand, plunging
his spurs up to the rowel in the flanks of his steed, and raising
his sword-arm in the air, each champion dashed furiously against
the other, dealing, as he passed him, a mandritta, or blow from
right to left, on his antagonist's casque, and then wheeling
suddenly round, performed a demi-volte with curvets, and
returning with the same fury as before, reiterated his stroke.
Upon the third encounter, executing a shorter demi-volte,
Crichton turned sharply round and faced his assailant. Continuing their curvets and voltes, each champion then discharged
a succession of imbrocatas and riversas upon his enemy's morion
and breastplate. No attempt on either side, on the onset,
appeared to be made to ward off those blows, but on the third
volte, Crichton directed a heavy stramazone (or cutting blow)
against Gonzaga's crest. The prince raised his estoc to beat
away the blow, but the weapon flew from his grasp, and so
terrible was the stroke, that Crichton's own blade shivered to
the hilt. Plucking his dagger from its sheath, and grasping it
in his right hand, each now spurred his steed close to that of
his antagonist. Accustomed to this species of encounter, the
animals stood stock-still. Crichton then grasped the left hand of
his enemy, and a deadly struggle ensued.

It was evident to the spectators that a few more blows would
now decide the conflict, and their interest rose in proportion.
Not a breath was drawn. Esclairmonde leaned over the balcony
with a look as if her own life hung upon that of her lover. Nor
could Catherine de Medicis, whose cause was leagued with that
of the opposite party, control her anxiety. At this moment, a
voice soft and low, in whose tones, altered as they were by
passion, she yet recognised those of Marguerite de Valois,
reached the ear of the Princess of Condé.

"I would give my soul to perdition," said the Queen of
Navarre, "to see the poniard of Gonzaga pierce the heart of
his enemy."

"For pity's sake—wherefore?" asked the princess, without removing her gaze from the combatants.

"To be avenged of thee," answered Marguerite in a hollow voice.

"Gracious heaven!" exclaimed the princess, "thy horrible wish is accomplished—he falls—he falls."

In the struggle it appeared that the dagger of the prince, glancing from the corslet of the Scot, had dangerously wounded the steed of the latter in the neck. The blood gushed in torrents from the deep gash, and the horse reeled with faintness. Pursuing an advantage obtained contrary to the laws of the combat, which forbade hurt to be done to the charger, Gonzaga threw himself furiously upon his antagonist, endeavouring to drive him beyond the boundary described upon the arena; but Crichton, feeling his steed totter under him, avoided the blow by leaning backwards, and disengaging at the same moment his feet from the stirrup, leapt to the ground, and ere the prince could regain his balance, seized him by the arm and dragged him from the saddle.

The conflict was now continued on foot. Blow after blow was dealt upon helm and cuirass. The tilt-yard rang like the forge of an armourer. Hacked off by the trenchant edges of the poniards, chips of the gold embossments and enamel strewed the arena, promising a rich harvest to the heralds. Gonzaga displayed all the address of a finished man-at-arms. In strength he was evidently inferior to his antagonist, but so expert was he in the use of the dagger, so dexterous in avoiding foyns and thrusts, which must have proved fatal had they taken effect, that the spectators felt doubtful as to the issue of the strife. At length, the poniard of Crichton, driven through the vantbrace of the prince, but without inflicting more than a trifling scratch, snapped in twain, and he appeared at the mercy of his opponent. Ruggieri lifted up his hands and uttered an exclamation of joy.

"Now Heaven be praised!" cried Catherine de Medicis, "the right will triumph."

"He is not yet vanquished, madam," exclaimed Esclairmonde, "and trust me, the right *will* triumph."

As she spoke, the prince advanced his dagger's point to the throat of Crichton, and glancing at him through the bars of his vizor, commanded him to yield.

"Yield!" replied Crichton fiercely; "it is a word I have never pronounced. Let this decide the combat."

And, with the broken blade of his poniard, he delivered so terrible a blow upon the morion of the prince, that head and casque appeared to be crushed by it. Gonzaga fell without sense or motion, a stream of gore flowing from out his vizor.

"Yield, prince," exclaimed Crichton, stooping over him, and snatching the dagger from his loosened grasp, "or, by Saint Andrew, you have breathed your last!"

But Gonzaga answered not.

At this moment the Duc de Nevers and the Vicomte de Joyeuse, followed by Montjoie and his attendant, spurred their horses to the spot.

"The victory is yours, Chevalier Crichton; slay him not," cried the duke, flinging himself from his steed. "Ha!" exclaimed he, as he regarded the motionless form of the prince, "you have destroyed the hopes of my brother of Mantua. By Saint Francis! you shall answer for the deed."

"If the prince is slain, he hath perished in the quarrel he himself provoked," replied Crichton sternly; "to yourself, my lord, or to others of his house, I will answer for what I have done."

"The prince, your nephew, has been fairly vanquished, my lord," said Joyeuse, "and the only felon stroke dealt during the combat was that by which yon bleeding charger was wounded."

"And that was accidental," said Crichton.

By this time the attendants had unclasped Vincenzo's helmet, and though stunned and wounded by the concussion, his life was evidently not in danger. Satisfied with this examination, the duke became eager in his apologies to the Scot for the impatience he had exhibited, and his excuses being courteously accepted, he next directed his followers to remove the senseless body of the prince from the field. While this took place amid the shouts of the spectators, and a loud flourish of trumpets, Crichton proceeded to the canopy occupied by the king and prostrated himself before him. Henri greeted him with a smile and, raising him from the ground, passed many encomiums upon the bravery he had displayed.

"You have approved yourself a loyal and valiant knight, Chevalier Crichton," he said, "and have fully established the truth of the charge you brought yesternight against the traitor Ruggieri, whose guilt admits of no further justification. *Quia transivit in rem judicatum, et judicatum debet inviolabiliter observari*, as is appointed by the ordinance of our predecessor, the good King Philippe le Bel, respecting the judicial combat. *Par la Mort-Dieu!* the Place de Grève shall blaze this night with his funeral pyre. Let him be removed to the Châtelet, and see whether the question will extract the truth from his lips."

"My gracious liege," said Crichton, "I crave a boon at your hands."

"Name it," replied the king; "if it refer not to one whom we will not name, it is yours ere asked."

"Let the punishment to which you have condemned the traitor Ruggieri be commuted into perpetual exile."

"Do I hear you rightly?" asked Henri, in surprise.

"Grant me his life, sire, upon the terms I shall propose to him," continued Crichton.

"He is in your hands—deal with him as you see fitting," returned Henri. "Bring hither the traitor," he added, speaking to his attendants, "and let him now be confronted with his accuser."

And, half dead with terror, the astrologer was dragged by his hooded attendants into the king's presence, amid the execrations of the spectators.

"Cosmo Ruggieri, thy guilt is fully approved," said Henri sternly; "thy sentence, whether of death or banishment, rests with the Chevalier Crichton. It is with him to pronounce thy doom. Down on thy knees, miscreant, and sue for grace. To me thou pleadest in vain."

Crichton approached the astrologer, who cast himself abjectly at his feet, embracing his knees, and striving to move his compassion with floods of tears. "Mercy," he cried, in a piteous tone.

"Thou wilt find none, unless thou provest obedient," replied Crichton; "arise, and listen to me." And as Ruggieri obeyed, Crichton whispered in his ear the conditions upon which he might look for clemency. The astrologer started and trembled.

"I dare not," he said, after a moment's pause, during which he stole a troubled glance towards the gallery.

"To the rack with him," said Crichton.

The hooded officials instantly darted upon him like kites upon a carcass.

"Hold!—hold!" cried Ruggieri; "I cannot brave that dreadful engine. I will do as you command me."

"Take him hence, then," commanded Crichton, "and let him remain with a sufficient guard within my pavilion until after the tourney."

"Your own lives shall answer for him," added Henri, as the astrologer was removed; "and now, *mon cher* Crichton," he added, "if you would effect the liberation of a captive princess from an enchanted castle, in which she is detained by magic arts, haste and equip yourself in fresh armour. Joyeuse will find you another steed in lieu of the one slain by the felon blow of your antagonist. Away, arm yourself, and join our ranks. And now, messeigneurs, for the Châtelet de la Joyeuse Garde! What, ho! Du Halde—my horse—my gallant Papillon."

Crichton joyfully departed to array himself for this new encounter, while the king, mounting his snow-white Arabian, proceeded to superintend the preparations for the grand estour. As he rode across the arena, a *billet* was presented to him by a page in the livery of Catherine de Medicis. Henri knit his brow as he perused it.

"*Peste!*" he muttered, "am I ever to be a puppet in my mother's hands?—By Saint Louis! this shall never be. And yet, all things considered, it may be better to concede this trifle. Du Halde," he added, beckoning to the chief valet, and speaking in an undertone, "get thee to Crichton's pavilion, and contrive some means for Ruggieri's instant escape. We desire not to be known in this matter.—Thou understandest—about it quickly."

Du Halde departed on his mission, and Henri, turning to his courtiers, with a smile that but ill-concealed his mortification, said, "It is our mother's pleasure, messeigneurs, that the grand mêlée be deferred till night. The defence of the Châtelet will, therefore, take place, as at first designed, by torchlight. Joyeuse, do thou give orders to this effect. Her majesty hath desired instant speech with us—on affairs of State," he added, in a sarcastic tone, "we presume—no matter—after our conference, which we shall certainly not prolong, it is our intention to essay a course with this *preux* Scottish knight, in honour of our fair Queen of the Lists."

With this, the monarch pressed forward, and dismounting from his charger, entered the royal gallery.

CHAPTER V

THE PAVILION

La reine vouloit persuader que ce pauvre prince, son fils, avoit conspiré
afin de le rendre odieux à chacun.

HENRI ETIENNE, *Discours Merveilleux.*

WHEN the armourer had completed his office, and Crichton,
attired in a magnificent suit of russet-coloured mail sent him
by the Vicomte de Joyeuse, was about to place his plumed
casque upon his brow and return to the tilt-yard, a page in the
royal livery suddenly appeared at the entrance of the pavilion
and announced the Queen-Mother. Ere the Scot could recover
from the astonishment into which he was thrown by this
unlooked-for visit, Catherine stood before him.

"My presence occasions you surprise, messire," said the queen,
with a gracious salutation, which Crichton haughtily returned,
"nor will that surprise be diminished when you learn the motive
that has brought us hither."

"To whatever motive I must attribute your majesty's present
condescension," returned Crichton coldly, "I am well aware,
from your smiles, that some new danger is to be apprehended."

"You wrong me by your doubts, Chevalier Crichton," rejoined
Catherine, in a tone of great courtesy and apparent candour;
"my enmity to you exists no longer. In vanquishing Gonzaga
you have vanquished me. I am here to acknowledge my defeat,
and I am assured that your nature is too chivalrous to refuse
mercy to a prostrate foe."

"Your majesty forgets our interview last night," said Crichton, regarding the queen distrustfully, "and the Machiavellian
precepts with which you unintentionally favoured me. Need
I remind you that 'words are the cloak 'neath which the sword
is hidden'; need I add, that under your present fair professions
I discern a dark and deadly purpose. Your majesty is no prostrate foe. And it is for me—not for yourself—to sue for clemency."

"You have nothing more to apprehend from me, messire,"
said Catherine, a slight shade passing across her majestic
features, "unless, indeed, you wantonly provoke my resentment.
I pledge my royal word that I am come hither to confer with
you in amity."

"That royal word was plighted to the brave and trusting
Coligni," rejoined Crichton; "how it was kept, the gory gibbet
of Montfaucon best can answer."

K 804

"Grant me patience, Heaven!" exclaimed Catherine, in an altered voice. "You will not then accept my assurance of friendship?"

"No, by the Saint-Barthélemy, madam," answered Crichton sternly.

Catherine's quivering lip proclaimed the struggle she underwent to repress her almost uncontrollable indignation. Skilled, however, in the mastery of her emotions, she did instantaneously repress it, and waving her hand to the attendants, who had withdrawn to the outlet of the tent at her approach, she was left alone with the Scot.

"Chevalier Crichton," she said, in a deep low tone, "you are brave—but your bravery amounts to folly. Of what avail are these idle taunts?—We understand each other."

"We do, madam," replied the Scot.

"And with this understanding, why should we not act in unison? Our interests require it. As friend or foe our purposes are so indissolubly connected, that to separate one were to destroy the other. So far you have succeeded. You are in a position to make terms with me. Propose them. Let not your ambition dread too high a flight. You have boasted that your ancestry is noble—regal——"

"The blood of the Stuart flows in my veins," said Crichton, proudly.

"If I have heard aright, your sire is——"

"Sir Robert Crichton, my father, is sole advocate to James of Scotland," interrupted Crichton; "our religious opinions are at variance, or I had never quitted my native land."

"You did ill to leave it in its season of calamity," said Catherine, "a prey to heresy and rebellion. One hand like yours, one voice potent as your own, might have availed to check, if not avert, this widely devastating storm. Your energies would, indeed, have been beneficially displayed in crushing that serpent brood which the pernicious zeal of the fanatic Knox has called into life. Had the tocsin of Saint-Barthélemy been rung from the towers of Edinburgh Castle; had our gentle daughter Mary dealt with her ruthless foes as we have dealt with the enemies of our faith, she would not now have been a captive to Elizabeth. Chevalier Crichton, your lovely queen weeps away her hours in prison. It should have been your aim, as faithful Catholic and loyal subject, to have effected her liberation."

"You have, unwittingly, touched upon a chord that vibrates

through my heart, madam," said the Scot, his colour mounting, and his glances kindling as he spoke. "To rescue my beloved queen from her oppressors, I would willingly lay down my life —nay, a thousand lives, if I possessed them! If her guard were thrice in number what it is—her prison yet more inaccessible— if she were lodged within the palace of her rival—or immured in London's impregnable tower, I would accomplish her deliverance, or perish in the attempt, did not an awful bar prevent me."

"What bar?" demanded Catherine, with some appearance of curiosity.

"A father's malediction!" replied Crichton, with a sudden change of tone. "Your majesty has spoken of the devastation which heresy has spread throughout my unhappy land. Her temples have been desecrated—the fire that burnt upon her ancient altars has been extinguished; her reverend priests have been driven forth—but this is not all. Into the bosom of her families these new doctrines have brought fierce and bitter dissension. Irreconcilable hatred has sprung up where love before existed. My sire (alas! that it should be so) has embraced the reformed faith. I have remained constant to the creed of my ancestry—to the creed of my conviction; and in behalf of that religion in the cause of my injured queen, I should have taken up arms, when I was of years to bear them, had not my sire placed between my sword and the hand that would have grasped it—his curse! With a father's malediction hanging over my head, I could not hope for success. Without a struggle I resigned the first, the dearest wish of my dawning life. In vain were prospects of ambition, clouded with heresy, and stained by rebellion, opened to me. In vain were proffers made me by those who would have purchased my services. I left my country, for whose weal I would have gladly bled—I quitted my paternal halls, to which a thousand tender recollections bound me— I vowed never to return to that country—never again to behold that home, till the schism of the one should be annihilated—the old rites of worship, once observed by the other, restored."

"You will never, then, see Scotland more," said Catherine; "she will cling to her false faith, as a libertine to the leman whose arts have ensnared him."

"Or, as her preachers affirm," rejoined Crichton, in a tone of scorn, "she is like the profligate who has abandoned the mistress and assumed the wife. But your majesty is right. Scotland will know no change. The homely creed she has adopted suits her homely people well. Austere in feeling as in manner, they will become hardened in heresy. The dogma promulgated by Knox —*plebis est religionem reformare*—roused the whole nation. The people *have* reformed their faith—and their creed is essentially plebeian. Stripped of its ornaments; robbed of its majesty and grace; its magnificent proportions, sculptured and reared by ages, destroyed; its venerable and hoary colouring, which time alone could impart, effaced; its odours scattered to the breezes; its traditions forgotten or despised; the worship of my country simple, naked, and, it may be, pure, no more resembles its ancient grandeur and sublimity, than the lowly temple of the Huguenot will bear comparison with the glorious edifices of Notre-Dame. A cathedral *is* religion. Who can enter its reverend aisles unmoved—who can gaze upwards to its vaulted roofs with thoughts that stray not heavenward! Mine be the antique fane—mine the time-honoured creed. Mine be the saint, the shrine, the solemn and melodious mass—mine the faith picturesque, poetical, beautiful. My native land I may never behold again—my father's blessing I may never receive—but the religion of Rome, entwined around my heart, endeared to me even by persecution, I will ever maintain."

"I applaud your zeal, messire," said Catherine. "To the brave man the soil he treads is his country. Be France the land of your adoption. Her faith is yet unchanged. Heaven grant it may continue so! The storm we have swept away is again gathering with increased power and fury. Lend us your assistance to dispel it—to uphold the religion so dear to you. In the reign of the Seventh Charles, who swayed the sceptre of this fair kingdom, one of your countrymen was, for his bravery displayed in the well-fought field of Beaugé, in Anjou, when the royal Clarence fell by his hand, created Constable of France—why should not a like dignity be yours?"

"Were such unhoped-for distinction mine, madam," said Crichton, smiling, "I should not be the first of my line who has been similarly graced. The valiant Earl of Buchan, the countryman to whom your majesty refers, by whose proud achievement the field of Beaugé was won, and by whom the baton of France was thenceforth borne, was (I hesitate not to proclaim it) my ancestor."

"Indeed!" exclaimed the wily queen, with well-feigned surprise. "Valour it seems is your inheritance. I rejoice to learn that you are a descendant of bold John of Buchan, whose chivalrous deeds my consort Henri II. has so often rehearsed to me. Why, I again ask, should you not tread in the steps of your ancestor? Why should not your hand grasp the marshal's baton? Why should not your voice lead on the chivalry of France to conquest? Why should not your vigilance maintain her ancient faith unsullied?"

Crichton returned no answer. His countenance glowed and his frame dilated, as Catherine, not insensible of the impression she had produced, continued: "Why should you not aspire to the hand of the fairest princess of her time? Why should not the lovely Esclairmonde be yours?"

"No more, I pray you, madam—tempt me not."

"Graced with the rank of marshal—allied to the royal house of Condé—enriched with the dowry which your bride will bring—would not even *your* ambition be contented?"

"Even in my wildest dreams my aspirations never soared so high," ejaculated Crichton. "A marshal of France!"

"Her leader!" said Catherine.

"That baton in my grasp which Bertrand du Guesclin, Olivier de Clisson, and the brave Boucicart bore—which Gaston de Foix, Brissac, and Montmorency wielded—that baton mine!"

"The legions of France beneath your command," added Catherine.

"Her legions!" echoed Crichton. "Ha! Saint Andrew! I see them rise round me! I see her fierce and fiery bands pour like a tide upon the plain. I see her chivalry arrayed before me— that peerless chivalry which Bayard led—ha! Montjoie! Saint Denis!—methinks I hear the battle-cry."

"Be Bayard's fortune yours."

"Bayard was reproachless, madam," returned the Scot, the glow which had lighted up his features suddenly fading away; "the name of Crichton shall be equally so."

"Your name shall not be stained, messire," said Catherine impatiently; "but in your dreams of ambition you have for-gotten—what we should least have expected you to forget— your tender aspirations."

"Esclairmonde!" exclaimed Crichton.

"Say rather the Princess of Condé," rejoined Catherine, "for her rank will speedily be acknowledged."

"Will *you* acknowledge it, madam?" demanded Crichton eagerly.

"At my own pleasure," returned the queen coldly. "Question not—but listen. The baton of France—the hand of the Princess of Condé are yours—on certain conditions."

"Hell hath her compacts," muttered Crichton, "and men have bartered their eternal weal for lighter offers. Your conditions, madam?"

"Have I your knightly word, that whether or not you accept the terms I am about to propose, your lips shall reveal no syllable I may utter?"

Crichton appeared lost in reflection.

"Have I your word?" repeated Catherine.

"You have, madam," returned the Scot.

"I trust you with my life, then—for I am well assured, that once plighted, you will not break that word."

"Your majesty may speak as to your confessor——"

"My confessor!" echoed Catherine derisively. "Think you I would entrust a secret—the betrayal of which would fill our city of Paris with scaffolds—would float her streets with blood —would crowd the dungeons of her Bastille, and the oubliettes of her châtelets with noble prisoners, to a crafty priest? No! there are secrets which must not even be breathed to heaven. Ours is one of them."

"And crimes too deep to be forgiven," said Crichton gloomily. —"Heaven grant your majesty propose not such."

"Be patient, messire," returned the queen, "and you shall hear what I *do* propose. You are already (no matter how!) in possession of my plans. I need not, therefore, tell you of my project for Henri's dethronement—of my scheme to place his crown upon the Duc d'Anjou's head."

"Thus much I know, madam," said Crichton.

"But you are not aware," continued Catherine, approaching more nearly to the Scot, and lowering her tone, "that Anjou is now in Paris."

"Within this city?—ha!"

"Within the Louvre — within the palace soon to be his own."

"Great Heaven!"

"Bussy d'Amboise, his favourite, has this morning arrived from Flanders. All goes well for us. We have the gold of Spain —the swords of Switzerland and Scotland—for the guards are *ours*. Our thousand agents, our spies and emissaries, are at work. They thread each quarter of the city. Our partisans collect together, and only await the signal to declare themselves. That signal will be given to-night."

"So soon!"

"Ay, so soon," reiterated Catherine triumphantly. "Nostradamus foretold that *all* my sons should be kings. To-morrow his prediction will be verified."

"And Henri?"

Catherine grew pale as death, and trembled so violently that she was compelled to lay her hand for support upon Crichton's armed shoulder.

"What of the king, your son, madam?" continued the Scot sternly.

"Of all my sons," exclaimed the queen, with a look of deep agony, and it might be compunction, "Henri hath ever been the most dear to me. The sickly François, the rugged Charles, found no place in my heart. But Henri, the fond, the pliant, the winning; Henri, ever devoted, ever deferential to my will; Henri, the graceful, the polished, the beautiful—whom Nature intended for a king, and for whom I have seconded Nature's intentions—he has ever been my favourite."

"And you will now destroy your own work; you will sacrifice your favourite son?"

"My safety requires it," returned Catherine, sighing deeply; "Henri has of late grown wayward and capricious. He refuses to follow my counsel—to acknowledge my sway. His minions have supplanted me in his esteem. Saint-Luc, Joyeuse, D'Epernon rule where I was wont to govern. The Salic law prevents the exercise of sovereign authority in my own person. I reign *through* my sons: if not through Henri, I must reign through François."

"Weighed against love of power, a mother's love is nothing," said Crichton.

"Against high resolves it *should* be nothing," returned Catherine; "against Fate it *is* nothing. Of what avail is my tenderness for Henri; of what avail are my regrets for his defection, of what avail is this hesitation to pronounce his doom? Chevalier Crichton," she continued, in a voice that froze the Scot's blood within his veins, "he must die!"

There was a terrible pause, during which each regarded the other fixedly.

"Horror!" exclaimed Crichton, at length recovering his speech. " Can *a mother* say this?"

"Hear me!" cried Catherine, "and learn with whom you have to deal—learn and tremble! By blood—my own blood, was my power obtained; by blood—my own blood, must it be maintained. Henri must die."

"By the hand that reared him?"

"No! mine might falter. I will find a surer arm to deal the blow. Listen," she continued, becoming perfectly calm, "by midnight all will be in readiness. Under various pretexts, and in various disguises, the leaders of Anjou's faction will, ere that hour arrives, have been introduced into the Louvre. Bussy d'Amboise has his own quarrel to avenge upon the king's favourites. His sword hath seldom failed him. He will deal with Joyeuse, D'Epernon, and Saint-Luc. The Duc de Nevers is ours already. Villequier and D'O are vanes that will shift with the wind. Henri alone remains—and he——"

"Well, madam?"

"Is reserved for your hand."

"For MINE!"

"I have prevailed upon him to defer the grand chivalrous emprise in which he takes part till midnight. Amid the conflict his lance will seek yours. Couch, then, your sharpened spear—cry 'Live François III.,' and strike! I know too well the force of your arm to doubt the fatal issue of the blow. That cry—that deadly stroke, will be the signal to Anjou—and to our party. They will respond to it. Henri's adherents will be exterminated —his crown will be his brother's."

"From the scene of carnage you depict, madam," said Crichton, "my mind flies back to days gone by—to the fair month of June 1559. Before the palace of the Tournelles, a splendid tournament is set forth to celebrate the nuptials of Elizabeth of France with Philip of Spain. A chivalrous monarch maintains the passage of arms against all comers. That monarch is your husband. That monarch is Henri II."

"No more—no more."

"That monarch demands a favour from his queen. Her scarf is sent him. He places it upon his corslet. He calls to the Earl of Montgomery to place his lance in rest. The earl obeys him. The combatants rush upon each other. The lance of Montgomery is broken——"

"Hold! I command you, messire."

"But a splinter hath pierced the brain of the ill-fated king," continued Crichton, heedless of Catherine's frowns. "He falls mortally wounded. You witnessed this fearful catastrophe, madam. You saw your husband hurled bleeding to the earth— and to a like fate you would now condemn your son—*his son!*"

"Have you yet done?"

"Think you I am an assassin, madam, that you propose to

me a deed from which even the ruthless bravo of your native Italy would shrink aghast?"

"If I propose a deed dark and terrible, I offer a proportionate reward," returned Catherine. "Stay!" she continued, drawing from her escarcelle a small roll ot parchment, to which a broad seal was appended, "here is your appointment."

"It bears date to-morrow."

"It will be ratified to-night," rejoined the queen, placing the document upon a tapestry-covered table which stood beside them. "Behold the royal signet—behold your title as Marshal of France! Your answer?"

"Is this," replied Crichton, suddenly drawing his poniard, and striking it through the parchment with such force that all trace of his name was effectually obliterated.

"Enough!" exclaimed Catherine, tearing the mutilated document from the board. "You shall learn anon whose wrath you have provoked."

"Threat for threat, madam," returned the undaunted Scot. "You may find in me a formidable enemy."

"Ha!" ejaculated the queen, pausing, "you will not betray my confidence? Your word is passed."

"It is," replied Crichton; "but your majesty forgets that Ruggieri is in my power."

Catherine smiled.

"Ruggieri will betray nothing," she said.

"He has sworn to reveal *all*, on condition that his life be spared," returned Crichton.

Catherine's brow darkened for an instant, but the same sinister smile still played around her lips.

"If my astrologer be your sole instrument of offence, messire," she said, "I have little to apprehend."

"Your majesty is confident," rejoined Crichton. "What, if I tell you that the packet containing the proofs of the Princess Esclairmonde's birth is found?—what if I add that your own letters to the Duc d'Anjou—your dispatches to the Prince Vincenzo di Gonzaga are now on their way to the king?"

"And if I answer—it is false!—false as your assertion that Ruggieri will betray me. That packet will never reach the king. That packet is in my possession. The Huguenot preacher, who was to have conveyed it to Henri, is my prisoner."

"The powers of darkness have not deserted your majesty, I perceive," said Crichton, with a look of astonishment.

"Nor those of earth," retorted Catherine, clapping her hands.

"Let Ruggieri be brought before us," she added, as the attendants appeared.

The men betrayed evident symptoms of alarm, and one of them stammered out something like an excuse.

"How is this?" demanded Crichton. "Have you dared to disobey his majesty's commands?—have you suffered your prisoner to escape?"

At this moment two of the hooded officials entered the pavilion.

"Where is the astrologer?—answer on your lives," said Crichton.

"We are come to seek him here, monseigneur," said the foremost of the twain.

"Here!" echoed Crichton, furiously.

"Yes, monseigneur," returned the man; "we had no sooner placed him in the guard-room than he disappeared; we know not how or where—and we thought he was as likely to be here as in any other place."

"I recognise your hand in this, madam," said the Scot, turning to Catherine.

The queen replied with a bitter smile: "The powers of darkness have not yet deserted us, you perceive, messire."

"The other prisoner, however, is safe enough," said the foremost official, as he drew back.

"What prisoner?" demanded Crichton eagerly.

"The heretic preacher," returned the man. "He is at hand if you wish to interrogate him." And without waiting for the Scot's reply, he motioned to his comrade, who, in his turn, motioned to someone without, and the curtain of the tent being drawn aside, with his arms bound with cords, and his whole appearance betokening great personal suffering from ill-usage, the venerable Florent Chrétien was dragged into the pavilion.

"His companion, the Englishman, escaped us," interposed the official who acted as spokesman, "owing to a fiend in the form of a dog, with fangs like a wolf, who fought by his side, and covered his flight. But he cannot have passed the gates of the Louvre—and we may yet secure him."

Crichton was about to rush to the assistance of the captive preacher to free him from his bondage. But a look from the old man restrained him.

"It is in vain, my son," said Chrétien; "do not draw down your blood likewise upon my head."

"The packet?" demanded Crichton, with frantic eagerness; "say it has not fallen into the hands of this remorseless queen—say you have given it to the Englishman Blount—say that he hastens with it to the king—say there is yet hope."

"Alas! my son, why should I deceive you? My mission hath failed. Our enemies triumph. They have pursued me sore. Like a bird I have fallen into their snare. The precious casket hath been stolen from me. There is no hope save from on high."

"Heaven will work no miracle in thy behalf, rank heretic that thou art," said Catherine; "the populace, robbed of the spectacle they anticipated in Ruggieri's execution by fire, will need a victim. They shall have one. The stake shall not have been planted, nor the faggots piled within the Pré-aux-Clercs, in vain. Abjure thine heresies, old man. Make thy peace above. Thy sentence is pronounced."

"I desire no better end," replied Chrétien; "my death shall be a testimony to the faithful."

"Your fanatic zeal blinds you, good father," said Crichton; "forsake your errors while there is yet time."

"Forsake them!" echoed the preacher, with fervour. "Never! Flames may consume my breathing body. Torture may rend my limbs asunder. But my lips shall never gainsay my heart. For a death like this, my whole life hath been a preparation. I am not taken by surprise. My house is set in order. I shall glory in my martyrdom. I shall rejoice to be numbered with the righteous, who have perished in the service of their God. It is thou, my son, who art in error. It is thou who art blinded and perverse. It is thou who art in danger of unquenchable flame. Let my words dwell with thee—let my spirit be upon thee. So shall I not die in vain; so shall thy own end be happy—be joyful as mine. Thou hast called me father—as a father I bestow my blessing upon thee."

"As a father—O God!" exclaimed Crichton, his eyes filling with emotion, and his voice faltering.

"Kneel down, my son; an old man's benediction, whatever may be his creed, cannot injure you." [1]

Crichton instantly threw himself at the preacher's feet.

"Heaven's grace descend upon your head, my son," said Chrétien, bending over him; "and may the dawning of a new light from henceforth break upon your soul!"

"My soul will never swerve from its fixed bias," replied

[1] These, or nearly these words, were addressed by the Pope Benedict XIV. to Horace Walpole.

Crichton, as he arose from the benediction. "I admire your constancy, but my faith is changeless as your own. I shall be no apostate."

"*Video meliora, proboque, deteriora sequor,*" sighed the old man. "Ah, my son, you are stubborn in unbelief. But my prayers will not be unheard, and your name, together with that of one dear to you as to myself, shall mingle with my latest breath. I shall expire in the hope of your spiritual regeneration. For thee, perfidious and bloody-minded woman," he continued, turning to Catherine, and regarding her with a terrible look, "a day of dreadful retribution is at hand. Thy portion shall be that of the idolatrous Queen of Judah. Evil shall be brought upon thee and shame. Thy posterity shall be utterly taken away. With blood hast thou polluted this city, and with thy own blood shall it be cleansed. 'Vengeance is mine,' saith the Lord, 'and I will repay.'"

"Peace, blasphemer," interrupted the queen, "and learn to thy confusion, that if the arm of heaven hath been manifested at all, it hath this day been declared in favour of the religion thou deridest. The leader upon whom the reliance of your miserable sect is placed—our chief enemy—hath been delivered into our hands. Ha! thou tremblest—have I found a way to shake thy inflexible spirit?"

"It cannot be!" exclaimed Chrétien, with a despairing look.

"It *is*," returned Catherine triumphantly; "we hold thy chieftain within our toils."

"Ah, fatal rashness!" cried Chrétien bitterly; "but I will not murmur against the decrees of Providence. I pray your majesty to send me forth; I am very faint."

"Take him hence," said Catherine, "and let it be proclaimed by sound of trumpet in each quarter of our faithful and Catholic city, that a Huguenot minister will be put to death by fire at midnight within the Pré-aux-Clercs. Let the ecclesiastical authorities receive instant intimation to attend. Here is your warrant," she added, delivering a written paper to the official.

"Your majesty hath delivered me the wrong order," said the official, glancing at the superscription of the scroll; "this is a warrant for the execution of Cosmo Ruggieri, Abbé of Saint Mahé, convicted of the crimes of *lèse-majesté* and sorcery."

"It will suffice," returned the queen, imperiously: "remove your prisoner."

Chrétien dropped upon his knees.

"How long, O Lord, holy and true," cried he, gazing earnestly

towards heaven, "dost Thou not judge and avenge our blood
on them that dwell upon the earth?"

And with these words his reverend head declined upon his
breast, while, supported by the two officials, he was borne out
of the pavilion.

"Your majesty, indeed, is an inexorable enemy," said Crichton,
gazing after the unfortunate preacher, with looks of the deepest
commiseration.

"And as unalterable a friend," returned the queen. "It is for
you now to determine, Chevalier Crichton, in which light I must
henceforth be viewed. A word ere we part. In Henri you have
a rival. He loves the Princess Esclairmonde."

"I know it, madam——"

"To-night she is his, or yours."

"*His* she shall never be."

"Then you accept my terms?"

At this moment the loud blast of a bugle was heard sounding
from the farther end of the tilt-yard.

"A knightly challenge!" exclaimed Crichton, listening for a
repetition of the notes.

"A *kingly* challenge," returned Catherine; "that trumpet
blast is the defiance of Henri of Navarre."

"Henri of Navarre!" echoed Crichton in astonishment. "He,
then, is the Huguenot leader whom fate hath delivered into
your hands."

"He is," replied Catherine. "I am indebted to chance for
this important discovery. One of my demoiselles, La Rebours,
as she rode to the Louvre, was struck with the resemblance of
a soldier in the train of the Baron de Rosni to Henri de Bourbon.
The circumstances was casually alluded to in my hearing. My
suspicions were at once aroused. Spies were instantly put upon
the scent, and I found that the soldier was the monarch in
masquerade. The secret must rest between ourselves, messire."

"Fear nothing, madam," answered the Scot; "my lips are
sealed."

"I learnt, also, that this foolhardy king was about to attend
the jousts held at the Louvre, for the express purpose of breaking
a lance with you."

"With me, madam?"

"Your renown as an expert tilter has, I conclude, reached his
ears, and he is resolved to put it to the proof. But hark! his
trumpet sounds for the second time. This conference must be
brought to a close. Your answer to my proposal?"

"It shall be delivered after the jousts."

"Our confidence in the meantime——?"

"Shall be held sacred. I swear it."

"Enough—after the jousts I shall expect you within the royal gallery. Place your hand, as if by accident, upon your poniard when you approach me. From the gesture I shall infer that you assent. *Dieu vous garde! messire.*" So saying, Catherine summoned her attendants and quitted the pavilion.

"What ho! my lance—my steed," shouted Crichton, snatching his helmet from the armourer, who had promptly answered his call. "Ha! Saint Andrew, my gorget, my gauntlets! By Heaven!" he murmured, "to cross a lance with the bravest prince in Christendom were reward enough for a thousand risks. Our Lady aid me in this essay!"

In another instant his equipments were completed, and, vaulting upon his steed, the Scot dashed through the entrance of the lists.

No sooner was the coast clear, than from beneath the tapestry-covered table, which stood in the middle of the tent, emerged first a long conical cap—then a fantastic visage in which drollery was strangely mixed up with apprehension—and lastly the odd-shaped parti-coloured person of Chicot—his teeth chattering and his limbs shaking.

"*Sang de cabres!*" he cried, after casting an anxious glance around. "I have stolen here to some purpose. Pretty revelations I have heard. A conspiracy on the eve of breaking forth!—our dear Henriot about to be transfixed with a lance as his father was transfixed before him. Had it been the cloister to which he was condemned, I should not have cared—he had always a taste for the frock—but assassination!—*Cornes de diable!* I am horror-stricken. Old Buridan was in the right to propound his sophism—'Reginam interficere nolite timere bonum esse.' It would be a praiseworthy act to put Queen Catherine out of the way. But Buridan's theories are out of fashion even in the Sorbonne. What is to be done? Luckily *I* have made no vow not to betray her majesty's confidence—and if I had, on an occasion like the present, I should not scruple to break it. What is to be done? I ask myself that question for the second time. I am sorely perplexed. Who will believe my tale? I shall be laughed at — cuffed — perhaps be put out of the way myself — the common fate of meddlers. I have it. I will abide the issue of the jousts, and then confer with this Scot—for I can guess what answer he means to give our Jezebel. How runs the pasquil?

'Twixt Catherine and Jezebel
The difference is small—
The one the plague of Israel,
The other plague of Gaul.
But if the fate of Jezebel
Our Catherine should befall,
The very dogs would (mark me well!)
Refuse to eat at all." [1]

And muttering these scurrilous strains as he went, the jester crept cautiously out of the pavilion.

CHAPTER VI

THE BÉARNAIS

Que direz-vous, fâcheux maris, de cette souffrance? N'aurez-vous point de peur, que vos femmes vous laissent pour venir à moi? ou n'estimerez-vous point plutôt que ce fût quelque lâcheté.—*Divorce Satirique.*

As Crichton rode into the tilt-yard he found Henri, encircled by his favourites, impatiently awaiting his return, and speculating upon the haughty defiance with which the walls of the Louvre yet resounded.

"Away, Montjoie—away, messieurs," cried the monarch, addressing the king-at-arms and the heralds; "do your devoir quickly, and bring us word what hardy champion dares to intrude within our lists. *Par la Mort-Dieu!* it would seem we hold a free passage of arms, and not private jousts. But this adventurer, whoever he may be, shall rue his temerity. Away! and let us know his title and condition. Ha! you are come," he added, as the Scot drew in the rein by his side. "We shall question you anon, messire, as to the nature of your interminable conference with our mother. We suspect from your looks that you have been hatching some treason against us. Is it so?"

"Sire!" exclaimed Crichton, reddening.

"By our faith your interview *hath* made you serious since you thus resent our jest," said the king, smiling; "and no wonder—for, certes, a *tête-à-tête* of any duration with her majesty the Queen-Mother is no laughing matter, even to ourself. However, upon the present occasion we ought to thank, rather than chide you, for detaining her so long, as her absence has enabled us

[1] From a bitter pasquinade in the *Journal of Henri III.*, entitled "Comparaison de Catherine et de Jezabel."

to lay closer siege to her lovely demoiselle than we should have cared to do in her presence. Apropos of the fair Esclairmonde, Chevalier Crichton, so soon as we have disposed of this unknown challenger, it is our intention to splinter a lance with you in her honour. We have no fears of your disloyalty you see, or we should not thus heedlessly place our life at your disposal."

"Be warned, sire!" said a deep voice, "and run no course to-day."

Henri started.

"Who speaks?" he ejaculated, turning with some misgiving, in the supposed direction of the sound. His looks of inquiry fell upon the frank countenance of the Vicomte de Joyeuse, which was charged with as much astonishment as his own.

"Remember your father's fate!" exclaimed the same deep voice now appearing to sound from a different quarter. "Beware!"

"*Sang-Dieu!*" vociferated the king furiously. "Who dares thus address us? Let him stand forth." But no answer was returned, nor was any movement made in obedience to Henri's mandate.

The courtiers eyed each other with glances of suspicion. No one, however, could tax his neighbour with having uttered the ominous words.

"Jesus!" exclaimed Henri, in a tone of some uneasiness, at the same time secretly crossing himself, "that voice recalls our idle terrors of last night. But there can be no sarbacane upon the present occasion."

"*Vive Dieu!* no, sire," cried Joyeuse, springing to the king's side. "But there may be other artifice."

"It may be well not to neglect the caution, my gracious liege," said Saint-Luc, who was almost as superstitious as his sovereign. "Charles le Bien-Aimé had his warning."

"And our ill-fated father, likewise," mused the king.

"Your majesty will not suffer yourself to be deterred from entering the jousts by this imposture," said Joyeuse. "Were I in your place, sire, I would show my contempt for this hidden traitor's counsel by seizing a lance and proceeding at once to the barriers."

"Joyeuse is in the right," said the Duc de Nevers, with a singular smile. "It were an impeachment of the Chevalier Crichton's loyalty to refuse him, upon such light grounds, the honour of a career with your majesty."

"It is an honour which I have not sought, Monsieur le Duc,"

returned Crichton sternly, "and I pray you to remember that the stroke by which Henri II. fell was *accidental.*"

"Speak not of it, *mon cher,*" said the king, shuddering.

> "Servans d'amours regardez doulcement,
> Aux eschaffaux anges de paradis——"

sang Joyeuse, anxious to reassure the pusillanimous monarch. "Think of the bright eyes that will watch your prowess, sire: think of the belle Esclairmonde."

Henri glanced towards the grand gallery; he there beheld the fair Princess of Condé, "the cynosure of neighbouring eyes," and his fears instantly vanished.

"Thou hast restored us, my brother," he said to the vicomte. "We will think of the mistress of our heart. Were it to be our last career we would no longer hesitate."

"It *will* be your last," said the deep voice, sounding yet more hollowly.

"Ha!" ejaculated Henri, relapsing into all his former terrors. "That voice again! This passeth a jest—if a jest be intended, and though we pardoned our buffoon Chicot's effrontery last night, think not we will tolerate similar freedom to-day. Look to it, messeigneurs, and let our hidden monitor, who lacketh the courage to discover himself, in his turn beware."

"Methinks your hidden counsellor displays more courage and forbearance in concealing himself," said Crichton, "than he would do were he to obey your mandate. He can have nothing to apprehend from your majesty."

At this moment, and while the utmost confusion prevailed amid the royal group, to Henri's infinite relief Montjoie and his attendant heralds returned. "Heaven be praised!" exclaimed the king. "If I am to be kept in the dark respecting this mysterious warning, my curiosity will, at all events, be gratified on another point of equal interest. Thou art welcome, Montjoie. Thy news!—the name and condition of this hardy adventurer? Yet hold! Ere thou speakest, I will wager the string of pearls against the knot of ribbons that flutters on the Chevalier Crichton's helm, that this champion is the Balafré."

"I accept your wager, sire," said Crichton. "Favour against favour."

"Decide, Montjoie," said Henri.

"Your majesty is the loser," returned the king-at-arms; "it is *not* the Duc de Guise."

"*Diantre!*" exclaimed Henri, reluctantly yielding the gage to

Crichton. "You are ever fortunate. It were vain to contend with one upon whom the capricious goddess constantly smiles."

"Certes, your majesty has lost a talisman which more than tempered steel would have been proof against my lance," rejoined the Scot, joyfully unhelming himself, and attaching the string of pearls to his casque.

Executed with consummate grace, this slight action was not unobserved by the fair princess by whom the ornament had been worn. Her situation enabled her to command the whole scene, and she witnessed with surprise the inexplicable conduct of the king towards his rival. Her astonishment was, however, speedily changed into admiration and delight as she beheld her lover's employment; and as she gazed upon his proud head, now divested of all covering save that afforded by his fair and flowing tresses; as she looked upon the stately and snow-white throat springing from out his "habiliments of war," like the moulded neck of Antinous; as she listened to the unrestrained praises of the dames by whom she was surrounded, and the louder plaudits of the admiring multitude; and as she finally encountered his enamoured gaze, and felt that he to whom all this homage was paid rendered homage alone to her—shall we injure her in the esteem of the fair reader if we say that something of self-elation mingled with her tenderer emotion? As Crichton replaced his bourginot upon his brow she waved her hand, and her salutation was instantly acknowledged by the Scot with a look and gesture of the deepest devotion.

Henri, meantime, turning to Montjoie, continued his interrogations respecting the strange knight.

"As permitted by the laws of chivalry, my liege," returned Montjoie, in answer to the king's inquiry, "this champion claims to be exempted from the disclosure of his name."

"And thou hast recognised his right to do so, we will be sworn?" said Henri in a petulant tone.

"In the due discharge of mine office, as your majesty's representative in the court of arms, I could not do otherwise," returned Montjoie.

"You have done well, sir," said the king, frowning.

"I have fulfilled my duty, sire," returned Montjoie bluntly; "your father, Henri II., of glorious memory, would not have thus rebuked me."

"Nor will his son," said Henri kindly. "Your pardon, my old and loyal servant. What title has this knight inscribed upon your rolls?"

"A strange one, sire—the Béarnais."

"The Béarnais!" exclaimed Henri in surprise. "This is some mockery. There is but one champion in Europe who has a right to that title, and he is not so much in want of warlike pastime, or so foolhardy, as to venture hither in quest of knightly adventures."

"The cavalier is, perchance, one of the King of Navarre's valiant captains, who has, for the nonce, usurped his sovereign's title," returned Montjoie; "it may be Chatillon or D'Aubigné."

"Is he unattended?" demanded Henri.

"No, my liege," answered Montjoie; "his companion is the King of Navarre's envoy, Maximilien de Béthune, Baron de Rosni."

"Ah! the Polydor of our cousin Alcandre," said the king, smiling.

"And the husband of the fair Dioclée," observed Joyeuse significantly.

"Madame de Rosni is still alive, I believe, though her husband threatened her with the dagger and the bowl when he discovered her inconstancy with Henri of Navarre—eh! marquis?" said Saint-Luc, addressing Villequier.

This was a home-thrust. The Governor of Paris, a few years back, had slain his first wife, Françoise de la Marck, for a like fault.[1] He endeavoured, however, to parry the stroke.

"The Baron de Rosni is a base and contented wittol," he said, with a sneer, "and merits his fate. Fortunate are they who possess spouses sufficiently ill-favoured to ensure their safety."

The laugh was now on the governor's side, for the baroness (as we have before remarked) was the plainest woman of her time.

Saint-Luc was about to make an angry retort to Villequier's raillery, but his petulance was checked by the king.

"No more of this, messeigneurs," said Henri. "Here come the Baron de Rosni and his unknown companion. I pray you observe them closely."

And as he spoke, two knights completely armed, and each followed by an esquire bearing his shield and lance, entered the *champ-clos*. The foremost of the twain, whose stature, originally large, was materially increased in bulk by the ponderous plates of steel in which his limbs were cased, was mounted on a fiery jet-black barb, which required the utmost efforts of his rider's powerful arm to restrain his impatience. The visor of the knight

---

[1] Cruentus sanguine uxoris, Pictavii ob improperatam sibi propudiosam vitam interfectæ.—THUANUS.

was closed, and through its narrow bars not even the flashing of an eye could be discerned. One uniform ruddy tint pervaded his equipments. From sallade to solleret, his harness was crimson-coloured. His panache of ostrich plumes, "longs et haulx," the sweeping caparisons of his charger, the feathered tufts that nodded on the chamfrin and croup of the lordly animal, the shield and battle-axe that hung at his saddle-bow, were all of the same sanguine hue.

Behind this champion, who, it is needless to say, was Henri of Navarre, rode an esquire in livery of similar complexion, bearing in his right hand a lance, on the point of which fluttered a small silken pennon, and on his left arm a buckler, painted with the simple flower so exquisitely described by a great poet of our time as

> A silver shield with boss of gold
> That spreads itself, some Faëry bold
> In fight to cover——

and surmounted by a diadem, with the following couplet traced in golden characters beneath it:

> J'aurai toujours au cœur écrite
> Sur toutes fleurs la Marguerite.

It was evident from the device that this posy was intended as an allusion to Margaret of Navarre.

The Baron de Rosni (better known by his subsequent illustrious title of the Duc de Sully) appeared in the same martial apparelling in which he was first introduced. His long two-handed sword—a formidable weapon, described by a skilful professor of the art of defence, Giacomo di Grassi, as being "four handfuls in the handle, or more, having also the great cross"—as still girt to his side. The housings of his steed, a powerful roan, were crimson and black in colour, while plumes of the same mixed hues crested his morion, the visor of which was raised.

"Yon knight is of larger make than Alcandre, my liege," said Joyeuse; "it cannot be he."

"By Saint Andrew!" exclaimed Crichton, who had witnessed the entrance of the two chieftains with rapturous enthusiasm. "The glowing trappings of yon *preux chevalier* remind me of the lay of the brave Louis de Beauveau (as charming troubadour as he was expert tilter), wherein he has depicted his own appearance at the jousts. Thus runs his ditty, if I remember rightly:

LES PLUS ROUGES Y SONT PRIS

I

Slowly unto the listed field I rode,
Rouge was my charger's wide caparison;
And the same hue that on his housing glowed,
Purpled my shield, my spear, my morion.

II

Rouge was my couvrechief, that swept the sward,
Rouge the tall plume that nodded on my crest;
And the rich scarf—my loyalty's reward—
Blushed, like a timorous virgin, on my breast.

III

My broad ensanguined shield bore this device,
In golden letters writ, that all might see
How for bold deeds will lightest words suffice,
And thus it ran—'Les plus rouges y sont pris.'"

"Have a care! *mon cher*," said Joyeuse, smiling at his friend's ardour. "See you not against whose shield the lance of yon doughty knight is directed?"

"Now, by Saint George!" replied Crichton, striking his spurs into his steed, and compelling him to execute a rapid succession of curvets. "I am right glad the appeal has been made to me."

"By the memory of my valiant uncle, François de Vivonne," exclaimed the Abbé de Brantôme, who, though not hitherto particularised, formed one of the group of courtiers in attendance upon the king, "you are the flower of knighthood, Chevalier Crichton, and appear to revive in your own person one of those hardy champions of François I., who, standing upon the very spot where we are now assembled, said, in admiration of their achievements:

Châteigneraye, Vieilleville, et Bourdillon,
Sont les trois hardis compagnons!"

"The saying would apply with equal force to the champions of our own time, dear abbé," returned Crichton, smiling. "The courage of the three renowned warriors you have named survives in their successors, the kingly courtesy of François is renewed in his grandson, and our own monarch might, with as much truth as his ancestor, exclaim:

Joyeuse, Saint-Luc, et D'Epernon,
Sont trois chevaliers braves et bons."

The three nobles smilingly acknowledged the compliment, nor did Henri appear less gratified than his favourites.

"What is all this?" cried Chicot, who had now found his way to the side of his royal master, "what miserable distich is that I hear? Talk of ancestors and descendants—pouah!—I, who am the descendant of the great Triboulet, who was fool to a greater fool, and upon whom my ancestor's cap and bells as well as his office have fallen—I, Chicot, buffoon in ordinary to

> Henri, par la grâce de sa Mère,
> Inerte Roi de France, et de Pologne imaginaire,

swear and declare upon my bauble, that

> Joyeuse, Saint-Luc, et D'Epernon
> Sont fous au merveilleux Crichton!

And there's a better rhyme, as well as sounder reason for you."

Henri of Navarre, meanwhile, followed by his esquire, having left the Baron de Rosni at the entrance of the tilt-yard, slowly traversed the arena, attracting universal attention, especially among the gentler sex, by his athletic and finely-formed figure, by the singularity of his equipments, and more than all, by his *vert-gallant* and amorous demeanour, which even danger could not subdue, nor bars of iron entirely conceal. The carelessness with which he bestrode his mettlesome and curvetting charger; the continual movements of his helmet from side to side, as his ardent glances wandered over the crowd of beauties; the majestic ease of his carriage, and a thousand indescribable graces, none of which were lost upon the spectators, worked wonders in his favour. Something, indeed, there was in the gallant Bourbon's manly form, that, under any disguise he might assume, never failed to awaken immediate interest in the female bosom. On the present occasion its effect was little less than magical, and as, he paused for a moment beneath the grand gallery, a perfect sensation was excited among its fair and frolic occupants.

"Who is he?" ran from lip to lip.

"It is the Duc d'Anjou," said Madame de Narmoutiers.

"It is Bussy d'Amboise," said Isabel de Montsoreau.

"It is the Duc de Guise," said la Maréchale de Retz.

"*Mon Dieu!* mesdames, yon knight's armour would encase all three," said Torigni, screaming with laughter. "You ought to know your old lovers better."

"Unless, like the Demoiselle de Torigni, we should have had so many as to have forgotten all save the last," returned the maréchale maliciously.

"*Merci, madame,*" rejoined the Florentine, "you are quite

welcome to attack my memory, so long as you compliment my attractions."

"What if it be the gendarme of the Rue Pélican?" sighed La Rebours.

"Your head has been running all the morning upon that soldier, demoiselle," remarked La Fosseuse, pettishly. "You thought him like Henri of Navarre, and now you think everybody like *him.*"

"Ah! if it should be the Bourbon, after all!" cried La Rebours, suddenly recovering her animation.

"Whoever he may be," replied Torigni, "he has decidedly the finest figure of any knight in the tilt-yard—the Chevalier Crichton not excepted."

"Name not the traitor in my hearing," observed Marguerite de Valois, whose attention this chance allusion to her lover's name had aroused.

"Our unknown cavalier appears in search of some dame from whom he may solicit a favour," said the Maréchale de Retz.

"And he is so like the Duc de Guise that *you* cannot possibly refuse him," rejoined Torigni.

"His glances are directed towards La Rebours," said La Fosseuse. "See, he moves."

"To me!" ejaculated La Rebours, crimsoning to the temples. "No," she added, with a look of disappointment, "it is to her majesty."

"And see you not the device on his shield," remarked Torigni, "and the motto,

J'aurai toujours au cœur écrite
Sur toutes fleurs la Marguerite.

He is, evidently, an aspirant to the smiles of our gracious mistress. Your majesty," continued the artful Florentine, addressing the queen in a low tone, "will have now an opportunity of fully revenging yourself upon your inconstant lover."

"You forget whom you address, minion," replied Marguerite, vainly endeavouring to hide her emotion under the mask of impatience; "once more I forbid you to allude to him."

At this moment, a page pressed forward, and bending the knee before the Queen of Navarre, tendered the homage of the unknown knight.

"The companion-in-arms of the Baron de Rosni," he said, "who solicits some slight token from your majesty, that he may splinter a lance in your behalf with the Chevalier Crichton."

"With Crichton!" exclaimed Marguerite, rising.

"I was in the right you see, madam," cried Torigni; but perceiving the fearful change that had taken place in the countenance of the queen, she checked her vivacity. "After all, she *will* avenge herself upon her lover," thought the demoiselle; "that look reminds me of the night when Guillaume du Prat, enticed by her caresses to the deed, for ever silenced the envenomed tongue of her enemy, Du Guast."

"This knight is the companion of the Baron de Rosni, thou sayst?" demanded Marguerite, with an abstracted air.

"His brother-in-arms, madam," returned the youth.

"He shall receive a gage from our own hand," said the queen, after a brief pause.

"He will value it the more highly," rejoined the youth. "Honoured by so fair a queen, his success in the career is certain."

"On my faith, *beau sire*, thou hast learnt thine office betimes," said Torigni, smiling.

"Let thy lord attend us within the chamber beneath this gallery," said Marguerite. "Demoiselles Torigni and La Rebours, you will accompany us."

The page arose and departed.

"May I crave a word with your majesty?" said Esclairmonde, approaching the queen.

"Your pardon, demoiselle," replied Marguerite haughtily, "we would pass."

And she quitted the gallery, followed by her attendants.

Having completed his survey of the fair occupants of the balcony, and dispatched the message we have just heard delivered, Henri of Navarre spurred his steed in the direction of the pavilion, before which, attached to a halberd struck deeply into the earth, was displayed Crichton's shield. Snatching a lance from his esquire, the monarch struck it against the targe with so much good will that the halberd and its clanging burden were at once borne to the ground; while, startled by the noise of the falling arms, his charger began to rear and plunge violently.

"*Harnibleu!*" muttered Henri, sharply applying his armed heel to the flanks of the unruly animal, and by a powerful effort reducing him to subjection. "This froward steed is evidently unused to the exercise of the tilt-yard. He starts at the clatter of steel as an unmanaged colt winceth at the lash of the *chambrière*. He may know his paces, but I doubt if I shall be able to bring him to the rest after the career. My sage counsellor Rosni had, I suspect, his own motives in persuading me to abandon my brave old Norman charger, whom the roar of a culverin, or the clash of a thousand pikes would not affright, and whom I can restrain with a silken thread, for this high-spirited and fantastic barb, because, forsooth, he has finer limbs, and a sleeker coat. The knave would gladly see me discomfited, that his own superior wisdom may, in future, be acknowledged. It shall go hard, however, if I do not, despite his ingenious stratagem, outwit him. At all events, I will not give him the satisfaction of perceiving the annoyance he has occasioned me. I have overcome greater obstacles than this rebellious animal presents—ay, and turned them to account, too. An enterprise without danger is of little worth. *Invia virtuti nulla est via* has ever been my device. And now for my lady's token! Sa ha! sirrah—take heed! You carry Cæsar and his fortunes."

Again applying the spur and checking the impetuous movements of his steed with an arm of iron, Henri, as deliberately as he came, returned to the grand gallery.

"Her majesty will bestow the token upon you with her own hand, monseigneur," said the page, advancing to meet him.

"*A la bonne heure!*" exclaimed the king. "This is exactly what I wished." And dismounting, he flung the rein to his esquire, and entered the scaffold with a light and joyous footstep.

"This way, sir knight," said one of the *huissiers* stationed at the portal. "The Queen of Navarre will give you audience within this chamber."

A tapestried curtain, suspended before an open valve, was then drawn aside, and the king found himself in the presence of his consort.

Henri of Bourbon was not wont to have misgivings where a lady was concerned. But the situation in which he was placed with his queen was rather embarrassing. It was a relief to him, therefore, to find that she was not alone. Having no such apprehensions, and not being aware who it was that stood before her, Marguerite immediately, on the king's appearance, dismissed her attendants. La Rebours lingered for an instant behind her companion, and as she passed the monarch, her embroidered handkerchief (it might have been by accident) fell to the ground. Henri stooped to raise it, and as he restored the perfumed *mouchoir* to its fair owner, his hand, divested of his gauntlet, contrived to encounter the taper fingers of the demoiselle. Assuredly it was *not* by accident that the pressure which he hazarded was so perceptibly returned.

"*Ventre-saint-gris!*" muttered the king. "This is the lovely dame whom I beheld in the Rue Pélican."

"I will stake my life that it is Henri of Navarre," thought La Rebours, glancing from beneath her downcast eyelids at the Bourbon's stately figure; "and if so," ran her meditations, as she quitted the room, "there can be no danger in trusting him with his queen. I need apprehend no rivalry in that quarter. Connubial devotion is certainly not Henri's foible."

If the monarch felt disconcerted at the idea of a *tête-à-tête* with his spouse, his embarrassment was not diminished when he found that this little piece of gallantry had not escaped her notice. His fears, however, were needless. Marguerite entertained no jealousy of *him*, though it suited her purpose to affect some slight pique.

"The kerchief of my demoiselle would seem to have a higher value in your eyes, messire," she said, "than any gage I could bestow, were it even a tress of my own hair to bind upon your helm?"

"You are mistaken, madam," returned Henri, in a feigned voice, but in the impassioned tone which he had ever at command, "the simple pearl is lovely in mine eyes; but the 'pearl of pearls' is that which wins my homage. As Jean de la Taille, from whom I have borrowed the scroll upon my shield, sings,

> Ce ne fut pas la paquerette,
> L'œillet, la rose, ni le lys:
> Ce fut la belle Marguerite,
> Qu'au cœur j'aurai toujours écrite.

Marguerite, your name is inscribed upon my heart as upon my buckler. Recall not your boon, I implore of you. Yield me that treasured gage, and you ensure me victory."

"If it *will* ensure you victory, it is yours," said Marguerite eagerly.

"What you refuse to love you readily accord to hate, I perceive," returned Henri. "You have some quarrel to avenge upon the Chevalier Crichton."

"The deepest a woman has to avenge," replied Marguerite. "I will not disguise from you, messire, that I have to requite a lover's inconstancy."

"Soh," thought Henry. "*I* am destined to hear my own dishonour proclaimed by lips which I cannot with propriety give the lie. I also have a quarrel to arrange with this Scottish knight," he added aloud, "and by consequence you could not have found a fitter champion to redress your wrongs. He has injured me as deeply as yourself."

"Impossible!"

"*Corbleu!* madam," returned Henri, "most men would consider my injuries the heavier. But I will not contest the point. You are, undoubtedly, the best judge as to which of us is the greater sufferer."

"I see to what you allude, messire," said Marguerite. "*I* have to complain of the perfidy of a lover—*you* of the infidelity of a wife."

"Precisely so," replied Henry.

"Wash out the stain upon your name in the traitor's blood," exclaimed the queen. "As to your faithless dame, if the death of her paramour will not content your vengeance, I swear, if she belong to the court of France, or to that of my royal husband, Henri of Navarre, her crime shall not pass unpunished."

"The guilt of the adultress shall not pass unpunished," rejoined Henri, gravely. "But it is well for my faithless dame that my plan of retribution differs from that proposed by your majesty."

"You love her, then, despite her fault?" said Marguerite.

"No," replied Henri mournfully. "But I *have* loved her—and for that remembered tenderness I will spare her."

"Your dame is fortunate in the possession of a lord so patient," returned Marguerite scornfully.

"She is more fortunate than she deserves to be, I must own, madam," answered Henri.

"You may repent this weakness when it is too late," rejoined Marguerite. "I comprehend not how a wrong like this can be forgiven."

"Would not these words pass sentence upon yourself, madam, were they uttered in the presence of the king your husband?"

"Speak not of Henri," said the queen. "He hath long divorced himself from my love. If I have been faithless consort, he has been faithless lord. He cannot complain. I *could* have loved him —but—no matter! It is not of *him* I would speak—but of yourself."

"Two persons closely connected," thought the king.

"Hear me!" cried Marguerite, clasping Henri's fingers with a hand that burnt with fever; "your dame has wronged you— you love her not."

"I have already confessed as much, madam. Open not my bleeding wounds anew."

"I do so but to heal them. Now, mark me. Let the result of this career be fatal to—to the Chevalier Crichton, and what I have of love is yours."

"*Ventre-saint-gris!*" mentally ejaculated Henri. "This is a novel reward for redressing my own injuries."

"How say you, messire?" demanded the queen impatiently.

"Can you doubt my answer? I accept your proposal. But what assurance have I of your sincerity?"

"My word—the word of an injured and vindictive woman—the word of a queen."

"When her injuries are redressed, the queen may forget what the woman has promised."

"The woman shall never forget that she is a queen, nor what is due to her as the sister, and the spouse of kings," returned Marguerite haughtily. "When I laid my commands upon the Baron de Viteaux to slay the ribald Du Guast; when I made the same proposal to him that I have made to you, he hesitated not.[1] But he had loved me long."

"*I* have loved you yet longer, Marguerite," rejoined Henri, in a troubled tone, "and I will do your bidding. But do not liken me to the assassin Viteaux."

"I blame not your incredulity, messire," said the queen, resuming all her softness and blandishment of manner; "it could not be otherwise. That I should affect to love one whom I never before beheld—with whose features—with whose name I am alike unacquainted—were to belie myself—to deceive you. But there is something in the tone of your voice that inspires me with confidence. I have unhesitatingly trusted you with the hidden purposes of my soul. As loyal knight you will not betray them. Obey my behests, and I will fulfil my promise. You ask for some token of my truth. Here is one will remove all doubts," and as she spoke, she took from her neck a carcanet of pearls, the lustre of which was eclipsed by the dazzling

---

[1] That these details are not exaggerated will be perceived by a glance at the subjoined account of the assassination of the Sieur Du Guast, taken from the *Journal de Henri III.*: "La reine Marguerite, piquée au vif, et animée encore par les plaintes de toutes celles que Du Guast avoit outragées, s'addressa à Guillaume Du Prat, Baron de Viteaux, alors caché à Paris, dans le Couvent des Augustins, pour un meurtre, qu'il avoit commis quelque temps auparavant en la personne d'Antoine d'Alègre; *elle l'engagea par ses caresses à devenir son vengeur.* Viteaux, pour faire son coup, choisit le premier de Novembre, veille de la Fête des Morts, parce que le bruit de toutes les cloches de Paris qui se fait entendre alors, étoit propre à cacher le bruit inséparable de l'exécution de son entreprise. Il se rend, avec quelques autres sur le soir, au logis de Du Guast, monte dans sa chambre, et le trouve au lit, où il le perce de plusieurs coups."

fairness of her skin; "this ornament was the gift of Henri of Navarre."

"*Diable!*" ejaculated the king.

"It was given me on our espousals—it is yours."

"Could Henri of Navarre have anticipated you would part with it thus, his hand should have been hacked off at the wrist ere he had bestowed it."

"How?"

"I crave your majesty's pardon. I have a strange habit of putting myself in the situation of other people, and for the moment fancied myself your credulous husband. Give me the chain."

"Remove your casque, then, and with my own hand I will attach the collar to it."

Henri appeared irresolute.

"Trifle not," said the queen, "but to the lists. And then death to the traitor, and confusion to your faithless dame!"

"Be it so," replied the king, unhelming himself, and gazing sternly at his consort. "Take back your own words, Marguerite, —confusion to my faithless dame!"

"Henri!" ejaculated the queen, gazing at him as if she beheld a spectre. "Pity—pity!"

"Be silent, madam," said the king; "this is my retribution."

Marguerite made an effort to control herself—but in vain. Her limbs failed her, and she sank senseless into the arms of La Rebours, who most opportunely flew to her assistance.

"Give me thy kerchief, *ma mie,*" said Henri to the demoiselle; "it shall be my gage instead of this polluted carcanet. And now, thy hand—nay, thy lips, sweet one; we shall meet again anon."

"Success attend your majesty," said La Rebours, as the king departed. "Give me joy, Torigni," she added, when the latter appeared, "my fondest hopes are realised."

"In what way?" asked the Florentine.

"Hush! her majesty revives—the intelligence is not for her ears."

"Is he gone?" gasped Marguerite.

"He has returned to the lists, madam," replied La Rebours.

"And my gage?" asked the queen.

"Is there," answered the attendant, pointing maliciously to the neglected pearls.

"Assist me to that fauteuil, Torigni," said the queen, withdrawing herself from the support of La Rebours. "If Crichton proves victorious in this conflict, bid the Demoiselle Esclairmonde attend me here."

CHAPTER VII

THE BARB

————La seconde venue
Guerry encor, j'en ay bien souvenance,
L'autre rompit, et depuis contenance
N'ot son destrier à la lice approcheir,
Et car long temps ne se peuvent touchier.

LOUIS DE BEAUVEAU.

CRICHTON, meantime, in answer to the defiance of the King of Navarre, instantly proceeded to the entrance of the lists, executing, as he rode thither, so many graceful curvets and high passades (which latter, according to Pluvinel, constitute "la vraye pierre de touche du bon chevalier, et du bon cheval") that the air resounded with the applause of the spectators, and the tide of popular opinion, which a breath will ever turn, again ran high in his favour.

Stirred by their shouts, and still more elated by the prospect of an encounter with his kingly and chivalrous antagonist; perceiving, also, that the Bourbon had dismounted, and that the pales (again hastily stretched across the area under the direction of the Vicomte de Joyeuse and Montjoie) were not yet firmly fastened to their supporters, the Scot called to his esquire, and taking his spear, with the ostensible purpose of breathing his charger, performed a brilliant course alone.

Nothing could exceed the rapidity and dexterity with which this pass was made. The animal seemed to obey every impulse of his rider. Starting from his post with a snort of wild delight, he launched into the career as if he would bear down all opposition by his fury. Crichton threw the rein upon his shoulder, and flung his heavy lance into the air—caught it—again tossed it aloft—and repeated this extraordinary feat for a third time, ere the haunches of his steed seemed to stiffen into marble on his arrival at the point of rest. Universal acclamations rewarded this triumphant exhibition of knightly skill.

But the admiration of the beholders amounted to the most rapturous enthusiasm as they witnessed what next ensued. The Scot shouted to the attendants and, in obedience to his command, the ring employed in the tourney was instantly attached to an elevated post, forming part of the framework of the lists. Executing a demi-volte with curvets, he again started on his career; again thrice hurled his spear aloft, and, maintaining throughout this gallant action an unaltered carriage of body, moving only the right arm, as occasion demanded, finally carried off the prize upon his lance's point. This performance (prolonged in description) was the work only of a few seconds.

The dames waved their kerchiefs; the sergeants of the guard clashed their halberds; the mob flung their caps into the air, without being so successful in regaining them as the Scot had been in the recovery of his spear; the bosoms of the youthful nobles beat high with ardour and emulation—even the members of the royal group were loud in their applauses.

"*Honneur aux fils des preux!*" exclaimed Brantôme, with transport; "that course was bravely executed."

"A marvellous exploit, certes, my dear abbé," said Henri. "Your valiant uncle, the Sieur de la Châteigneraye, with all his address in horsemanship, and expertness in the management of arms, could scarcely have achieved that amazing feat."

"It may not occur to your majesty's recollection, but precisely the same feat as that we have just witnessed *was* performed by the Sieur de la Châteigneraye in the presence of your royal father," returned Brantôme. "My brave uncle has been surpassed by no knight, living or dead, in vigour and address."

"Save by Gui de Chabot, abbé," cried the jester, with a scoffing grimace. "The *coup de Jarnac* has passed into a proverb. It will be fortunate for our dear Henriot if the *coup de Crichton* do not supersede it."

"A truce to this!" said the king; "thy jesting is ill-timed."

"Good counsel is generally so, *compère*," retorted Chicot. "If, however, after this specimen of Crichton's consummate skill, like yon unknown knight, you are so madly adventurous as to tilt with him, I shall say of you, what one wiser than I am said of the king, your father:

Sire, vous n'estes plus, vous n'estes plus que cire!"

"You shall say what you please of us, *scélérat*," returned the good-humoured monarch, laughing; "if we *do* hazard the safety of our royal person, and endanger our hitherto untarnished reputation as a knight, by entering the lists with this invincible Scot, whom Satan certainly abetteth. But see! his foolhardy challenger again takes the field—ha! *Mort-Dieu!* what is this? Our Béarnais (if he *must* be so designated) tears the silken streamer from his spear, and casts it beneath his charger's hoofs."

"Observe, also, my liege, that he replaces it with a kerchief," interposed Brantôme; "and note, moreover, that this kerchief has not the golden fringe which is worn by the Queen of Navarre. Her majesty, whose colours he hath rashly assumed, has evidently refused him a favour—ha!—ha!"

"There is nothing extraordinary in that, Seigneur Abbé, seeing that the Admirable Crichton is in the case," returned Chicot. "I warrant me, if *thou* hadst been his opponent, this cavalier's suit would not have been fruitless. Let it suffice that he *has* a gage—no matter what—or whence obtained—

> What a queen hath denied him,
> A *quean* hath supplied him:
> And the favour he beareth
> No favourite shareth:
> His choice is a right one
> With kerchief a white one,
> To tilt against Crichton."

"By Phœbus! gossip!" exclaimed the king. "Thou rhymest like Frère Jean, *en cramoisi*. But hark! the charge is sounded. Montjoie's arrangements are completed. *Allons!* messeigneurs. Hola! Du Halde, my warder! Hast thou contrived Ruggieri's escape?" he added, in a whisper.

"He is already without the Louvre, my liege," returned the chief valet, in the same tone.

"The fair Esclairmonde is ours, then!" ejaculated Henri, with triumph.

And, followed by his favourites, he proceeded to the canopy and took his seat upon the throne.

By this time the area of the tilt-yard was cleared of its numerous intruders. The marshals of the field hastened to their tribunal; Montjoie hurried to the estrade reserved for himself and his attendants; while each cavalier sought to secure for himself an advantageous position for the approaching spectacle. For the moment all was bustle and clamour. But, above the shouts of the various officers, stationed (it would seem in all ages), not so much to preserve order as to increase confusion, the trampling and neighing of steeds, and the jingling of martial equipments, arose the loud fanfare of the trumpeter, making "young pulses dance" with its stirring notes.

As the blast died away, profound silence ensued. The two champions and their esquires alone occupied either extremity of the barriers. Each regarded his antagonist with curiosity. On the part of Crichton the feeling was one of enthusiastic delight: on that of Henri of Bourbon admiration was chilled by deep sense of wrong. Nevertheless, his frank and noble nature could not resist the Scot's high claims to consideration; and as he narrowly scrutinised his matchless symmetry of figure, and consummate grace of demeanour, he, who was no harsh judge of woman, felt half disposed to overlook his consort's fault.

"*Ventre-saint-gris !*" he mentally ejaculated. "A likely galliard to please the fancy of a queen—and worth a thousand such migniard voluptuaries as the *baladin* La Môle, or that grand *dégoûté* Turenne. I could forgive his attentions to Marguerite. But there is our fair cousin of Condé—I *must* punish his presumption in that quarter. Sa ha! the devil is in his steed."

Crichton now drew his visor over his glowing cheek, and repressing the tumultuous emotions of his heart, with a light and steady hand placed his lance in its rest. The trumpet sounded for the second time, and Henri was about to follow the Scot's example, in expectation of the signal of assault, when, affrighted by the kerchief fluttering over his head, his fiery charger, disregarding all restraint, broke from his post, and dashed headlong into the area.

Expert in all martial exercises, the chivalrous Bourbon was one of the most perfect horsemen of his time, and his arm was endowed with no ordinary vigour, but neither skill nor strength availed him on the present emergency. Encumbered by his lance, which he was unwilling to throw aside, he could only employ his left hand in coercion—while, deeply mortified and irritated at the occurrence, his efforts were in the first place directed rather to the punishment than the subjection of his unruly steed—and this made matters worse. Each application of the spur was followed by a fierce and violent plunge. The infuriated animal reared, jerked, winced, and resorted to every vicious practice and stratagem to dislodge his rider. In this he failed. But, in his turn, his rider failed in compelling him to approach the lists.

At this juncture, and just as the monarch, full of wrath against his counsellor Rosni, began to despair of accomplishing his point, assistance was afforded him from a quarter whence it could have been least anticipated. Perceiving the Bourbon's inability to govern his charger, Crichton rode towards him—and in a tone of the highest courtesy proffered to exchange steeds with him, expressing, at the same time, his perfect conviction that he could achieve the animal's subjection and carry him safely through the course.

"By the soul of Bayard!" returned the Bourbon, with equal courtesy, "fame hath not belied you, Chevalier Crichton. Your proffer is worthy of a brighter age of chivalry, and should have

L 804

been made to a worthier knight than myself. In acceding to your proposal I feel that I acknowledge my defeat. In any case you are victor in point of generosity. Nor will I by a refusal rob you of additional honour." So saying, he flung himself from his charger's back.

"It follows not, because I may be the more expert horseman, that I shall also prove the more expert tilter," returned Crichton, dismounting.

"If you overcome the impetuosity of this froward beast, you will accomplish a feat more difficult than that of Alexander of Macedon," rejoined the Bourbon. "But if you succeed in bringing him to the pales, look well to yourself—I promise you the reception due to so valiant a champion:

> Les plus jolis n'ont pas à leur plaisance
> Aucune fois l'honneur et le renom."

"You will find me no *fainéant,*" replied Crichton. "Nor do I think so lightly of your prowess as to neglect your caution."

At this moment the Baron de Rosni, attended by Montjoie and Joyeuse, rode up to them.

"Sire," said Rosni in a whisper, "I pray you take my steed."

"Stand back, sir!" returned the Bourbon coldly.

"Chevalier Crichton," said Rosni, turning to the Scot, "mount not that ungovernable horse—my charger is at your service."

Crichton replied by vaulting into the saddle of the King of Navarre, and giving the rein to the barb, he careered round the tilt-yard, as if he was borne by one of the winged horses of the sun.

"Courage, *mon Admirable,*" cried Joyeuse, looking after him, with a smile.

Vain were the efforts of the nigh frantic steed to shake his firm-seated rider; he had to strive against one with whom contention was ineffectual. Crichton, for the moment, allowed him to expend his fire. He then struck spurs fiercely into his sides, and compelled him to execute upwards of twenty caprioles in a breath. His fury now visibly abated and the Scot completed his mastery by another career and a swift succession of curvets. The next moment the animal stood controlled and motionless at the entrance of the lists.

The loudest plaudits would have followed this achievement had not all clamour been interdicted during the actual progress of the jousts. As it was, an irrepressible murmur testified the wonderment and delight of the spectators.

The clarion now sounded for the third time and the combatants started on their career. Both lances were splintered by the vehement shock of their encounter. But no injury was sustained on either side. A similar result followed the second atteinte.

"Give me that painted spear, it is of tougher wood," said Crichton to his esquire, while the trumpet was blown for the third assault. And couching his lance, as he again sprang forward, he directed it, with unerring aim, against the crest of his antagonist's morion.

The result of the career was decisive. The shock was more violent than those of the preceding rencounters. The lance of the Bourbon, whose mark had been the centre of the Scot's helm, again shivered to the handle, while the stroke of Crichton, into which he had thrown all his force, would unquestionably have unhorsed his adversary, had not the helmet of the monarch, which had never been firmly fastened since his interview with his queen, yielded to the blow and rolled to the ground.

"*Bon Dieu!*" exclaimed Henri III., rising. "It *is* the Béarnais —it *is* our brother of Navarre. We should recognise that Bourbon nose among a thousand. What ho!—our steed! our steed!— Where is our mother?—where is her majesty, Catherine de Medicis? We would speak with her, ere we confront the hardy traitor. Surround us, messeigneurs, and let our bodyguard be trebled. Some conspiracy may—nay, *must* be on foot. What think you of it, Villequier, and you, cousin of Nevers? See to the outlets of the tilt-yard. Suffer none to go forth, or to enter. By Saint Hubert! we have snared a tiger."

Crichton, meantime, had reined in his steed, and returned to the Bourbon. "Sire!" he said, speaking in a low, determined tone, "I have, unwittingly, betrayed you to your foes. But if you will confide in me, I pledge myself to accomplish your deliverance."

"My counsel to your majesty," interposed Rosni, "would be to hasten to the king your brother, and if possible obtain permission to depart with your escort ere he have time to confer with the Queen-Mother. It is your only hope."

Henri averted his head from his confidant. "Chevalier Crichton," he said, addressing the Scot, "I will trust you. There is my hand."

"If I take it not, sire," replied Crichton, "your majesty will understand my motive, when I say that the eyes of Catherine de Medicis are upon us."

"True," replied the Bourbon, "and those of our fair cousin of Condé, also—hem! chevalier."

CHAPTER VIII

THE ENGLISHMAN

Where'er I wander, boast of this I can,
Though banish'd, yet a true-born Englishman.
SHAKESPEARE, *Richard II.*

THE majestic and remarkable countenance of Henri of Navarre (a face, once seen, not readily forgotten) had been instantly recognised by the majority of the assemblage, and such of the crowd as were unacquainted with his features speedily gathered his title from the general vociferations. Coupled with various and most discordant epithets, his name now resounded from every quarter. Some applauded his bravery and bonhomie; some derided his imprudence and temerity; others railed bitterly and loudly against his heresies and apostacy from the religion of Rome (whose tenets Henri, not over-scrupulous on matters of faith, embraced or renounced, as circumstances required); others, on the contrary, silently and devoutly hailed him as the champion of their creed. A few there were, who fancied they discovered in his sudden appearance in the midst of his foes a signal for an insurrection and massacre, in retaliation for the sanguinary day of Saint-Barthélemy, and held themselves in readiness to obey his mandates; while another, and more numerous faction, deeply interested in all events affecting their project, regarded the occurrence as singularly inauspicious. Catherine de Medicis alone viewed the discovery without surprise or dismay.

Popular by his affability, generosity and manliness (qualities which afterwards won for him the affectionate appellation—yet hallowing his name in the breast of every true Frenchman—of "le bon roi"), the Bourbon, even during the period of his detention within the Louvre, had attached no inconsiderable party to his cause; and amongst the youthful and light-hearted nobles then present, there were many whose zeal would have prompted them to declare themselves in his favour, had any attempt been made upon his life. The situation, therefore, of the intrepid monarch, who, attended by Crichton and Rosni, remained unmoved, with his hand upon the pommel of his sword, and a smile upon his lips, was not fraught with so much peril as at first sight would appear.

Joyeuse and D'Epernon, with several of the immediate and

loyal adherents of Henri III., flew to each outlet of the tilt-yard, reinforced the guard, and issued the king's commands to allow none to enter or to pass forth from the arena.

Before these orders could be obeyed, a man of robust appearance and square, stout make, rushed upon the ancient, or standard-bearer of the guard, plucked from his side a long two-handed sword, leaped over the palisades of the lists, and, followed by a huge dog, made the best of his way in the direction of Henri of Navarre.

The action was too suddenly and too swiftly executed to be prevented. But the flying figure of the man catching the eye of the Vicomte de Joyeuse, he struck his spurs into his charger, and dashed in pursuit with the intention of cutting him down. Nothing could have prevented the fugitive's destruction but the timely assistance afforded by his four-footed companion. Just as Joyeuse had overtaken him, and was about to discharge a blow, which must have proved fatal, the career of his steed was checked by the dog, whose fangs were suddenly fixed within the nostrils of the terrified animal. At the same moment the man turned and stood upon his defence.

With eyes starting from their sockets, veins distended, flanks quivering, head borne to the ground by the weight of the dog, and nostrils gushing with blood, the poor horse uttered a shrill neigh, sounding almost like a scream, but attempted neither to move nor to free himself from his fierce assailant. Exasperated beyond endurance at the condition of his steed, Joyeuse directed his next assault against the hound.

"Hold!" exclaimed Blount. "Touch a hair of my dog's hide, and, by Saint Dunstan! I will no longer stay my hand."

Joyeuse replied by aiming a downward blow at the Englishman. Blount received the stroke upon the edge of his sword, and returned it with such good effect that the vicomte's rapier was beaten from his grasp, and whirled to some distance.

"Call off thy dog, villain," shouted Joyeuse furiously, "or thou shalt repent it. Ha! *Vive Dieu!*" he added, as several of his attendants rode up, "seize him! If he resists, show him no quarter—yield, madman!"

"Never!" replied Blount stoutly, "were they ten times their number. I ask no quarter, and will yield to no man, or men. It shall not be said that an Englishman sued for mercy, while his hand could wield a sword. Come on, then, my masters—one and all—and try the force of an English arm. Your sires have felt the weight of our blows at Crécy and Poitiers—and their sons shall find that our bull-dog breed is not degenerated, or his country disgraced, in the person of Simon Blount."

"Why do you hesitate?" thundered Joyeuse.

"*Why* do they hesitate?" echoed Blount, in a taunting tone, at the same time flourishing his tremendous blade with the greatest ease over his head. "Because I *am* an Englishman. They are six and I am one. They are mounted, I on foot. They have sword and partisan—I, sword only. They are Frenchmen —I am an Englishman. By my troth! we are fairly matched."

"Silence him!" cried Joyeuse.

But this was no such easy matter. The inert but sturdy Islander was now fairly roused from his habitual lethargy. His arm and tongue were alike in motion. He answered with a roar of defiance.

"Silence me! quotha. E'en let them, if they can! But they have good reasons for their forbearance. Their memories serve them too faithfully. They recollect the bygone times of the Regent Bedford—when a French noble was obliged to doff his cap to an English churl. Old Rabelais has told them of our thirst—and at whose cost we allayed it."

"Cravens! will ye bear this?" cried Joyeuse. "He says truly —ye are six to one."

"It was the same at Agincourt," retorted Blount, "and ye know by whom that day was won."

"That day was not won by big words, sirrah," rejoined Joyeuse, amazed at the Englishman's audacity.

"Right!" exclaimed Blount, waving his sword, as if selecting a mark. "I thank you for the hint. I have already talked too much."

"Dispatch this hound with your pike, Baptiste," shouted Joyeuse, "and liberate my wounded charger."

The man instantly obeyed and thrust his partisan through the throat of Druid. Severely, but not mortally wounded, the courageous brute still maintained his grasp.

"Hew him in pieces!" vociferated Joyeuse. "It is the nature of the accursed animal to cling thus, while aught of life remains."

Another man-at-arms now took up the attack, and in his endeavour to cleave asunder the dog's skull, which he was only prevented from effecting by the resistance made by his thick hide, struck off his right ear and fore-paw.

Blinded by his own blood, and frightfully mutilated, Druid kept his hold with unflinching tenacity.

"Saint George for England!" shouted Blount. And as he spoke, his sword whistled through the air, and the man-at-arms fell headless to the ground. "Here is a sweet morsel for thee.

Druid," he added, with a savage laugh, at the same time spurning with his heel the gory head, which had dropped near him. "Come hither, sirrah, quick!"

Obedient to his master's call, the dog yielded that compliance which he had refused to commands, enforced by sharpest blows, and at once set free the vicomte's charger. Uttering a piercing cry, the latter animal galloped, with uncontrollable speed, to the farther end of the lists, where, fortunately, his career was stopped by one of the heralds, and Joyeuse was enabled to dismount.

Blount's assailants were now reduced to five. But he was on all sides surrounded, and fresh foes were pouring against him from each quarter of the tilt-yard. Undismayed by numbers, and supported by his constitutional phlegm, he viewed his probable end with indifference, and resolved to meet it as became a brave man, and a denizen of that island nook, which, in the words of the greatest of her sons, "breedeth very valiant children."

"Would I were with my back against a wall," he thought, "I would take far greater odds, and give them ruder welcome than they bring. As it is, with this long poking-iron so luckily obtained, I will carbonado some of their doublets after a fashion in which they were never slashed before. *Gules* shall predominate over *or* and *azure* in their emblazoned coats."

And as these reflections ran through his mind, his sword again described a tremendous circle, in the course of which it encountered the various weapons of his antagonists, who were thrusting and striking at him from all points, and finally descending upon the shoulder of the halberdier, by whom Druid had been first wounded, the man, cloven almost to the girdle, fell to the ground.

"*Habet!*" cried Blount, laughing, and again whirling round his ensanguined blade.

In the midst of this gladiatorial display, which was regarded by the beholders, even of the gentler sex, with the same fierce and thrilling interest that prevailed amongst the witnesses of the terrible entertainments held within a Roman circus, we shall take breath for an instant to describe more fully the weapon used by our English combatant. We have before adverted to the treatise of Giacomo di Grassi [1]—

> ———A man of great defence,
> Expert in battles, and in deeds of armes—

and we shall now give the manner of wielding the two-edged

[1] *Giacomo di Grassi, his True Arte of Defence.* First written in Italian by the foresaid author, and Englished by I. G., Gentleman, 1594.

sword, as delivered by the Italian professor. In the words of his quaint translator we are told that "one may with it (as a galleon among manie gallies) resist manie swords, or other weapons. And it is accustomed to be carried in the citie, as well by night as by day, when it so chaunceth that a few are constrayned to withstand a great manie. And because his weight and bigness require great strength, therefore those only are allotted to the handling thereof which are mightie and bigge to behould, great and stronge in bodie, of stout and valiant courage. Who (forasmuch as they are to encounter manie, and to the end they may strike the more safelie, and amaze them with the furie of the sword) do altogether use to deliver great edge-blows, downright and reversed, fetching a full circle or compass therein, staying themselves sometimes upon one foot, sometimes on the other, utterlie neglecting to thrust, and persuading themselves that the thrust serveth to amaze one man onelie, but these edge-blows are of force to encounter manie. The which manner of skirmishing, besides that it is most gallant to behold, being accompanied with exceeding swiftness in deliverie (for otherwise it worketh no such effect), it is also most profitable, not properly of itselfe, but because men considering the furie of the sword, which greatly amaseth them, are not resolute to doe that, which otherwise they could not choose but doe."

All that Di Grassi has here so graphically depicted, was performed by Blount—and more than this; for so great was his activity and dexterity—so nimble was he in the management and recovery of his weapon—so tremendous was its sweep, "being of the compass of ten arms or more," that in the space of a few moments he had disabled a third opponent, and beaten off the others.

"Hurrah!" he shouted, with lusty lungs, tossing, as he spoke, his bonnet into the air. "Hurrah! for England, and God save Queen Bess."

At the same time, as if partaking of his master's triumph, Druid upturned his mangled visage, and uttered a loud and exulting howl.

"Poor fellow!" said Blount, his heart smiting him as he heard the sound. "Thou art sorely hurt, but I have amply avenged thee," he added, looking grimly around; "we can at least die together—thou wouldst never survive thy master."

The faithful dog understood this appeal. His fierce howl changed to a piteous moan.

"Peace, sirrah!" cried Blount angrily; "no whimpering. Thou art wounded, or I would bestow a buffet on thee for thy cowardice. An English bull-dog—and whine?"

The red flame in the dog's eyes at this reproof blazed yet more fiercely, and his fangs were instantly displayed.

"Why, that is right," cried Blount, in a tone of approval.

Whereupon, shouldering his gigantic blade, and keeping his eye steadily fixed upon the movements of his foes, though menaced with immediate, and, it would seem, inevitable destruction, in order to show his utter disregard of the peril in which he stood, he began to carol in a rough, but not inharmonious voice, the following homely stave:

DRUID

I

Through the world have I wandered wide,
With never a wife, or a friend by my side,
Save Druid—a comrade staunch and tried:—
Troll on away!
Druid, my dog, is a friend in need,
Druid, my dog, is a friend *indeed*,
Druid, my dog, is of English breed!
More need I say?
Troll on away!

II

Druid would perish *my* life to save,
For faithful Druid like fate *I'd* brave,
The dog and his master shall find one grave.
Troll on away!
Life! I heed not its loss a feather!
And when black Atropos snaps *my* tether,
She must cut *twice*—we'll die together!
No more I'll say,
Troll on away!

In enumerating the good and evil qualities of Henri III., we have before mentioned his singular predilection for the canine species. His attachment to dogs was as strong as his aversion to cats. Upon the commencement of the skirmish just described, the royal train, by their sovereign's command, had halted, and Henri's attention throughout had been attracted towards Druid, whose courage and fidelity he could not sufficiently admire and applaud. It was owing to this circumstance that Blount remained so long unmolested.

"What would I give for a follower so faithful!" said the king. "Such a hound were worth a whole pack of barbets and spaniels, with my two favourites, Citron and Chatelard, at their head.

I *must* possess him. Miron will speedily heal his wounds. But
how shall we get rid of his master, without doing the dog
further mischief?"

"Let your harquebusiers fire upon the knave, my liege,"
said the Duc de Nevers, in a low tone; "and, if a stray ball
should reach the Béarnais, your majesty will have an enemy the
less. Maurevert is behind us, armed with the same caliver with
which Coligni was wounded. A look will suffice for *him*."

"Thanks, fair cousin," returned Henri, "but we are in no
such hurry. We see no reason to suspect treachery on the part
of our brother of Navarre. He appears as much diverted as
ourself with this fray. Besides," he added, smiling, "we have
not yet consulted our mother upon the expediency of a step
so important in its consequences."

"I will answer for her majesty's approval," returned the
duke hastily.

"*You!*" exclaimed the king, with a look of surprise. "Are
you our mother's confidant, Monsieur le Duc? What reason have
you to suppose she would desire the death of the Béarnais?"

"Because," replied Chicot boldly, "he is like the wrong king
unexpectedly turned up at Primero; he spoils the order of the
cards, and ruins the game."

"*Parbleu!* what game, *compère?*" demanded the monarch.

"Your majesty forgets the dog you are anxious to save,"
interrupted the duke, darting an angry glance at the jester;
"another moment and it will be too late."

"Right!" cried Henri. "Command your men-at-arms to stay
their swords, and let a company of harquebusiers advance."

The king's orders were instantly obeyed. The soldiers, who
had rushed to the assistance of their comrades, reluctantly
withdrew. A dozen harquebusiers, attired in richly emblazoned
doublets of crimson frieze, girded in at the waist by broad
leathern belts, from which depended matches of lighted tow;
with great ruffs round their throats, pale green hose upon their
lower limbs, and roses of ribbons, almost as large as the shoes
they covered, upon their feet; each carrying on his right arm
a huge bell-mouthed musket, and on his left a forked staff
intended to support it—this troop, headed by Maurevert, the
hired assassin of Charles IX. (and surnamed *le Tueur du Roi*),
swiftly advanced, ranged themselves in two lines by the side
of the king, planted their forks in the ground, pointed their
artillery against the Englishman's breast, and awaited only
the royal mandate to fire.

Blount witnessed these proceedings without dismay. When he saw the death-dealing tubes levelled against him, he stooped to the ground and, catching Druid in his arms, breathed the words of his song:

> The dog and his master shall find one grave!—

fully prepared to meet his fate.

"Hold!" exclaimed Henri. "Some fiend hath put it into the knave's head to defeat our object. Bid him surrender at discretion, Maurevert. Once get possession of his dog, and deal with him as you list. But I charge you, on your life, do the animal no further injury."

Maurevert stepped forward. Blount, however, sturdily refused to yield up his sword.

At this moment, and while Henri, ever irresolute when resolution was required, hesitated to give the signal to the harquebusiers, Crichton rode up. "I will disarm him, sire," he said, "if I have your majesty's permission to do so."

"Gramercy! *mon cher*, you have our permission at once, and to slay him, too, if it please you, provided you harm not the dog."

"One will scarcely succumb without the other, I suspect, my liege," replied the Scot. "We shall see."

Saying which, he dismounted, and giving his steed to the charge of an attendant, advanced towards Blount.

"Are you mad?" he said sternly, as he arrived within a few paces of the Englishman, "that you adopt this braggart posture? Yield! and I may yet preserve your life."

"I should hold it foul scorn were such words to pass my lips, even at *your* bidding, Chevalier Crichton," replied Blount doggedly.

"Fool!" said the Scot, in a low and significant tone, "this is but a feint. Throw down your sword. I will be your safeguard."

"Were I to do so it would seem as if I yielded," rejoined Blount; "and I would rather die a thousand deaths than these accursed Frenchmen should be able to crow over me."

"Defend yourself, then," exclaimed Crichton, plucking his rapier from the scabbard.

"If I fall by your hands I shall die the death I would have chosen," replied Blount. "Yet think not I will perish tamely. I hold it too good luck to cross swords with you, not to approve myself worthy of the honour. But our blades are ill-matched. I cannot fight without equal arms."

"I have helm and corslet," answered Crichton; "you have neither buff jerkin nor steel cap. The advantage is on my side."

"Down, Druid," said Blount, quitting his hold of the dog; "stir not—use neither tooth nor claw. Chevalier Crichton," he added, in a tone of some emotion, "if I fall—this hound——"

"I understand," replied Crichton. "I will be his master."

"No!" said Blount. "I meant not that—dispatch him."

"Waste no more words in this idle parley," returned Crichton, fiercely. "My blows are for men, not dogs. Again, I say, defend yourself."

"Saint George for England!" shouted Blount, fetching a compass with his sword that dazzled the eyes of the beholders like a flash of lightning. But rapid as was this circle—not so swift was it as the corresponding movement of the Scot. Instead of endeavouring to avoid the blow, or to encounter its force, where it was most dangerous, at a distance, he at once rushed in upon the Englishman, met the edge of his weapon in mid-sweep with a stoccado, and nothing daunted that his own rapier was hurled from his grasp, clutched with his left hand the wrist of his adversary, and with his right fearlessly catching hold of his enormous blade, by a violent downward jerk wrested it from his grip.

Thus far Druid had obeyed his master's orders, and crouched inoffensively at his feet—but now instinctively comprehending his danger, he flew with such violence against Crichton's legs, that had they not been plated in steel, he must have withdrawn his attack from Blount to defend himself from his follower. "Lie still, sir," cried the Englishman furiously. And setting his foot upon the dog's back, he pressed him, notwithstanding his desperate struggles, forcibly to the ground. "You are the victor," he continued, addressing Crichton. "Strike!"

"I have accomplished all I desired," replied the Scot, "in disarming you."

"I will not yield," said Blount sullenly. "You had better finish me."

The words were scarcely uttered, when his arms were suddenly seized from behind by a couple of halberdiers, who had stolen upon him unawares, and a stout sword-belt, slipped over his wrists and drawn tightly together, prevented any further resistance on his part. At the same moment, a sash, tied in a noose, and flung over the head of Druid by a third man-at-arms, made the brave animal likewise a prisoner.

"Harm neither," said Crichton, addressing the guards, "but await his majesty's pleasure—and see! he approaches."

"Draw near to me, I pray you, Chevalier Crichton," said Blount, gazing earnestly at the Scot; "I have something to communicate, which, in my confusion, I had forgotten."

"I know what you would say," returned Crichton, making a gesture of silence; "all is lost!"

"The devil!" exclaimed Blount, with a look of disappointment. "My labour, then, has been in vain. It was merely to bring you these tidings that I adventured within the lists."

"Heed not that, good Blount, but pacify your dog," said Crichton, noticing, with uneasiness, the violent efforts of the animal to free himself, by which he was well-nigh strangled; "on *his* life hangs your own."

"True," replied Blount, taking the words literally, "it does so." And he addressed an angry declamation to Druid, who instantly became passive in the hands of his captor.

CHAPTER IX

THE TWO HENRIS

Premier Soldat. Le Béarnais a peut-être promis de retourner à confesse. Ca serait heureux, tout de même—il me fait l'effet d'un bon compère de roi! *Deuxième Soldat.* Le nôtre n'a pas mauvais air non plus sur sa grande jument — mais il sent trop le jasmin.—*La Mort de Henri III.*

UNWILLING to hold any private conference with the King of Navarre until he should receive some information of Catherine's disposition towards him, and "perplexed in the extreme" that no message had, as yet, arrived from her majesty, Henri III., uncertain what line of policy he ought to pursue, and glad of any pretext to gain further time, instead of advancing to question the Bourbon, as he had originally intended, bent his course towards the captive Englishman. This plan, however, was defeated. Henri of Navarre, yielding tardy compliance with the earnest solicitations of Rosni, who represented, in the most moving terms, the perils and calamities in which his present fatal obstinacy must necessarily involve himself, his people, and his religion, came suddenly to the resolution of throwing himself upon the generosity of his royal brother. Accordingly, when Henri III. turned aside to confer with Blount, he stuck spurs into his charger, and rode towards him.

A greeting of apparently fraternal warmth passed between the two monarchs. Though each, in secret, distrusted the other, both deemed it prudent to assume an air of unbounded confidence and goodwill. Dissimulation formed no part of the Bourbon's frank and loyal character. But his long experience of the perfidy and insincerity of the race of Valois, while it prevented him from being Henri's dupe, satisfied him that any advantage which might accrue to him from the interview, could only be attained by the employment of similar artifice. Throwing himself, therefore, instantly from his steed, he attempted with the greatest cordiality, to take the hand of the king, with the intention of proffering the customary salutation.

Henri III., however, drew back his steed as he approached. "Your pardon, my brother," he said, with a gracious smile; "we would cut off our right hand could we suspect it of heresy, nor can we consent to take yours, tainted as it is with that contagious leprosy, unless we first receive assurance from your lips that you are come hither, like the prodigal son, to confess your indiscretions, to implore our forgiveness, and to solicit to be received once more into the indulgent bosom of our holy Catholic, Apostolic and Roman Church."

"Sire," replied the Bourbon, "I own that I am in much the same predicament as the unfortunate wight to whom you have likened me. I have, at this moment, more nose than kingdom—more care than coin—more hope than faith—more regard for your majesty than the religion you propose——"

"And more regard for your body than your soul, I fear, my brother," interrupted Henri III., gravely shaking his head, and telling a bead or two upon his rosary.

"That is to say, he has more regard for his mistress than his queen," said Chicot. "You are right, *compère*. Our Béarnais will never be saved unless the good old faith of the Gentiles comes round again, and new altars are raised at Cnidos and Paphos, to the goddess he worships."

"Certes, thou malapert knave, I am a heretic in no creed in which beauty is concerned," replied the Bourbon, laughing; "and amid yon gallery of fair saints, there is not one to whom I would refuse adoration."

"I could point out one," cried the jester.

"I defy thee," said the Bourbon.

"Your queen!" returned Chicot.

Even Henri III. could not help joining in the mirth occasioned by this sally of the jester.

"Ribald!" exclaimed the Bourbon, laughing louder than the rest. "Thy fool's cap alone protects thee from my resentment."

"My fool's calotte is a better defence than many a knight's casque," answered Chicot. "For the love I bear her majesty of Navarre, I will exchange it for thine, and throw my marotte into the bargain. Thou wilt need both on thy next encounter with the Admirable Crichton."

"Wilt thou throw thyself into the bargain, knave," asked the Bourbon, "and follow my fortunes?"

"Of a surety, no!" replied the jester. "That were to quit the master for the valet; the provost for the prisoner; the falconer for the quarry."

"*Pardieu! compère,*" said Henri III., in a tone of raillery, "art thou so blind to thy own interest as to tarry in our service, when an offer so brilliant is made thee by our brother of Navarre? Bethink thee of the eminence to which thy wisdom and decorum must, necessarily, promote thee, amongst the synods of the Huguenots, and the sage councils of the court of Pau!"

"I never leap in the dark, gossip," replied Chicot. "It were the province of a wise man to go in quest of danger. I am a fool, and prefer safe quarters at home."

"Wholesome advice may be gathered even from the mouth of fools, you perceive, brother," said Henri III. "May I now inquire to what fortunate circumstance I owe the unexpected happiness of this visit? I have been singularly misinformed about you and your proceedings. I am told you are an enemy —I find you our best of friends. I learn that you are at the head of a hostile army, putting my towns and subjects to fire and sword—I find you as blithe companion as ever, and almost unattended. My last accounts are, that you are barricaded within the walls of Pau, or Nérac; my next are gathered from your own lips within the walls of the Louvre. See how one may be deceived."

"Your majesty is not deceived in my expressions of friendship," replied the Bourbon cordially. "Will it please you to command your gentlemen to stand farther off?"

"Excuse me, my brother, if I venture to retain my attendants," replied Henri III. "I am curious to question this bold knave," he added, glancing at Blount. "You may reserve your tale, if you please, for the ear of our confessor, whom you will permit me to recommend, in the hope of accomplishing your conversion."

"Your confessor, sire!" ejaculated the Bourbon, knitting his brow.

"And at the tail of the priest the headsman," added Chicot, "You will not then fail to profit by his instruction, and for the third time get rid of any scruples of conscience. The laconic message of his late majesty Charles IX. to your cousin, Henri of Condé, had other merits besides its conciseness."

"What message was that, gossip!" asked Henri III., affecting ignorance.

"*Messe, mort ou Bastile!*" replied the jester. "Our Béarnais will remember it by the token, that about the same time he abjured his own Calvinistic heresies."

"*Ventre-saint-gris!* thou scurrilous varlet," cried the Bourbon fiercely. "If thou darest to push thy mischievous pleasantry further, not even thy own insignificance, or thy royal master's presence, shall prevent my inflicting due chastisement upon thee."

Alarmed by the menacing aspect of the King of Navarre, with a grimace of mixed terror and defiance, Chicot, like a snarling cur, apprehensive of the heels of a noble steed he has annoyed beyond endurance, now turned tail, and retreated to the protection of his master, who was secretly delighted with this specimen of his skill in the "art of ingeniously tormenting."

"Since you decline answering my inquiries respecting the motive of your visit, brother," said Henri III., in his blandest accents, "I will not press the point. But I trust you will not object to remaining near my person till I return to the banquet?"

"Your majesty has only to command me."

"And as you have no attendants excepting the Baron de Rosni, I give you your choice of six of my own gentlemen, who will continue constantly by your side."

"I understand your majesty. I am a prisoner."

"I did not say so, brother. Choose your attendants."

"My choice is readily made, sire. I shall name but one—the Chevalier Crichton. I leave the nomination of the others to *him*."

"*Fœnum habet in cornu,*" muttered Chicot, "a wittol's choice!"

"You could not have made a better election," observed Henri III., with a smile.

"I think not," said the Bourbon.

"I am *sure* not," added Chicot. "Forgiveness becomes a Christian prince. Madam Marguerite will highly applaud your generosity and placability."

"Peace, droll!" said Henri III. "And now, brother," he continued, in the same honeyed tone he had previously adopted, and which by those who knew him was more dreaded than the most violent bursts of indignation, "as the jousts are at an end, and you will have no further occasion for it, I entreat you to resign your sword to the custody of him whom you have appointed your principal attendant."

"My sword, sire?" exclaimed the Bourbon, recoiling.

"Your sword, brother," repeated Henri III. blandly.

The King of Navarre looked around. On all sides he was invested by danger. The whole circle of the area in which he stood bristled with pikes and spears. Above the halberds of the Switzers rose the javelins of the Scottish guards, and above the javelins of the Scots gleamed the long lances of D'Epernon's gallant Gascon troop. Here was stationed a company of archers —there a band of harquebusiers. On the right were arrayed the youthful nobles, under the command of the Vicomte de Joyeuse, readily to be distinguished by their gorgeous apparel and fluttering pennons; on the left was drawn out the sumptuous retinue of the Duc de Nevers. Nor was this all. A nearer circle of the king's body-guard encompassed him. Every hand was upon a sword-hilt—every glance fixed upon him. As he carelessly noted all this hostile preparation, the Bourbon turned towards his counsellor Rosni, who stood leaning upon the handle of his sword immediately behind him. Not a word—not a sign were exchanged between them. But the monarch understood the meaning of the cold stern look of his counsellor. At this moment the rolling of drums, mingled with the sound of other martial instruments, was heard from the outer courts of the palace.

"Hark! the tambour!" exclaimed Henri III. "Fresh troops have entered the Louvre."

"By your command, sire?" asked the Bourbon in a tone of displeasure.

"Our subjects are careful of our safety," answered Henri III. evasively.

"They *ought* to be so, sire," replied the Bourbon; "your majesty has well earned their love; and when were the people of France ungrateful? But against whom are all these precautions taken? Is the Louvre in a state of siege, or have the burgesses of your good city of Paris broken into revolt?"

"No, brother, our good city is at present free from faction or tumult, and it is our intention (with the aid of Heaven) to maintain its tranquillity undisturbed."

"You cannot suppose I would be the instigator of disorder,

sire," said the Bourbon. "I have drawn the sword to protect the rights of my people, and to uphold their persecuted creed, not to wage war upon your majesty. On any terms which shall secure to my subjects the immunities and religious toleration they seek, I will, at once, enter into a compact of truce with your majesty, and place myself in your hands as a hostage for the due observance of its conditions."

"Sire!" exclaimed Rosni, grasping his sovereign's arm. "Each word you utter is a battle lost."

"Your majesty will not now suspect me of disloyalty," continued the Bourbon, disregarding the interruption.

"I suspect nothing, brother — nothing whatever," said Henri III. hastily; "but I will sign no truce—enter into no compact which shall favour, or appear to favour, the dissemination of heresy and sedition. To tolerate such a faith were to approve it. And I would rather command a second Saint-Barthélemy; rather imitate the example of my brother, Philip II. of Spain; or pursue the course pointed out to me by my cousin of Guise and the gentlemen of the League, than in any way countenance a religion so hateful. I am too good a Catholic for that, brother. My reign has been (for my sins) disturbed by three great troubles. My brother of Anjou and his faction; the Balafré and his Leaguers; you and your friends of the reform."

"Sire!"

"I know not which of the three has been the most vexatious, Anjou with his claims, Guise with his pretensions, or you with your exactions. I shall be glad to put an end to *one* of these annoyances."

"I have exacted nothing but what was my due, sire," replied the Bourbon bluntly.

"So saith Anjou; so saith the Guise; so say all rebels."

"Rebels, sire!"

"Fret not yourself about a word, brother. Your own conduct will best prevent the application of the term, if you deem it injurious."

"Sire," replied the Bourbon, drawing himself up to his full height, and regarding his royal brother with a glance of undisguised scorn and defiance, "you have done me deep wrong in stigmatising me as a rebel. It is false. I am none. Rashness, insane rashness—if you please—is all that can be laid to my charge. I came hither attended only by the Baron de Rosni, whose person, as my ambassador, guarded by your passport, is sacred: and as I came I should have departed, had not an accident occasioned my discovery. No thought of treason was in my breast. Nor had I other motive save a desire to splinter a lance with one whose prowess I doubted, with as much justice, it appears, as your majesty now exhibits in questioning my sincerity."

"You mistake me, brother. Heaven forbid I should question your fealty."

"Your actions contradict your words, sire," returned the Bourbon. "It is evident from the threatening demeanour of your attendants, from the hostile disposition of your troops, as well as from the orders you have issued, that you *do* distrust me, and that you have more reason to apprehend my influence with the populace, in the event of an insurrection, than you care to admit. Your alarm is groundless. Had I come as an enemy, I should not have come alone. I am the contriver of no plot, the leader of no faction; nor, amid yon vast assemblage, could I point out the features of a single adherent, though I nothing fear, if my war-cry were once raised, I should find friends enow to rally round my standard. Yester-morn, with but a dozen followers, I entered the gates of Paris: to-day, with but *one*, those of the Louvre. And to-morrow's dawn shall find me and my scanty train far on our way to my territories, if I have your majesty's permission to depart peaceably."

"In the meantime, brother," said Henri III., "I would gladly learn what induced you to quit those territories to which you are now apparently so anxious to return? I can scarcely flatter myself that a desire to hold this interview with me was your sole motive."

"So far from it, sire, that I repeat it was my intention to have remained strictly incognito, had not my own heedlessness betrayed me. The object of my hare-brained journey I will no longer disguise. When I deserted the Louvre," he added, his brow relaxing to a slight smile, "there were two things which, in my haste, I left behind me."

"Ah! what were they, brother?"

"The mass and my wife, sire. For the loss of the former I felt little concern. The want of the latter was a more serious grievance. And having failed in my previous remonstrance, made through the Sieur Duras, I thought the fault might rest with my envoy. Accordingly, I resolved——"

"To come yourself," interrupted Henri III., laughing heartily. "A wise determination, certes. Still, I fear your suit has proved as unsuccessful as ever, though backed by your own solicitations."

"His majesty is certain of gaining his cause, now that he has employed the Chevalier Crichton as an advocate," cried Chicot. "It is exactly three years since the Sieur Duras came to Paris on this fool's errand, and then Bussy d'Amboise sent him back again, like Panurge, 'avec une puce à l'oreille.' The same result would have followed his own application had it not been for this masterstroke. Of all men, Henri of Navarre ought to be the last to forget the maxim, that

> A husband out of season
> Is a husband without reason!"

"Let not these taunts annoy you, brother," said Henri III. "You shall have both your lost matters. But I cannot restore the one without the other."

"I will have neither, sire."

"You are changeable, brother."

"It may be so, sire," replied the Bourbon coldly; "but I have the same aversion to a faithless woman that I have to a consecrated wafer."

"I have at all events made you the offer," said Henri III. angrily. "And now, Chevalier Crichton," he continued, addressing the Scot, who had remained near him, a silent, but deeply interested observer of the scene—"advance!—arrest him!"

These words, uttered in a sharp, abrupt tone, produced a startling effect upon the group. Saint-Luc and D'Epernon drew their swords, closing in on either side of their sovereign. The Bourbon uttered a single exclamation, and placed his hand upon the hilt of his own weapon. His arm, however, was again forcibly withheld by Rosni.

"Remember, sire," said the baron, in a deep whisper, "your sacred pledge to your people, and to your God. One false step, and your subjects are without a ruler—your Church without a defender. Be warned!"

"Quem Deus vult perdere prius dementat," said Chicot.

Crichton meanwhile stirred not, but watched steadily the movements of the King of Navarre. "Must I repeat my orders, messire?" asked Henri III.

"No, sire," replied the Bourbon. "I will relieve the Chevalier Crichton from his embarrassment. Here is my sword."

The Scot received it with a profound salutation.

"Keep it," continued the Bourbon; "you need not blush to bear it."

"I blush to receive it, sire," returned Crichton, scarcely able to repress the emotions swelling within his bosom.

"And now for the other captive and his dog," said Henri III.

"Hold, sire," exclaimed the Bourbon. "Ere this conference is broken up, I have a secret of importance to disclose to you. I would willingly have imparted it to your ears alone. But since you refuse me a private audience, I am compelled to proclaim it openly."

At this moment the shifting glances of Henri III. fell upon the Duc de Nevers. The latter was evidently ill at ease, and approaching his sovereign, said, in a low emphatic tone:

"This interview were better concluded, sire."

"I think otherwise, fair cousin," returned the king, whose curiosity was awakened. "May I venture to trust myself alone with him for a few moments?" he whispered. "He is unarmed."

"By no means, sire," returned the duke; "he has a poniard."

"True," returned Henri III., "and he is not unskilful in its use, as I have seen. His strength, too, greatly exceeds my own —and though his bearing is frank and loyal, it were most imprudent implicitly to confide in him.—Speak, brother," he continued aloud. "I am impatient to hear your disclosure."

"Your majesty drives me to the course I now adopt," returned the Bourbon haughtily; "the shame I would willingly spare the queen your mother I will no longer spare her."

"Will you endure this insolence, sire?" said the Duc de Nevers, alarmed at the King of Navarre's commencement.

"Heed him not," returned Henri III.; "her majesty will give herself little concern about *his* reproaches."

"What I would have requested," continued the Bourbon, who had paused for a moment, "I now demand. In the name of my cousin, Henri I. of Bourbon, Prince of Condé, whose person I here represent, I require from your majesty the liberation of his sister, unjustly detained a captive within the Louvre by the Queen-Mother, Catherine de Medicis."

"*Mort-Dieu!* brother," exclaimed Henri III., "you are strangely deceived in this matter. Our mother has no such captive."

"Contest not the point, sire," whispered the Duc de Nevers, who was now relieved from his own apprehension. "Promise her liberation."

"Your majesty has been, designedly, kept in ignorance of the circumstance," said the Bourbon.

"Well, brother," returned Henri III., with affected bonhomie, "if your representation be correct, we pass our word for the freedom of the princess."

As this speech was uttered, a slight exclamation of joy escaped Crichton. But when the king glanced towards him, his eyes were riveted upon the Bourbon's sword.

"Add to your boon, sire," said the King of Navarre, "for which I thank you as heartily as if my own liberty had been included in it, and suffer the princess to set forth, at once, from the Louvre, under your safe-conduct. My own escort shall, with your majesty's permission, act as her convoy to Henri of Condé."

"Why this extreme urgency, brother?" asked Henri III. doubtfully.

"Because," replied the Bourbon, "while she remains in the power of Catherine de Medicis, her life, her honour are in danger."

"Beware how you scandalise our mother," returned Henri III. with warmth. "These are dark accusations."

"They are made in broad daylight before your assembled nobles, sire, and will not be unremembered."

"Nor unrequited," answered Henri III. frowning. "Proceed, brother."

"I am a soldier, not a courtier, sire," continued the Bourbon. "My steel corslet is seldom exchanged for a silken pourpoint— my rude speech as seldom takes the garb of flattery. Your majesty will bear in mind that you have forced me to make this charge in public. I am prepared to answer to the queen your mother for my accusation, and to approve it. Your royal word is passed for the liberation of the princess. That is enough for me."

"What are we to think of this mystery?" demanded Henri III. of the Duc de Nevers.

"That his majesty of Navarre's wits, as well as his discretion, have deserted him, my liege," returned the duke. "I am sufficiently in the confidence of her majesty the Queen-Mother to assert, unhesitatingly, that there is no such princess."

"You are sure of it, fair cousin?"

"As of your majesty's existence—as of the presence of yon Bernese bear."

"You have already relieved me. I began to fear that I had, in some way or other, committed myself."

The Bourbon, meanwhile, conferred an instant apart with his counsellor. "Thou wilt command this escort, Rosni," whispered he, "and say to the Prince of Condé that——"

"I quit not your majesty's side for any prince or princess," interrupted Rosni.

"How, sir?"

"Spare your frowns, sire. I can be as obstinate, on occasion, as your majesty."

"Stay with me, then, my faithful friend," replied the Bourbon, pressing the hand of his counsellor, "and let our recent difference be forgotten. Thou hast my full pardon."

"When your majesty has obtained your own forgiveness, it will be time enough to extend the same grace to me," rejoined Rosni, bluntly.

"Chevalier Crichton," said the Bourbon, turning in displeasure from his confidant, "will you escort the Princess of Condé to her brother?"

The Scot's colour mounted to his temples at the proposal. "Your majesty has already appointed me to the post of your chief attendant," he returned, in a voice of constrained calmness; "I cannot accept both offices."

"Nor can I consent to part with you, *mon cher*," said Henri III. approvingly. "To put an end to this discussion, brother," he continued, addressing the Bourbon, "if you will find the princess, I will undertake to find the convoy."

"*A la bonne heure!*" cried the King of Navarre. "My task will be readily performed. Behold her!" he added, pointing to the royal gallery.

"Behold whom!—you cannot mean——?"

"In the queen of the lists—in the fair Esclairmonde your majesty beholds the sister of Henri of Condé—my cousin—*your* cousin, sire."

"*Mort et damnation!* Esclairmonde my cousin! Esclairmonde a Princess of Condé!—Were it so—but you do not, cannot expect us to credit your assertion, unsupported by proof, upon a point like this?"

"I *have* proofs, sire—proofs of her illustrious birth—of her capture as an infant by Tavannes—of her detention within the Louvre by Catherine—proofs which will carry conviction even to the mind of your majesty."

"Produce them, brother, produce them!" cried Henri III., trembling with agitation.

"Let your guard, by sound of trump, summon before your presence Messire Florent Chrétien, a preacher of the Reformed Faith and the spiritual adviser of the princess; he is within the Louvre—he is in possession of these proofs."

"Ha! think you to delude us by the devices of the evil one—of his minister?" vociferated Henri III. "Think you we would place the fabrications of this miserable hypocrite against the word of our mother? Think you we will endure the presence of a heretic, and a propagator of heresy, knowing him to be such? Let him take heed how he approaches us—how he defiles the hem of our garment—how he pollutes our palace. The Grève hath an axe—the Pré-aux-Clercs a stake—Montfaucon a gibbet. He shall have his choice of the three; the sole grace a false and perjured Huguenot may look for at our hands."

"Be all three his portion and mine, if he deceives you, sire," returned the Bourbon. "Let him be summoned. I will abide the issue."

"Be it so," replied Henri III., as if he had suddenly decided upon the course he ought to pursue.

"Your guard must seek him within the dungeons of the Louvre," said Crichton. "He is a prisoner."

"A prisoner!" echoed the Bourbon, starting.

"A prisoner!" repeated Henri III. joyfully.

"He is in the hands of Catherine de Medicis," continued the Scot.

"And the documents?" demanded the King of Navarre eagerly.

"Are also in her majesty's possession," returned Crichton. "Florent Chrétien is adjudged to the stake."

"Will you now forgive yourself, sire?" asked Rosni, in a low tone.

"Away!" ejaculated the King of Navarre, stamping his foot upon the ground with wrath. "*Ventre-saint-gris!* is this a season for reproaches? Your majesty, I am well assured," he added, indignantly appealing to his royal brother, "will see fit to reverse this most unjust judgment. Chrétien is innocent of all crime."

"Of all, save that of heresy, it may be," returned Henri III., "than which no guilt is more heinous and unpardonable in our eyes, and of which, even by your own showing, he is culpable. Our mother has acted in conformity with our wishes, and in furtherance of the interests of the true faith, in condemning this Huguenot preacher to expiate his offences against Heaven at the stake; and, were our sanction needful, it should be readily accorded."

"Vive la messe!" cried the courtiers.

"You hear, brother," said Henri III., smiling. "Such are the sentiments of every good Catholic."

"Will you violate the majesty of your own laws, sire?" demanded the Bourbon. "Have you no regard for the sanctity of the pledges voluntarily given for the security of your Protestant subjects?"

"Hæreticis fides non servanda est," rejoined Henri III. coldly.

"It follows then, sire," said the Bourbon, "that your royal word, passed to me for the liberation of the Princess Esclairmonde, is not binding upon your pliant conscience?—ha!"

"Satisfy me that she *is* a princess, and I will keep my faith with you, albeit you *are* a heretic, brother. Produce your proofs, and I repeat, she is free."

"Your majesty may safely make that promise now," returned the Bourbon scornfully.

"If *I* produce those proofs ere midnight, will you fulfil your word, sire?" asked Crichton, advancing.

Henri III. was visibly embarrassed.

"You cannot retreat, my liege," whispered the Duc de Nevers.

"But, fair cousin," returned the king in an undertone, "we would rather part with our crown than Esclairmonde—and this accursed Scot would outwit the devil."

"He will not outwit Catherine de Medicis, sire," said the duke. "I will put her upon her guard."

"How says your majesty?" demanded the Bourbon.

"Our word is already passed," returned Henri III.

"Enough!" said Crichton, retiring.

At this moment the Vicomte de Joyeuse approached.

"I am the bearer of a *billet* from the Queen-Mother, sire," he said, presenting a sealed dispatch to the king.

"*Peste!*" exclaimed Henri III. as he glanced over the contents of the latter. "We have been too precipitate, fair cousin," continued he, addressing the Duc de Nevers. "Her majesty counsels us to treat the Béarnais with all courtesy and consideration."

The duke replied by a shrug of the shoulder.

"Nay, this is not all," added the king; "she entreats us to restore his sword."

"And your majesty will, of course, comply with her request."

"*Pardieu!* no, cousin."

"Remember the fair Esclairmonde, sire."

"Ah! you are right," returned Henri III. hastily. "That name at once decides me. I know not what credit is to be attached to this story of the lovely demoiselle's birth. It is possible it may be true. But true or false, it is plain, if I would hope to succeed in my designs upon her, I must now, more than ever, yield implicit obedience to my mother's behests."

"Wisely resolved, sire."

"A reconciliation with the Béarnais will not be difficult," pursued Henri III. "His choler is as readily appeased as aroused. You shall see how easily we will cajole him. A fair word or so will make all smooth between us. Approach, brother," he continued, addressing the King of Navarre in a friendly tone; "I have done you wrong, and am eager to make you reparation."

"Sire!" exclaimed the Bourbon, springing eagerly forward.

"Your hand, brother."

"It is the hand of a heretic, sire."

"No matter! it is a loyal hand, and as such I clasp it. Nay, withdraw it not, good brother. I wish all my court to perceive that we are on terms of amity together—especially my mother," he added, aside.

"Vive le Roi!" cried the courtiers. And the shout was echoed by a thousand voices.

"I have deprived you of your sword," continued Henri III. "You cannot reclaim your gift from the Chevalier Crichton. I pray you, therefore, to wear this blade for my sake," he added, unbuckling his rapier, the hilt of which was studded with diamonds, and presenting it to the King of Navarre. "Promise me only that you will not draw it against a subject of France."

"I will wear it for your defence, sire," replied the Bourbon. "Your majesty's kindness will not allow me for an instant to doubt your sincerity, but I would gladly learn to whom I am indebted for this sudden alteration in your sentiments."

"To one whose intercession you scarcely merit," returned Henri III. with a gracious smile—"to the Queen-Mother."

"*Jour de Dieu!*" exclaimed the Bourbon, "to her!"

"Pardon the unworthy reception I have given you. I was taken by surprise, and could not divest myself of certain misgivings, which this letter has wholly dispelled. I will make the best amends in my power."

"Grant me the life of Florent Chrétien, and we are quits, sire."

Henri III. was again perplexed.

"His life is in my mother's hands," he said. "Make your appeal to her. You stand well with her, it seems. I never interfere between her majesty and the objects of her displeasure. Yet stay! if you can induce this Chrétien to abjure his heresies, I think I may venture to promise you his life."

"You have ratified his doom, sire," said the Bourbon, retiring.

"What think you of this change, Rosni?" he added, as he rejoined his counsellor.

"I like it not," returned Rosni. "The friendship of this Vilain Herodes is more to be dreaded than his enmity. But you have confided in him——?"

"Bon gré, mal gré," answered the Bourbon.

"How have I played my part, my cousin?" asked Henri III. of the Duc de Nevers.

"To admiration, sire," replied the duke.

"You are a flatterer. But I am weary of this conference. Bring forward our captive and his dog. 'Twill divert my thoughts to question him."

"Take heed, *compère*," cried Chicot; "you will not find that dog so carefully muzzled as the great bear of Berne."

CHAPTER X

THE MISSAL

——Que toute trahison sur le traître retombe!
VICTOR HUGO, *Hernani.*

BLOUNT, who had been strictly guarded during the conference previously detailed, and had endured, with stoical calmness, all the petty persecution, in the shape of taunts and blows, that his captors chose to inflict, was now dragged into the king's presence. Druid followed as closely at his heels as the sash by which he was restrained would permit him to do.

"Before you bestow yon caitiff's head upon the executioner of the Châtelet, my liege," said Joyeuse, "it may be well to interrogate him as to the motive of his daring action. I can scarcely think, with all his reckless courage, that it proceeded from mere bravado. My own opinion is," he added, lowering his voice, "that he is charged with a message to the Béarnais— in which case your majesty may elicit some important information from him."

"I will essay, *mon enfant*," replied Henri III., "but I despair of success. Look at his stubborn visage and resolute bearing, and say if threats are likely to shake him? That man would perish rather than play the traitor."

And so it proved. Blount refused to return other than a surly monosyllabic response to the monarch's inquiries.

"Remove him to the Grand-Châtelet," said Henri III.

impatiently, "and let the question ordinary and extraordinary be proposed to him."

"It will extort nothing," rejoined the Englishman firmly.

"I was right, you perceive, *mon cher*," said the monarch, turning to his favourite.

"I will find a way to wring his secret from him, my liege," replied the vicomte. "I see where his vulnerable point lies."

And he whispered to the king.

"You have hit it," returned Henri, laughing; "but proceed not to extremities."

"Leave him to me, sire," said Joyeuse. "Draw thy sword," he added, addressing the man-at-arms by whom Druid was guarded, "and upon each interrogation which this obstinate traitor may decline to answer, hew a limb from his hound."

The weapon of the halberdier flashed in the air.

"Devils!" cried Blount, in a voice that sounded like the roar of a lion, at the same time exerting himself with so much force as to burst asunder the leathern thong that confined his arms. "What would you have me do?"

"Reply, without disguise, to his majesty's interrogations," said Crichton, advancing towards him.

"Well, then," returned Blount, "to spare my dog unnecessary suffering, I will do that which I would not have done to preserve my own flesh from the hot pincers, or my bones from the grinding wheel—I *will* speak—though, by the rood! I have nothing to reveal. I might have borne to see Druid perish," he muttered, "but to behold him die by piecemeal—no—no, I could not endure *that*."

"What brought thee hither, thou contumacious varlet?" demanded Henri III. "Wert thou not aware that thy life would pay the penalty of thy rashness?"

"I was fully aware of the consequences of the step I took," answered the Englishman. "But the desire to serve a friend was paramount to any consideration of danger."

"What friend, sirrah?"

"I have been too bold, perhaps, to term him such," returned Blount, "but death levels all distinctions, and mine is so near at hand, that I may claim some exemption from worldly forms. My fidelity will, I nothing doubt, ensure me a worthy place in his remembrance."

"Thy devotion to whom, sirrah?" demanded Henri III. impatiently. "To the King of Navarre?"

"To the Chevalier Crichton, sire."

"To Crichton!" echoed Henri, in astonishment. "*Morbleu!* Joyeuse," he continued, addressing the vicomte, "this Scot exercises an unaccountable influence over his fellows. Here is a sturdy knave, who derides the dungeon and the rack, ready to lay down his head for the love he bears him. By what magic is this accomplished?"

"By the magic of manner, sire," returned Joyeuse. "Was ever smile beheld so captivating—was ever demeanour witnessed at once so courteous and so dignified, as that of Crichton! Add to the charm of manner, the ennobling and heroic spirit of chivalry breathing from his lightest word and action—weaving its spell around him, and inspiring all who approach with kindred ardour, and you have the secret of his witchery over the minds of men. It was the same with Bayard—the same with Du Guesclin—with Charlemagne, and with Godefroy de Bouillon. Some men there are for whom we would willingly live: others for whom we would as readily die. Crichton is among the latter."

"You have merely drawn the distinction between friendship and devotion, *mon cher*," replied Henri, turning, with a look of displeasure, towards Blount. "Thy intelligence must have been of vital import, sirrah," he added, pursuing his inquiries, "since it could not be delayed till the jousts were ended?"

"My errand was nothing more," answered Blount carelessly, "than to apprise the Chevalier Crichton that a packet on which he set some store, and which, after incurring various risks, had been strangely found, was again as strangely lost."

"Is that all thou knowst concerning it, *mon maître*?"

"I know that it has proved a fatal charge, sire. All who have meddled with it have come to ill. It was lost, as it was won, at the point of the sword. To the breast of him who first grasped it, it brought a poniard; to the next who received it, the stake; and to myself, it is like to bring the axe. May like calamity alight on her into whose possession it hath now fallen."

"Your majesty will, perhaps, next question him as to his acquaintance with the contents of the packet?" interposed Crichton.

"By no means," returned Henri, frowning. "I perceive your drift, and have heard enough to convince me that the testimony of this traitor is suborned. Hola! Larchant," he continued, addressing one of the officers in attendance, "let the prisoner be conveyed to the Châtelet, and thrown into the *Fin d'aise,* where, if he expire not within the week, the headsman may release him from further torture."

"Yours are tender mercies, sire," returned Blount, smiling disdainfully.

"Let the hound be cared for," continued Henri.

"Is he not to go with me?" asked Blount, starting.

"Hence with the prating knave!" exclaimed the king furiously.

Blount suddenly broke from his guards, and prostrated himself at the king's feet.

"I do not ask for mercy, sire," he cried. "I know my life is forfeited, and justly; but oh! separate me not from my faithful companion."

Henri wavered. If he *had* a heart, it lay on the side on which the Englishman now assailed him.

"Thou lov'st thy dog?" he said musingly.

"Better than my life."

"'Tis a good sign!—Thou *shouldst* be honest. I cannot, however, grant thy request. Refusal here is mercy. The poor animal would only howl beneath thy carcass, and it may console thee to learn that, in changing masters, he will find one who will not value him less than thou dost, while he is better able to protect him. Stand back! *mon maître.*"

"My dog is no courtier," replied Blount, rising; "he will serve no second master. What ho! Druid."

This summons, followed by a short, sharp whistle, brought Druid instantly to the Englishman's feet. The scarf was round his throat, and in his teeth he held a large fragment of the apparel of the man-at-arms, which he had torn off in effecting his liberation.

"I knew no bonds would hold thee, brave fellow," said Blount, caressing his dog, who, in his turn, fondly licked his master's hand. "We must part, old comrade."

Druid looked wistfully in his face.

"For ever," said Blount slowly, "for ever!"

"Away with him," cried Henri, "but take heed you harm not the dog. I would not lose that noble animal for a prince's ransom."

"A moment, sire, and he is yours," ejaculated Blount, over whose open and manly countenance a sullen cloud had now spread. "It is hard to part with a friend whom one has long cherished. This dog," he continued, with difficulty mastering the emotion, which was proclaimed by sundry twitches at the corners of his mouth, "will feed from no hand but mine; will answer to no call but mine; will fight at no bidding but mine. I must teach him obedience to his new master. You will find him tractable enough when I have done with him."

"I will take every care of him," said Henri, somewhat affected by the scene.

"Fare thee well, Druid!" murmured Blount; "and now," he added gently, "lie down, lie down, old friend."

Druid crouched upon the ground.

Swift as thought Blount placed his foot upon the dog's body, as if about to crush him to the earth, and with both hands seized the scarf entwined around his throat. Though he perceived the action, and might have guessed its intent, Druid offered no resistance. His eyes were fixed upon his master. The noose was tightened, and in another instant the fate of the brave dog would have been sealed, but for the intervention of Crichton, who forcibly arrested the Englishman's arm.

"Desist!" he whispered. "I promise to dispatch him, if aught befall thee."

"You promise more than you can perform sometimes, Chevalier Crichton," returned Blount sullenly. "You undertook to free me from any peril I might incur in the execution of your orders. My head is now within reach of the axe."

"Thy own madness has brought it there," rejoined Crichton, sternly. "Release thy dog, or I abandon thee to thy fate."

Blount, with some reluctance, relinquished his hold of the scarf. "Where is the missal which I entrusted to thy care?" continued the Scot.

"Where you placed it—next my heart; where it will remain while that heart beats."

"Saint Andrew be praised!" exclaimed Crichton joyfully. "Anticipating they would search thee and discover that book upon thy person, I allowed matters to proceed thus far. But no injury should have been done thee. Deliver it instantly to the king."

Crichton retired, and Blount drew a small richly-gilded volume from his doublet. "Sire!" he said, addressing Henri III., "this book, confided to me by the Chevalier Crichton, dropped from the folds of the packet about which you have just questioned me. It was committed to my charge because, upon ascertaining it was a mass-book of the Romish Church, Messire Florent Chrétien refused to receive it. I am a Catholic. And were I not, I have no such scruples. It would seem to belong to your majesty. The vellum cover is emblazoned with a royal crown—with the lilies of France, and with the letters *C* and *H*."

"*Pardieu!* it is our mother's missal," exclaimed Henri III.

"It is her cipher linked with that of the king our father. Give me the book, Du Halde."

"Your majesty will not touch it," said the Duc de Nevers, turning pale; "it may be poisoned."

"I will be the first to open it, if you have any such apprehensions, my liege," interposed Crichton.

"I have no fear," replied the king. "From these pages I derive health and succour, not bane. Ah! *Mon Dieu!*" he exclaimed, as his eye rested upon a leaf on which certain mysterious characters were traced. "Have I chanced upon the serpents' nest?"

"What have you discovered, my liege?" asked Joyeuse.

"A plot!" vociferated Henri III. "A conspiracy against our crown—against our life!"

Universal consternation prevailed amidst the assemblage. Many mysterious and suspicious glances were interchanged by the nobles, and a look of intelligence passed unobserved between Crichton and the King of Navarre.

"By whom is this plot contrived, my liege?" asked the Duc de Nevers, with quivering lips.

"By whom think you, Monsieur le Duc?—by whom think you?" thundered the king.

"By the Guise?"

"By our father's son—by the Duc d'Anjou."

There was a deep silence, which no one cared to break except the Bourbon, who coughed slightly in an ineffectual attempt to conceal his satisfaction.

"I have long suspected my brother's treachery," said Henri, after a pause, during which he appeared greatly disturbed; "but I have here evidence of his guilt under his own hand."

"It is a letter you have found, sire?" inquired the Duc de Nevers anxiously.

"Ay, my cousin," returned the king in a deep whisper, "it *is* a letter!—a letter from Anjou to our mother—a letter of treason and blood penned upon these sacred pages—a letter devised by the demon, inscribed upon the word of God!"

"It is a forgery, my liege. The Duc d'Anjou is incapable of a crime so monstrous and unnatural. I will answer for his innocence with my head."

"Answer for yourself, monseigneur," replied Henri in a freezing tone, at the same time speaking in a voice so low as to be inaudible to his attendants, "you will find it no easy matter. The characters in which this letter is traced reveal

the writer. They are secret characters, known only to myself
—my mother—and this arch-traitor. They were contrived for
the security of my own dispatches from Poland, when Charles
stood towards me as I now stand to Anjou; and when my
mother betrayed him, as she has here betrayed me. These
characters cannot have been fabricated, neither can they be
deciphered without a key. Look at this writing! To you it is
incomprehensible as an Egyptian hieroglyphic: to me legible
as the *billet* of a mistress. And see! a leaf is wanting. Where
was our mother's letter—here is Anjou's answer. Jesus-Maria!
if I had any doubts left, this would remove them. I am doubly
betrayed."

"My gracious liege——"

"Anjou is guilty of *lèse-majesté* and felony in the highest
degree—and shall die the death of a traitor—as shall all who
have favoured, or are engaged in this foul conspiracy—even
though I flood the Louvre in the noblest blood of France. The
scaffold and the block shall not be removed from these courts,
nor shall the headsman cease his labour till he has utterly
exterminated this hydra-headed monster of rebellion. Hitherto
I have been easy, forgiving, merciful. It has availed nothing.
Henceforth I will be relentless and inflexible. The ordinance of
my ancestor Louis XI., which condemns him who is guilty of
misprision of treason, to like doom with the traitor, is not yet
abrogated. You have answered for Anjou with your head. Take
heed I claim not the pledge. It is already forfeited."

"Your suspicions cannot attach to me, sire," faltered De
Nevers. "I have been your loyal follower ever."

"My suspicions!" echoed the king in a tone of irony. "*Par
la Mort-Dieu!* monseigneur, I *suspect* you not—I am *assured*
of your treachery."

"*Malédiction!* this to me, sire?"

"Be patient, fair cousin. Another such intemperate exclamation, and my guard shall conduct you to the Bastille."

"Your menaces alarm me not, sire," replied the duke, who
had now recovered his composure, "conscious as I am of my
innocence, and of the groundlessness of the charge preferred
against me. The name of Gonzaga has never yet been coupled
with that of traitor. Were I aware of any conspiracy against
your majesty, I would denounce it, though my own son were
its leader. And if I should march hence to the scaffold with
which you have threatened me, my last prayer should be for the
uninterrupted prosperity and long continuance of your reign."

M 804

"Judas!" muttered the king between his teeth; "the plot is better organised, and nearer its outbreak, than I deemed it, if he is thus confident. I must proceed with greater caution. *Qui nescit dissimulare, nescit regnare. Vive Dieu!* cousin," he continued, placing his hand familiarly upon the duke's saddle-bow, and regarding him with a look, in which distrust was skilfully veiled by an expression of friendliness, "your warmth would almost persuade me I have wronged you in suspecting you of defection. If it be so, you will know how to overlook the error. Environed as I am by faction and sedition—surrounded by perfidy in all shapes and all aspects—by rebels in the mask of brothers—traitors under the cloak of counsellors—assassins in the guise of friends; when those I have most loved, most honoured, most rewarded, are the first to desert, to betray me; when those bound to me by the strict ties of duty, and by the stricter ties of affinity, forget alike their allegiance and affection; when the hand that once caressed me brings the poniard to my bosom; and the lips, from which the fondest maternal endearments have flowed, command my destruction, I may be forgiven if I should mistake a loyal follower for a deadly enemy, and for a moment question the stainless honour, and mistaken, though not wholly unrequited, fidelity of Gonzaga."

"My services, however requited," replied the duke with some asperity, "should have secured me from these unmerited taunts. But since they who should be nearest to your highness in your love are visited with the extremity of your indignation, I am content to disregard the affront."

"You do wisely, monseigneur," rejoined the king, with a smile of derision. "*I* need not remind you this is not the first time I have detected and defeated Anjou's treasonable schemes. I need not tell you of the revolt which was to have followed my return from Poland to the throne of France; of the ambuscade which beset my route; of the assassins who were balked of their victim. I need not tell you of my brother's capture, interrogation and confession; of the decapitation of La Mole and Coconnas, and of my mistaken clemency. Catherine de Medicis in those days watched over my safety with zealous care. Now she has instigated a rebellion she was then prompt to crush. Would to Heaven Anjou had yielded to the promptings of his own dark heart and strangled her, as he intended to do, when she embraced him in his prison at Vincennes."

"Sire, your resentment carries you too far. Catherine de Medicis is still your mother. To her you owe your crown."

"*Oui-dà*, monseigneur, and to *her*, also, I might owe my abdication and dethronement, if she would permit me to finish my term of life in the seclusion of a cloister. Think you I know not *whose* hand has hitherto grasped the reins of empire—whose voice has swayed my councils—whose mandates have controlled my edicts—whose policy has influenced my actions? Think you I deemed, when Catherine resigned the regency of this realm to me, she resigned also its sovereign sway? *Pardieu!* if such has been your opinion, it is time you were undeceived. I owe her much, but she owes me more. I am indebted to her for the name of king: she has to thank me for the powers of royalty. If I have preferred an existence of enjoyment and repose (as much repose, at least, as is ever allotted to princes) to the cares and responsibilities of active government—if I have sought to dispel my *ennui* by a thousand trifling occupations— if the pursuits of pleasure, the exercises of devotion, the companionship of favourites and of mistresses, have engrossed my attention—though my people may have some reason to complain, my mother has none, because such a course has been consonant to her inclinations. I have submitted all to her disposal. But, if I am rudely awakened from my dream of security—if I find that the arm which defended me has become hostile—that what I have quietly yielded is to be forcibly wrested from me—that not even the semblance of rule is to be left, what wonder if I start, like one from a trance, and, banishing from my breast all feelings, save those akin to justice and retribution, prepare to wreak my vengeance upon the heads of the aggressors?"

"Calm yourself, my liege."

"*Tête-et-sang!* I *am* calm enough, as you will find anon, monseigneur. I pardoned my brother's first transgression— restored him to my love—bestowed upon him in appanage the dukedoms of Berri and Anjou, the earldoms of Touraine and Maine, and refused only his solicitation for the lieutenant-generalship of the kingdom. I had good reasons for my refusal. I reserved that high post for some adherent, trustworthy and meritorious as the Duc de Nevers."

"Sire," replied the duke, in confusion, unable to divine Henri's real meaning, and fearful of some snare being laid for him, "I have already received too many proofs of your favour."

"Bah!" exclaimed the king, with ill-disguised irony. "I never till now sufficiently appreciated your services or fidelity. True, I thought, in raising you to your present elevated position—in entrusting my Piedmontese army to your command—in appointing you to the government of Pignerol, Savillan and La Perose; in placing certain wealthy benefices at your disposal; in granting you a heavy pension from the coffers of the State, and investing you with the cordon of the Saint-Esprit which hangs from your gorget; in doing all this I imagined I had made some slight return for your unremitting zeal and devotedness. But I perceive my mistake. I have yet a greater service to exact: I have yet a higher reward to offer."

"The service I can conjecture," said the duke, after a pause—"the reward——"

"The post I refused to Anjou. My refusal made him a traitor. My grant shall make you loyal."

"Sire!"

"Your brevet shall be signed to-morrow."

"I should prefer it to-day," replied the duke significantly. "To-morrow it may be out of your majesty's power."

"Ha!" exclaimed Henri, with a thrill of apprehension, "is my peril then so imminent? Mary Mother protect me!"

"In the Virgin's name," whispered the duke, "I beseech you to maintain your composure. You are surrounded by the spies of Catherine de Medicis, whose glances are fixed upon your every look and gesture, whose ears are on the alert to catch each word you let fall. Still appear to suspect me, or I shall become as much the object of their vigilance as your majesty. You are on the brink of a precipice. My arm alone can arrest your fall."

"How shall I evince my gratitude?" said Henri, vainly endeavouring to repress his agitation.

"By the fulfilment of your promise, sire."

"Doubt it not—doubt it not, my cousin. You shall have your appointment on my return to the Louvre. I swear it by Saint Louis, my patron! And now relieve my anxiety. You have put me on the rack——"

"Your majesty must excuse my saying more at present," returned the duke evasively. "I have already said too much. Your cabinet will be the fittest place for my further disclosures. Here I dare not breathe them. Meantime, do not disquiet yourself. I will answer for your safety."

Henri darted an angry and distrustful glance at the wily De Nevers. "Who will answer for your honesty, Monsieur le Duc?" he said.

"San Francesco, my patron," replied the duke, smiling.

"Where is the Prince Vincenzo?" demanded Henri.

"He has been removed by his attendants to the Hôtel de Nevers," answered the duke. "Heaven be praised, his wound is not dangerous."

"'Tis well!" exclaimed Henri. "And now take heed, cousin. To-morrow you are chief in command of our armies, or," he added, in a deep, determined tone, "the Duke of Mantua will have to lament his son and brother."

"As you please, my liege," rejoined De Nevers, with affected indifference. "I have warned you, and you will find my warning fearfully verified if you neglect it. Arouse the suspicions of Catherine de Medicis, and all is lost. Her party is stronger than your own. Her majesty, I perceive," he continued, carelessly looking in that direction, "has quitted the grand gallery. She has remarked our conference, and dispatched a secret messenger to ascertain its object. It must be brought to a close. Pardon my freedom, sire. Danger is not ceremonious."

"So I find," said Henri.

"Be ruled by me, my liege," continued the duke, "and your crown shall be preserved without risk—without bloodshed. I will meet plot with counter-plot, stratagem with stratagem, and turn the weapons of your adversaries against themselves. One life only shall be sacrificed."

"The life of my brother?" faltered Henri.

"No, sire; that of your rival in the affections of Esclairmonde—that of the Chevalier Crichton."

"*Sang-Dieu!* though I shall not regret to be freed from a rival so formidable as Crichton, I see not how his destruction will ensure the success of your schemes."

"On him rests the chief reliance of Catherine de Medicis—of the Duc d'Anjou. On him devolves the terrible part of your assassination."

"Jesus!" exclaimed Henri, smelling at a flacon which he took from his escarcelle.

"He must die."

"In Heaven's name let him die, cousin. Order his instant execution, if you think proper."

"In good time, my liege. And now let me counsel your majesty to command some of your youthful nobles and gentlemen to enter the lists, or to engage in such knightly exercises as may induce your lynx-eyed mother and her *mouchards* to conclude our *tête-à-tête* has had reference only to the business of the tilt-yard."

"Well thought of, cousin," replied Henri. "But can you not devise some better expedient than the withdrawal of our loyal attendants from our side at a critical conjuncture like the present? I dare not—will not hazard it."

"What say you to a combat of animals, sire?" insinuated De Nevers. "Many months have elapsed since the gentle dames of your court had an opportunity of witnessing a spectacle so delightful. It will afford them the highest gratification, and answer our purpose admirably. Suppose you make trial of the strength and ferocity of the African lion, sent by Philip II. of Spain, against the tigers lately presented to your majesty by the Grand Signor Amurath III., or, if you think that match unequal, against the pack of German wolves——"

"Or Italian foxes," interrupted Henri. "No, De Nevers; were the lion worsted, I should hold it an evil omen. I have often heard of the extreme hardihood of an English bull-dog in the fight; I will now put it to the test."

"Bravo!" exclaimed the duke.

"I have a wild Spanish bull, black as Pluto, and fierce as Chiron," continued the king; "he shall sustain the hound's attack. Bid his keepers bring him forth, and chain him to the stoutest post they can find in the lists. *Mort-Dieu!* 'twill be brave sport," he added, rubbing his hands with pleasurable anticipation.

De Nevers bowed and retired. Henri gazed after him a moment in silence, and then addressing his chief valet, said quickly, "Follow him, Du Halde, and let me know with whom he converses. Take note of all he does. Away!—Strange!" he muttered, "everything, whether of love or peril, in which I am concerned, seems to hinge upon Crichton."

"Not at all, *compère*," said Chicot, who had overheard the latter part of the monarch's self-communion; "he is your destiny."

"How, gossip?"

"In his hand rest your crown—your life—your mistress."

"Sirrah!"

"Henriot," said the jester, with a look that ill became his wonted laughter-moving visage, "for the first time in my life I am serious."

"And the last, I hope, gossip," returned the king.

"No, *compère*, I shall be more serious when I am buffoon to François III. By my bauble! I had rather they should carve me a monument like that of Thevenin de Saint-Ligier, the faithful fool of Charles V., at Senlis, than what I fear should happen. And it *will* happen unless you profit by my caution."

"And what *is* thy caution, my poor gossip?"

"Place your faith in Crichton, *cher Henriot*," whispered the jester. "Otherwise I shall certainly lose one of the best of masters, and France will as certainly gain one of the worst of kings."

Struck by the jester's unfeigned, though ludicrous, emotion, Henri seemed to reflect for a short time. He then motioned the Scot to approach him. "Chevalier Crichton," he said, "to your charge I entrust this missal. I may require you to produce it hereafter. But understand me, and you too, messeigneurs," he added, looking round, "the suspicions entertained of treasonable intentions on the part of my brother have been entirely dispelled by the Duc de Nevers. I recall my accusation, and beg of you to dismiss it from your remembrance."

A murmur of astonishment and displeasure was heard among the courtiers.

"Have I your majesty's permission to defy the Duc de Nevers to the combat," said Crichton, unable to repress his indignation, "and to extort from his own lips an avowal of his treason?"

"It is needless, *mon cher*. He has cleared himself from all imputation of guilt."

"You are the dupe of this wily Italian, my liege," returned the Scot, with warmth; "he is a felon knight and disloyal gentleman."

"The duke is absent, messire," said Henri, anxious to put an end to the discussion.

"On his return I will hurl the epithets in his teeth."

"Be that task mine," cried Joyeuse. "You have won honour enough. My sword is eager to leave the scabbard."

"I have a vow to defend his majesty against all traitors," exclaimed Saint-Luc, "and claim the right of challenge."

"His be the right who first shall affront the caitiff," shouted D'Epernon, striking spurs into his charger.

"Agreed!" cried Joyeuse, following the baron's example. "We shall see who will be first in the race."

"Hold! messeigneurs," ejaculated Henri authoritatively. "Let no one stir from hence on pain of our sovereign displeasure."

"*Vive Dieu!*" exclaimed Joyeuse, chafing with vexation. "Your majesty shows more favour to traitors than to your loyal followers."

"Be patient, *mon enfant*," returned Henri, smiling graciously. "Your devotion and that of my other faithful friends shall not be forgotten. Meantime, I forbid all further allusion to this matter. After the banquet we shall hold a secret council, at which thou, Saint-Luc, D'Epernon, Crichton and, I trust, my brother of Navarre, will assist. Till then, keep guard upon your speech and actions. Chevalier Crichton, a word with you."

"By my patron, the Evangelist," said Saint-Luc, shrugging his shoulders, "I am completely in the dark."

"And I," rejoined D'Epernon. "Henri seems bewitched. Like a love-sick damsel he will—and he will not. He evidently distrusts De Nevers, and yet will not avow his suspicions."

"He has good reasons, doubtless, for his caution," observed Joyeuse. "I will be sworn this false duke has betrayed his own party, and purchased Henri's favour with the heads of his colleagues. I am, moreover, of opinion, that in lieu of a peaceful mêlée by torchlight, we shall have a sanguinary conflict with swords and sharpened lances. So much the better! Perish the Medicis and her train of Italian imposters, priests, poisoners and panders. If we can free Henri's neck from this intolerable yoke, he will indeed become a king."

"And thou?" interrupted D'Epernon, laughing.

"A duke, peradventure," returned Joyeuse. "*En attendant,* we are to have a duel between two *raffinés* in the art of offence. The horns of the bull will, I trust, avenge the injuries inflicted by the teeth of that accursed hound on my gallant charger Bavieca."

"The hound will be the victor, for a thousand pistoles," cried Saint-Luc.

"I am for you," replied Joyeuse eagerly.

"Let us look at him," said D'Epernon; "methought he was sorely wounded by your men-at-arms."

"That will not prevent his fighting," said Saint-Luc. "These dogs are the bravest in the world, and will fight as long as life endures."

Upon which the three nobles directed their coursers towards the Englishman, at whose feet Druid still crouched.

"What think you of all this, Rosni?" said the King of Navarre to his counsellor.

"That mischief is brewing, sire," replied the baron, knitting his brows, "and that the Valois is either a knave, or a fool—perhaps both."

"It is easy to see that a storm is gathering," rejoined the

Bourbon. "But it will pass harmlessly over our heads, and may, perhaps, facilitate our evasion."

"It may so," returned Rosni gravely.

Henri III. meantime conferred apart with Crichton. "Guard that missal," he said, continuing his instructions, "as you would the hidden letters of her you love; as you would a tress of her hair, or a glove from her hand; as you would guard holy relic or charmed amulet. I may require it anon."

"I *will* guard it as I would the honour of her I love, sire," returned Crichton haughtily. "It shall be wrested from me only with life."

"When the bull-fight is ended," said Henri, "depart secretly from the Louvre, and proceed to the Hôtel de Nevers. Here is my signet. Display it to any of the captains of the guard, and such men-at-arms as you may require will attend you. Arrest the Prince Vincenzo——"

"Sire!"

"Interrupt me not. Arrest him, I say, and let him be conveyed in a litter to the palace. I will give orders for his further custody. This done, rejoin us at the banquet."

"Sire," rejoined Crichton, regarding the king with a searching glance, "whatever commands you may impose upon me, I will obey. I would, however, counsel you to adopt measures widely different. I am at no loss to discover your design. It is unworthy of the grandson of François I.—of the son of Henri II. Unmask these traitors, and let them perish by the death they merit. Sever the web they have woven around you with the sword. But do not resort to this perfidious Machiavellian policy— treachery against treachery, in which the winner is the loser— or you will find, when too late, that you are not so profoundly versed in its mysteries, or so intimately acquainted with its thousand shifts and expedients, as the subtle queen with whom you have to contend."

"We shall see," replied Henri, angrily. "What I now require is obedience, not counsel."

"*Quicquid delirant reges*," cried Chicot, who had stolen upon them unawares. "I am now more than ever convinced of the wisdom of the sage who wrote that kings are fools, and fools are kings. Mark the intimate relationship between us.

> Kings are fools, and fools are kings,
> Majesty does foolish things,
> While from Folly wisdom springs.
> Majesty her sceptre swings,
> Folly soon her bauble brings;

Majesty to tinsel clings,
Folly bells of silver rings.
Crowns and coxcombs, fools and kings
Are inseparable things:
Where kings govern Folly rules,
Fools are kings, and kings are fools!''

At this moment a loud bellowing roar, followed by general plaudits, announced the appearance of a new combatant within the precincts of the tilt-yard.

CHAPTER XI

THE BULL

J'ay ouy conter que feu son père luy faisoit mesler en tous ses mangers et boires de la poudre d'or, d'acier et de fer, pour le bien fortifier; ce qu'il continua si bien jusqu'à l'âge de douze ans, qu'il le rendit ainsi fort et robuste, jusqu'à prendre un taureau par les cornes, et l'arrester en sa furie.
BRANTÔME, *Hommes Illustres*, discours lxxxii.

A MENAGERIE, in the olden time, was considered an indispensable appendage to regal state. Sauval relates, that from the reign of Charles V. to that of Louis XII., there existed in the Rue Froidmantel, immediately behind the Louvre, a building "où soulaient estre les lions du roi." When the ancient palace of the kings of France was in part destroyed to make way for the magnificent structure erected upon its site by Pierre Lescot, and later known as the old Louvre, this *vivarium*, removed to one of the outer courts, was greatly increased by Francis I., and carefully maintained by his successors. Here, on grand occasions, conflicts took place between the savage occupants of the various cages, and the atrocities of a Roman amphitheatre were, in some degree, revived. Here the inhuman Charles IX., in whose bosom the soul of Nero was lodged, frequently repaired with his favourites to indulge his insatiable appetite for carnage. Here, brilliant crowds assembled; and the courage and devotion of a lover were sometimes severely tested by his mistress, who, dropping her glove into the scene of strife, made its restoration the price of future favours.

An exploit of this description, attended with more than ordinary peril, marked the commencement of Crichton's amour with Marguerite de Valois. A combat of animals had been commanded. Scaffoldings, reared around the court, were graced with the flower and loveliness of the land. A fiercely contested fight, between the ruler of the forest and the sole disputant

of his sway—the striped tiger—had terminated in the defeat
of the latter. With mane erect and paw heavily imposed upon
the lacerated breast of his antagonist, the kingly brute, still
growling with rage, glared defiance at the assemblage; when,
amid the hush of silent admiration that succeeded his victory,
was heard the light musical laugh of the Queen of Navarre,
and the next moment her embroidered kerchief fell at the feet
of the slaughtered tiger. The curiosity of the spectators to
ascertain whose faith was to undergo this dread ordeal was
not long ungratified. Exclamations of terror burst from many
a gentle lip as the figure of a youthful cavalier was discovered
within the arena. To the terrible encounter in which he was
about to engage, this youth brought only a poniard, and a
short Spanish mantle swathed around his left arm. His finely
formed limbs had no other defence than was afforded by a
rich attire of velvet and saye, while his fair uncovered locks,
floating over his shoulders, added to the noble and poetical
beauty of his countenance. He looked like Ogier le Danois
before the lion-guarded seats of Avalon. With a swift and resolute
step he advanced towards his foe, who awaited his approach
with grim, but majestic, composure. He had attained the object
of his quest; his foot was placed on the kerchief; his eyes were
fixed steadfastly upon the kindling orbs of the lion. At this
juncture—and when scarcely a breath was drawn by the spectators—a page at the back of the scaffold was seized with
sudden faintness, and uttered a piercing cry. So absorbing,
however, was the interest of the passing scene, that no one
heeded him, and he fell back deprived of sense. Better had it
been for that page he had never revived! Roused by the cry,
the lion menaced his fatal spring. With a roar that shook the
rafters of the gallery, he prepared to dart upon his intrepid
enemy. But the cavalier evaded the attack. As the furious
beast bounded against him, he sprang to one side, and, with
marvellous force and skill, plunged his dagger deeply into the
animal's throat. The wound was not mortal. Lashing his sides
with rage, the lion returned instantly to the charge. On this
occasion, the cavalier flung himself on the ground, and, as the
animal passed over his prostrate body, inflicted another and
surer stroke. The roseate hue, which, during the combat, had
deserted the blooming cheek of Marguerite de Valois, returned
with added lustre as the cavalier, on bended knee, shortly
afterwards sued for the prize he had so dearly won. Marguerite
smiled upon him, as she granted his request, as only queens

(and queens who love) *can* smile, and that smile was *then* in his esteem held cheaply purchased by the hazard he had run.

On the same night the page we have described as overcome by emotion beheld another conflict between the cavalier and the most celebrated duellist of his day, *le bien raffiné* Bussy d'Amboise —at that time the avowed favourite of the Queen of Navarre. In this second encounter he was fortunate as in the first. He disarmed and slightly wounded his adversary. Quitting this rendezvous, which took place in a retired walk within the gardens of the Louvre, the cavalier entered the palace, still warily followed by the page. He was admitted, with some mystery, to the apartments of Marguerite de Valois. Framing a thousand excuses, the page awaited his return within a corridor. It was a night of lengthened torture, for the gallant appeared not till dawn, when, with a quick and buoyant step, he passed the miserable witness of his *bonne fortune*.

"Why follow you not your master, the Seigneur Crichton, good youth?" said Aubiac, Marguerite's confidential valet, to the page, who remained like one stupefied. "The coast is clear —away!"

"Call him not my master," replied the page, bursting into an agony of tears, and tearing his raven curls. "I serve him not—I love him not—I will forget him. As to your royal mistress," he continued, glancing with fury at the door, "may my curse fall upon her; may she endure the anguish I have endured; may she pass one such night as I have passed." And with these words he rushed from the corridor.

"Ha! ha!" laughed Aubiac. "I see how it is—a girl in disguise —over head and ears in love with this handsome Scot, whom all the women rave about, though for my part I see nothing extraordinary in him. However, as Madam Marguerite admires him, I suppose he *has* merits I cannot discover. From hence-forth the Sieur Bussy is dismissed, and for three weeks, or, it may be, three days, the Sieur Crichton will reign in his stead. *Maugrebleu!* I must take care that pretty vixen does not find her way here again. Of all plagues a jealous woman is the most intolerable; and of all women, your woman of intrigue is the most jealous. Madam Marguerite is the most jealous woman I have the honour to know. The malediction of that unhappy damsel is likely enough to attach to her. Where have I seen that lovely face before? Those dark eyes are certainly not unknown to me. She looks like an Italian: ah! I have it— I recollect her. She is the principal actress of the Hôtel de

Bourbon. A fine girl i'faith. This Crichton *is* fortunate. I should prefer her to the queen."

Aubiac was right in the conjecture. It *was* the Gelosa.

To return. Within the menagerie previously described, the Duc de Nevers sought out the warlike beast destined to sustain the attack of Druid. Captured amid the Sierra Morena, this wild mountain bull—one of the fiercest of his untamable race—was so little subdued in spirit by confinement, that it required considerable address to approach him, and it was only by entirely excluding light from his den, that his keepers were enabled to bind and blindfold him. In this state—now rushing madly forward, now suddenly halting, with lip curled upwards, nostrils distended, head bent down, and tail erect—foaming, butting, bellowing, and leaping—girt, as to his neck and shoulders', with a strong tether of ropes, so disposed that he could neither break loose from his bondage nor injure himself by its pressure, the furious animal, exasperated by the shouts of the spectators, reached the middle of the arena, where he was speedily attached to the central and stoutest stake in the lists. This done, the covering was withdrawn from his eyes.

Dazzled by the sudden transition from obscurity to sunshine, the bull appeared for a moment bewildered. He then uttered a sullen, ominous moan, which, in the opinion of the experienced, gave unquestionable assurance of resolution and ferocity. His vigour could not be doubted. In make he was perfect. Broad-chested, wide - fronted, straight - backed, thick - necked, well-hammed — curled, shaggy, tufted; his tremendous energies were plainly written in every limb. In colour, from the points of his short, sharp, wrinkled horns to his pawing hoofs, he was black as the steeds of Pluto. The old Syracusans would have chosen him as an acceptable sacrifice to that Deity. Glaring around the assemblage with eyes of flame, tossing the sand over his shoulders, and lashing his sides with his tail, he all at once changed his moan into a fierce prolonged roar of defiance. This challenge was instantly answered by a growl deep and terrible as his own.

Before, however, we attempt to describe the combat, we will repair for a few moments to the outer ranks of the spectators, composed of the burgesses, the scholars, and others of the commonalty of Paris.

"*Valeme Dios!*" exclaimed a swarthy-visaged knave, with a broad-leaved, rusty sombrero pulled over his beetle brows, pressing forward as he spoke to obtain a nearer view of the bull.

"A noble animal, and of a good heart, I'll be sworn. He is of the right breed and make. I know his stock well. He comes from the mountains of Estremadura; from the heights of the Guadalcana, where range herds of the finest steers in Spain—*ciertamente!* I have seen a hundred such when a grand bull-fight has been held in the Plaza at Madrid, in the presence of his most Catholic Majesty, Don Felipe, and by the black eyes of my mistress it was a glorious sight!"

"No doubt of it, most veracious Don Diego Caravaja," rejoined a bystander, turning round, and disclosing the cynical countenance of the Sorbonist. "But what brings you here, my hidalgo? I was told you had entered into the service of Ruggieri, on the last day of his compact with Sathanas, and were to be hanged from the walls of the Grand-Châtelet, at the precise juncture that the faggots of the old sorcerer were lighted in the Place de Grève. *Pardieu!* I am glad to find I was misinformed."

"Never believe idle rumours, *amigo,*" said the Spaniard, twisting his moustache after a threatening fashion. "Ruggieri is free, and the hemp is yet unsown that shall form my halter. I, the familiar of a magician—foh! Hark ye, *compañero,*" he added, mysteriously, "I am in the service of the Queen-Mother."

"You have quitted the devil, then, for his dam," replied the Sorbonist, with a sneering laugh. "But i'faith, man, whether you have escaped the noose of the hangman, or the clutches of the fiend, I am delighted to see you. I am only sorry we shall lose the agreeable spectacle of your master's—I beg pardon—Ruggieri's execution. Because I had a wager with our comrade, the Bernardin, who stands by my side, that the Prince of Darkness would, as a matter of policy, deliver so serviceable an agent from the midst of his fiery torment."

"Which wager you have indubitably lost, *compaing,*" laughed the Bernardin, "for the black prince has clearly interfered in his behalf by releasing him before he has even snuffed the odours of the resinous torches. *Sapristi!* I would you had laid a like stake on Caravaja. I should have been a double winner—ho!—ho!"

"Whoso wagereth on my neck, had better look to his own," said the Spaniard coolly, at the same time tapping the hilt of his long Toledo in a significant manner, "or there may be more slitting than choking of weasands. A truce, however, to jesting. I am in no mood for it. In regard to the execution, you will not be disappointed, señors. The Pré-aux-Clercs will not want a bonfire to-night. Ruggieri's name has been erased from the warrant, and that of Florent Chrétien substituted."

"*Io triumphe!* let me embrace thee for the intelligence," cried the Sorbonist. "I had vowed that old sinner's destruction. Better one heretic should perish than a thousand sorcerers. There is some hope of the conversion of the latter. Besides, it will be a pleasant pastime to him.

> Tormenta, carcer, ungulæ,
> Stridensque flammis lamina,
> Atque ipsa pœnarum ultima
> Mors Lutheranis ludus est—
> Ridebat hæc miles Dei."

"*Chito!*" whispered Caravaja, placing his finger on his lips, and again assuming a mysterious air, "this is not the only spectacle you will behold to-night."

"Indeed!" exclaimed the Sorbonist, elevating his eyebrows into an expression of surprise. "What goodly sight is in reserve?"

"May I trust you?" demanded the Spaniard, yet more mysteriously.

"You may, if your disclosure be not treasonable," returned the scholar, mimicking the tone and gesture of his companion.

"Treasonable or not, I *will* confide in you," replied Caravaja, in a low voice. "See you these rose-nobles?" he added, thrusting his hand into his doublet, and exhibiting, under the shadow of his cloak, which he held over them, a glittering handful to the greedy eyes of his companion.

"Whose throat are you bribed to cut?" asked the Sorbonist spitefully.

"Thine, if thou amendest not thy speech, *amigo*. But listen to me, and I will tell thee how to replenish thine empty pouches. I have discovered the true El Dorado. Lend me thine ear."

The Sorbonist complied. He soon became deeply interested in Caravaja's communication.

"And is this to take place to-night?" he inquired, as the Spaniard concluded.

Caravaja nodded.

"And the whole court is to be turned topsy-turvy?"

Caravaja nodded again.

"And thine office—our office, I should say—if I join you—is —the word sticks in my throat—the assassination of Crichton?"

Caravaja nodded for the third time, adding a slight cough by way of emphasis.

"By Barabbas! I like it not," said the Sorbonist, as if struck with contrition. "I would not stick at a trifle—but this is crime on too grand a scale for my fancy."

"Choose," returned Caravaja, pointing alternately to the purse and a poniard. "I have but to name thee to one of Catherine's *mouchards*, of whom there are plenty around us, and the chances are shrewdly against thy reaching the Sorbonne in time for vespers."

"Of two evils the wise man electeth the lesser," replied the scholar. "After all, one king is as good as another. *Le roi est mort—vive le roi!* I am with you. I will be a conspirator. There is something antique and Roman in the idea of overthrowing a tyrant. It will be as amusing as the *jeu de coupe-tête.*"

"*Bueno!*" exclaimed the Spaniard. "To-night thou shalt help to rid us of a foe. To-morrow thou mayst, peradventure, fill the place of one of these minions of the Sybarite. The scarf I will give thee anon. The word is——"

"Hark!" cried the Bernardin, interrupting their conference. "The sport is about to begin. You will lose it altogether if you stand so much aloof. May the devil direct the bull's horns to the heart of that accursed hound for the fright he gave me at the disputation yesterday!"

Leaving these worthies to struggle for a good station to view the fight, we shall now return to the arena.

Druid, meantime, had not remained inactive. No fiery champion ever evinced more impatience at the sound of hostile bugle, than he displayed on hearing the roaring challenge of the bull. His fury could scarcely be restrained, and his efforts to break loose became at length so violent, that Blount was compelled to take him in his arms and forcibly restrain him. Covered with dust and blood—the thick gore slowly dropping from his unstanched wounds, his head swollen, his right eye closed—the poor brute presented a deplorable spectacle. But neither suffering nor exhaustion affected his courage—he was still fierce and terrible as heretofore. To the questions put by the youthful nobles by whom he was surrounded, the Englishman refused all response, until the Vicomte de Joyeuse casually remarked "that it was impossible the dog could fight long in that condition—he must speedily give in."

A slight smile of derision passed across Blount's features.

"I would I were as sure of my freedom as I am of Druid's endurance," he said. "He is thoroughbred. And I would stake my life—if my life were my own to stake—that when once he has pinned the bull, nothing will move him. You may hew him

in pieces, from tail to jowl, and, while life lasts, the fangs
will cling."

The nobles were laughing loudly at this boast, when Henri III.,
attended by Crichton, who still continued on foot, approached.

"Thy hound is in a sorry condition, *maître*," said the king,
in a compassionate tone; "dost think he will face his foe?"

"I am assured of it, sire," replied Blount.

"Thou hast vaunted his courage," continued Henri; "if he
is victorious I give thee free pardon. If he loseth the battle
thou diest."

"I am well contented," answered the Englishman.

The monarch and his retinue then proceeded to take up a
position immediately in front of the bull, leaving an interval
of some ten paces between them and the enraged animal, who
eyed their movements with a look of malignant curiosity,
redoubling his clamour, and vainly endeavouring to disengage
himself from his bondage. All at once he became still—his
glaring orbs seemed fascinated; he ceased bellowing, and giving
a loud snort, that scattered the foam over his dusky shoulders,
lowered the points of his horns.

The spectators next beheld a man, bearing a dog in his arms,
advance from the ranks. At his approach the bull brought his
broad front almost to a level with the sand.

Like his antagonist, the dog had left off growling. There was
something formidable in the sudden silence of these two savage
beasts, who had up to that moment filled the tilt-yard with
their roaring.

Arrived within fitting distance of the hostile party, Blount
deposited his burden upon the ground.

"Upon him!" he cried; "thy country's honour is at stake."

But Druid stirred not.

"How, sir!" exclaimed Blount angrily; "hast thy valour
degenerated since I brought thee to this craven country? Ha!
I see," he added, changing his manner; "*I* am to blame, not
thou." Upon which he clapped his hands together smartly
twice or thrice, and uttered a shrill and peculiar cry.

Exasperated by these sounds, the bull slightly raised his
head. The instant he did so, Druid, who had watched his opportunity, sprang furiously upon him, and made good his hold by
fixing his teeth in the thick and fleshy covering of his antagonist's
eye. Bellowing with rage and pain, the wounded animal sought
to free himself from his persecutor by violently dashing his
head to the earth, plunging it between his legs, shaking and

tossing it in the air. His efforts were in vain. Crushed, bruised, and gored, Druid relinquished not his grip.

The spectators were in ecstasies. Henri III. laughed till the tears filled his eyes. The Bourbon, who stood on his right hand, appeared equally to enjoy the spectacle.

"By my bauble!" cried Chicot, thrusting himself between the steeds of the two monarchs, "'tis royal sport! and worthy the illustrious beholders. A goodly conclusion to a chivalrous spectacle—ha—ha! The *sotie* after the tragedy—the *charivari* after the widow's espousals. May it end as well as it hath begun! Yon huge *cornuto*," he added, darting a malicious glance at the King of Navarre, "appears, as yet, to have the worst of it."

"Rail on, knave," returned the Bourbon, laughing good-humouredly; "thou art welcome."

"Fear me not," rejoined Chicot; "I am of the bull-dog breed myself:

Ut canis a corio nunquam absterrebitur uncto,

I never relax—once bit, hold tight. Attend!

> The horns of a bull,
> The sword of a fool,
> The heels of a mule,
> Make a King of Misrule.
> But of crown should he be shorn,
> Who weareth wittol's horn;
> Better queen had never suckled him,
> Than other *quean* should cuckold him!"

The jester did not wait to see what effect these ribald strains produced upon the subject of his satire, but diving under the charger of his own sovereign, disappeared.

A loud shout was now raised. The bull had obtained a momentary advantage over his assailant. By a tremendous effort—attended with considerable detriment to his own hide—he succeeded in dislodging Druid, whom he flung to a great height above his head. Fortunately, the brave hound escaped the deadly points that awaited his descent, but he fell so heavily to the ground, that few imagined he would rise to renew the conflict—an opinion which was further strengthened when the bull, bending his knees, dropped upon Druid's body before he had time to recover himself, and strove to crush him by his ponderous weight. At this juncture the voice of the Englishman was heard in encouragement of his luckless companion.

"What ho! Druid—what ho!" he cried; "bestir thyself, or the knees of that accursed brute will force all the breath from thy

body. By Saint Dunstan! I can scarcely forbear my hand. Up!
man—and rouse thee—or it is all over with both of us."

Henri III. was no less disturbed.

"*Mort-Dieu!*" he ejaculated. "The brave hound will be
slain, and I shall lose one, who might have proved my trustiest
follower. Fool that I was to command this fight."

"Had you not better throw down your warder, gossip?"
said Chicot, suddenly appearing on the left hand of the king;
"the chivalrous bull will probably attend to your behests—
and withhold the stroke of mercy. Down with it!—the base
cur yields."

"'Tis false, thou yelping limmer, he does *not* yield," exclaimed
Crichton, who, stationed also on the left of Henri III., had
watched the contest with lively interest. "Seest thou not the
maddened beast hath, in the blindness of his fury, driven his
horns deeply into the soil, and not into the dog's reins. And
mark how Druid struggles with his huge oppressor, like Typhon
with the rocks of Jove—or Hercules with the Cretan bull. Look!
he *has* extricated himself!—ha!—bravely done!—bravely done!
—to the assault! staunch hound!—to the assault! Fix thy keen
and tenacious fangs within his leathern nostrils. 'Tis done!—
'tis done!—there thou wilt cling till thy foe sinks from exhaustion. The victory is thine. By Saint Andrew!" he added, with
warmth, "I would rather assail the bull myself, than that
noble hound should perish."

"Your assistance is needless," replied Joyeuse, whose hilarity,
occasioned by Druid's recent perilous position, had become
overcast by the present aspect of the fray; "I fear I shall lose
my wager as well as my charger."

"Certes, if you have backed the bull, you will infallibly lose,"
said the Scot, laughing, "for see! even now he staggers, and
exhibits symptoms of faintness."

"There I differ with you, *mon cher*," rejoined the king. "To
me he appears as if he were collecting his energies for some
mighty effort. Remember, this is no stall-fed, scant-winded
steer."

Druid, as will have been gathered from the foregoing discourse,
had again made good his hold upon the nostrils of his antagonist; and such was the effect of his combined weight and
strength, that he contrived to detain the bull, for some little
space, in the kneeling posture he had just assumed. No sooner,
however, did the latter animal regain his feet, than, nigh
frantic with wrath and agony, he resorted to every expedient

that desperation suggested, of freeing himself from his relent
less assailant. Worn out, at length, with repeated fruitless
attempts, he became comparatively tranquil; and it was this
cessation from strife that Crichton had construed into relaxing
energy, but which was rather, as the king had surmised, the
preparation for a mightier struggle.

"Saint George for England!" shouted Blount, whose sanguine
anticipations had also deceived him—"the victory is ours. A
few minutes must decide the conflict—hurrah!"

But the next moment the Englishman's countenance fell—
the smile of exultation fled from his lips. He perceived his
error. Renewing the combat with a fury that showed his vigour
was undiminished, the bull tore the ground with his hoofs—
filled the air with his blatant cries—tossed his head as if a thousand hornets were buzzing about his ears—and shook the stake
to which he was attached, as if he would uproot it.

"*Cornes de Diable!*" screamed Chicot; "'tis a pleasant sight
to witness the fantastic gambols of yon amiable beast, and
equally diverting to listen to his music. 'Fore Heaven! he
danceth the couranto more deftly than the Chevalier Crichton
—ha!—ha!—ho!"

"Is the fastening secure, think you, *mon cher* Crichton?" said
Henri III., noticing with uneasiness the violent strain produced
upon the rope by the ceaseless struggles of the bull.

"Have no fear, sire!" returned the Scot, advancing a step or
two in front of the king. "I will place myself between your
majesty and the possibility of harm."

"Gramercy," rejoined Henri, smiling graciously; "and calling
to mind your former exploit in the Court of Animals (which,
en passant, cost me somewhat dear in the life of my noblest
lion), I cannot doubt your ability to cope with a beast of inferior
power. I shall, therefore, rest under your protection as securely
as behind a rampart."

"*Vivat!*" cried Joyeuse, "the bull wins!"

"And the calf," added Chicot.

As he spoke, the applauses, resounding on all sides, were
suddenly checked, and a wild cry of alarm, mingled with
screams from the female portion of the assemblage, arose. Druid
was again tossed aloft, and the bull, instead of awaiting his fall
to gore and trample him as heretofore, gave a headlong dash of
such force that the rope, though of almost cable thickness,
snapped in twain close to his throat, and, thus liberated, the
animal commenced a mad scamper on the arena. The first

obstacle he encountered was Blount, whom he instantly over-threw. He paused not, however, to molest him, but rushed in the direction of Henri III.

"The king!—the king!" cried a thousand eager voices. "Save the king!"

But this seemed impossible. Ere a pike could be hurled, a bolt fired, or a sword drawn, the bull had reached the spot occupied by the monarch, and Henri's destruction would have been inevitable, if an arm of iron had not interposed between him and the danger with which he was menaced. That arm was Crichton's, who threw himself unhesitatingly upon the furious animal, and seizing his wrinkled horns, by the exertion of his almost superhuman strength arrested his career.

Amid the turmoil that ensued, the voice of the Scot was heard sternly exclaiming, "Let no one touch him — I will achieve his subjection alone."

Thus admonished, the crowds, who had flocked to his assist-ance, drew back.

The struggles of the bull were desperate—but unavailing. He could neither liberate himself, nor advance. Suddenly, from acting on the defensive, Crichton became the assailant. Calling into play all the energies of his muscular frame, he forcibly drove his opponent backwards.

"It is time to bring this conflict to a close," he thought, holding the bull's head, immovably, with his right hand, while with his left he sought his poniard.

He then glanced towards the king. Surrounded by the bristling halberds of his guard, Henri looked on at his ease.

"*Pollicem verto,*" cried Chicot, "let him dispatch his enemy, *compère.*"

The royal assent given, scarce another moment elapsed before the bull, mortally wounded by a blow dexterously stricken between the vertebræ of the neck, fell to the ground. Thunders of applause succeeded.

The royal cortège then formed into two lines, and Henri rode forth to greet his preserver.

"Chevalier Crichton," he said, "to you I owe my life. No Valois was ever ungrateful. Claim some boon, I pray you, at my hands."

"Sire," replied Crichton, smiling, as he unhelmed himself to wipe the dust and heat from his brow, "my demands will not exhaust your treasury. I ask only the life of that man," pointing to Blount, who, with folded arms and a dejected air, stood alternately regarding the carcass of the bull and Druid, who, stunned by his fall, had with difficulty limped to his feet. "He will suffer punishment enough in the mortification occasioned by his dog's defeat."

"It is yours," replied Henri.

"Your majesty will not separate the faithful hound from his master," continued the Scot.

"As you please," sighed the monarch. "I cannot refuse your request." Crichton threw himself upon his knee, and pressed Henri's hand gratefully to his lips.

"My thousand pistoles, Saint-Luc," said Joyeuse gleefully.

"They are not fairly won," replied Saint-Luc. "I appeal to D'Epernon."

"'Tis a drawn wager," returned the baron; "and in future I recommend both of you to back a Scottish right arm against bull or bulldog."

CHAPTER XII

THE PRIZE

Quand ilz furent tous devant sa presence,
Et à genoulx pour sa face choisir,
Le roy d'armes en très grant révérence
Lui dit ce qu'il s'ensuit, et à loisir:
Sire, avecques le vostre bon plaisir
Et licence d'autre part obtenue,
La pastourelle est devant vous venue
Pour le grant pris delivrer orendroit
A cellui qui sans doutance y a droit,
Et de dehors desservi l'ara mieux.
　　　　LOUIS DE BEAUVEAU, *Le Pas de la Bergière.*

Two sergeants of the guard now advanced, leading a steed, to which the carcass of the slaughtered bull was promptly attached by means of cords, and dragged out of the arena.

A pursuivant-at-arms, clothed in a sumptuous casaque flowered with the lilies of France, next approached; and, reverentially inclining himself before Henri, demanded, in the name of the Queen of the Lists, his majesty's licence to close the jousts. Permission being graciously accorded, the pursuivant, accompanied by a couple of trumpeters, who gallantly did their devoir, proceeded towards the pavilions, and removing the shields of the combatants, delivered that of Crichton to his esquire. This done, the judges of the field, marshalled by Montjoie, descended from their tribunal, and gravely directed their course towards the grand gallery, into which they were ceremoniously ushered.

Crichton, meantime, looked on in silence. Indescribable emotions swelled his bosom. The stirring notes of the trumpet rekindled all his fire. Much as he had done to distinguish himself, he burnt for new opportunities of displaying his prowess, and would gladly have splintered another lance in honour of the bright eyes he worshipped.

"What would life be," ran his self-communion, "without ambition—without fame—without love?—hopeless slavery—and prolonged torture. I for one could endure not its burden. My life shall be computed by days, not years; with me hours shall play the part of days—moments of hours. I will crowd into each moment as much of active existence as that moment will comprehend, nor will I know pause till fate shall for ever check my impulses. I reverence age, but I desire not its honours. I would rather die covered with glory than bowed down by years. Were I to perish now, I should have lived long enough. And if I can achieve the deliverance of her, to whose love my heart is forbidden to aspire—but for whom alone it can ever beat; if I can free yon brave monarch from his thraldom, and that inconstant, yet not ungenerous voluptuary, from the peril in which he stands—I care not if this day be my last."

As these thoughts swept through his mind, the countenance of the Scot—ever the faithful mirror of his emotions—took a slight cast of sadness, and Henri, inspired by jealousy, having narrowly scrutinised his features during this momentary reverie, fancied he could detect the secrets of his inmost soul.

"It will not do to trust him," thought the king, "his passion is stronger than his loyalty. Hola! Chevalier Crichton," he added aloud, and in a tone of raillery, "while you are studying your next ode, or preparing a thesis for the schools, we, less philosophical, less poetical mortals, are dreaming only of the speedy appearance of the Queen of the Lists to award the chief prize of the tourney. I have some notion upon whom it will be bestowed. Attend me to the tribunal. Lover as I am of etiquette, it would ill become me to break through prescribed forms upon an occasion like the present, when I have fairer dame to grace my lists than ever yet rewarded valour, and braver knight to receive the meed of victory than ever yet won prize from dame!"

With this high-flown compliment, Henri rode slowly towards the canopy, where he dismounted, and took his seat upon the fauteuil, placing the King of Navarre on the tabouret at his right. Crichton remained standing on the lowest step of the scaffold.

Presently the inspiring bruit of clarions and other martial instruments was heard from that quarter of the tilt-yard in which the grand gallery was situated. The barriers were hastily removed; the halberdiers ranged themselves *en haie*; and admittance was given to a troop of fair equestriennes, whose personal charms were scarcely less to be apprehended than the weapons of their knightly predecessors. At the head of this radiant band, which, like the burst of a sunbeam, diffused smiles and animation as it proceeded, three figures were distinguished, each so beautiful, yet each so different in style of beauty, that the admiration of the beholders was divided, and the judgment perplexed, as to whom the palm of surpassing loveliness ought to be assigned. In the fine and delicate features, the exquisite fairness of complexion, the soft blue eyes and gentle regards of her who rode on the right, the spectators recognised and hailed their queen, the virtuous but lightly-esteemed Louise. In the fuller form and more majestic deportment, in the ravishing grace, the jetty tresses, and dark languid glances of the queenly dame on the left, no one failed to detect the gorgeous Marguerite de Valois. Murmurs of impassioned homage pursued her. The very air respired of love as she passed; and there was not a cavalier of the thousands who gazed upon her, but would have perilled his life for a favouring regard. Marguerite, however, was insensible to the general idolatry. A smile was on her lips, witchery was in her looks, but in her heart raged the undying worm of jealousy.

Between the two queens, on an Isabelle-coloured palfrey, richly caparisoned with blue velvet bordered with pearls, rode Esclairmonde; and if a preference was shown by the assemblage, it was towards the lovely princess, whose attractions, although they did not excite the fiery admiration roused by the voluptuous fascinations of Marguerite de Valois, awakened a sentiment of far deeper devotion. Immediately behind this captivating trio rode Catherine de Medicis, who displayed the admirable symmetry of person for which she was celebrated—a charm not to be impaired by time—as well as the proficiency as an equestrian, for which she was equally noted, in the management of a fiery Arabian. In the languishing looks of the beautiful blonde, on the left of the Queen-Mother, the King of Navarre was at no loss to discover his new conquest, La Rebours; while, in the sprightly brunette at her right, admirers, too numerous to particularise, claimed a more intimate acquaintance with Torigni.

Preceding the Princess of Condé, and bearing a white wand, together with the grand prize of the tourney, a magnificent diamond ring, which he ostentatiously displayed to the spectators, marched the pursuivant. The judges of the camp, headed by Montjoie, and followed by a band of pages and trumpeters, brought up the rear of this brilliant cavalcade.

Arrived within a short distance of the royal canopy, the jocund troop came to a halt, and formed a long line in front of the king, of which Esclairmonde constituted the centre. Rapid as thought, the page of each dame, attired in her colours, then advanced, and placed himself at the bridle of her steed. Executed with great precision and quickness, this manœuvre produced an agreeable effect, and was loudly applauded by the gallant Bourbon, whose eye wandered over the fair phalanx in a manner that plainly evinced of what inflammable material his valiant heart was composed.

"*Ventre-saint-gris!*" he ejaculated. "Such a legion would be irresistible." Just then his ardent gaze chanced upon his queen. "*Peste!*" he added, averting his glances, "the snake will always intrude itself into Eden."

It was, in sooth, a pleasant sight to look upon that array of lovely dames (Catherine's famous "*petite bande*"), and to mark their different attractions, now so forcibly, yet so advantageously, contrasted—each acting as a foil to the other—each unconsciously contributing to her neighbour's fascination. Oh! how various are the aspects of beauty—how beautiful are all its aspects!

Making his way through the press, Montjoie now bent the knee before Henri, and repeating a formula similar to that of the pursuivant, entreated permission for the Queen of the Lists to award the prize to him who had demeaned himself the most valiantly in the jousts; concluding with the almost unnecessary assurance, that all would be done "with loyalty and justice." To this solicitation Henri vouchsafed a gracious response, and the king-at-arms having fulfilled his duty, retired.

Holding the bridle of Esclairmonde's palfrey, the pursuivant next led her towards Crichton, who, perceiving the intention of the princess, advanced to meet her, and threw himself at her feet. Taking the ring from the pursuivant, Esclairmonde then placed it upon the finger of her lover. The Scot joyously arose.

The reward to which he looked forward with most eagerness was yet to be conferred.

Amid the thunder of acclamations that succeeded, the voices of the heralds were heard exclaiming, "À Crichton!—à Crichton! —largess! largess!"

The Scot motioned to his esquire. Raising the shield of his master, the youth filled it with broad golden pieces, which he distributed amongst the officers of the tilt-yard, who thereupon redoubled their joyous vociferations.

While this was passing, Montjoie, with stately step, drew near the principal group of this vast and resplendent picture.

"Remove your helm, sir knight," he said; "the Queen of the Lists desires to thank you for the fair courses you have run in her honour, and to bestow upon you the priceless reward of your prowess."

A deep blush mantled Esclairmonde's cheek as Crichton obeyed the injunctions of the king-at-arms. The next moment he felt the glowing lips of the princess pressed upon his brow. That salute annihilated all his prudential resolutions. He forgot their disparity of rank—his own danger—her perilous position. He did not relinquish the hand she had confided to him—but, in the delirium of the moment, raised it to his lips.

Esclairmonde was equally agitated. Suffused with blushes, and anon becoming white as marble, palpitating, faint, she could scarcely maintain her seat upon the unruly palfrey, and in order to prevent mischance, Crichton deemed it necessary to pass his arm around her waist. The situation was rather embarrassing, and awakened the ire of the two monarchs.

"Esclairmonde," whispered Crichton passionately, "you are mine."

"I am—I am," returned the princess, in the same tone. "I would abandon my newly-discovered title—my rank—life itself, rather than my love."

"I have the queen's assent to our espousals," rejoined Crichton, in an altered voice. "She has promised me your hand—on certain conditions."

"On what conditions?" asked Esclairmonde, tenderly regarding her lover.

"Conditions which I cannot, dare not fulfil—conditions which involve the sacrifice of my honour," replied Crichton gloomily. "Esclairmonde," he added, in accents of despair, "the dream is passed. You are the Princess of Condé. It is madness to indulge these vain hopes longer. I may serve you, but I may *not* love you—farewell!"

"Stay!" exclaimed the princess, detaining him with a gentle grasp. "I have a painful, a dreadful duty to fulfil to-night. I have to take an eternal farewell of one who has been a friend, an adviser, a father to me."

"Of Florent Chrétien?"

"Intelligence of the martyrdom to which he is adjudged by the merciless Catherine has just reached me. An hour before midnight I shall be within his cell to receive his parting benediction," she added, with some hesitation, and gazing at the Scot with eyes that swam with tears.

"Were it to encounter certain destruction I would be there," returned the Scot fervently.

"And you *will* encounter certain destruction if you carry this presumptuous passion farther, Chevalier Crichton," said Henri of Navarre, advancing towards them. "You cannot plead ignorance of the exalted station of the maiden to whose love you aspire. The bright blood of the Bourbon will never mingle with that of a Scottish adventurer. Your pardon, fair cousin," he continued, addressing Esclairmonde in a conciliatory tone, "it is with extreme reluctance that I interfere in an affair of the heart. I would rather forward a lover's suit than oppose it, especially the suit of a cavalier so accomplished as Crichton. But I must act as the Prince of Condé would have acted. Take this decision, then, from his lips. The daughter of Louis of Bourbon can only bestow her hand upon her equal."

"The daughter of Louis of Bourbon will only bestow her hand upon him she loves," returned Esclairmonde, with a spirit such as she had never before exhibited; "and your own experience of her race will inform you, sire, that her heart is as little likely to be controlled as her hand."

"As I expected," rejoined the Bourbon; "but it cannot be. It is one of the curses of exalted birth that the hand and the heart can never go together."

"And why should they be divided in this case," asked Catherine de Medicis, advancing, "if my consent be given to the match?"

"For a sufficient reason, madam," said Henri III., joining the group; "because *our* pleasure is otherwise; and because we forbid the Chevalier Crichton, on pain of banishment from our presence—from our kingdom—as he would escape the doom of a traitor, and a dungeon within the Bastile—again to approach the Demoiselle Esclairmonde in the character of a lover. We shall see whether he, or you, madam, will venture to disobey us."

"Henri!" exclaimed Catherine, in amazement—"this to me?"

"You are our mother—but you are also our subject, madam," returned the king coldly. "We have issued our commands—it is for you to see them obeyed."

Catherine did not reply. Her glance fell upon Crichton, and an almost imperceptible smile passed across her features. At the threat of the monarch the Scot's hand instinctively sought his poniard, upon the hilt of which it now rested. When too late, he perceived his error, and the false constructions put upon the action by the queen.

"If you will set at rest the question as to the illustrious birth of the Demoiselle Esclairmonde, madam, I am content to obey the mandates of the king," said Crichton. "On your decision," he added, with a significant look, "must rest her fate."

"The time is arrived for the acknowledgment of her birth, which you have truly said *is* illustrious, messire," replied Catherine, glancing triumphantly at her son. "Esclairmonde is a princess of the blood royal of France. She is a Bourbon. Let the King of Navarre take note of my words; let all remember them; and let those who reverence the memory of Louis I., Prince of Condé, incline themselves before his daughter."

Obedient to the intimation of Catherine, a crowd of nobles pressed forward to kiss the hand of the newly discovered princess; and many there were, who, upon that occasion, forgot their ancient enmity towards the great champion of the Protestant Church, in the admiration excited by his lovely descendant.

"Well, sire," said the Bourbon, turning to Henri III., "*I* have found the princess. Of course *you* will find the convoy."

"*Peste!*" exclaimed Henri angrily. And motioning to Du Halde, he issued his commands to close the jousts.

"The princess is yours," said the Queen-Mother, aside to Crichton.

This assurance, however, gave little encouragement to the Scot. He felt that his passion was hopeless. And the despair which love without hope must ever inspire took possession of his soul.

The flourish of trumpets which immediately succeeded afforded some relief to his oppression. Silence being proclaimed by this warlike prelude, the pursuivant advanced, wand in hand, and uttering thrice the preliminary "*Oiez,*" informed the noble assemblage that the jousts were brought to a conclusion

—that his majesty bade them all to the banquet within the Louvre—and that in lieu of the emprise of the Châtel de la Joyeuse Garde, and the grand mêlée by torchlight, the king would hold a masque and fête within the palace.

This announcement was received with general surprise and chagrin.

"How is this, my son?" said Catherine in a troubled voice. "Have you abandoned the chivalrous spectacle to which you looked forward with so much pleasure? Methought you were about to exhibit your own matchless skill as a tilter in the *courses à la foule.*"

"*Par la Mort-Dieu!* madam," replied the king, in a tone of raillery, "the masque will be more in character with the strange scene we have just witnessed than the mêlée. Besides, the tilt-yard is not the theatre for our display. The lists are unlucky to our race. We remember our father's fate—and shall in future avoid the lance."

"Ha! betrayed," muttered Catherine. "But the traitor shall not escape my vengeance."

"To the Hôtel de Nevers, *mon cher,*" said Henri, turning to Crichton, "and arrest the Prince of Mantua. Interfere not with our passion," he added, in his blandest accents, "and we have no favour to refuse you."

Amid renewed fanfares of trumpets, the splendid assemblage then separated. But the troop of laughing dames did not return in the strict array it came. The ranks were disordered, and in place of a page, by the side of each bright-eyed equestrienne rode a favoured cavalier. Henri III. took the lead with the reluctant Princess of Condé; the Bourbon attached himself to La Rebours; while Crichton returned to the pavilion, where the armourer proceeded to free him from his knightly habiliments.

As the two monarchs quitted the tilt-yard, loud shouts were raised of "*Vive le roi! vivent les rois!*"

"You hear, Rosni," said the Bourbon, addressing his counsellor.

"*Vivent les rois!* 'tis a good augury."

By and by three figures alone remained within the precincts of the arena.

"Since the mêlée is abandoned, thy scheme falls to the ground, my hidalgo," said the foremost, who was no other than the Sorbonist.

"Perdition!" exclaimed Caravaja, twisting his moustache, after his wonted ferocious fashion. "I know not what to think of it. I would give my soul to Sathanas, that that accursed Scot should fall in my way."

"The compact is concluded," said the Bernardin, "for lo! he appears."

And as he spoke, Crichton, attired in a pourpoint of velvet and short Spanish mantle, issued from the pavilion. He was followed by Blount, bearing Druid carefully in his arms, and directed his steps towards the outer court.

"After him," cried Caravaja, drawing a knife, and placing it in his sleeve. "*A muerte!*"

CHAPTER XIII

THE DUNGEON

Paolo. Aurait-il abjuré?
Elci. Pas encore.
Paolo. Mais cet acte il n'est que différé?
Casimir Delavigne, *Une Famille au temps du Luther.*

THE Louvre once enclosed within its walls a number of subterranean cells, appropriated to the confinement of prisoners of State. Into one of these gloomy receptacles Florent Chrétien had been thrust. Deprived, by the rigour of his persecutors, of the consolation which had ever been afforded him in hours of affliction by reference to the "healing balm" of Scripture, the good man passed the brief space allotted him on earth in deepest prayer. As the time drew nigh when his dreadful sentence was to be carried into execution, his devotions were interrupted by the entrance of one of the hooded officials, who introduced a masked female into the dungeon, and then silently departed. The dull light of a brazen cresset suspended from the ceiling imperfectly illumined the apartment, and a few moments elapsed ere Chrétien, whose eyes had been closed in earnest supplication, could distinguish the muffled object that stood before him.

"Is it you, my daughter?" he asked, as the figure remained stationary.

"It is," replied Esclairmonde, unmasking; "but I feared to disturb your devotions."

"Approach," rejoined the preacher; "your name has mingled with my prayers, let your voice also ascend with mine towards the throne of mercy. The sands of my life are almost run out. Each moment is precious. I have much counsel to give you.

But ere I offer such precepts for your guidance as may be needful for the spiritual welfare of one whose passage will be longer than mine own through this Vale of Tears, I would fain invoke a blessing on your head."

Esclairmonde knelt by his side. The benediction was besought and bestowed. The voice of the princess joined in the fervent petition for heavenly grace that succeeded. Scarcely, however, was their devout employment brought to a close—scarcely had the holy man begun to address himself to those instructions which he deemed it necessary to impart to his religious pupil, when the door again opened, and the hooded official, having introduced another figure enveloped in a large mantle, departed as noiselessly as he had entered the chamber.

"He comes!" cried Esclairmonde.

"The executioner?" asked Chrétien calmly.

"The Chevalier Crichton," returned the princess.

"He here!" exclaimed Chrétien, a slight shade passing across his benevolent countenance.

"He is here to bid me an eternal farewell," sighed Esclairmonde.

"Princess of Condé," said the preacher, with some severity, "it *must* be an eternal farewell."

"You have said it, good father," replied Esclairmonde, in a tone of sorrowful resignation.

"Your rank forbids an alliance so disproportionate, even if the Chevalier Crichton's religious opinions coincided with your own," pursued Chrétien.

"Alas!" murmured Esclairmonde, "our creeds are adverse; a wide disparity of rank exists between us; but our hearts are indissolubly united."

"You love him, then, most tenderly, my daughter?"

"Love him!" echoed the princess passionately. "Father, to you I look to strengthen me in the resolution I have taken. This interview is my last."

"I will not fail you, my daughter," replied the old man kindly. "Think only that he is the enemy of your faith, and that were you united to him he might interfere with the important services it may hereafter be in your power to render to your persecuted Church. The thought that will most alleviate the anguish of my latest moments is, that I have sown the good seed within your bosom, which, in due season, shall bring forth a plenteous harvest for our suffering people. Princess of Condé, promise me solemnly that you will never wed a Romanist."

"Esclairmonde," said Crichton, advancing.

"Hesitate not," said the preacher severely, "or you are lost. Promise me."

"My soul is wedded to the Reformed Faith," replied the princess firmly; "and I here vow never to bestow my hand upon a Catholic."

"Amen!" responded Chrétien fervently.

A deep groan burst from the bosom of the Scot.

"Chevalier Crichton," said Esclairmonde, "you have heard my vow."

"I have," replied the Scot mournfully.

"Hear me yet further," continued the princess. "My zeal— my love—my gratitude, prompt me to lay aside feminine reserve. When I desired that our final interview should take place in the presence of this reverend man, it was that I might address you freely; it was that I might avow my love in the presence of one whose holier aspirations have not rendered him insensible or indifferent to the frailties of his fellows; it was," she added with some hesitation, and blushing deeply as she spoke, "in the hope that our united efforts might induce you to embrace the religion I profess; and that as convert to a faith, the purity of which your severest judgment must acknowledge, I might, without violation of my conscientious scruples, though in disregard of the elevated position I am compelled to assume, offer you my hand, and request him from whose lips I have imbibed the precepts of truth and humanity, which inspire me at this moment, to affiance us together before heaven."

"You have spoken with a voice of inspiration, my daughter," said Chrétien with a benignant smile, "and I have offered no interruption to your words, because they flow from a source whence true wisdom only springs. You have appealed to me in a manner which I cannot resist. Your heart, I know, is already betrothed to the Chevalier Crichton. Let him cast off the bondage to which he has so long heedlessly subjected himself. Let him not view religion through the medium of the senses, but by the purer light of the sacred Scriptures. Let him abjure the errors and idolatries of Rome, and exert the mightly intellectual powers with which he has been entrusted for the noblest purposes from on high—in the advancement of the true faith, and your betrothment shall not, for one moment, be delayed."

"Crichton," inquired Esclairmonde tenderly, "is this our last meeting, or are we for ever united?"

"It is our last," replied the Scot, in a despairing tone, "if the condition annexed to the continuance of our love be my apostasy, Esclairmonde, for you I would make any sacrifice consistent with honour and rectitude of principle. For you I would resign those projects of ambition which have hitherto engrossed my soul; for you I would repress that desire for universal distinction which has ever formed the ruling passion of my existence; for you I would be aught but a renegade to my faith—a traitor to my God. Glory has been my guiding star; my gaze has been steadfastly fixed upon it; I have steered my barque by its rays. Fame is dearer to me than life; love is dearer than fame; but honour is dearer than love. Listen to me, Esclairmonde. You are the Princess of Condé. Your rank is the most illustrious in France; but that rank has had no influence in engaging my affections. My heart was yours when our stations were supposed to be equal; my heart is yours now a barrier is placed between us. I can neither cease to love, nor feel increase of passion. To me you are unchanged. To me you are the orphan Esclairmonde. Rank can add nothing to your beauty, as it can detract nothing from it. To link my fate with yours was to realise the wildest dream of my youthful imagination. It were to attain at once the goal to which I have aspired. It were to raise me to the proudest pinnacle of felicity to which man may attain."

"Reflect," said Chrétien.

"I *have* reflected," returned the Scot. "Think not my fixed resolve upon a point involving my eternal welfare has been the result of inconsiderate caprice — think not because I have clung to the faith of my fathers, through trials, of which this, though the severest, is not the most formidable—think not it has been from a perverse adherence to wrong; think not, because you are strong in your own belief—a belief which I regard as false and pernicious—that I am not equally inflexible. I have disputed on the tenets of my faith with my sage preceptor, Buchanan, and he has failed to convince me of my errors. I am a Catholic from conviction, and as such, am as fully prepared as yourself to embrace the alternative of death rather than departure from that religion which is derived from truth, and sustained by holiest tradition."

"If the great Buchanan has failed to work your conversion, my son, my endeavours must prove ineffectual," returned the preacher, shaking his head; "nevertheless, I will essay——"

"It is in vain," replied Crichton sternly. "My martyrdom is past—yours is to come, old man. I have twice endured temptation

N 804

to-day—I have twice resisted it. The hand of the Princess of Condé was to have been the price of my disloyalty—the same hand has been made a lure to drag me to perdition."

"Say rather to direct you to salvation," rejoined Esclairmonde. "Oh! Crichton, if I have any influence over your heart I would now exert it—if, as the humble instrument of the divine will, I can wean you from the dangerous and idolatrous creed to which you are bigoted, the whole of my future life shall evince the extent of my gratitude and devotion."

"Esclairmonde!" exclaimed Crichton mournfully. "For that creed I have quitted my father's roof—for that creed I have braved a father's malediction—for that creed I now renounce all I hold dear on earth. We must part for ever."

"Crichton, you love me not."

"Let the sacrifice I have just made attest my love," returned the Scot bitterly. "Tempt me not, Esclairmonde. My bosom is torn asunder by conflicting emotions—my brain reels—I cannot support this struggle longer. Your own lips shall seal my fate."

"Be mine, then."

A shudder ran through Crichton's frame.

"I am lost," he murmured.

"No, you are saved," replied the princess triumphantly; "kneel with me at the feet of this holy man."

"Hold!" exclaimed Chrétien. "This must not be. Gladly as I would number the Chevalier Crichton among the faithful servants of the true God, his conversion must be accomplished by other influence than that of the passions. Evil means cannot work good ends. The faith which is not the result of conviction is little better than hypocrisy. Differing as I do with him upon essential points of religious credence, I applaud the Chevalier Crichton's constancy—nor would I attempt to shake it save by arguments such as my brief span of life will not permit me to employ; and I must think better of a creed which can strengthen the bosom of one so young against snares and temptations that hoary zealots might have found it difficult to resist."

"Your hand has arrested my downfall, good father," said Crichton.

"I rejoice at it, my son," replied the preacher. "Fly while your resolution still continues. I would not incur your reproaches. You must part from the princess, but not, I hope, for ever. A time—not far distant—may arrive when your opinions will undergo a change, and when she may bestow her hand without violating her sacred promise."

A tear stood in Esclairmonde's eye as she regarded her lover, and, unable to control herself, she fell into his outstretched arms.

"When I uttered that fatal vow, I pronounced my own sentence of death," she cried.

"Alas!" returned Crichton, "I would have prevented it—but it is now too late."

"It is," rejoined Chrétien, in a severe tone. "Depart quickly. You interrupt my devotions. I would prepare for eternity."

"Father," said Crichton, "I trust you will have a longer period for that preparation than your persecutors would allow you. Your life is of more consequence than mine; the services which you can render the Princess Esclairmonde are greater than I can render her. Live, then, for her."

"You speak in parables, my son," returned the preacher, in surprise.

"Take this mantle and this ring," said Crichton, "and your evasion is easy. It is the signet of the king. Display it to the guard at the portals of the Louvre, and the gates will fly open at your approach. Waste no time, but muffle up your features and figure in this cloak."

"And you?"

"Heed me not. I will remain here in your stead."

"I cannot accept freedom on such terms, my son."

"Hear me, good father," replied Crichton earnestly. "You go not forth alone. Esclairmonde must accompany you. If she returns to the masque she is lost."

"Gracious Heaven!" exclaimed the preacher.

"Henri's plans are so contrived that she cannot escape him. The King of Navarre is the dupe of his royal brother, and will unwittingly increase the risk, if not precipitate the fate of his new-found cousin, in the wild scheme he has devised for her flight. Catherine de Medicis is occupied with her own dark designs. But she will not interfere with, if she declines to forward, those of her son. An hour hence the Louvre may be the scene of fiercest strife. But an hour hence it may be too late to save the princess from dishonour."

"And your life will be the sacrifice of your devotion?" said Esclairmonde. "No, I will rather return to the banquet, and place myself under the protection of Henri of Navarre."

"He is unable to protect you," replied Crichton. "Fear nothing for me."

"Why should not you accompany the princess, Chevalier Crichton?" asked the preacher.

"Question me not, but go," replied Crichton hastily: "her life, her honour is endangered by this delay."

"I will not consent to your destruction," said Esclairmonde passionately.

"You destroy me by remaining," rejoined Crichton; "a moment more, and it may be too late."

As he spoke, the iron door revolved upon its hinges, and a *huissier*, bearing a flambeau, entered the cell, and in a loud voice announced "The king."

Accompanied by Marguerite de Valois, Henri III. immediately followed this announcement. A malicious smile played upon the features of the monarch as he noticed the dismay of the group at his appearance. "You were right in your conjecture, sister," he said, turning to the Queen of Navarre; "our stray turtle-doves *have* flown hither. The prison of a Huguenot is as favourable, I find, to the assignations of love as the bower of a Phryne. Messire Florent Chrétien might, perhaps, have found fitter occupation for his latest moments than to assist at such a rendezvous. But it is quite in character with his doctrines. His meditations, however, shall not be longer disturbed. The damps of this cell strike chilly on my senses after the perfumed atmosphere I have quitted. Princess of Condé," he continued, advancing towards Esclairmonde, who recoiled at his approach, "the masque claims your presence."

"Sire," replied the princess firmly, "I will rather remain a captive for life within this dungeon than return to your polluted halls."

"Obey him," whispered Crichton; "I may yet be able to deliver you from this perilous strait."

"Our attendants are at hand, fair cousin," said the king, significantly; "I neither mean to detain them as prisoners, nor to endanger my own health, by longer continuance in this unwholesome vault."

"Go, my daughter," said Chrétien. "The Power that watches over innocence will protect you. Fear nothing."

"Your hand, fair cousin," said Henri impatiently.

"Your majesty will not refuse to conduct me to the King of Navarre?" said Esclairmonde, reluctantly complying with the monarch's request.

"Of a surety not," rejoined Henri smiling; "but you will

find him so completely engrossed by the languishing regards of
La Rebours, that he will scarcely desire your company."

"Indeed!" exclaimed the princess starting.

"Chevalier Crichton," said Henri pausing, "you have
disobeyed our injunctions. Henceforth you are banished from
our presence."

"Henri," interposed Marguerite de Valois, "for my sake
overlook his fault."

"For *your* sake, Marguerite!" returned the king, in surprise;
"a moment ago you would have changed his banishment to
death."

"Tax me with inconsistency if you will, but grant my request."

"*Souvent femme varie*," returned Henri laughing; "be it as
you please. To banish him from the revel might tend to throw
a shade over its gaiety. Retain him by your side, and I am
content. *Allons.*"

"Marguerite," said Crichton, as the Queen of Navarre took
his arm, "your generosity has saved your brother's crown."

"If it has revived your love, I am satisfied," returned Marguerite tenderly.

"You may revive it, my queen," said Crichton.

"In what way?" demanded Marguerite, trembling with
eagerness.—"But I can guess. You require my assistance to
free the Princess of Condé from her present danger. You shall
have it."

"Yours is a noble heart, Marguerite."

"It is a faithful and a fond one, Crichton. Trifle not with
its tenderness."

"If I survive this night, my life is yours."

"Survive it, Crichton!—what mean you?"

"I am half distracted, Marguerite. But linger not. Henri is
already gone."

"And Esclairmonde," added the queen, with a look of jealous
reproach.

Many minutes had not elapsed after their departure, when
Chrétien, who had again addressed himself to his devotions, was
aroused by the harsh voice of the hooded official, who commanded him to arise. The good man instantly obeyed. The cell
was filled with a crowd of figures in sable robes and masks.

"Thy last hour is come," said the official.

"I am prepared," returned Chrétien, in a firm tone. "Lead
me forth."

While the hands of the preacher were bound together, the

voice of a priest, who formed one of the dismal group, thundered forth the following psalm: "Exurge, quare obdormis, Domine? exurge, et ne repellas in finem: quare faciem tuam avertis? oblivisceris tribulationem nostram: adhæsit in terra venter noster: exurge, Domine, adjuva'nos, et libera nos."

Chrétien was then conducted through a variety of intricate passages to the edge of the Seine, now lighted up by the lurid glare of the torches borne by the expectant crowds on the other side of the river, and being placed in a barque was rowed swiftly over to the Pré-aux-Clercs, where a fierce shout of exultation welcomed his arrival.

"Kindle the pile," shouted a thousand voices; "let the heretic die!"

"We are starved to death," cried the Sorbonist, "and want a fire to warm us—to the stake—quick—quick!

> Death to the Huguenot!—faggot and flame!
> Death to the Huguenot!—torture and shame!"

The red glare which shortly afterwards tinged the inky waters of the Seine was the reflection of Chrétien's funeral pyre.

CHAPTER XIV

THE CONSPIRACY

Dis-moi, mon maître, comment crois-tu que finira cet imbroglio?
L. VITET, *Les Barricades.*

WHEN the royal party returned to the masque the festivity of the evening was at its height. The music was breathing its softest strains—the cavaliers were whispering their most impassioned love-speeches—the dames were making their tenderest responses. The universal freedom that prevailed gave the revel somewhat of the character of an orgy. Esclairmonde shrunk back as she beheld the licence of the scene, and would have retreated, had retreat been possible. But Henri hurried her quickly onwards.

"The King of Navarre is seated near yon beaufet," he said. "His right hand grasps a goblet, while his left is passed around the waist of his mistress. We shall be rather in the way. No matter. I am ready to commit you to his care."

Esclairmonde hesitated.

"At all events we had better wait till he has finished his

song," continued Henri, "for it is evident from his gestures that he is pouring forth his passion in verse. In the meantime, you will oblige us by resuming your mask, fair cousin."

As the princess complied with the monarch's request, Henri of Navarre arose. Taking the hand of his partner, he hastened to join the dancers, and was quickly lost to view.

"You must, perforce, remain with me a few moments longer," said Henri; "let us take our station within yon embrasure, whence we can command the room, and as soon as the bransle is ended, I will summon the Béarnais to our presence."

Esclairmonde suffered herself to be led towards the window. As they proceeded thither, Henri ventured to take her hand within his own.

"Sire," she said, gently endeavouring to withdraw it from his grasp, "I will only consent to remain with you, on the condition that you do not renew the suit which has hitherto so much distressed me."

"Your condition is a hard one, fair cousin, but I will strive to obey you."

The princess looked around for Crichton. Amid the crowd of gay masks, however, that surrounded her, she could not discern his stately figure, or that of Marguerite de Valois. "He has left me," she mentally ejaculated; "that royal siren has regained all her influence over his soul."

Henri divined her thoughts. "My sister has imposed no such condition on her lover as you would impose on me, fair cousin," he said. "Their quarrel is evidently arranged, and he is restored to his old place in her affections."

"Sire!"

"They have disappeared. Shall we pay another visit to the oratory?"

"Suffer me to join the Queen-Mother, sire. I perceive her majesty in the farther *salon* conversing with the Duc de Nevers."

"With de Nevers," repeated Henri angrily. "No, *ma mie*, I cannot part with you thus. I have a word or two to say respecting this Admirable Scot. A little more this way, fair coz. I would not be overheard. What if I tell you that Crichton's life hangs on your compliance."

"His life, sire?" gasped Esclairmonde.

"Your hand alone can arrest the sword that trembles o'er his head."

"You terrify me, sire."

"I would not do so, *mignonne*," replied Henri; "on the contrary, I wish to reassure you. Princess," he added passionately, "it is in your power to save him."

"I understand your majesty," said Esclairmonde coldly.

"Not entirely," returned the king; "you may divine my motive, but you scarcely, I think, foresee the proposal I am about to make to you. I must premise by recounting the history of my earliest amourette. Renée de Rieux, my first mistress, before I beheld her, had disposed of her heart to Philippe Altoviti."

"Spare me this recital, sire."

"She is now his consort. You love the Chevalier Crichton. On the same terms you shall be his bride."

"I am the daughter of Louis of Bourbon, sire."

"The Chevalier Crichton shall be a peer of France."

"Were the King of France to sue for my hand I would refuse him!" replied Esclairmonde haughtily. "Let him seek out his minions among those complaisant dames who, because he *is* a king, have nothing to refuse him."

"You have sealed your lover's fate, fair cousin," rejoined Henri. "Du Halde," added he, motioning to the chief valet, "bid the Duc de Nevers attend us."

"Sire," said Esclairmonde, becoming pale as death, but speaking in a firm tone, "take heed how you proceed to extremities. I am a woman, and a threat from me may weigh little with your majesty. But, if from mere jealous anger, and on no just ground, you adjudge a knight, loyal and true as Crichton, to a shameful death, such vengeance as one of my sex *may* take, I will have. Look to it, sire. My threat is neither an idle nor a light one."

"*Par la Mort-Dieu!*" exclaimed Henri. "If I had entertained any doubts as to your origin, fair cousin, the spirit you have just displayed would have removed them. The fire of the old Bourbons is not extinct. I accept your defiance. Crichton dies— or you are mine. Decide, for here comes his executioner."

"I answer, as the Chevalier Crichton would," replied Esclairmonde, "Death rather than dishonour."

Whatever reply Henri meditated was cut short by a merry peal of laughter from a party of frolic dames who occupied a fauteuil near them, and the voice of the Abbé de Brantôme was heard reciting the following lines, which produced a very edifying effect upon the fair auditors:

LOVE'S HOMILY

Saint Augustin, one day, in a fair maiden's presence,
Declared that pure love of the soul is the essence!
And that faith, be it ever so firm and potential,
If love be not its base, must prove uninfluential.
Saint Bernard, likewise, has a homily left us—
(Sole remnant of those, of which fate hath bereft us!)
Where the good Saint confers, without any restriction,
On those who love most, his entire benediction.
Saint Ambrose, again, in his treatise, *De Virgine*,
To love one another is constantly urging ye;
And a chapter he adds, where he curses—not blesses—
The ill-fated wight who no mistress possesses!
Wise De Lyra, hereon, makes this just observation,
That the way to the heart is the way to salvation;
And the farther from love—we're the nearer damnation!
Besides, as remarks this profound theologian
(Who was perfectly versed in the doctrine Ambrogian)—
He, who loves not, is worse than the infamous set ye call
Profane, unbelieving, schismatic, heretical.
For, if he the fire of one region should smother,
He is sure to be scorched by the flames of the other!
And this is the reason, perhaps, why Saint Gregory
(The Pope, who reduced the stout Arians to beggary)
Averred—(keep this counsel for ever before ye)
That the lover on earth has his sole purgatory!

PERORATION

Let your minds then be wrapp'd in devout contemplation
Of the precepts convey'd by this grave exhortation;
Be loving, beloved, and never leave off—it's
The way to fulfil both the law and the prophets!

To return to Crichton. Upon entering the grand *salon* the Scot detached himself from Marguerite de Valois, and hastily resuming his mask, proceeded with a quick step in the direction of the Queen-Mother. Catherine, at that moment, was engaged in deep conference with the Duc de Nevers, and the Scot was enabled to approach her unperceived. Stationing himself behind a pillar, his quick ear failed not to catch each word of their discourse, though it was carried on for the most part in whispers.

"And the Duc d'Anjou, you say, madam, alarmed at the discovery of his letter contained in the missal, has quitted the Louvre without striking a blow?" said De Nevers.

"The moment I received your *billet* I dispatched it to him by a faithful messenger," returned Catherine. "Apprehensive of discovery, he fled."

"Confusion!" muttered the duke; "his head was to have been the price of my lieutenant-generalship. Henri will dare nothing against the Queen-Mother."

* N 804

"You are thoughtful, Monsieur le Duc," said Catherine suspiciously.

"I am full of regret that our plot is defeated," replied De Nevers.

"It is not *utterly* defeated," answered the queen.

"Indeed!"

"What Anjou dared not do I will execute alone."

"You, madam?"

"Failing in my attempts upon the honesty of our incorruptible Scot, I have found a hand as sure as his, and less reluctant. Hold your partisans in readiness, De Nevers. Henri dies to-night."

"And your majesty can fully rely upon the instrument of your will?"

"Fully," replied Catherine. "He is a Spanish bravo, accustomed to the use of the stiletto—and will not need to repeat the blow."

"'Tis well," rejoined the duke—"and the signal?"

"Will be the king's assassination," said Catherine. "Mark me, De Nevers. I will contrive that Henri and Crichton shall enter the oval chamber together. The assassin is already posted behind the arras. As the king passes he will strike. Do you and your attendants rush in at the cry and dispatch the Scot. Hew him down without mercy. Henri's death will lie at his door."

"It shall be done, madam."

"Ah! here comes Du Halde. We must separate."

Possessed of the plans of his enemies, Crichton hastened back to Marguerite de Valois, who awaited his return with impatience. "To the oval chamber, my queen," he said. "Quick—quick."

"Wherefore?" demanded Marguerite.

"Henri's life is menaced by an assassin," replied Crichton. "I must seek him, and apprise him of his danger."

"Henri is there already," returned Marguerite. "He has this moment entered that chamber with Esclairmonde."

"Ha!" exclaimed Crichton, darting from her. "I may be too late to save him."

It will be necessary to return for a moment to the Princess of Condé. After rejecting Henri's proposal in the disdainful manner described, and in order to escape from his further assiduities, while he lent an attentive ear to Brantôme's homily, Esclairmonde retired into the embrasure, and throwing open the window, stepped forth upon the balcony. A terrible spectacle was presented to her view. In the midst of a bright and spiring flame which mounted high in the still air of night, brilliantly illuminating a confused mass of threatening figures, hung a black and shapeless object. The princess turned aside in horror. Just then a loud exulting roar arose from the multitude. The remains of the martyred Chértien had dropped into the devouring element. Esclairmonde heard no more. She fell, without sense, into the arms of Henri, and, by his command, was instantly conveyed to the oval chamber.

When Crichton arrived at the doors of this chamber he found them closed. Two *huissiers* stationed before them peremptorily refused him admittance.

"Follow me," said Marguerite de Valois; "I will show you a secret entrance to the room."

Passing through a suite of apartments with the rapidity of thought, Crichton and the queen reached a small ante-chamber, in the corner of which, a suite of tapestry having been removed by Marguerite, a masked door was disclosed. Another valve admitted them to the oval chamber.

"Help!" exclaimed Henri, who, pursued by Caravaja with a drawn dagger in his hand, flew in the direction of the sound. "An assassin! help!"

"*Sangre de Dios!* I have missed my first blow," cried the Spaniard, catching hold of Henri's mantle; "but this shall find the way to thy heart, tyrant."

But as he uttered the words, the sword of Crichton passed through his body, and he fell heavily upon the person of the king, which he deluged with his blood.

"Crichton!" exclaimed Esclairmonde, aroused from her insensibility by Henri's outcries. "Ah! what do I behold?— the king assassinated!"

"No, fair cousin," replied Henri, extricating himself with difficulty from the grip, which death had not relaxed, fixed by the Spaniard upon his cloak. "The Virgin be praised, I have escaped without injury—though not without alarm. Chevalier Crichton, let those doors be thrown open."

The command was obeyed, and the monarch, pale, trembling, and covered with blood, was revealed to the general gaze. By his side stood Crichton with his drawn sword in his hand, still giving ghastly evidence of the execution he had done. Amid the universal consternation that prevailed, the voice of the Duc de Nevers was heard exclaiming:

"The king is mortally wounded—the assassin stands before us. It is Crichton. Slay him! Cut him in pieces!"

"Hold!" ejaculated Henri, checking the movement of his faction. "I am unhurt, messieurs," he continued, addressing the guard. "I command you to attach the person of the Duc de Nevers, whom we accuse of *lèse-majesté* and treason.—Madam," added he, turning to Catherine, "you will answer me on the same charges."

"At once, and boldly, my son," replied the Queen-Mother. "You are deceived. The sole traitor stands by your side. I will prove the Chevalier Crichton guilty of the crimes you have imputed to me."

"Let Cosmo Ruggieri stand forth," said Crichton.

At this summons the astrologer forced his way through the crowd.

"What hast thou to advance against me?" demanded the queen imperiously.

"That you have conspired against the life of the king, your son, and against his crown," returned Ruggieri firmly, "and that the Duc de Nevers is your accomplice. Will your majesty deign to regard this scroll?"

"It is thine own condemnation, Ruggieri," said Henri, glancing at the document; "thou art deeply implicated in this conspiracy."

"I deny it not," replied the astrologer; "let equal justice be dealt upon all who have betrayed you."

"Ruggieri," said the king, "thy doom is the galleys. De Nevers shall lose his head. "For you, madam," he added, looking at the Queen-Mother. "I will reflect upon your sentence."

"I am content," said Ruggieri, with a look of gratified revenge; "one of these accursed Gonzagas will fall by my hands."

"Away with him," said Henri. "Chevalier Crichton," he added, embracing the Scot, "you are my preserver, and henceforth my brother. I have played the tyrant and the libertine long enough. I will now endeavour to assume the part of the generous monarch. The hand of the Princess of Condé is yours— ha! what means this hesitation?"

"Sire!" a greater obstacle than you have raised divides us," replied Crichton; "our creeds are different."

"What of that?" said Henri of Navarre, who had joined the group. "Marguerite de Valois is a Catholic; I am a Protestant."

"An excellent example, certes," said Chicot, screaming with laughter.

"There is one favour which you *can* confer, sire, and which I can accept," said Crichton.

"Name it."

"The freedom of the King of Navarre."

"It is granted," replied Henri, "on condition that he takes his queen with him."

"Excuse me, sire," replied the Bourbon. "I have too much consideration to separate her from the Admirable Crichton. Fair cousin of Condé, you will accompany me. His majesty has promised you a fitting escort."

"I have," replied Henri; "but I would rather find her a fitting husband."

"Crichton," said Esclairmonde, blushingly turning towards her lover, "have I your dispensation if I break my vow?"

"From the bottom of my heart," replied Crichton passionately. "And I begin to find I am not so staunch a Catholic as I fancied myself when I quitted Florent Chrétien's cell."

"I would be of any creed for the woman I love," said the Bourbon.

"And I," said Henri III.

"Then no more need be said about the matter," cried Chicot. "Let us send for a priest at once. He will remove every difficulty. Points of faith are easily settled where love plays the umpire."

APPENDIX

DURING Crichton's residence in Venice in the autumn of the year 1580, when, as he himself has told us,

Dum procul a Patria Hadriaci prope litora Ponti
Consedi,———

when his eloquence had electrified the Doge and the assembled signory—when he had disputed *in utramque partem* upon the subtle doctrines of the Thomists and Scotists (*a parte rei, et a parte mentis*) with the learned Padre Fiamma, *e con molti altri valorosi prelati*, in the presence of the Cardinal Ludovico d'Este, the patron of Tasso, and the brother of Alfonso II., Duke of Ferrara; had discussed with the Greek theologians, in the house of the Patriarch of Aquileia, the mysterious subject of the procession of the Holy Ghost, overwhelming his opponents with the weight of authorities which he adduced; had astonished the ready Italian improvisatore by a faculty more wonderful than his own; had confounded the mathematician, the astrologer and the cabalist; had foiled the most expert swordsman, and the most brilliant wit at their own weapons—when his grace and beauty had captivated many a fair signora, and his unequalled prowess in the revel and the masque had driven many a rival gallant to despair; and when, at length, satiated with enjoyment, and crowned with success, to escape from the enervating allurements of the sea Phryne, he crossed her blue lagoons, and secluded himself in some villa on the Brenta, to prepare for that final triumph which he was destined so gloriously to achieve in the three days' disputation held in the Chiesa San Giovanni e Paolo; then it was, that Aldus Manutius, prompted by his ardent admiration of the youthful Scot, or urged to the task by the curiosity of his noble correspondent, furnished Jacomo Buoncompagno, Duke of Sora, an eminent patron of men of letters, and brother to the reigning pontiff, Gregory XIII., with the following particulars of the *mostro de mostri*:

383

RELATIONE *della qualità di* JACOMO DI CRETTONE *fatta da* ALDO MANUTIO *al* DUCA DI SORA *ad x Ottobre* 1581 [1]

LO SCOZZESE detto Jacomo di Crettone è giovane di xx anni finiti alli 19 d'Agosto passato, grande di statura, di pelo biondo, e d'aspetto bellissimo. Possiede diece lingue, la Latina più bella et più pronta di quella di Monsignore Moretto,[2] la Francese ed Italiana in eccellenza, la Greca bellissima e ne fa epigrammi, l'Hebrea, la Caldea, la Spagnuola, la Fiamenga, Inglesa, Scozzesa, e intende la Tedesca. Possiede Filosofia, Theologia, Mathematica, ed Astrologia, e tiene tutti i calcoli fatti sin ad hoggi per falsi. Di Filosofia e Theologia ha disputato più volte in questa Città con li primi letterati di questa professione con stupore di tutti. Ha perfettissima cognitione della Cabala, e di memoria tale che non sà che cosa sia il dimenticarsi ed ogni oratione udita da lui recita a parola per parola. Fa versi all'improviso di tutti li metri, e di tutte le materie vulgare e latine e ne fa improvise e belle. Ragiona di cose di stato con fondamento. Cortegiano con maraviglia e gratissimo nelle consultationi, soldato à tutta botta, e ha speso due anni in Francia alla guerra con carico assai honorato; salta e balla per eccellenza; armeggia e giuoca d'ogni sorta d'armi e ne ha fatto qui la prova; maneggiatore aggarbato di cavalli, giostratore singolare, di sangue nobile anzi per madre Regale Stuardo.[3] Ha disputato con greci in casa del Nuntio e del Patriarca d'Aquileia in materia della processione dello Spirito Santo con grande applauso e con grandissima copia d'autorità di Dottori e consigli come Aristotele e commentatori alle mani recitando le facciate intiere non che le righe greche.

[1] Relazione delle qualità di Jacomo di Crettone fatta da Aldo Manutio all Illustrimo ed eccelentissimo S. Jacomo Boncompagno Duca di Sora e Gover. Gen. di S. C. In Venegia, MDLXXXI. Appresso Aldo.

[2] The famous Marcus Antonius Muretus, the friend of the Manutii, and one of the most profound scholars of his day. He was succeeded in the Roman chair of philosophy by the younger Aldus. The wonderful skill of Muretus in Latin versification will readily be conceived when it is stated that he palmed certain scenes of his own composition upon the learned Joseph Scaliger as fragments of two ancient comic writers, Attius and Trabea, which that great philologist unhesitatingly introduced into his edition of Terentius Varro.

[3] Compare the above description with the following passage from the *Dedication to the Paradoxes of Cicero*, subsequently published by Aldus: "Magna sunt ista profecto, et inaudita, mediocria tamen, si cetera spectemus; quod, scilicet decem linguarum, multorum idiomatum, omnium disciplinarum cognitionem ante vigessimum primum ætatis annum, sis adeptus; et digladiandi, saltandi, omnium gymnasticarum exercitationum, et equitandi studia, tanta cum alacritate ingenii, animique humanitate, mansuetudine, et facilitate conjunxeris, ut nihil te admirabilius reperiri possit. Sed non innumerabiles vitæ tuæ transactæ laudes; non mirificam illam coram Serenissimo Principe ac Illustrissimis Venetæ Reipublicæ proceribus actionem; non subtilissimas tuas de Theologia, philosophia et rebus Mathematicis, disputationes in plerisque maximorum hominum concessibus, recensebo; non tantorum hominum ad te videndum concursum, ut olim Platoni a Sicilia revertenti, relicto Olympico spectaculo, tota Atheniensium celebritas occurrisse fertur; cum te omnes, signo rubeæ Rosæ, quod tibi natura circa dextrum lumen impressit, tamquam unicam et raram in terris avem, homines cognoscerent."

Sà tutto S. Thomaso, Scoto, Thomisti e Scotisti a mente, e disputa in utramque partem, il che ha fatto felicemente l'altro giorno col Padre Fiamma, e con molti altri valorosi Prelati alla presenza di Monsignore Illustrissimo il Cardinale da Este. Volse il Patriarca e la Signora udirlo e ne restarono maravigliosi e stupefatti; da S. Serenità fù premiato di 200 scudi. In somma è mostro de mostri, e tale che molti udendo così fatte qualità in un sol corpo benissimo proporzionato e lontano dalla malinconia fanno di molte chimere. Hieri si ridusse fuori in villa, per stendere due mila conclusioni le quali in tutte le perfettione vole mantenere qui in Venetia nelle Chiesa di S. Giovan e Paolo; fra due mesi tutto il mondo corre per udirlo.

There is only one perplexing point about this letter; and if I could follow my Uncle Toby's advice to Corporal Trim, and "leave out the *date* entirely," much tedious speculation might be spared. For the genuineness of the edition in my possession —that it is actually, as its title states, *appresso Aldo*—I cannot vouch. Counterfeits of the productions of this celebrated press are too numerous and too skilful to suffer me to hazard such an assertion. But at all events it is, beyond doubt, a facsimile of the original. Obtained from Milan, my copy consists of a few leaves, yellow with age, with the device of the elder Aldus on the title-page, and purports to have been printed "in Venegia, MDLXXXI." The memoir is not mentioned by Renouard; nor is it included in the small quarto volume of the letters of Aldus Manutius, published at Rome, none of which, as Dr. Black observes (for I have not seen the collection), is written prior to 1585. Having premised thus much, I shall proceed with my reasons for the emendation of the date, which, I conceive, should be the *tenth of October*, 1580, *not* 81. From another contemporary authority (a manuscript chronicle cited by Serassi, the writer of which evidently derived his information from Aldus) we learn that Crichton reached Venice "nel mese d'Agosto del 1580." Coupling this intelligence with the final passage of the *Relatione*, "fra due mesi tutto il mondo corre per udirlo," we have the exact period of his arrival and departure, and my hypothesis is confirmed. He remained in Venice two months. And here I may note that the *Affiche* (the date of which is 1580) is made, owing to its faulty punctuation, to announce to the learned world that Crichton's disputation in the Church of Saint John and Paul would take place *within two months*; whereas we are expressly told by Aldus Manutius, who was not only the adviser, but a spectator, of this memorable controversy, that it commenced on the day of Pentecost, 1581. Aldus, indeed, seems to refer to some such panegyric as this *Relatione*, when he states in the *Dedication to the Paradoxes of Cicero*, "nunc vero etiam lætor, toti Italiæ, et orbi fortasse terrarum universo perspectum esse judicium de te meum, ET EA QUAE CUM HUC VENISSES SCRIPTIS COMMENDAVI"; and mark what follows, "quæ tibi ipsi, ac nonnullis acerrimis censoribus, aspera atque injucunda videbantur. Nam, licet tum amorem malui ostendere, quam prudentiam, nunc ambo, cum amicis tuis, tum inimicis, si qui amplius tam feri atque inhumani reperiuntur, manifesta sunt, postquam tua virtus tam clarum sui splendorem diffudit." Influenced by a desire to serve his friend, the great printer may have allowed his letter to the Duke of Sora to be widely cir- culated, and perhaps connived at its publication by the brothers Guerra, for which injudicious zeal he appears to have incurred the censure, as well of the high-minded object of his adulation, as of those envious detractors, which a celebrity like that of Crichton was certain to awaken. That Dr. Black, after a careful investigation of the collected letters of Aldus, could only dis- cover this solitary passage, which he thinks may relate to Crichton: "Sa V. S. Illustrissima, che io sempre functus sum officio cotis, o deve ricordarsi dello Scozzese, il quale gode la benignità, e liberalità di cotesta Republica, favorito anche da lei, che si mosse e per favorir lui, e per obligar me"—proves nothing. Aldus might not probably desire to introduce his letter to Buoncompagno in a volume containing a similar eulogy on the Polish Crichton, Stanislaus Niegossevio, addressed to the same nobleman.

It follows, from what has been advanced, that upon the validity of the evidence afforded by Aldus Manutius—whether considered as the author or originator of the *Affiche*, the *Relatione*, the *Manuscript Chronicle*, or the *Dedication to the Paradoxes* (for they are one and the same thing), rests Crichton's claim to that glorious epithet by which he has since been distinguished. His mighty intellectual powers are attested by Astolfo and Scaliger; but his universal accomplishments and personal graces are recorded by Imperialis, Dempster, David Buchanan, Johnston, and other later writers on the testimony of Aldus.[1]

[1] It may be curious to glance at the different terms of eulogy applied to Crichton by various authors. By Aldus Manutius, in the *Relatione* and the *Affiche*, he is styled "mostro de mostri"; by the same writer, in the *Dedication to the Paradoxes of Cicero*, "unicam et raram in terris avem"; and in the address prefixed to the *Dialogue de Amicitiâ*, "divinam plane juvenem"; by Astolfi, "mostro maraviglioso"; by Imperialis, "sæculi monstrum—orbis phœnix—dæmonium prorsus"; by Scaliger, "ingenium prodigiosum"; by Boccalini (satirically), "il portento di natura"; by

And that testimony, notwithstanding it has been impugned by Doctors Kippis and Black, has been satisfactorily shown by Mr. Fraser Tytler to be unimpeachable.

If any proof, indeed, were wanting of the sincerity of Aldus's affection for, and admiration of, his friend, it would be found in the following pathetic lament, which (deceived by a false rumour of Crichton's death) he inscribed to his memory:

ALDUS MANUTIUS TO THE MEMORY OF JAMES CRICHTON

O Crichton, it is just that praise should attend thy memory, since we have been deprived of thee by an untimely death! Who is there that did not admire thee in life? who that does not mourn thee dead? *While alive, the judgment I had formed of thy merits was my honour and advantage; and now that thou art no more, my grief is immeasurable.* Would to God thou wert yet alive, and that this fatal land (though the native country of Virgil) had never possessed thee! For such has been our wretched destiny, that the same land which to him gave birth, should in this latter year deprive thee of life (*alas, in thy twenty-second year, a span of existence, though sufficient for thy glory, yet too short for us*). For ever shall I revere thy memory! For ever shall thy image be present to my eyes! To me thou wilt ever be the same, ever cherished in my heart, as in the affections of all worthy men! God grant that thy lot above may be the consummation of heavenly felicity, as on earth thou wert ever attached to what was of heavenly origin, and ever employed in the contemplation of such objects. *O melancholy day, the third of July!* This to thee I write, from this melancholy sojourn on earth, to that heavenly habitation, with my earnest prayer for every blessing to thy spirit.[1]

The date of this affectionate tribute is the 4th of November, 1583: it is prefixed to the Aldine edition of *Cicero de Universitate.* I mention these circumstances because they are important to the consideration of two unedited poems of Crichton, which have fallen into my hands, to which I shall now proceed.

I do not know how I can better introduce the subject than in the words of Mr. Tytler. "Serassi," says this gentleman,[2] "an author of high character for accuracy, asserts that he has amongst his miscellanies an 'Epicedion,' written on the death of the Cardinal and Saint, Charles Borromeo, by James Crichton, a

Rotinus, "Phœnix Critonius"; by Ronconius, "ingenio Phœnix"; by Dempster, "miraculum orbis"; by Johnston, "omnibus in studiis admirabilis"; by Abernethy, "juvenis incomparabilis"; and by Sir Thomas Urquhart he was first entitled "THE ADMIRABLE CRICHTON."
[1] This translation appears in Dr. Black's *Life of Tasso.* It was furnished by Lord Woodhouselee.
[2] *Life of Crichton,* pp. 211–13. Second edition.

Scotsman, and printed the very day after his death. Serassi copies the title of this 'Epicedion' verbatim, and evidently must have had it before him when he wrote the passage. All supposition of mistake upon his part is thus nearly precluded. The coincidence of the two names, *Jacobus Critonius,* the additional appellative *Scotus,* and the circumstance that the elegy was written, printed, and published the day after the death of the cardinal, fixes the poem upon James Crichton of Cluny, as the improbability of the supposition that there should have been another Scotsman of the name of James Crichton in Italy, in the year 1584, possessed of the same remarkable facility in poetical composition, is quite apparent. And lastly, the subject on which this elegy was composed, renders any error almost impossible. Had it been a poem on any indifferent subject, or a prose work relating to any disputed point in physics or in morals, we might have been allowed to conjecture that the date 1584 was erroneous; but the death of the Cardinal, Charles Borromeo, fixes us down to a certain time. An 'Epicedion' on this venerable character could not have been written anterior to the year 1584. On the one hand, therefore, we have Aldus, Imperialis, and all his succeeding biographers, fixing the death of Crichton to the year 1582 or 1583; on the other hand, we have it asserted, that the Admirable Crichton, on the 4th of November, 1584, composed an 'Epicedion' on the Cardinal Borromeo. On which side the truth lies, must be left for future writers to discern."

To this I answer by producing the "Epicedion" in question.

EPICEDIUM ILLUSTRISSIMI ET REVERENDISSIMI CARDINALIS CAROLI BOROMÆI, AB IACOBO CRITONIO SCOTO, ROGATU CLARISSIMI, SUMMAQUE IN OPTIMUM PASTOREM SUUM PIETATE, VIRI, IOANNIS ANTONII MAGII MEDIOLANEN. PROXIMO POST OBITUM DIE EXARATUM. DE CONSENSU SUPERIORUM. [MEDIOLANI. EX TYPOGRAPHIA PACIFICI PONTIJ. MDLXXXIII.]

> Heu pullâ clamyde, et scissis Elegia capillis
>   Prodeat, et calamos Egloga nacta nigros.
> Nox erat, et mœstas agitabam pectore curas,
>   Horaque me noctis tertia vexat atrox.
> Nulla datur requies; sed mens insana vagatur
>   Semper, et objectis horret imaginibus.
> Ast tandem sero declinant lumina somno,
>   Et (dolor) obrepunt somnia dira mihi.
> Namque fretum ingressus portu prodire videbar,
>   Quique ratem regeret Navita nullus erat.
> Hic Ephyre, Drymo, Cydippe, Glaucia, Doris,
>   Xanthia, Cymodoce, Lysis et Opis erant.
> Hæc velut in gyrum duplicato poplite fertur,
>   Remigat hæc pedibus, nec resupina jacet.

Intonat horrisono Cœlum se murmure miscens,
  Hinc Notus, hinc Boreas, Africus inde ruunt.
Involuere diem nubes, cæcæque tenebræ
  Insurgunt, et nox ingruit atra salo.
Deficit eximio spoliata carina Magistro,
  Atque procellosis ingemit icta notis.
Extimui, steteruntque comæ, et timor occupat artus,
  Proh dolor, en veris somnia mixta noto.
Proh stupor, Arctois peregrinus Scotus ab oris,
  Nauclerum Latii defleo jure pium.
Flete viri, lugete senes, discindite vultus
  O pueri, heu juvenes imbre rigate genas.
Stridulus emissis certatim ululatibus æther
  Horreat, et finem non habeant gemitus.
Quales cum Troiæ jam tum Fortuna labaret,
  Iliades scisso crine dedere Nurus.
Ne mea suspensum teneant te metra, benigne
  Lector, Christigenæ Navita, puppis hic est.
CAROLUS Insubri BOROMÆUS sanguine cretus,
  Cui virtus claro stemmate major erat.
CAROLUS æterno BOROMÆUS Numine fultus,
  Et miseræ gentis dux foret ille suæ.
Non prece, non pretio, non vi sed cœlitus almum,
  Illius texit purpura sacra caput,
Menteque perpetuâ Christum spectabat IESVM,
  Purpureos inter gloria summa Patres.
Non aliter quàm vel radiis solaribus æther
  Cynthia vel bigis nox taciturna suis.
Scilicet Insubres vitiorum mole ruentes,
  Erexit præsul dexteritate pius.
Erectosque manu validâ fulcivit Ephebus,
  Contudit et sacra Relligione scelus.
Hunc Deus elegit solidæ pietatis alumnum,
  Ut magnus patriæ splendor ubique foret.
Sæpiùs ille homines mediâ de morte recepit,
  Quum pestis latè serperet atra Lues.
Ille Dei classem remis, velisque carentem
  Instituit medio fortius ire freto.
Et licet extinctus sit corpore nomine vivit,
  Cujus fama nitens pulsat utrumque polum.
In quo virtutes fixere sedilia cunctæ,
  De vitiisque ferunt alta trophæa Deo.
Integritas animi, placidoque modestia vultu,
  Et nullis probitas contemerata malis.
Despectusque sui, legis respectus avitæ,
  Providus, et casto plenus amore timor
Factis culta fides, non solis fumea verbis,
  Sed supero accensas quæ dat ab igne faces.
Aures nobilibus mites præbebat; egenis
  Consuluit pariter nobilis ille parens.
Ergo non alio fas est hunc nomine dici.
  Quàm sua, quo, pietas nota sit, atque fides.
Sic virtute sua clarus, nec carmine nostro,
  Laude nec alterius clarior esse potest.
Haud equidem varios cristallina globa colores
  Tot dabit, hic morum quot simulachra nitent,
Et tamen (o Pietas) vitales exuit auras,
  Et cœli proprias itque reditque vias.
Eheu nil valuit fugientem sistere vitam,
  Ah nil morte homini certius esse patet.

Illa malis requiem, metamque laboribus affert,
 Omniaque alternas constat habere vices.
Sic pluvialis hyems, Zephyro spirante recedit,
 Sic pia nauclerus præmia vester habet.
Admonet ecce Deus, Deus æthere missus ab alto,
 Currat ut in portus tuta carina suos.
Intereà Præsul visit pia fana Varallæ,
 Ut præsagus olor fata subire parans.
Sanctè, quem dederat, cursum Natura peregit,
 Molliter ossa cubant, spiritus astra colit.
Quem nunc felicem, terris pelagoque relictis,
 Fatidico cecinit Delphicus ore Deus.[1]

EPICEDIUM
ON THE
CARDINAL CARLO BORROMEO

I

With black funereal robe, and tresses shorn,
 O'erwhelmed with grief, sad Elegy appears;
And by her side, sits Ecloga forlorn,
 Blotting each line she traces with her tears.

II

'Twas night!—long pondering on my secret woes,
 The third hour broke upon my vigil lone;
Far from my breast had sorrow chased repose,
 And fears presageful threatened ills unknown.

III

Slumber, at length, my heavy eyelids sealed;
 The self-same terrors scared me as I slept:
Portentous dreams events to come revealed,
 And o'er my couch fantastic visions swept.

IV

Upon the shoreless sea methought I sailed,
 No helmsman steered the melancholy barque:
Around its sides the pitying Nereids wailed,
 Cleaving with snow-white arms the waters dark.

V

Cydippe, dolphin-borne, Ephyra fair,
 And Xanthia leave their halcyon-haunted caves,
With Doris and Cymodoce to share
 The maddening strife of storm-awaken'd waves.

VI

Drawn, unresisting, where the whirling gyre
 Vexes the deep, the ship her prow inclines;
While, like a pharos' gleam, the lightning's fire
 Over the raging vortex redly shines.

[1] A free translation of this Elegy follows. Another copy alluded to by M. Eyriès (the writer of the article on "Crichton" in the *Biog. Universelle*) is preserved in the Bibliothèque du Roi at Paris, of which I have procured a transcript, agreeing in all respects with yet another impression obtained from Milan.

VII

Mix'd with the thunder's roar that shakes the skies,
  Notus and Africus and Boreas sound;
Black wreathing clouds, like shadowy legions, rise,
  Shrouding the sea in midnight gloom profound.

VIII

Disabled, straining, by the tempest lashed,
  Reft of her storm-tried helmsman's guiding hand,
The vessel sinks!—amid the surges dashed,
  Vainly I struggle—vainly cry for land!

IX

Alas! stern truths with dreams illusive meet!
  Latium the shipwreck of her hopes deplores!
The pious leader of the Insubrian fleet
  I mourn—a wandering Scot from Northern shores!

X

Weep, youths! weep, aged men! weep! rend your hair!
  Let your wild plaints be on the breezes tost!
Weep, virgins! matrons! till your loud despair
  Outbraves her children's wail for Ilion lost!

XI

In that wreck'd barque the Ship of Christ behold!
  In its lost chief the Cardinal divine,
Of princely Lombard race [1]; whose worth untold
  Eclipsed the lofty honours of his line.

XII

His suffering countrymen to rule, sustain,
  By the All-wise was Borromeo given;
And he, who stoop'd not dignity to gain,[2]
  Derived his high investiture from Heaven.

XIII

Bright as the sun o'er all pre-eminent,
  Or Cynthia glittering from her star-girt throne,
The saintly Charles, on truths sublime intent,
  Amid the purple hierarchy shone.

[1] Saint Carlo Borromeo was born at Arona, near the Lago Maggiore, the loveliest of Italian lakes, on 2 October, 1538. His family was, and long continued to be, the most illustrious in Lombardy. It derives, however, its proudest distinction from its connection with the virtuous cardinal and his exalted nephew Federigo, whose sublime character has been of late so exquisitely portrayed by Manzoni. If ever man deserved canonisation, it was the subject of this elegy, whose whole life was spent in practices of piety; and whose zeal, munificence, wisdom, toleration and beneficence have conferred lasting benefits on his creed and country.

[2] He was made Cardinal and Archbishop in his twenty-third year by his uncle, Pius VI., who had resigned several rich livings to him twelve years before.—Eustace, *Classical Tour through Italy.*

XIV

The Christian fleet, devoid of helm and sail,[1]
  He mann'd and led where roughest billows roll;
And, though no more, his virtues wide prevail,
  Their sacred influence spreads from pole to pole.

XV

His was the providence that all foresees,
  His the trust placed, unchangeably, above,
His strict observance of his sires' decrees,
  Rapt adoration, and fear-chasten'd love.

XVI

The faith in practice, not profession, shown,
  Which borrows all its glory from on high
Was his: nor did his holiness, alone,
  Consist in outward forms of sanctity.

XVII

A willing ear unto the nobly-born,
  Nobler himself, he ne'er refused to yield;
Nor, Jesus' meek disciple, did he scorn
  The humble prayer that to his heart appealed.[2]

XVIII

Can no remembrance dearer than his name
  Bequeathed us, link his memory with the earth:
Nor can my praise add lustre to his fame—
  Proud heritage of unexampled worth![3]

[1] Borromeo found the diocese of Milan in the most deplorable state of disorder. But with a vigorous and unsparing hand he reformed all ecclesiastical abuses. "C'est ainsi," observes M. Tabauraud, the writer of his life in the *Biog. Universelle*, "que l'Eglise de Milan, tombée dans une espèce d'anarchie depuis quatre - vingts ans que ses archevêques n'y résidaient pas, reçut en peu d'années cette forme admirable qui, par la vie toute angélique de son clergé, la rendit le modèle de toutes les autres Eglises. Tant de réformes ne purent se faire sans de grands obstacles, qu'il surmonta par sa fermeté, sa patience et son imperturbable charité."

[2] So unbounded was Borromeo's charity that he sold his principality of Oria, and distributed the proceeds amongst the poor.

[3] The private virtues of Saint Charles, that is, the qualities which give true sterling value to the man, and sanctify him to the eyes of his Creator —I mean humility, self-command, temperance, industry, prudence and fortitude—were not inferior to his public endowments. His table was for his guests; his own diet was confined to bread and vegetables; he allowed himself no amusement or relaxation, alleging that the variety of his duties was in itself a sufficient recreation. His dress and establishment were such as became his rank, but in private he dispensed with the attendance of servants, and wore an under-dress, coarse and common; his bed was of straw; his repose short; and in all the details of life he manifested an utter contempt of personal ease and indulgence.—EUSTACE.

XIX

When o'er his desolated city fell
The livid plague's inexorable breath;
Oft, in the lazaretto's tainted cell,
Fervent, he prayed beside the couch of death.[1]

XX

As through the fane the pale procession swept,[2]
Before its shrine he bent in lowliest wise;
Imploring Heaven, in mercy, to accept
His life, for them, a willing sacrifice.

XXI

When from the assassin's arm the bullet sped,
He blench'd not, nor his deep devotions stopt;
"Be not dismay'd in heart!"—the anthem said,
He rose—the bullet from his vestment dropt![2]

XXII

Not in the prism more varied hues reside,
Than bright examples in his course are traced:
Alas! his longer sojourn here denied,
His guiding star is from its sphere effaced.

[1] During a destructive pestilence he erected a lazaretto, and served the forsaken victims with his own hands.—EUSTACE.

[2] The incidents described in this and the following stanza do not occur in the original. As, however, they appear necessary to complete the picture of the holy Primate's career presented by the poem, I have ventured upon this introduction. These actions, as well as his heroic devotion to the plague-stricken in the lazaretto, mentioned in the preceding verse, form subjects for part of the eight magnificent silver bas-reliefs which adorn the vaulted roof of the gorgeous subterranean chapel in the Duomo at Milan, where the body of the saint reposes enshrined amid "barbaric pearl and gold." During the period of the plague, Borromeo was indefatigable in his exertions to arrest the terrible calamity. "Cherchant," says M. Tabauraud, "à désarmer la colère du ciel par des processions générales, auxquelles il assistait nu-pieds, la corde au cou, les yeux fixés sur son crucifix, qu'il arrosait de ses larmes, *en s'offrant à Dieu comme une victime de propitiation pour les péchés de son peuple!*"

[2] The ecclesiastical reformation effected by Saint Charles met, as was natural, with considerable opposition on the part of the corrupt and disorderly priesthood, and he became the object of their bitterest animosity. "Les plus opposés à la réforme," writes M. Tabauraud, "suscitèrent un frère *Farina*, qui se posta à l'entrée de la chapelle archiépiscopale, où le Saint Prélat faisait sa prière avec toute sa maison; et, au moment où l'on chantait cette antienne: *Non turbetur cor vestrum neque formidet,* l'assassin, éloigné seulement de cinq ou six pas, tire un coup d'arquebuse sur Saint Charles, à genoux devant l'autel. A ce bruit, le chant cesse, la consternation est générale; le Saint, sans s'émouvoir, fait signe de continuer la prière: il se croyait cependant blessé mortellement, et offrait à Dieu le sacrifice de sa vie. *La prière finie, il se relève, et voit tomber à ses pieds la balle qu'on lui avait tirée dans le dos, et qui n'avait fait qu'effleurer son rochet.*"—*Biog. Universelle.* The holy primate endeavoured, ineffectually, to preserve Farina and the instigators of his crime from the punishment they merited. They were put to death, and Pius VI. dissolved the order (*Gli Umili*) to which they belonged.

XXIII

Alas! life's ebbing tide no hindrance knows!
With man is nothing certain but to die!
Mortality, alone, presents a close
Immutable, 'mid mutability.

XXIV

As, in some stream remote, the swan expires,
Breathing, unheard, her fate-foreboding strain,
So the declining Cardinal retires
To steep Varalla's solitary fane.[1]

XXV

Like the fair flower that springs from winter's crust,
Lombards! your Primate bursts his earthly chains;
And, in his Father's mansion with the Just,
A portion and inheritance obtains.[2]

XXVI

Within his chosen tomb calm may he sleep![3]
Beatified, aloft, his spirit soars!
While Virtue's loss irreparable, deep,
With reverential grief the Muse deplores.

The authenticity of this poem cannot for an instant be disputed. It bears the strongest internal evidence of emanating from the same mind that conceived the *Appulsus ad Venetam*; and the *vexata quæstio* so long agitated, as to Crichton's having survived the perilous nones of July may be now considered finally settled. As an extemporaneous effusion (and its author *twice* intimates that it is to be so esteemed), it must be allowed

[1] The Monastery of Monte Varalla is situated in the Piedmontese states, near the banks of the Sesia. Thither Saint Charles retired immediately previous to his dissolution, attended only by his confessor, the Jesuit Adorno—and returned thence to Milan in a dying state. "Franciscum Adornum Societatis Jesu plurimi fecit qui cum in extremo vitæ curriculo per dies plurimos, quo tempore in Monte Varallo meditationibus se totum tradiderat CAROLUS ab ejus latere nunquam discesserit."—VALERIO, *Caroli Cardin. Borromæi Vita.* Antoine Godeau, Bishop of Grasse, who has written the life of the illustrious Primate, gives the following particulars of his melancholy visit to the Monastery: "Encore que toute la vie de SAINT CHARLES fust une retraite mentale, toutefois il avait accoutumé d'en faire une locale tous les ans en quelque monastère écarté, où il employoit quelques jours pour faire une revue sévère de sa vie, et pour prendre un nouvel esprit de zèle et de piété. Avant que de s'en retourner à Milan, il voulut passer au *Mont Varalle*, dont nous avons parlé, et y faire ses exercices."—*Vie de S. Ch. Borromée*, liv. ii. chap. dernier. M. Mellin, in his *Voyage dans le Milanais*, describing the mountain oratory of Varese, observes: "On va de là à *Varalle*, où les Histoires de l'Ancien et du Nouveau-Testament sont figurées dans cinquante-deux chapelles."

[2] The earthly pilgrimage of Saint Charles terminated on 4 November, 1584, at the age of forty-six years. He was canonised by Paul V. in 1610.

[3] "Cupiens hoc loco sibi monumentum vivens elegit."—*Epitaph inscribed upon Borromeo's tomb by his own desire.*

to be a remarkable production. Its versification is singularly fluent and harmonious, and it breathes a spirit of tender melancholy perfectly in unison with the subject. It was dashed off at a heat, at the request of a friend, with its writer's characteristic rapidity; and, if we should fail to discover passages of such transcendent beauty as might be expected from a genius of an order so high as that of Crichton, we must bear in mind the disadvantageous circumstances under which, in all probability, it was composed. The grief of the youthful Scot was, I am persuaded, no poetic fiction. Be this as it may, his reputation will suffer no diminution from the connection of this "Epicedion" with his name.

> Famigeras iterum Critonius exit in auras
> Et volat ingenio docta per ora virûm.

Not only, however, was Crichton alive in November 1584— not only on the death of the divine Borromeo did he pour forth his elegiac strains, but in the succeeding month we have further proof of his existence and unabated poetical powers in the following congratulatory address, with which he celebrated the induction of Gaspar Visconti to the archiepiscopal see of Milan.

JACOBI CRITONII SCOTI AD AMPLISSIMUM AC REVERENDISSIMUM VIRUM GASPAREM VICECOMITEM [1] SUMMA OMNIUM ORDINUM VOLUNTATE, AD PRÆCLARAM ARCHIEPISCOPATUS MEDIOLANEN. ADMINISTRATIONEM, DELECTUM.

GRATULATIO [2]

> Primus in Exequiis ferali carmine Scotus
> Pastoris dolui funera mœsta pii.
> Funera mœsta pii BOROMÆI Præsulis ah ah,
> Deplanxit tristi nostra Thalia stylo.
> Aspice post nimbos, nitidum quàm sæpe reducat
> Vectus Lucifero Cynthius axe, diem.
> Namque salo pridem Navis spoliata Magistro,
> More poetarum, fluctibus obruitur.
> Sævit hyems, venti ingeminant striduntque rudentes,
> Sollicitoque tremunt corda pavore virum.
> Nec spes ulla fuit melior, quin deficit omnis
> Naucleri posito, turba, magisterio.
> Nec quicquam nisi vota facit divosque deasque
> Orat, ut afflictis rebus adesse velint.

[1] Gaspar Visconti, a prelate eminent for learning and piety (though thrown into the shade by the superior sanctity of his immediate precursor and successor, Saint Charles and Frederick Borromeo) was appointed to the archbishopric of Milan on 29 November, and consecrated during the ides of December 1584 (*vide* SAXII *Series Archiepisc. Mil.*, tom. iii.), the period when Crichton's congratulatory poem was published. A translation of the address will be found in the ensuing page.

[2] Mediolani, ex. Typographia Pacifici Pontii, MDLXXXIII.

Tanta sed æterni fuerit clementia Patris
  Ut non humanas deseruisset opes.
Sic pelagi tandem compescuit Æolus æstus,
  Atque reluctantes traxit in antra Notos.
Et caput exeruit formosior æquore Titan,
  Illuxit votis mille petita dies.
Ecce velut fulgur media quod nocte coruscat,
  Alter adest præstans navita puppis, Iö.
Cujus opes magnas, virtus et gloria longè
  Exuperant, hujus non levis urbis honor.
Rostra Rotæ,¹ Romæ, rectâ ratione rotabat,
  Rimantique ratem relligione reget.
Colloquio præsens præsentem denique novi,
  Sensibus injecit qui pia vincla meis.
Præsule ter felix o nunc Insubria tali,
  Inclyta cui virtus cernitur esse parens.
Quem propriis ultrò tendentem laudibus, omnes
  Hoc norunt sacrum promeruisse jubar.
Currite jam cives, dignis ornate lapillis,
  Nobile, facundum, conspicuumque caput.
Exoptatus ades patriæ rectorque paterque
  Gaspar præsignis nomine reque Comes.
Quid potuit mœstæ contingere lætius Urbi?
  Qui suavi pasces pectora nostra cibo.
Participes hujus concurrunt undique gentes
  Lætitiæ, et cura est omnibus una tui,
Deponunt luctus, et te succedere gaudent,
  Nam cui succedis non latet orbe viros.
Illum Sarmaticus Boreas, et Caucasus asper
  Protulerit, Charites qui neget ore tuas.
Magnanimum sydus, tu gloria splendor avorum,
  Tu generis columen, portus et aura tui.
Integritas morum, pietas, facundia, virtus,
  Musa, tibi probitas, dexteritasque placent.
Relligione Numam, antiquum gravitate Catonem
  Augustum illustrem nobilitate refers.
Hinc te Gregorius, summi qui Numinis instar,
  Clavigerâ, reserat regna beata, manu.
Eximio magnus donavit munere Pastor,
  Ut tegat emeritas sacra Tiara comas.
Auguriis sibi quisque animum felicibus implet,
  Exoptat longos, et tibi quisque dies.
Critonius Scotis Arctoæ in finibus oræ
  Progenitus, Gaspar, gratulor ecce tibi,
Sis felix, carmenque meum lege fronte serenâ,
  Gaudebit, Præsul, Musa favore tuo.

V. Idus Decembris (1585).

TO GASPAR VISCONTI

I

When her fair land with grief o'erspread,
  Insubria mourn'd her Primate dead;
When Borromeo to the tomb
  Was borne 'mid all-pervading gloom:

¹ The well-known Papal court called the Rota. Gaspar Visconti was one of the twelve judges, as we learn from Saxius, who says that he proceeded to Rome—*ut una cum auditoribus quos vocant* Rotæ Romanæ *in eo insigni sapientum collegio consideret.* The reader will admire the singular alliterative splendour of this couplet.

When dimm'd with tears was every eye,
When breathed one universal sigh
The sorrowing lyre for him who slept,
I first—a Scottish minstrel—swept.

II

The night is pass'd, and dawn awakes,
Bright Cynthius through the vapour breaks
And Lucifer, with cheering beams,
From out his golden axle gleams.
Where late upon the raging sea
The wild winds rush'd tumultuously;
And the frail barque by surges tost,
Her tempest-braving helmsman lost,
Her timbers strain'd, her canvas riven,
Wide o'er the weltering waste was driven;
While her pale crew, with fear aghast,
Gazed (as they deem'd) on heaven their last!
With shrieks their hapless fate bewailing!
With prayers the threatening skies assailing!—
——A change is wrought!—hushed are the gales,
A soft and summer calm prevails;
And the glad ship, in safety, glides
Over the gently-rolling tides.
In troops o'er the ocean's broad expanse,
Day's rosy harbingers advance;
Bland Eolus careers the wave,
Fierce Notus hurries to his cave;
Young Titan from the waters springs,
With new-born lustre on his wings;
And over all things shines that sun,
Whose light a thousand vows have won.

III

Iö! with shouts the deck resound!
Iö! another chief is found!
Another leader hath been sent
To rule the Christian armament;
Whose firmness and undaunted zeal
Ensure uninterrupted weal:
Whose voice the Roman Rota sway'd,
Whose laws that synod sage obey'd;
Whose hand will guide with equal ease,
Religion's barque through stormy seas:
Whose power in exhortation shown,
Whose wisdom I myself have known;
When by his eloquence subdued,
In admiration lost, I stood.
Rejoice, thrice-happy Lombardy!
That such a chief is given to thee!
A chief so free from aught of sin,
Virtue might be his origin:
Whose heavenly purpose, onward-tending,
Whose resolution—calm, unbending,
Shall lead thee through the shades of night
To realms of everlasting light.

IV

Haste, Milanese! your Primate greet!
Prelates! your leader fly to meet!
Run, maidens! youths! let each one bring
Some gift, some worthy offering!
Surrounding nations hail your choice,
Surrounding nations loud rejoice!
Like him, whom ye have lost, was none
Save him your choice has fall'n upon!

V

A father fond, a ruler wise
GASPAR, in thee, we recognise:
Thy name, VISCONTI, seems to be
An earnest of prosperity.
To us thou art in our distress,
As manna in the wilderness.
Inhospitable Caucasus,
Sarmatian Boreas rigorous,
Seize on the caitiff, who denies
Thy all-acknowledg'd charities!
A glory art thou, and a star,
A light, a pharos seen afar!
And, clothed with majesty divine,
Shalt prove the pillar of thy line.
High rectitude and prescience
Are thine, and wide beneficence;
A Numa in thy sanctity,
A Cato in thy gravity,
Augustus in nobility.
Hence the High Pontiff Gregory,[1]
Who holds of Paradise the key,
For thee earth's chains hath cast aside,
For thee heaven's gate hath opened wide;
Milan's white robe hath round thee spread,
Her mitre placed upon thy head.

VI

In thy blest advent all men see
Of peace a certain augury:
All tongues are clamorous in thy praise,
All prayers are for thy length of days.
Amid the crowd, I, CRICHTON, born
On Caledonian shores forlorn,
Not all unknown, congratulate
Thee, GASPAR, on thine honour'd state.
Perpetual happiness be thine!
Thy bright, approving smile be mine!
Nor let thy taste, severe, disdain,
Primate, this welcome-breathing strain.

Unnoticed by, and evidently unknown to all his former
biographers, this congratulatory poem closes the intellectual

[1] Gregory XIII., the Pope by whom Gaspar Visconti was appointed to
the archiepiscopal see of Milan.

career of the Admirable Crichton.[1] All beyond is wrapped in obscurity.

To the consideration of the present and the preceding performance should be brought a knowledge of Crichton's strong devotion to the Church of Rome; to that ancient faith—shorn of its glory in his own land, for which, after encountering those unhappy differences adverted to be Aldus (*prælia domestica contra te suscitata quæ cum patre gessisti*), and rejecting the brilliant offers held out to him by the leaders of the popular faith, whose cause and opinions his family had embraced, he had so long absented himself from his country, his friends, his home.[2]

Attached to the Church of Rome, he was necessarily attached to her priesthood. Milan, under the sway of the divine Borromeo, became the model of ecclesiastical jurisdiction. To Milan, Crichton repaired. His grief for the loss of the exalted primate was deep and heartfelt; his rejoicing at the appointment of his successor, whose piety he himself, as he informs us, had approved:

> Whose power in exhortation shown,
> Whose wisdom, I myself have known,
> When by his eloquence subdued,
> In admiration lost, I stood—

was unfeigned—and if the verses just quoted do nothing more, they at least prove that the adherence to the faith of his ancestry, which sent him forth a wanderer from their heresy-girt halls, was still unchanged.

Efforts have been made on the part of some recent writers to shake the celebrity of the Admirable Scot, by assailing the few poetical pieces which he has left us, and by measuring the grasp of his intellect by this unfair standard. This is to judge of the fire of Sappho by her twin odes; of the comic humour of Menander by his fragments. The prejudices of the learned biographer of Tasso must indeed have been blinding, if he could see no beauties in the *Appulsus*—no inspiration, no poetic verve, no classic taste and feeling in the odes to Massa and Donatus. It is not, however, from what remains to us of his writings, but from the effect produced upon his contemporaries (and *such* contemporaries), that we can form a just estimate of

---

[1] Any further information respecting Crichton will probably be derived from the voluminous manuscript letters of San Carlo Borromeo, preserved in the Ambrosian Library at Milan; from the letters of Sperone Speroni, in the edition of Forcellini, which have not come under my observation; or from some contemporary memoir or correspondence published at Mantua.

[2] *Quod scilicet regno, patria, domoque, ob Catholicæ fidei ardorem, tam-longe abes.*—ALDI, *Dedicatio in Paradoxa Ciceronis*

the extent of Crichton's powers. By them he was esteemed a miracle of learning—*divinum plane juvenem*: and we have an instance in our own times of a great poet and philosopher, whose published works scarcely bear out the high reputation he enjoyed for colloquial ability. The idolised friend of Aldus Manutius, of Lorenzo Massa, Giovanni Donati, and Sperone Speroni, amongst the most accomplished scholars of their age; the antagonist of the redoubted Arcangelus Mercenarius and Giacomo Mazzoni—(whose memory was so remarkable that he could recite entire books of Dante, Ariosto, Virgil and Lucretius, and who had sounded all the depths of philosophy)—could not have been other than an extraordinary person; and we may come to the conclusion respecting him, arrived at by Dr. Johnson, that "whatever we may suppress as surpassing credibility, yet we shall, upon incontestible authority, relate enough to rank him among prodigies."

FINIS

MADE AT THE TEMPLE PRESS LETCHWORTH IN GREAT BRITAIN

Printed in the United States
104277LV00003B/63/A